What Agreement Is There Between the Temple of God and Idols?

WHAT AGREEMENT IS THERE BETWEEN THE TEMPLE OF GOD AND IDOLS?
The Accidence of Sin and Idolatry

James Venezia

The Christian Exceptionalism in Counseling Series ™

EXULTANTIS PRESS

NEW YORK

What Agreement Is There Between the Temple of God and Idols?: The Accidence of Sin and Idolatry. Copyright TXu 1-944-558 © 2015 by James Venezia

The Christian Exceptionalism in Counseling Series™. Trademark 2015 by James Venezia

Published by EXULTANTIS PRESS, NEW YORK

All rights reserved, including the right to reproduce this book or portions thereof in any form whatsoever.

Available in print and electronic-book formats through Amazon.com:
    ISBN 978-0-9961181-4-9 (paperback)
    ISBN 978-0-9961181-1-8 (electronic book)

Unless otherwise noted, Scripture taken from the HOLY BIBLE, NEW INTERNATIONAL VERSION ®. Copyright © 1973, 1978, 1984 by International Bible Society. Used by permission of Zondervan. All rights reserved.

The author can be contacted at jamesvenezia@yahoo.com.

Second edition, 2016

Cover picture: *A Sculpture Gallery*, Lawrence Alma-Tadema, 1867

Printed in the United States of America

"What agreement is there between the temple of God and idols? For we are the temple of the living God. As God has said: 'I will live with them and walk among them, and I will be their God, and they will be my people.'" (2 Corinthians 6:16, emphasis added)

The Christian Exceptionalism in Counseling Series™

Welcome, dear reader, to *The Christian Exceptionalism in Counseling Series*™. This material is written to be accessible to both the neophyte as well as to the counseling aficionado. The first book in the series, *Ask for the Ancient Paths: From Art to Artifice to Arisen*, serves as a comprehensive introduction to biblical counseling. It is written as an overview of the Bible's creation-fall-redemption paradigm. The second book, *What Agreement Is There Between the Temple of God and Idols?: The Accidence of Sin and Idolatry*, explores sin and idolatry so as to eradicate it. The third book, *The Days of Reckoning Are at Hand: From Fig Leaf to Olive Branch to Laurel Wreath*, focuses on application in which one will find a more in-depth handling of diagnosis, as well as analysis of pressing topics such as suffering and loneliness.

My hope is that these books will not serve to merely inform, but rather will implement God's work of change in those he claims as his own. If you are already a Christian (one personally saved through Jesus' death upon the cross) then this series will advance God's sanctifying work in, and through, you. If you are not yet a believer then this series functions as an apologetic persuasion. The hope is that through this material you will see the unfathomable power of Christ-centered counseling, and in response find new life in him.

Wedding Procession, Gustave Brion, 1873

Ask for the Ancient Paths: From Art to Artifice to Arisen

Chapters

1. The Exordium to Biblical Counseling

2. The Counseling Ambition

3. The Centrality of Scripture in Counseling

4. The Gospel as Inception Point: From Immorality to Immortality

5. Redefining the Pygmalion Effect: Exploring the Image of God in Man

6. Man Before the Face of God: The Imperium of the Psyche

7. The Needs Imperative

8. What Has Jerusalem To Do With Vienna?: The Case Against Psychology

9. Integrationism: The Modern Day Babylonian Captivity

10. The Third-Way of Sanctification: From Abominable to Indomitable

Appendix: A Sanctification Plan

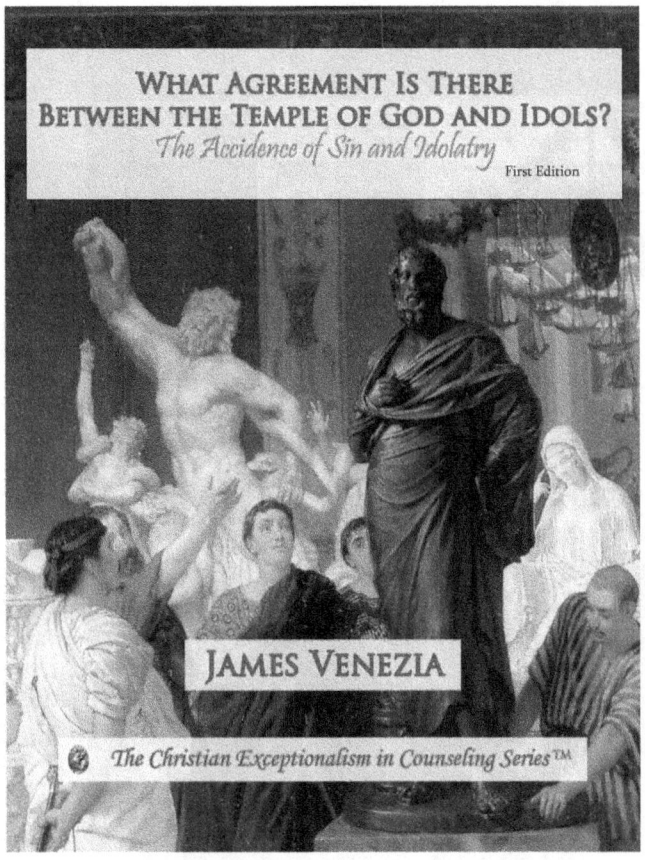

*What Agreement Is There Between the Temple of God and Idols?:
The Accidence of Sin and Idolatry*

Chapters:

1. Deliver Us from Evil

2. The World, the Flesh, and the Devil: Assessing the Threat Matrix

3. Total Depravity: This Imperiled Arcadia

4. Hamartiology: Sin in All Its Ignobility

5. Metaphors for Sin

6. Uncovering Idols of the Heart: Make Us Gods to Go Before Us

7. The Idolatry Doppler Shift

8. The Search for Eldorado Ends: Repenting of Idols of the Heart

9. Marauding Visigoths: The Autocratic Self

10. A Nouthetic Analysis of Moses

Appendix: The Demon Possession Case Study

The Days of Reckoning Are at Hand: From Fig Leaf to Olive Branch to Laurel Wreath

Chapters:

1. Memories Preserved in Amber: Adopting God's Retrospective

2. Suffering: The Kintsugi Objective

3. The Hobgoblin in the Inglenook: Assessing Loneliness

4. The Umbilicus of Personal Relationship with Christ

5. Navigating the Counseling Fjord: Preliminary Reconnaissance

6. The Basic Plotlines Which Emerge in Counseling

7. Artisanal Counseling: A Foray into Methods

8. Diagnosis: Vanishing Secrets

9. Emerging from the Chrysalis: Issues the Counselor Observes and Seeks to Change

10. Counseling and the Church: Syndicating the Vision

Also by the Author

*The Lord Kept Vigil That Night:
An Exposition of the Parable of the Lost Son*

*Rescue Us from the Present Evil Age:
Array of Hope*

*Hurl All Our Iniquities
into the Depths of the Sea*

Contents

Preface	xxi
Acknowledgments	xxv
Introduction	1

1. Deliver Us from Evil — 7

"The Human Race Has Improved Everything Except the Human Race"	7
Views on Evil	9
Analysis of the Christian Perspective on Evil	13
The Nature of Common Grace	16
Common Grace in Balance	20

2. The World, the Flesh, and the Devil: *Assessing the Threat Matrix* — 25

"Everything that Kills Me Makes Me Feel Alive"	25
The World's Gods	27
The Church of the World	29
The World's "DNA"	32
The World's Motives	35
City as Incubator of the World	38
The World's Entertainment	39
The World's Handmaiden: Hollywood	40
The World's Cantata	41
The World's Legerdemain: Science	42
The World System: Intrusive Government	44
The Web of Lies Surrounding Government Intrusion: "Our Father, Which Art in Washington"	46
The Slavery Cycle	47
The Triumvirate of Evil	51
The Devil Doesn't Dance in the Pale Moonlight; His Name is Not Mr. Scratch and He Doesn't Wear Prada®	54
Case Study: Balaam and Balak as Tropes of Satan	58
The World's Singular Obsession: Destroy Faith in Jesus Christ	62
Excursus: The Amish	63
Jesus Has Overcome the World, the Flesh, and the Devil	64

3. TOTAL DEPRAVITY: *This Imperiled Arcadia* — 67

- Introduction — 67
- The Root of Total Depravity — 68
- Understanding the Nature of Depravity — 72
- Total Depravity — 79
- Depravity Through the Lens of Proverbs — 87
- Excursus: Does Material Poverty Predispose One to Repentance and Faith? — 90
- Sin as Assault upon Mankind's "Very-Goodness" — 92
- Christ Reverses Man's Total Depravity — 95
- In Christ the Body Will Be Resurrected — 97
- In Christ the Conscience Is Revived — 98
- In Christ There Is Relational Renewal — 98
- In Christ the Spirit Is Rekindled — 99
- In Christ the Reason Is Realigned — 99

4. HAMARTIOLOGY: *Sin in All Its Ignobility* — 101

- Introduction — 101
- The Bible's Handling of Sin — 102
- Case Study: Parents Picking-up Their Children — 103
- Exploring the Issue of Sin — 104
- Various Indicators That Each Is a Sinner — 109
- Five Symbols of Sin — 120
- Fallen Man Believes Finiteness Is His Problem — 122
- Drawing Back the Veil on Moralism — 126
- Case Study: Joseph's Naïvite — 128
- Society's Artificial Demarcation for Normal and Abnormal — 130
- Sin as Comprehensive State of the Heart — 142
- Vital Truths Regarding Sin — 145
- The Broken Window Theory on Sin — 150
- Sin's Downward Spiral — 152
- Satan's Devices for Minimizing the Severity of Sin — 155
- Case Study: The Contours of Blame-Shifting and Hypochondriacal Sin — 156
- Is There a Hierarchy of Sin? — 158
- The Clench and Conflict of Sin — 159
- Sin Harangues the Sinner — 161
- Sin as Pillaging Visigoths — 162
- Sin's Great Ravishment: Insanity — 163
- Sin Bears a Lifetime of Regret — 165
- Razing the Strongholds of Sin — 166

5. Metaphors for Sin — 169

Introduction — 169
1. Sin as misdirected worship — 170
2. Sin as inverting or blurring the Creator-creation distinction — 171
3. Sin as slavery to evil — 174
4. Sin as addiction to self-worship — 175
5. Sin as prostitution to false gods — 176
Case Study: Is There a Fundamental Gender Asymmetry with Regard to Sexuality? — 178
6. Sin as lust of the flesh — 180
Case Study: Sexuality Forbidden in Leviticus 18 — 181
7. Sin as rebellion and hatred directed toward God — 183
8. Sin as demand and war against God — 184
9. Sin as seeking the gift over the Giver — 186
10. Sin as a state of exile — 188
11. Sin as building one's own kingdom — 188
12. Sin as defacing the temple of one's body — 190
13. Sin as making God "small" and people into giants — 192
Case Study: An Analysis of Abraham — 193
14. Sin as hiding and seeking covering — 197
Case Study: Technology as a Form of Covering — 198
15. Sin as standing on a false authority — 205
16. Sin as false rest and false peace in the things of the world — 206
17. Sin as an inverted sense of reality — 208
18. Sin as foolishness — 210
19. Sin as friendship with the world — 211
20. Sin as pollution — 212
21. Sin as a set of lenses — 213
22. Sin as being a people of the eye — 213
Further Development of the Lust of the Eye — 220
The Heart-Eye Feedback System — 223

6. Uncovering Idols of the Heart:
Make Us Gods to Go Before Us — 225

Introduction — 225
The World Is Not Enough — 226
The Heart as Living Rorschach Image — 227
Pockets of Atheism Within the Heart — 230
Worship Patterns — 231

Idols of the Heart and the Vanity Fair	233
The Heart's Fine and Gross Motor Movements	233
Idolatry and the Quest for Happiness	236
Idolatry as Uncreation	239
Idolatry as Zoetrope	240
The Idolater as Covenant Maker	241
The Pantheon of Gods	243
The Idol's Allure	245
Typical Idols	248
The Smorgasbord of Idols	253
Excursus: The Rise of Gluttony	254
Idols and the Array of Sins They Spawn	255
Case Study: Amnon and Tamar: Idolatry and Hatred	256
Plumbing the Depths of the Idol Mine	257
Excursus: Barbie® in Iran: The Clash of Idols	259
Idols in Counterbalance	260
Case Study: The Golden Calf: Idolatry in All Its Malevolent Glory	262

7. The Idolatry Doppler Shift — 271

1. Distracted	272
2. Disrupted	273
3. Dense	273
4. Dull	274
5. Dependent	275
6. Defenseless	276
Case Study: Contrasting Armor	277
7. Deserted	279
8. Desolate	280
9. Disappointed	281
Excursus: The Growth of Personal Wealth and Dissatisfaction	282
10. Distressed	284
11. Depressed	284
12. Divided/Divisive	285
13. Deceived	287
14. Darkened	288
15. Demanding	289
16. Desperate	290
17. Desirous	290
18. Delusional	292
Excursus: Delusional Idolatry	293
19. Defiant	295

20. Deceitful	295
21. Devious	296
22. Debauched	297
23. Defiled	297
24. Disgraced	298
25. Detestable	299
26. Damaged	300
27. Defeated	300
28. Destroyed	301
29. Devoured	302
30. Dead	303
Conclusion	303

8. THE SEARCH FOR ELDORADO ENDS: *Repenting of Idols of the Heart* — **305**

Uncovering Idols: Back to the Basics	305
The Idol's Circle of Safety	312
The Idolatry Bell Curve	313
How Idols Masquerade as Sanctification	315
The Herod Effect	316
Becoming Vulnerable to the Truth	319
The "Heisenberg Uncertainty Principle" of Biblical Counseling	322
Pinpointing Idols for Extraction	323
Laying Siege to Buttressed Idols	325
Dismantling the Pantheon One God at a Time	327
A Tree Metaphor for Idolatry	330
A Tree Metaphor for Redemption	331
Case Study: Applying the Tree Metaphor	332
The Call to Repentance	336
Repentance Explored	338
Repentance Implemented: The Quail and Serpent Approaches	339
Incentivized Repentance: Gratitude Reversal	340
Building Faith on a Solid Foundation of Repentance	342
Worship Recidivism	343
The Counselor's Role in Exposing Idolatry	347
The Trap of Fig Leaf Counseling	349
Idolatry and the Exemplar	350
Recasting the Worshipping Core	352
Excursus: The Day of Atonement	354
Vanquishing the Ghost of Attila the Hun	355

9. MARAUDING VISIGOTHS: *The Autocratic Self* — 359

Jesus Exposes Each Person's True Identity	359
Three Aspects of Self	361
Modern Culture's *Lingua Franca*	363
The Rise of Self-Celebration	371
The Toxic Delusion of Believing in Oneself	373
Excursus: Automobile Ownership and Self-Obsession	377
The Proliferation of Self-Love	378
Narcissism: Self-Love in the Extreme	380
Excursus: The Veblen Effect and Vanity	383
The Curse of Self-Love: Burning Insecurity	384
Excursus: The Dunning-Kruger Effect	386
The Curse of Self-Love: Crippling Comparison with Others	387
Case Study: The Explosion of Love Addiction	390
Scintillating Self-Denial	391
The Self-Esteem Reign of Terror	394
Case Study: King Nebuchadnezzar: One Afflicted with Himself	396
Self-Esteem's Deception	399
The Low Self-Esteem Label: "I Have So Many Talents but I Just Can't Remember Where I Hid Them"	403
The Counselor's Charge	405
Excursus: Counterculture as Manifestation of Self-Pride	407
Counseling Those with Perceived Low Self-Esteem	407
How Does the Christian Rightly Tell Others of God's Love?	409
The Christian Possesses That Which Is Far Greater Than Self-Esteem	410

10. A NOUTHETIC ANALYSIS OF MOSES — 415

Liberation from Egypt: The Call of Moses	415
Interpreting Moses' First Four Statements	416
Moses' Conclusion: Defiant Distrust	420
Moses' Misplaced Priorities and Squandered Opportunities	423
Moses' Blindness to Foreign Gods Among the People	424
Moses' Strategic Error: Serving as Civil Judge	427
Moses' Squandered Opportunity to Shepherd Hearts	428
Moses' Recumbent Fear of God, Recalcitrant Fear of Man	430
In Living by Sight Moses Remained Blind To People	432
I Wouldn't Have Seen It If I Hadn't Believed It	434
Case Study: Numbers 32: The Transjordan Tribes	436
Concluding Remarks	439

EPILOGUE	443
APPENDIX: THE DEMON POSSESSION CASE STUDY	447
THE AUTHOR	473

Preface

At the time of this writing, Christians throughout the Middle East are being harassed, tortured, and killed. Millions of Iraqi Christians have fled to the mountains to escape the persecution of a marauding state. With all the bloodshed, chaos, and suffering experienced by many Christians, what could this book possibly offer a beleaguered people seeking to survive in a profoundly contused world?

One of my many objectives is to shatter typical stereotypes surrounding biblical counseling. One such stereotype is that it only addresses "First World problems," the plight of the housewife whose husband no longer pays attention to her, the cry of the father whose son is distant and detached, the ache of a retiree coping with loneliness. While these are anguishing problems in their own right, they hardly compare to the genocide of Christians in the Sudan, the imprisonment of underground church pastors, or the ongoing brutal murder of Coptic and Armenian Christians.

The Sword of Damocles, Felix Auvray, d. 1833

Biblical counseling is not about smoothing out cosmetic emotional problems. It is not focused on "boutique" solutions to life's idiosyncrasies. In this regard it bears no substantive resemblance, in either form or content, to secular psychology. Biblical counseling dives to the heart of the human plight and problem. It seeks out the root of humanly nested evil, to uproot and destroy it, all the while respecting persons in their specific giftedness, calling, challenges, and situation in life.

Neaera Reading a Letter
Henry J. Hudson, d. 1912

Thus, biblical counseling is able to counsel those who suffer because it offers Christ-centered relationship within the context of the human dilemma. Far from a Pollyanna, the Bible understands the human condition because it sees the vexing problems of evil, sin, and idolatry with crystalline clarity. This is why the Christian worldview is able to diagnose and resolve the human condition; it builds upon a savior who made himself into the image of evil in mankind's place so as to vanquish that evil and deliver man from it.

My sincere hope is that this book will be used by Christ to vanquish the wickedness in and around you, to deliver you from evil as you experience the wonder of ever-deepening relationship with a good God.[1]

In reading *What Agreement Is There Between the Temple of God and Idols?* please keep the Bible at your side. It is crucial that this text be seen as building upon the foundation of Scripture. The better the reader knows Scripture, and the more closely he reads Scripture in conjunction with this text, the richer and more vivid this counseling model will become.

One may notice frequent sections throughout the book labeled, "case study" and "excursus." What is the difference? A case study is so denoted because, following the natural trajectory of the chapter, it offers an opportunity for deeper study and reflection. An excursus is similar except that it is more tangential. It may be a cultural,

---
[1] Matthew 6:13

historical, literary, artistic, or scientific reference which is fascinating to consider, but not as directly relevant. Thus, an excursus offers a rest-stop in which to exercise the imagination.

> While I encourage the reader to study all three books in *The Christian Exceptionalism in Counseling Series™*, each is designed as a stand-alone unit, and most of the constituent chapters are, to some degree, stand-alone. The reason is that each topic is positioned on a tripod of the Bible's creation-fall-redemption paradigm.[2]

Finally, I have included over 400 pieces of classical artwork throughout the entire series. This art is intended to more persuasively marshal the imagination, to offer the mind a reprieve from propositional truths, to extend the delight of magnificent fare. In most instances, the art is simply a creative augmentation to the topic at hand. If a painting helps expand one's grasp of the concept, then it has served this work's purpose.[3] But please don't allow style to overwhelm substance.

> "'What is the use of a book,' thought Alice, 'without pictures or conversations?'" (*Alice in Wonderland*, Lewis Carroll)

Isaac Newton (1642–1726) humbly stated, "If I have seen farther than others it is because I stand on the shoulders of giants." This presentation stands on the shoulders of the Christian Counseling and Education Foundation (CCEF) in Willow Grove, Pennsylvania. This is my contribution, and I hope, my gift to the biblical counseling movement which serves Jesus Christ so faithfully. In all essentials of the faith my thinking aligns precisely with CCEF, not out of blind compliance, but out of sincere conviction. This work, like theirs, is triumphantly gospel-centered to its core.

Spotlight on the Second Edition

The first edition of *The Christian Exceptionalism in Counseling Series™* was officially launched on June 20, 2015. Since that time, myriad edits, updates, and additions have been applied. ("…Of writing many books there is no end…"[4]) As stated previously, reading this material is, to the extent that it accords with Scripture, an encounter with the person of Jesus Christ, not just knowledge about him, but to be confronted and searched by him. In this sense, this material is not so much informative as it is formative.

---

[2] This I describe as the fractal method of counseling in the third book in this series, *The Days of Reckoning Are at Hand: From Fig Leaf to Olive Branch to Laurel Wreath*, chapter 7: "Artisanal Counseling: A Foray into Methods."

[3] Please note that nearly all the artwork included in these books could be classified as "classical." On occasion, classical artwork contains nudity. While that nudity is never gratuitous, where it is conspicuous, it has been discretely covered so as to maintain the book's modesty. This covering is not an attempt to alter the painting, but simply to guard those readers who might otherwise be tempted to sin.

[4] Ecclesiastes 12:12

In the course of this work's advance, at crucial junctures, there have been pronounced spiritual attacks. Yet, despite the setbacks, an invisible hand presses this work forward. With each seemingly insurmountable obstacle, an unanticipated breakthrough emerges. The sense of God himself prospering this work, and seeking to bring it to fruitful completion, has invested me with a towering Christ-centered confidence, an indomitable perseverance, and an unspeakable joy in the final result.

As a side note, it has been an intriguing case study to observe reactions to this work over the past several months. It would appear that this material functions like a prism clarifying those who desire to know, and be known, by Christ. I can only surmise that with each turn of the page Jesus' own winnowing fork is at the threshing floor, an axe to the root of the heart, the disentangling of faith from apostasy. May he will and work to further his kingdom in each who encounter this series.

Please contact the author at jamesvenezia@yahoo.com with questions or comments on this series.

Like Sherlock Holmes it is time to don the deerstalker hat and insert the meerschaum pipe to investigate the psyche!

S. D. G.
January 20, 2016

> "But even if I am being poured out like a drink offering on the sacrifice and service coming from your faith, I am glad and rejoice with all of you." (Philippians 2:17)

Acknowledgments

Thank you to my parents, Peter and Jo-Ann, for providing me with the opportunity and encouragement to write. They have read more of my writing than anyone I know and have taught me a great deal about the perseverance and discipline required to complete such a task. My father also proofread a considerable quantity of this text. I am grateful for his assistance.

Singing to the Reverend, Edmund Blair Leighton, d. 1922

Thank you to many Christ-centered teachers for their priceless mentoring and instruction. Their voices echo throughout this book series because they echo throughout my faith. They each, in distinctive ways, have continually reintroduced me to Jesus through, not just their formal instruction, but in their daily experience of knowing, and being know by, Jesus. Their collective counsel serves as a perennial corrective, encouragement, and scriptural realignment to my heart.

"Never trust a scholar who won't tell you who his teachers were." (Aristotle)

This book series is a celebration of Jesus Christ's work in and through Westminster Theological Seminary. Westminster set me on the right path early in life, a path that continues to lead me into ever richer experiences of Christ. With warm gratitude I thank Westminster for its care for my soul and for the abundant harvest it has produced in and through so many.

Introduction

More than ten years ago I contracted a severe virus. I know exactly when and where I caught it. I had just started a new job in which my desk was positioned directly below an air-conditioning vent which blasted Arctic-cold air. One day, in the distance between my parked car and the office, I was caught in a torrential downpour. I was drenched to the bone. As I sat at my desk with cold air buffeting the back of my neck I felt a sudden chill. I knew I had just gotten sick. I could feel the illness enter my body.

Sure enough, that night I came down with a fever and by morning I had a sore throat. This began what would become a nine-month viral infection, plunging me into the depths of despair before I would finally find healing. The illness progressed from a sore throat to swollen neck glands. It then migrated into ducts under my arms before finally taking up residence in glands behind my knees. The virus had burrowed its way into my lymphatic system. Naturally, I had been sick many times in the past and, like most people, given enough rest and proper nutrition, my body had always healed itself. However, this illness was not receding. In fact, with each passing week, it worsened.

The Wounded Cavalier (detail)
William Shakespeare Burton, 1855

Those who have suffered with a serious viral infection know that often the illness shows itself with almost random intensity. Some days one feels newfound energy and assumes that the illness is fading. He might go for a run or take care of those errands he has been putting off. However, this exertion leaves one debilitated the following day, or sometimes for several days.

(This condition is typically labeled "chronic fatigue syndrome," although it is obvious to me that the root cause is an unidentified virus.)

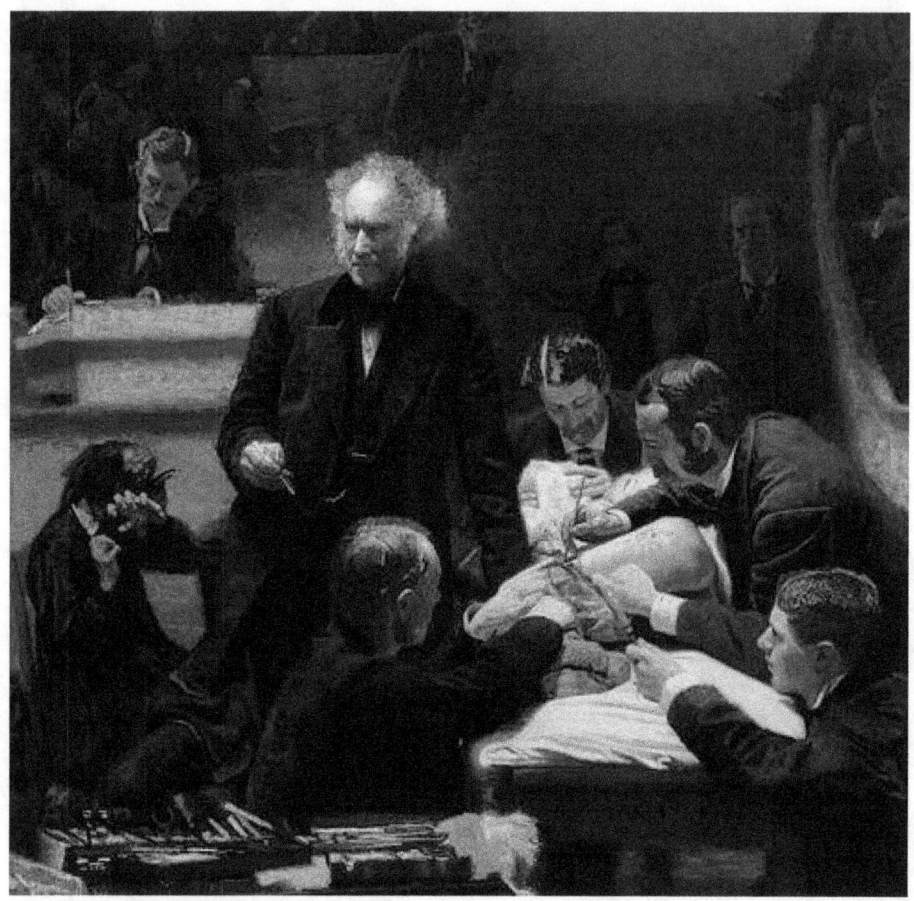

Dr. Samuel D. Gross (The Gross Clinic), Thomas Eakins, 1875

I saw several physicians, each recognized specialists in his field. I was evaluated by four internal medicine specialists, an endocrinologist, a hematologist, and an epidemiologist. I even made an appointment with the world-renowned Mayo Clinic in Boston. No one had any idea what was wrong with me. I did not bear any ostensible symptoms except severe fatigue and swollen glands. I was at a healthy weight and my face had full-color. A few of the doctors assumed I was a hypochondriac. One told me I just needed to get outside more often and get more exercise. Another, despite my protestations, insisted I was depressed and tried to prescribe Prozac®. (He even went so far as to state that denial is a sure sign of depression.). Still another told me I ought to be tested for HIV. I told him I am chaste and have never had a blood transfusion. He cast a jaundiced eye in my direction. The physicians each denied that my glands were swollen, when, knowing my own body, the swelling was as plain as day to me.

After five months of deepening despair, my mother suggested that I see a chiropractor for an evaluation. Having nothing to lose, I made an appointment. As I lay facedown, the doctor placed his clasped hands between my shoulder blades. He delivered a sudden thrust into my back. I heard a loud cracking sound, as if he had snapped several twigs between his hands. Yet, oddly, there was no pain. At that very instant I felt health return to my body. I knew that some passageway, some conduit, had been released of its blockage, that my body was restoring itself. This was the first step in a long road to recovery. It would take another four months of rehabilitation to finally return to full strength.

The point of this story is not to cast aspersions on the evidence-based medical community. (Without doubt, each physician I met was well-intentioned and has offered life-saving assistance to many.) Nor is this a sales-pitch for holistic medicine. The point is to draw an analogy between this episode and the dynamics of the human psyche. There was a discrete moment when I knew I had fallen ill, and another moment when I knew my health was being restored. Likewise, the psyche, under the aegis of sin, somehow knows that it is ill. Sin induces a kind of "chronic fatigue" within the soul, so that one feels a "viral infection" inhabiting him. Just as my illness terrified me, so too, each sinner is terrified of the evil resident within himself, an evil which he knows to be present, but against which he finds himself powerless.

Where is healing to be found? There is only one means: rebirth in Jesus Christ. This rebirth initiates a healing process in which the soul gains strength through the experience of God's forgiveness, and through the concomitant extension of forgiveness to others.[1] This promise of forgiveness, and the ability to in turn forgive, is delivered to sinners through Jesus' death on the cross.

Sadly, psychology, which presumptuously claims authority over the psyche, attempts various methods to restore the soul's strength. One method is to deny the existence of a soul altogether, to reduce every psychosis to somatic triggers. (This is a form of scientific materialism which exercises supreme command over psychology.) Another method is to simply offer coping mechanisms or pragmatic advice ("You just need to get outside and exercise more.") Still others resort to the psychopharmacological (i.e. Prozac®). Most of my physicians tried to convince me that I was not sick at all (at least not in the way that I knew myself to be). In the same way, psychology seeks to convince mankind that he is not sick in the way that God knows him to be. In fact, most of what God calls illness psychology calls health, and that which God calls health, psychology might label as illness.

Psychology's methods only exacerbate the underlying problem and finally frustrate the sinner, because they never strike at the root cause ("the liberation of some deep passageway"). Thus, the healing for what psychology terms "mental illness" is found along an ancient path: faith in a man who lived some 2,000 years ago, claimed to be God, and proved himself as such. It is through faith in Jesus that the soul finally finds

---

[1] Matthew 6:9-13

healing. Those who have been brought from death to life know that health has entered their souls, that healing is being effected, and that the underlying illness is mislabeled (not "chronic fatigue syndrome" but an invidious viral infection of the worshipping heart).

> "…Jesus said to them, 'It is not the healthy who need a doctor, but the sick. I have not come to call the righteous, but sinners.'" (Mark 2:17)

This text, *What Agreement Is There Between the Temple of God and Idols?: The Accidence of Sin and Idolatry*, is not written to condemn, but to diagnosis the most profound and prevalent human condition, sin. The objective is to finally bring permanent and pronounced healing. I pray that just as that odd sound of snapping twigs brought healing to my body, so too, this book might apply the right thrust so as to snap the central blockage within each reader's soul, to initiate or intensify a Christ-directed healing process. Through this work may you discover the nature of your sin, its choking miasma, its grotesque architecture, its Stygian darkness, and may you find emancipation from it.

> "Instruct the wise and they will be wiser still; teach the righteous and they will add to their learning." (Proverbs 9:9)

The Accidence of Sin and Idolatry

- 1 -

Deliver Us from Evil[1]

Expulsion, Moon and Firelight, Thomas Cole, 1828

"The Human Race Has Improved Everything Except the Human Race"[2]

Beginning in 1949, Lewis Fry Richardson (1881–1953), noted British mathematician, attempted to build a statistical model for the frequency of war. He studied every known international conflict from 1815 to 1945 hoping to uncover patterns. He sought to understand the timing of conflicts, the casualties they inflict, and most importantly, when they might occur again.

In Richardson's analysis he looked at economics, geography, language, political systems, and religions. For example, he studied the length of the shared border between warring nations, and the condition of their diplomatic relations in the lead up

---

[1] For additional discussion of evil as it relates to suffering see "The Search for Answers in an Evil World" in the third book in this series, *The Days of Reckoning Are at Hand: From Fig Leaf to Olive Branch to Laurel Wreath*, chapter 2: "Suffering: The Kintsugi Objective"
[2] Adlai Stevenson (1835–1914)

to war. Richardson hoped to develop a mathematical model which would, in theory, accurately predict the incidence of international conflict.

Building upon Richardson's research, physicists and mathematicians apply similar analysis to the frequency of modern terrorism. They hope to see mathematical patterns emerge which will predict the location and timing of future conflicts and the probability of casualties. (Of course, the U.S. State Department keeps a keen eye on these findings.)

Cain Slaying Abel
Johann Karl Loth, d. 1698

From the Bible's perspective such analysis is misguided. The starting point for understanding mankind is its open war with its Creator. Thus, mankind's earthly wars are often an overflow of its cosmic conflict. Who can understand the times and seasons, the methods and madness, of the heart?[3] It is foolishness to try to quantify that which is unquantifiable as there are forces at play which social science can never comprehend. Evil is not a mathematically-defined occurrence but embodied in a person (Satan) who marshals persons (mankind) to engage in a life-and-death struggle with God himself.

Today, we understand the physics of an expanding universe and the mysterious behavior of quarks. We know how to create vaccines and custom genes, replace body parts and build space robots. Our knowledge of life and the universe continues to grow dramatically in every field imaginable, except one. We don't understand evil – what it is, how it works, and why it so routinely and effortlessly ruins our lives. Put another way, we don't understand ourselves. Despite the human race's extraordinary capacity for invention and progress, we clearly have a millennia-old blind spot in this one

---

[3] Ecclesiastes 9:3

all-important area.[4]

Everyone experiences evil firsthand yet few have a sound explanation for it. Each person has been subject to evil's viciousness and in turn has perpetrated evil upon others. In this sense each person is both an Abel and a Cain, victim and victimizer. (This is not saying that each person is a mixture of good and evil, a common Christian fallacy.) Being subject to evil often makes people bitter and hostile; perpetrating evil makes them profoundly guilty. Each realizes that what has been done to him is of the same ilk as what he has done to others, and yet none has any answer in himself for why he would perpetrate that which he knows to be evil.

> "Or those eighteen who died when the tower in Siloam fell on them – do you think they were more guilty than all the others living in Jerusalem? I [Jesus] tell you, no! But unless you repent, you too will all perish." (Luke 13: 4, 5)

Views on Evil

How does one understand evil? What follows are various perspectives on evil.

1. Buddhism holds that all passions should be extinguished and the desired outcome of life is Nirvana, non-existence. In this same way, evil does not really exist. It is just an illusion.

> In Buddhism the lotus blossom symbolizes enlightenment because, like one who is enlightened, it "rises in purity and beauty above the pond's muck [the material world]…"
>
> In Buddhist philosophy evil is symbolized with three animals: the cockerel representing desire, the pig representing ignorance, and the snake representing anger.

2. Greek philosophers (Plato and Aristotle), and those who relied on them (Origin and Aquinas), taught that evil is a privation, a lack of the good. In this view, evil is merely the absence of good, like a hole in cloth. Evil is not a thing and does not have substance in itself. This puts the blame squarely upon God's creative work. God fashioned a universe with voids in which good does not exist.

Plato (c.428 – c. 348 BC) considered the material world, including the human body, to be evil. This means that evil is woven into the creation itself. In this view, evil is no longer the result of human culpability, but the result of being passively subject to an evil body. This makes mankind into a tragic hero, one who has no choice but to sin.

---

[4] David Kupelian, *How Evil Works: Understanding and Overcoming the Destructive Forces That Are Transforming America* (New York: Threshold Editions, 2010) ix.

Like Greek philosophy, Gnosticism (a forth century heresy) saw the physical world as evil, and God, its creator, as setting a trap for humanity.[5]

3. The Enlightenment philosopher Gottfried von Leibniz (1646–1716) called this world "the best of all possible worlds."[6] However, the universe, like a machine, simply breaks down; it is unavoidable. So for von Leibniz, evil is merely a failure in the machinery of the universe, such as a thrown cog or broken lever. Evil occurs because of an inherent weakness in the creation – a design flaw or fragility in its very fabric. Additionally, according to von Leibniz, God calibrated the perfect proportion of good and evil so that good would unmistakably manifest itself. For von Leibniz, this universe is simply the best that God could do, given the exigencies of highlighting good.

> On January 23, 1556, 830,000 Chinese in Shanxi province perished in an earthquake. According to von Leibniz's line of thinking this is merely the result of the inevitable breakdown of the universe, a chance occurrence with no deeper meaning. In fact, the Lisbon earthquake of 1755 conclusively shattered von Leibniz's theory (that this is the best of all possible worlds) since the earthquake was thought to unleash unrelenting evil with no sense of any possible good.

If this is the best possible world, then the greatest good is dependent upon evil, for God could not create the greatest possible good without evil. But the greatest good, God himself, is infinitely holy, separate and independent of evil. He in no way requires evil to accomplish the good, the best, or the perfect.

> "The optimist thinks this is the best of all possible worlds. The pessimist fears it is true." (J. Robert Oppenheimer)

4. Romanticism saw society as evil, but individuals as innocent and blameless, evil mysteriously entering society through unknown means. Romanticism makes evil a vague abstraction.

> In Romantic author Mary Shelley's (1797–1851) novel, *Frankenstein* (1818), there is a monstrous creature which perpetrates evil. In keeping with Romantic ideals, the creature was not corrupted by his own depravity but by the evils of a harsh and cruel society. The monster was merely the victim of a dehumanizing culture, and therefore not to blame for his conduct.

5. According to Karl Marx (1818–1883), co-author of *The Communist Manifesto* (1848), evil is found in a capitalist economic system that keeps workers (the

---

[5] Joseph Schimmel, Fight the Good Fight Ministries
[6] Gottfried Wilhelm von Leibniz, *Theodicee* (1710)

proletariat) in a state of subservience to owners (the bourgeoisie).

6. The neo-orthodox theologian Karl Barth (1886–1968) described evil as a mysterious, ill-defined shape of which one can never know the boundaries. Evil is like a "place" which does not exist in the three-dimensional universe, an intrusion or overlay into space and time.

7. The Christian view asserts that evil is embodied in a person, Satan. Like all people, evil has a mind; it acts with intent; it has force. Evil is not passive, nor an illusion. It is active and motivated; it hates; it schemes; it rationalizes; it articulates. Evil was first embodied in Satan and later in humans. Humans can act as vessels of evil, even though they were never designed for that purpose. As mankind harbors and nurtures evil within himself he soon resembles its first perpetrator, Satan.

The Abduction of the Sabine Women, Nicolas Poussin, 1634

Before the creation only God existed. Therefore, evil did not exist from all eternity; it is not ultimate or necessary for the existence or knowledge of good. However, there is a veil of mystery surrounding Genesis 1:2 in which the earth was "formless and empty," with "darkness over the surface of the deep." There seems to be some kind of "evil" which God overcame in his creative work, a reclaiming of matter from the hands of chaos. Yet, the Bible offers no information on the origin of evil. In terms of evil's chief, Ezekiel 28 informs that Satan, God's highest ranking angel, entertained megalomaniacal ideations (desires to be God himself) and was cast from heaven as a bolt of lighting.[7] The first evil (as distinct from the first sin) was the pride of wanting to usurp God's sovereignty, wanting to sit on the throne of heaven. The reader is not given any additional understanding than this.

> The Christian worldview does not state that God voluntarily gave up some of his power to ensure human autonomy.[8] Man's "power" is derivative power, not that which he has created for himself.

Since evil is embodied in a person it functions as all persons do, to achieve some end, to gain mastery over the universe, to be god. According to the Christian perspective, man is powerless against the advances of evil; he will invariably succumb to its temptations. Yet, it is fascinating to note that Hollywood movies almost always present evil as being defeated in the end. In fact, it is a forgone conclusion that evil is finally vanquished with regard to the human spirit. (This underlies nearly all story-telling.) However, this concept is hijacked since only Jesus' death on the cross makes such an assumption reality. As only Jesus could defeat evil, mankind must implicitly rest in Jesus' accomplished work on the cross. Thus, while the world denies Jesus' death as the conclusive triumph over evil, it trades in the savior's currency.

> Evil is like a parasite that seeks human beings as its vector. As the parasite feeds off of the vector it transforms it into the essence of the parasite itself. Mankind was intended to exhibit the character and traits of a holy, wise, and loving God. However, as mankind allows evil to dwell within himself he exhibits the character and traits of Satan, the purest manifestation of evil.
>
> The Chinese philosopher Mencius (372–289 BC) wrote, "For a man to give full realization to his heart is for him to understand his own nature." What is mankind's nature? The Bible describes the heart as: "proud,"[9] "insane,"[10] "arrogant,"[11] "rebellious,"[12] "deceitful,"[13] "wicked,"[14] "weak,"[15] "foolish,"[16] and "evil."[17] Philosophy may at times catch glimmers of the heart's condition, but it cannot understand it, and certainly can never cure it.

Only the Bible understands evil in its full extent, its mechanics and machinations, its

---

[7] Luke 10:18
[8] William Edgar, *Reasons of the Heart: Recovering Christian Persuasion* (Presbyterian and Reformed Publishing, 2003) 101.
[9] Proverbs 21:4
[10] Ecclesiastes 9:3
[11] Isaiah 10:12
[12] Jeremiah 5:23
[13] Jeremiah 17:9
[14] Jeremiah 17:9
[15] Ezekiel 16:30
[16] Romans 1:12
[17] Hebrews 3:12

cunning and craft. The Bible understands that in the face of evil mankind is powerless in his own strength, that when men and evil meet evil always enjoys mocking victory. In his sinful state mankind is subject to evil's traps, curse, and consequence so that all human effort to vanquish evil is utterly futile.

> "And I declared that the dead, who had already died, are happier than the living, who are still alive. But better than both is he who has not yet been, who has not seen the evil that is done under the sun." (Ecclesiastes 4:2, 3)

Evil is so vicious, so wicked, so terrifying, that only the death of God himself could destroy it. When one looks upon Jesus Christ hanging on the cross one sees the utter heinousness of evil.[18] Evil is something so unfathomable that only the mutilation, humiliation, and death of God could denature it, could strip its power, could unwind its cunning. Through his death, Jesus conclusively defeated the eternal consequences of evil making it possible for those who follow him to share his victory over Satan.[19]

Therefore, the cross is not a talisman to ward off evil (that is the contrivance of godless superstition). The cross symbolizes Jesus himself invading the human heart so that it no longer functions as a terror cell for Satan. Jesus actually lives within the hearts of believers so that they are progressively delivered from evil to holiness. Thus, Jesus springs the Hobbesian trap positioned between man and God; what was once a hostile standoff has become a joyful homecoming.

> "Be self-controlled and alert. Your enemy the devil prowls around like a roaring lion looking for someone to devour." (1 Peter 5:8)

Analysis of the Christian Perspective on Evil

During the Western Han Dynasty (206 BC – AD 220) in Runan County, the Ruhe River was inhabited by a devil which afflicted villagers with a plague. To get rid of the devil, a boy named Huan Jing climbed a southeast mountain to visit a powerful god. The god agreed to show Huan Jing how to defeat the devil. He gave him a pack of cornus leaves and chrysanthemum liquor. Huan Jing then returned home and instructed the villagers to climb a mountain to wait for the devil to appear. As the devil approached he was dazed by the scent of the cornus and liquor. Then Huan Jing was able to slay the devil. Thus, started the tradition of climbing mountains on the Double-Ninth Day (重九節).[20]

This legend views evil as though it could be vanquished with elements from the creation (in this case, cornus leaves and chrysanthemum liquor). This is indicative of

---
[18] Isaiah 53:3
[19] Colossians 2:15
[20] Ren Xiu Hua, *Classic Legends of Traditional Chinese Culture* (2009) 21-23.

mankind's stance toward evil; it is viewed as that from which mankind can save himself using elements in the creation (garlic, a cross, a silver stake to overcome Dracula, for example). In this sense, mankind bears a perilous tendency to trivialize evil, to grossly mischaracterize it, and to profoundly misjudge its full extent. Evil can never be overcome through any element in the creation. It is a spiritual power which only God himself can crush. As evil also inhabits humanity, likewise, only God can destroy this power within man.

> "Is God willing to prevent evil, but not able? Then he is impotent. Is he able, but not willing? Then he is malevolent. Is God both able and willing? Whence then is evil?" (Epicurus).

The Fire, Jean-Pierre Alexandre Antigna, 1851

Consider a person who has experienced evil at its worst. As this person assesses the various options for evil he may grow indignant. How could evil be an illusion? How could it be merely a privation of the good? How could it be simply a mechanical breakdown of the universe? All of these options just feel wrong; all of these answers deal humanity an indignity. Evil feels fiercely active.[21] It is intent on destruction and its moves forward with intelligence and power to accomplish its task. When

---
[21] Job 1:7; 1 Peter 5:8

Christianity speaks about evil as a person, with a will and a mind that plans and acts, this simply feels like the correct understanding. Only Christianity recognizes evil in all its fury and ferocity, something seemingly so indomitable and intractably fascistic that only one act could destroy it - the death of God himself. In what way does the Christian view of evil offer hope both to those who are subject to it and to those who perpetrate it?

> All that is necessary for the triumph of evil is that good men remain silent. (adapted from Edmund Burke)

To one who has suffered at the hands of evil, to one who has looked into its terrifying face and has tasted from its bitter cup, only the Christian worldview fully dignifies this experience. Only Christianity sees evil as it really is, and offers a solution that would heretofore seem unconscionable, that God himself would hang on a cross to obliterate its power (while allowing its presence to continue). To one who has been placed into an iron-maiden of torment only the cross offers release, comfort, and permanent deliverance. Only in the indignity of the cross is a dignity extended to the human experience of evil. (Incidentally, it is my contention that the Christian view of evil increasingly falls on deaf ears as mankind lives out a humanistic delusion. As humanity feeds on a steady diet of secular humanism it loses sight of evil, and all its unrelenting fury. In other words, false views of evil gain ascendancy as people forget what evil really is and in its place substitute counterfeits of evil.)

> "Satan trembles when he sees the weakest saint upon his knees." (William Cowper)

When the Christian encounters evil, should he avoid it, work to contain it, try to peacefully co-exist with it, or seek to destroy it? Romans 12:21 is clear, "Do not be overcome with evil, but overcome evil with good." Responding to evil with evil only serves to increase its presence on earth.[22] The Christian has been given a power to overcome evil so as to stop its advance. So, as evil is perpetrated, and seeks to replicate itself, the Christian responds with good performing a kind of cosmic onychectomy (declawing).

Jesus promised that the Christian would be subject to persecution from the world. What's more, as the Christian grows in holiness he will be more thoroughly subject to that persecution in both quantity and quality.[23] However, he has been given the means, by the power of the Holy Spirit, to vanquish evil through humble obedience to his Savior. Thus, the Christian participates in the destruction of evil, not through fighting it on its own terms, but through an abiding faith in Christ. At times that will mean proximate avoidance, containment, and even moments of co-existence, but the

---

[22] Jay Adams, *How to Overcome Evil* (Presbyterian and Reformed Publishing, 2010) 45.
[23] Jay Adams, *How to Overcome Evil* (Presbyterian and Reformed Publishing, 2010) 49.

Christian's ultimate goal is always evil's complete obliteration, anywhere and everywhere he finds it. In Christ, the believer has been given a power, not of this world, to strip evil of its force and persuasion. He is to take full advantage of what he had been given in Christ; to do any less is to sinfully serve as evil's complice.

The Shepherd David
Elizabeth Bouguereau, c. 1895

> Can God make a rock so large that he cannot lift it? Yes, there are things that God cannot do. He cannot lie; he cannot perpetrate evil; he cannot deny himself.

In the cross of Jesus Christ evil and good came together as never before in the history of creation. In Jesus' crucifixion mankind witnessed the greatest evil that could ever be perpetrated – the brutal murder of God himself. In Jesus' crucifixion mankind also witnessed the greatest good that could ever be imagined – God dying to save his enemies. God returned good for evil *a caelo usque ad centrum* ("from the sky to the center of the earth"). At evil's worst, God showed his best.[24]

> "Evil often triumphs, but it never conquers." (Joseph Roux)
>
> "Do not repay evil with evil or insult with insult, but with blessing, because to this you were called so that you may inherit a blessing…" (1 Peter 3:9)

The Nature of Common Grace

Consider the fact that animals do not prepare their food; they simply eat that which they find naturally. Humans, on the other hand, prepare food using various techniques and spices, all with attention to color and presentation. Doesn't it appear that "someone" designed the natural world in such a way that foods would exist in a diverse and pleasing array of textures, colors, aromas and tastes? Isn't it obvious that the natural world was masterfully infused with a richness and artistry of culinary

---

[24] Jay Adams, *How to Overcome Evil* (Presbyterian and Reformed Publishing, 2010) 49.

delights which enhance the human experience? This is further evidence that humans are not the product of blind evolution but rather are the beneficiaries of a carefully laid out plan for the universe.

This observation about the inherent artistry of the universe, serves as a fitting introduction to the issue of God's common grace. The doctrine of grace could be summarized as "God's rewards at Christ's expense." Common grace (like the two other forms of grace - prevenient grace and special grace), is equally a gift at Christ's expense and, more specifically, is God's good gifts to reprobate mankind, his unmerited favor even to those who deny him, reject him, and ultimately hate him. The *locus classicus* for the doctrine of common grace is Matthew 5:45, "…that you may be sons of your Father in heaven. He causes his sun to rise on the evil and the good, and sends rain on the righteous and the unrighteous." On account of Jesus' sacrifice on the cross, and because of the Father's incomparable love for his Son, mankind is afforded a refuge from God's unmitigated wrath, offered unmerited favor that he might turn to God in faith.

> Mankind shows a tendency to attack that which is weak and vulnerable. This is not normative but results from the igneous intrusion of sin into the human heart. God however comforts, protects, and strengthens the weak and,[25] through his common grace, restrains the evil within men so that they often do the same. In fact, God prioritizes the forlorn indigent and the humble outcast in his efforts to save mankind,[26] while opposing and thwarting the proud and self-aggrandizing.[27]

Additional Scripture on common grace:

1. In Exodus 9:19, the Lord warned Egypt of a coming plague.

   > 'Give an order now to bring your livestock and everything you have in the field to a place of shelter, because the hail will fall on every person and animal that has not been brought in and is still out in the field, and they will die.'

   It is fascinating that God, as an act of common grace, warned Egypt of his own judgment upon them. Those among Pharaoh's officials who feared the Lord heeded the warning.[28] Thus, as an act of grace, God even warns those who are rightly under his judgment to flee from impending wrath.

---

[25] Psalm 82:3; 116:6
[26] Matthew 5:3
[27] James 4:6
[28] Exodus 9:20

2. "This is what the wicked are like – always carefree, they increase in wealth." (Psalm 73:12)

3. "Though grace is shown to the wicked, they do not learn righteousness; even in a land of uprightness they go on doing evil and regard not the majesty of the Lord." (Isaiah 26:10)

4. Luke 2:10 recounts, "But the angel said to them, 'Do not be afraid. I bring you good news of great joy that will be for all the people.'" This is the nature of Jesus' birth, death, and resurrection, good news for *all* people throughout the world as the blessing of his incarnation would be felt throughout the entire creation.

5. "If you then, though you are evil, know how to give good gifts to your children, how much more will your Father in heaven give the Holy Spirit to those who ask him!" (Luke 11:13)

6. "Yet he has not left himself without testimony: He has shown kindness by giving you rain from heaven and crops in their seasons; he provides you with plenty of food and fills your hearts with joy." (Acts 14:17)

> Christopher Columbus (c. 1451–1506) wrote, "It was the Lord who put into my mind the idea of sailing to the Indias. All who heard of my project rejected it with laughter and ridicule. There is no question that God inspired me." This might be seen as a manifestation of common grace.

Common grace offers a taste, a hint, of the bounty of fellowship with God. God's intention, in fact, is that his common grace would function as a prelude to the gospel.[29] The idea is to lavishly bless mankind so that he will turn to God in repentance for such unmerited favor. Mankind, under the tyranny of sin, is offered a palimpsest of God's goodness and character, both in the external world and in his internal being, so that he would run to God in faith. Thus, the goodness of God juxtaposed with a world under the bitter curse of evil should drive sinners to repentance. Birds build nests even in dead trees.

A heightened appreciation for common grace emerges when one catches glimpses of its absence. (Murphy's law, "Anything that can go wrong, will," highlights something of this absence.) After the fall, when evil entered the creation, the world should have become a hell-like habitat, overrun by threats, pain, suffering, loss, and degradation in every place, at every time, to the highest degree. However, God, in his common grace, restrains both the evil within man and cosmic evil. For example, the ten plagues on Egypt (in Exodus 7:14-11:10) offer a grainy picture of a world without God's

---

[29] Clair Davis, "Doctrine of Man" class, Westminster Theological Seminary, Philadelphia, Pennsylvania

common grace, a time of unrelenting wrath upon the earth, a world without restraint, consumed by uninhabitable places, overrun by destructive forces, punctuated by catastrophic events, and ultimately cankered by agonizing death.[30] In the same way, the world today, too, could become a theater of calamity in which each day is marked by heightened tragedy, vexing annoyances, and unimaginable loss, if not for Christ.

> As a result of the fall, in Eden the ground was cursed;[31] in the land of Canaan the ground was blessed. The Bible's description of Canaan functions as a metaphor for common grace as the land seemed to exhibit a kind of reversal of the fall. Canaan seemed to, in some way, be shielded from the consequences of the fall so that even God's enemies living in the land benefited from its abundance. Canaan's fruit was sizable, the people grew tall and strong, and their cities were fortified.[32] The land's blessings seemed to accrue to its inhabitants regardless of their status before God.

Bonaparte Crossing the Alps
Paul Delaroche, 1848

One looks upon evil despots as the worst of men, yet each person harbors the same fundamental propensity to hatred, murder, and abandonment to evil. Each is a Caligula (AD 12–41) in waiting. There are two reasons that one does not become a functional tyrant. The first is on account of God's common grace which restrains evil within the heart. The second is that each person, thankfully, does not possess the means by which to act out his destructive ideations. This, too, is grace, that God limits human ability to act upon its own evil

---

[30] It is fascinating to note that God even finds a way to be glorified through the wicked and their destruction. Exodus 14:4 states, "And I will harden Pharaoh's heart, and he will pursue them. But I will gain glory for myself through Pharaoh and all his army, and the Egyptians will know that I am the Lord."
[31] Genesis 3:17
[32] Numbers 13:27, 28

desire, not affording the means to fully express the rebellion within.[33] Thus, it is God's grace and greatest gift to each person that he does not grant him what he wants. Man's limitations in ability, opportunity, and resources are a towering display of God's goodness.

> I find it fascinating that Jesus even had mercy on demons, allowing the legion evil spirits possessing the demoniac to inhabit a herd of swine.[34] Thus, common grace extends to the *entire* creation (even to Satan and his minions), that none should suffer unduly. God shows his unfathomable goodness even toward that which is pure evil.

One could think of common grace as tidal breaks running parallel to the shore. Such breaks, checking the ocean's surging mass and taming its fury, offer a measure of calm. This is the effect of God's common grace upon the world (often mediated through faithful Christians), a kind of tidal break to the world's unrelenting evil, moments in which veins of evil are staunched so that they cannot extend any further. However, a tidal break is limited; it may dampen the ocean's power and presence, but it does not eliminate its destruction. Likewise, common grace offers some bulwark but, by God's fiat, its effect is limited.

> American exceptionalism (the idea that America was the first nation in the history of the world in which its citizens were protected from the encroachment of government) was only possible because an overwhelming majority of the population exhibited a profound and abiding faith in Jesus Christ. This has always been the basis for the Constitution's success and the motivation for American freedom, something never before seen in the history of the world (hence the exceptionalism). However, as faith in Jesus Christ slowly dies in the American theater, so crumbles the foundation for its exceptionalism. Without faith in Jesus Christ, the Constitution cannot long endure as the federal government will arise as social savior, shredding the Constitution's delicate balance. As faith in Jesus erodes so does the freedom which once accompanied it. (It is actually God's mercy to remove certain freedoms where faith in Jesus does not exist, since those freedoms soon become a noose around the people's necks.)

Common Grace in Balance

While the doctrine of common grace is crucial for understanding God's dealings with fallen mankind, Christians often concede too much too it. Christians tend to view common grace as a catch-all or umbrella concept by which to cast favorably any medical, scientific, literary, educational, or social achievement which appears to

---
[33] Genesis 11:7, 8
[34] Mark 5:12, 13

benefit society. However, many fail to see that what often passes under the guise of common grace is in reality a blight and scourge upon humanity.

For example, much of what passes under the stamp of medical advance actually destroys the body or the psyche. Because they often do not understand the nature of some types of medicine, its treachery as a world system, and its inherently man-centered directive, Christians blindly praise God for this gift to humanity. While reconstructive surgery (medicine which maintains or repairs the basic structure and integrity of the body) is beneficial, other forms of medicine are detrimental, such as chemical-based psychotropic medications (that which seeks to in any way alter the body's design features). What Christians often call a gracious gift may be the exact opposite.

The point is that common grace easily becomes a blinding concept not permitting the Christian to critically analyze and evaluate the mechanics of a world system operating around him, without Christ, and against Christ. Christians are easily beguiled by the world's stratagems when they attempt to be naïvely irenic and winsome. Efforts to be falsely gracious (replete with the appearance of secular-style tolerance) form lacunae in the Christian's understanding leaving him vulnerable to traps set by the world.

> Anywhere in the world in which one finds effective hedges against evil people thrive. Sometimes those hedges are legitimate governments, biblically-sound church authority, or even well-crafted social structure. At other times those hedges are draconian intrusions such as totalitarianism, mob rule, or economic extortion. One way or another mankind finds a way to hem in social evils. Where that hem is God-directed it will prove a blessing; where it is man-centered it will prove a curse.

Common grace must not be construed in such a way that it has nothing more than a canceling effect upon God's other statements, or undermines the Bible's assertions about the consequences of sin ("Do not be deceived: God cannot be mocked. A man reaps what he sows."[35]). Common grace cannot become a type of *deus ex machina* in which God suddenly and decisively delivers the wicked from the wages of their sin.[36] For example, Proverbs 14:30 is clear, "The heart at peace gives life to the body, but envy rots the bones." Proverbs 28:1 states, "The wicked man flees though no one pursues, but the righteous are as bold as a lion." There are consequences to sin (most pointedly within the heart); chasing false gods often brings bitter ramifications and life-altering repercussions.

Consider the following statistic. Ninety percent of American households own at least

---

[35] Galatians 6:7
[36] The *deus ex machina* (literally in Greek: "god from the machine") is a plot device found in ancient Greek tragedy in which a seemingly intractable dilemma is suddenly and abruptly solved with the contrived and unanticipated intervention of an unforeseen element such as one of the gods.

one Bible (the average household has three), but only twenty-six percent of Americans read the Bible daily. People enter and exit those households; they discuss matters; they laugh and cry; they make purchases; they watch television and they surf the internet. All the while, a Bible may sit on a backroom bookshelf gathering dust year after year, decade after decade. As family members go about their daily routine, the truth sits right there in their midst. The answer to life's murky questions remains within arm's reach but often, on account of distracted hearts, a world away. Thus, for the ninety percent the truth is present; for the twenty-six percent the truth is known (presumably).

Don Giovanni and the Statue of the Commander
Alexandre Evariste Fragonard, c. 1835

John 8:32 states, "Then you will know the truth, and the truth will set you free." Often, well-intentioned Christians quote the second half of this verse ("the truth will set you free"), while neglecting its qualifier in the first half. The truth does not set one free; it is one's *knowledge* of the truth that sets one free. The truth cannot set one free unless he knows it. This distinction pierces to the heart of this common grace discussion since truth is not a magic wand setting everyone free. That dusty backroom Bible is not a sacred amulet to ward-off evil. It has no power to change lives unless it is opened and read with eyes of faith. Only those who rightly weigh and appropriate the truth are set free. In other words, God does not universally negate the effects of the fall, but specifically negates those effects in those who avail themselves of the truth. God does not blindly cancel out the effects of sin separated from repentance and faith (a coming to know the truth).

Back to the central point, common grace should not act as a glossing agent, seeking to mitigate the God-induced mechanics of the created order, especially the effects of evil upon the heart. A sound hermeneutic permits the full force of Scripture to take hold and apply itself so as to expose the dire condition, import, and peril of sin. Thus, common grace should not become a set of blinders causing one to tacitly overlook the deadly consequence of life outside of God's provision.

- 2 -

THE WORLD, THE FLESH, AND THE DEVIL:
Assessing the Threat Matrix

The Course of Empire: Destruction, Thomas Cole, 1836

"Everything that Kills Me Makes Me Feel Alive"[1]

The world system is Satan-orchestrated war with God. Sinful nature, the flesh, craves the things of the world, and in so doing strengthens the devil's hold over humanity. Satan is the great adversary, liar,[2] and destroyer who seeks to obliterate God's work in the most cunning, vicious, and violent ways. Thus, three concepts work in tandem, the world (comprehensive system), the flesh (willful and complicit participant), and the devil (prime-mover and mastermind). In Matthew 13: 38, 39, Jesus used an agricultural metaphor to describe this. He likened the world to a field, the devil as a sower, and the evil-doers who arise (those of the flesh) as the weeds. Additionally, 1 John 5:19b states, "…the whole world is under the control of the evil one." One could think of the world, the flesh, and the devil in orchestral terms. The world is the music score, the flesh is the musicians, and the devil, the conductor. The musicians willfully obey the conductor in bringing the score to life.[3]

---

[1] Lyric from "Counting Stars," One Republic, 2013
[2] John 8:44
[3] Getting somewhat creative, one could think of the world as lightning, the flesh as the monster, and the devil as Frankenstein, the mad scientist.

> If one cannot define the enemy, one cannot defeat the enemy.

The world could be thought of as a cosmic cult, a grand system of compliance to Satan's objectives, methods, and will. In this way, the world might be labeled "corporate flesh." It loves what God hates, and hates what God loves. It calls good evil and evil good.[4] The world is marked by mixing and mingling that which should not be mixed and mingled. In other words, the world joins that which should be separated and separates what should be joined.[5] In this way, the world is a reversal of God's created order. It is a pressure, movement, or motive to return to "Day Zero" of God's creative acts,[6] a glorification of chaos, rebellion, and worshipping Satan and his work.

Leviticus 19:19 could be considered a metaphor for the world. The Lord commanded his people not to mate different kinds of animals, not to plant a field with two types of seed, and not to wear clothing woven of two kinds of material. This verse points to the animal world (fauna), the plant world (flora), and human culture. Thus, it encompasses the entire known world. God seeks to maintain the sanctity of his creative brilliance. For example, God established each animal and plant according to its kind.[7] It is God's good pleasure to maintain this order. However, in its war with God, the world perverts the created order, mixing what ought not to be mixed, and in the process destroys something of the creation's beauty. This perversion affects animal life, plant life, and human design. The parable of the weeds in Matthew 13:24-30 recounts how "an enemy" (the devil) sowed weeds in a field of good seed.[8] This is indicative of Satan's work, to mix, confuse, and ultimately ravish what God has done.

God's creation is perfect; man tampers with it to his detriment. Mankind only detracts from the creation when he attempts, through his own reason, to improve upon it. Consider every supposed technological advance. Any of those advances which does not comply with God's created order invariably forms rips and tears in the creation with dire consequence. In fact, the world system attacks God's created order with ruthless intent. Thus, every human creation which competes with God's is, to some extent, an attempt to either depreciate or worship the creation.

Consider also that God upholds the purity of his creation (through a continual process of either separating or joining) for the larger purpose of forming a backdrop for the gospel. The gospel's pure, unadulterated, and unmingled message is amplified by God's creative fiat. The creation and gospel function in tandem, and under the same

---

[4] Isaiah 5:20
[5] Cornelius Plantinga, Jr., *Not the Way It's Supposed to Be: A Breviary of Sin* (Wm B. Eerdmanns Publishing Co. 1996)
[6] This idea of "Day Zero" from Douglas Green, Westminster Theological Seminary, Philadelphia, Pennsylvania
[7] Genesis 1:11-25
[8] Matthew 13:39

themes of simplicity, purity, and perfection. For example, justification by faith and faith's subsequent good works are distinct aspects of salvation (the latter being evidence of the former)[9] which are to remain strictly separated.[10]

The World's Gods

In man's sinful nature, he hates God and convinces himself that God is not worthy of worship. In making God distant and irrelevant, man searches for a proximate god, one who comforts and exculpates him in his nagging travail of the soul. The following are some of the world's legion gods:

1. Atheism

2. Autonomy - man as law unto himself serving as his own judge

3. Monism (the body with no spirit, a derivative of scientific materialism) – a focus on the physical; denying mankind's eternal nature, while deifying the mind and that which pleases the body

4. The worship of self

5. Aesthetics (appearance, beauty, image)

6. Gratuitous pleasure – a consumption with lust

7. Materialism

8. The love of money – the relentless pursuit of money with little regard for ethical concerns

> "Do not store up for yourselves treasures on earth, where moth and rust destroy, and where thieves break in and steal. But store up for yourselves treasures in heaven, where moth and rust do not destroy, and where thieves do not break in and steal. For where your treasure is, there your heart will be also." (Matthew 6:19-21)

9. Competition for survival – the denial of a Creator who pours out grace upon his creation

10. Power – the unmitigated desire for control over others

---

[9] James 2:14-26
[10] Matthew Henry Commentary, Bible Study Tools, 2012

11. Relativism – the belief that all religion is manmade and therefore essentially equivalent and irrelevant

Entering the Mosque, Edwin Lord Weeks, 1885

12. Scientism – blind faith in science, technology, and medicine as mankind's saviors

> Isaiah 46:1 states, "Bel bows down, Nebo stoops low; their idols are borne by beasts of burden. The images that are carried about are burdensome, a burden for the weary." There are two gods mentioned in this verse, Bel and Nebo. Bel, the Babylonian god of war, sun, weather, destiny, and creation, was worshipped with prostitution and child sacrifice rituals. Nebo was the Babylonian god of learning, astronomy, and science.[11] It is fascinating that Isaiah mentions these gods in tandem, and that both are "burdens to the weary." The modern world also worships at the feet of a god like Nebo, and that god continues to burden its acolytes.

---

[11] *NIV Study Bible* (Zondervan), Table 8: "Major Idols Mentioned in the Old Testament"

13. Utilitarianism – the focus on pragmatism with little regard for deeper moral concerns

Matthew 4:8, 9, states, "Again, the devil took him to a very high mountain and showed him all the kingdoms of the world and their splendor. 'All this I will give you,' he said, 'if you will bow down and worship me.'" Satan stands behind each of the world's gods so that they uphold a common theme: oppose God and glorify Satan.

The Church of the World

Nothing exemplifies the world's worship and message like a modern New Year's Eve celebration. New Year's Eve has the look and feel of a bacchanalia evangelistic meeting, soaring praise of the world, the flesh, and the devil. This past New Year's Eve, I was invited to a friend's house where guests sat around a television anticipating the Times Square ball drop. In the countdown to the New Year, various entertainers performed. Upon completing his number, one musician stepped forward and said, "I have a message for everyone this New Year – love yourself!" The crowd roared.

That musician succinctly expressed his religion, voiced his faith commitment, and there is no better summary the world's message and mission than to simply love oneself. While this message sounds innocent enough (and therein lies its brilliance) what is really being communicated is – hate God. (The love of oneself and the hatred of God are opposite sides of the same coin, the love side merely serving as a clever disguise for the hate side.[12]) With those two words the world's voice, Satan's voice, and the voice of the flesh merge into a single clarion call to deify mankind.

Under the dictates of Satan (who seeks his own worship) the world establishes its own "church" with its own gospel, moral code, traditions, values, sermons, and evangelism. This secular church seeks to legitimize the "cravings of sinful man, the lust of the eyes, and the boasting of what he has and does."[13]

There are patterns which emerge when the secular church "gathers for worship." One's conscience is seared as he begins to sing with a chorus of other world worshippers. As all sing together they legitimize and affirm one another in their sin.[14] At first one's sin piques his conscience, but when everyone else is doing the same there is an atavistic acceptance of sin. Thus, the world seeks, with all the means at its disposal, to blunt one's innate sense of guilt before a holy God.

> The world breaks down worship resistance slowly and progressively. It ushers

---

[12] For a comprehensive discussion of self-love see chapter 9: "Marauding Visigoths: The Autocratic Self"
[13] 1 John 2:16
[14] This concept from Edward Welch, Westminster Theological Seminary, Philadelphia, Pennsylvania

mankind from theism to deism, from deism to atheism, and finally from atheism to Satanism.[15] Theism is the belief in a Creator God, to whom man is morally accountable. Deism makes God into a distant Creator, from which mankind is autonomous. Atheism removes God altogether, creating a worship vacuum. Filling the vacuum, Satan then installs himself as the creator. A proponent of occultism, Aleister Crowley (1875–1947) said that Satanism can make anyone feel like a "rock star." That is the world's ultimate objective to make each person feel like a demiurge.

The Chariot Race, Alexander von Wagner, c. 1882

Consider 2 Corinthians 4:4, 5:

> The god of this age has blinded the minds of unbelievers, so that they cannot see the light of the gospel that displays the glory of Christ, who is the image of God. For what we preach is not ourselves, but Jesus Christ as Lord, and ourselves as your servants for Jesus' sake.

Satan's shifting shadows and the darkness within the heart of mankind function in tandem to promote deception. In league with Satan, and under the dictates of sin, mankind fails to see evil for what it really is, a counterfeit of good. Man's sin is his religion blinding him to his worship predicament, shielding him from the state of his heart, so that while in the death-grip of slavery he feigns freedom.[16]

In 1919 the Amish collectively decided not to have their homes connected to electrical power lines. They felt that electricity would bring easy access to the allurements of the world therein imperiling their relationship with God and fracturing their community life. In a certain regard, the Amish show wisdom far in

---

[15] This progression borrowed from an unknown source.
[16] G. C. Berkouwer, *Sin* (Grand Rapids, Michigan: Wm. B. Eerdmanns Press, 1971) 237.

> excess of many other Christians. They recognize that no supposed worldly advantage is worth even a modicum of temptation to sin. Thus, the Amish sagaciously reject that which would normally be to their advantage in order to obtain that which eternally is.

As a kind of church, the world preaches sermons. The following are a sampling of the world's "sermons":

1. One's desires and cravings are good, indulge them at will.

2. One is incapable of loving others until he has been loved by those who owe him love.

3. One can be satisfied if he just has a little more. Keep indulging desires and one will eventually be filled and content.

4. Build boundaries between oneself and unhealthy situations and relationships.

5. One needs love, companionship, and sex or one can never be a complete person.

6. The one who successfully glorifies himself is the world's victor.

One of the world's principle blinding agents is a continual shift in, what might be termed, "language landscapes." When speaking of human relationship, the world takes on the language of psychology. When addressing human origins, the world adopts the language of evolution. When speaking of human need, the world assumes the voice of humanism. The world adopts the voices of hedonism, scientific materialism, liberalism, feminism, Marxism, or any other "ism," to suit the context. However, each language, while varied in contour and texture, is unified in a singular mission – oppose the gospel and deify mankind.

As a fascinating sidebar, in this shifting language landscape, the church of the world routinely distorts God's Word for its self-serving purposes. For example, Matthew 25:29 states, "For everyone who has will be given more, and he will have an abundance. Whoever does not have, even what he has will be taken from him." The world distorts this verse into a sociological term called the "Matthew effect," or accumulated advantage.[17] This term describes how, for example, eminent researchers routinely receive more credit than unknown colleagues, even if their work is similar. Likewise, those who are already renowned garner more attention, even if their work is in no way superior to that of others.

---

[17] This concept from sociologist Robert K. Merton (1910–2003), 1968

However, Matthew 25:29's intent has nothing to do with the worldly gain which accrues to the renowned. It focuses on the blessing of living by faith, the assertion that those who show faith will reap an abundance of blessing. while those who live for the world (those who "do not have"), will experience the curse of a life separated from God. The world grossly misinterprets God's Word, twisting and folding it into "origami" of its own imagining.

Finally, the world cannibalizes itself. The very message which it offers as living bread is the same message which devours those under it. For example, children today are often taught to have self-confidence, to believe in themselves, to assert themselves. It is this very message which vitiates against raising properly adjusted and content children. The world's lies hobble its inhabitants, casting them into an abyss of confused, fractured, and afflicted worship. The world's message finally spoliates those who adhere to it.

> Each person is born a slave, born into a prison he cannot smell or taste or touch, a prison for the soul. (adapted from "The Matrix," (movie) 1999)

The World's "DNA"

The Goldsmith Ladies on the Way to Boulogne in a Car
Julius LeBlanc Stewart, 1897

Between 1890 and 1908 the automobile was a toy for the affluent. From 1908 to 1925 it was a utilitarian vehicle for the masses. By 1925 it became a statement of personal style and an expression of taste. Ford Motor Company missed this decisive shift in

American culture, while General Motors exploited it. GM devised marketing innovations such as:

1. Purchasing a car on credit
2. Leasing
3. Using one's current car as the down-payment for a new one
4. Planned obsolescence - building cars to last only a relatively short period of time
5. Model years
6. A hierarchy of models
7. A fixed price regardless of demand

While Ford was a master of innovation, GM was a genius of marketing. At the end of the day marketing triumphed in the increasingly media-driven society of the 1920s.[18] This points to something of the world's methods, to manipulate consumers into spending through evermore sophisticated marketing techniques. The world seeks to keep consumer's slaves to purchasing, and uses any manipulative tactic to this end. The advent of advertising, marketing, and media was a bonanza for the world system as it could increasingly wield lethal weapons in the domination of the human heart.

> "There is no greater human power shaping the affairs of mankind than competition." (Henry Clay)

The media specializes in repeating boilerplate statements, infectious sound-bites, to characterize events. These statements function like mantras to keep the public brainwashed, thinking that events are accurately characterized by those statements. If a target statement is repeated enough times it is blindly believed as axiomatic truth, setting and baiting a Hobbesian trap in the culture war. An excellent example is any time the abortion debate is raised the term "the war on women" is inserted with regard to the pro-life position. Thus, the two concepts have become inextricably linked in the public consciousness so that any mention of the pro-life position is reflexively defined as a war on women.[19]

The world is largely composed of four main elements:

1. False religion (psychology, evolution, etc.)

2. Oppressive government (high taxation, maintaining control through licensure, regulation of borders, control of commerce and trade, defining national values and heroes, promoting the love of money as a societal panacea, advancing

---

[18] H. W. Brands, *Masters of Enterprise* (New York: Free Press, 1999)
[19] These media techniques are the work of mastermind Saul Alinsky (1909-1972) as found in his work, *Rule for Radicals: A Pragmatic Primer for Realistic Radicals* (New York: Random House Publishers, 1971)

forms of story-telling (such as the exploration of outer-space, which keeps the populace bewildered and subdued), and maintaining control over education using humanistic psychology)

3. Mind-control education (compliance to homogeneous knowledge, defining academically acceptable lines of argument, controlling debate within an academic elite using esoteric terms so as to exclude unwanted voices)

4. Mesmerizing media (entertainment, image, stilted story-telling)[20]

Some of world's sub-elements include:

1. The corporate world (control of commodities, advertising)
2. Finance (ownership, money-supply)
3. Scientism (stealth religious perspectives made to appear as objective knowledge)
4. Medicine (the manipulation and destruction of health)
5. Fashion (aesthetics, image)
6. Food production (inducing obesity and deliberate impairment of the body)

A Summary of the World's "Geography"

Primary Elements	False Religion (psychology, evolution)	Government (promote social panaceas)	Secular Education (beat the mind into submission; standardize thought)	Media (dazzle, confuse, beguile, mesmerize)
Secondary Elements	1. Corporations	1. Military	1. Homogenize knowledge	1. Media-driven storytelling
	2. Scientism	2. Taxation (the control and redistribution of wealth)	2. Set the terms of acceptable academic debate	2. Need and lust-inducing advertising
	3. Nationalism	3. Licensing boards	3. Maintain discussion within an academic elite	3. Obsession with aesthetics; image as enslaving

---

[20] For further discussion of the world's use of the media see the excursus, "The Rise of Media-Generated Need" in the first book in this series, *Ask for the Ancient Paths: From Art to Artifice to Arisen*, chapter 7: "The Needs Imperative"

	4. Humanism	4. Control of commerce	
		5. Define national values and heroes	
		6. Promote the love of money as universal panacea	
		7. Maintain a particular definition of medicine and control it with licensure	
		8. Food production as means of control of human health	*The Shadow* Edmund Blair Leighton, 1909

While the world follows Satan's intent and drive, its details and particulars bend to the will of mankind. Thus, while the world is Satan's idea, its specifics are man's craft. In this way, there is an inextricable link between individual sin and corporate sin so that the world's depravity is a macroscopic manifestation of the heart's microcosm.

The World's Motives

Nature abhors a vacuum. Likewise, the world cannot tolerate anyone not conformed to its image and intent. Thus, the world seeks to keep every person worldview homogeneous, in lockstep, compliant, and subservient to an overall system, while allowing for cursory and inconsequential individualism. As each person assumes a station in life, the world hates those who think outside of their allotted role, who deviate from the established system or plan. It fights viciously to keep each blinded and enslaved to futile pursuits, to keep its subjects chasing illusory wealth and meaningless pleasures.

False religions, intrusive governments, humanistic education, and propagandized media all work in tandem to maintain this stranglehold on the world's citizenry. It is through these institutions that the world seeks to equalize evil's pressure so that mankind's experience of intrinsic and extrinsic evil is seamless. In other words, the world seeks to uniformly replicate itself in each person so that that which one experiences in the world is exactly that which lives inside of oneself. In this way worldview conflict and motivational strife are eliminated. Incidentally, this is why

Jesus warned that the world would hate believers;[21] believers represent an external-to-internal pressure gradient. By means of their citizenship they embody something of a world vacuum, a bulb of worship defiance which the world cannot invade.

> "We all live under the same sky, but we don't all have the same horizon." (Konrad Adenauer)

Like a Procrustean bed, the world system is upheld by every non-Christian, whether directly or indirectly, so that he is a willful participant on account of his unwitting alliance with Satan. Thus, the world is a grand conspiracy aligned against God and his people, a paroxysm of willed order lent the appearance of disorder.[22] The Christian will generally be hated by, and at war with, the world system (although the world may at times tolerate Christians on account of God's common grace).[23]

The world system has four chief motives:

1. Sear the conscience so that it no longer correctly adjudges right from wrong
2. Institutionalize idols of the heart
3. Falsely exonerate the sinner from guilt before a holy God
4. Anneal these three internal conditions into societal institutions so as to maintain a stranglehold on the heart

> "If they can get you asking the wrong questions, they don't have to worry about answers." (Thomas Pynchon)

The world, in all of its various manifestations, obsessively zeroes-in on and guards these motives. With fanatical compulsion, the world attempts to make the enemy something other than oneself, to exonerate the self so as to escape blame before a holy God. God's work is always in the opposite direction, to implicate the self as guilty and in need of repentance. The Bible therefore impresses upon its reader the need to see the great enemy within.

> One could think of his conscience as a moral compass. A compass operates by means of an internal magnet. The world places another magnet next to that compass so that it gives a false reading. The closer the competing magnet the greater the disruption. Thus, the more one loves the world the greater his worship distortion.

The world deflects attention from man's true psychic state, emboldening him to assign blame to any source outside of his own conscience. Thus, the world's focus is toward

---

[21] Matthew 10:22; John 15:18
[22] This concept from Rene Magritte (1898-1967)
[23] John 15:18

that which is extrinsic to the conscience, so as to sidestep and exonerate the conscience. The Bible, however, directs itself toward the conscience, seeking to confront it so as to bring the sinner to crisis and therein recognize his desperate need for God's mercy.

For example, psychology, the handmaiden of the world, erroneously makes sexuality a basic human need and its expression, regardless of marriage commitment, a normal activity. Those who are abstinent by moral choice are considered in some way deficient, subject to some form of unhealthy suppression, and living in denial of their nature. Psychology has elevated sexuality to a non-negotiable need because it seeks to destroy God's absolute morality. According to God's Word, the unmarried person is fully expected to remain chaste. That is not abnormal, but rather the normal function of God's design vis-à-vis the human psyche. God calls the unbetrothed to exercise self-control, restraint, and patient self-denial. Likewise, God calls the betrothed to express their sexuality, not out of pagan lust,[24] but in mutual love. Thus, the world perverts, twists, and denigrates God's standard to suit a specious definition of true humanity.

The Lady of Shalott
William Holman Hunt and Edward Robert Hughes, 1905

> "The most dangerous falsehood is the slightly distorted truth." (G. C. Lichtenberg)

In summary this is the world's cartography, a master schema that keeps people on the leeward side of sin's mountain, permanently separated from the "hydrologic cycle" of Christ, forlorn and forgotten in an existential desert. In finding Christ, the sinner is

---
[24] 1 Thessalonians 4:5

shown the wayward side of the mountain, showered in life-giving rains so as to produce abundant fruit. The world, with all of its flourish and fury, seeks to separate the believer from that fruit.

What is the most dangerous thing in the world's eyes? What does the world hate more than anything? The gospel. Why? Because those who have given themselves to Jesus Christ, who are submissive to his will, cannot be controlled. The world wants more than anything to enslave people to its will and whim. The gospel breaks the enslavement mechanism and matrix so that the world loses its power and persuasion over hearts and minds.

> The blockbuster movie, "The Matrix" (1999), envisions a computer-generated social system which controls the earth's inhabitants. In the movie that which is thought to be tangible does not really exist, as everything is a digital illusion. This is not the Bible's worldview. The Bible presents the world, the flesh, and the devil as actual, as existential realities which keep mankind in bondage. Evil does exist, and its work is not just an illusion to be renounced through mental discipline. It is for this reason that Jesus Christ entered the world as God incarnate, and actually battled and defeated Satan through means of a physical cross. Since evil exists, salvation came, not through greater mind-control, but through the material entrance of God himself into history.

City as Incubator of the World[25]

In recent years numerous housing developments have arisen in my area. The typical construction technique is to clear-cut the forest, bringing down every last tree over several acres. The roads are constructed, the houses are erected, and saplings are replanted on newly-laid sod lawns. It occurred to me that this is exactly how the world operates with regard to the subjects of Satan's kingdom. The world's objective is to "clear-cut" each person so that he loses all connection with his head, the God of heaven. Once everyone has been stripped of his purpose, and disenfranchised from his nascent image-bearing, he is then "replanted" for the world's purpose, in the world's image.

The world uses various means to achieve this clear-cutting. For example, it increasingly herds people into cities so that they are easier to label, brainwash, and control. The urban landscape keeps life as distracted as possible so that inhabitants rarely consider the purpose and meaning of their lives. The city is saturated with entertainment so as to keep the mind numb and unreasoning. The city dangles the allure of fast pleasure with impunity, the promise of burgeoning wealth, and the lie of sophistication and advancement. In time urban dwellers are reduced to mere stumps of

---

[25] For further discussion of the city see "Sin as Building One's Own Kingdom" in chapter 5: "Metaphors for Sin"

humanity, no longer able to focus on anything outside of themselves.

Cities standardize and concentrate the world's brainwashing. The city standardizes the world's delusion that salvation is found in money or pleasure, so that avenues to wealth and sensuality are clearly laid out. The city concentrates its message through a barrage of images plastered on every commodifiable surface. It is through this standardization and concentration that the city incubates world automatons, those who often see themselves as renegades, but are actually foot-soldiers marching in lockstep with the grand delusion.

> "If I'm free, it's because I'm always running." (Jimi Hendrix)

The World's Entertainment

The Rod of Aaron Devours the Other Rods, James Jacques Joseph Tissot, c. 1902

Consider Exodus 7:10-12, in which Aaron threw his staff down in front of Pharaoh and it became a snake. Pharaoh then summoned his wise men, sorcerers, and magicians who performed the same feat by their secret arts. Each threw down his staff and it became a snake. But Aaron's staff swallowed up the others. Exodus 7:22 then records that the Egyptian magicians, in imitation of God's first plague, turned the Nile to blood by their secret arts. Later, in Exodus 8:7 these magicians, again by their secret arts, made frogs spring up on the land in imitation of God's second plague. However, in an attempt to reproduce the third plague, Exodus 8:18 states, "But when the magicians tried to produce gnats by their secret arts, they could not..." In Exodus 8:19 the magicians admitted to Pharaoh, "This is the finger of God."

Later in Leviticus 19:31 God warned, "Do not turn to mediums or seek out spiritists, for you will be defiled by them." Mediums and spiritists, like Egypt's wise men, sorcerers, and magicians, employed various methods to keep the population in bondage to lies. They pronounced auspicious and inauspicious days; they predicted future events, and warned of supposed impending evil. This is all Satan's artifice to keep the foolish mired in superstition, wonderment, amusement, enquiry, mystery, and hidden elements of the phenomenal world. People seem to thrive on this tension and release of tension in their daily lives.

The wise men, sorcerers, and magicians entertained the Egyptians with their secret arts. These charlatans used fine sounding words to "tickle" the ear; the sorcerers summoned spirits with a frightful curiosity, and the magicians dazzled and thrilled with shadows and light. The modern world, like its ancient Egyptian counterpart, also employs wise men, sorcerers, and magicians for its purpose. The world's so called wise men are the academics, the scientists, and the psychologists. Its sorcerers are the storytellers who offer superstition and mystery. Its magicians pull the levers of the entertainment and media networks. But unlike Pharaoh's magicians who, in recognizing the finger of God, admitted the limits of their legerdemain, the modern world works with a brazenness that knows no bounds, bewitched by rakish delusion.

> "Now the Spirit expressly says that in later times some will depart from the faith by devoting themselves to deceitful spirits and teachings of demons," (1 Timothy 4:1)

The World's Handmaiden: Hollywood[26]

In past epochs China was conquered by foreign invaders such as the Mongols and Manchus. To repel these threats China built the Great Wall, amassed armies, and forged alliances. Today, however, there is a far more insidious foreign invader – the media. It does not force its way in with brute power, but invades with sweet enticements, seductive allurements, and the promise of mastery over one's fears. This is an immeasurably more effective means than physical conquest as it makes the conquered believe that he is the conqueror.

While former-president Dwight Eisenhower (1890-1969) coined the term the "military-industrial complex" to describe the mechanism by which the modern capitalist economy functions, a new term has arisen in the twenty-first century, the "entertainment-industrial complex." Today, modern economies are largely driven by

---

[26] For further discussion of this topic see the excursus "Psychology Reads Like a Hollywood Movie Script" in the first book in this series, *Ask for the Ancient Paths: From Art to Artifice to Arisen,* chapter 8: "What Has Jerusalem To Do With Vienna?: The Case Against Psychology"

entertainment, so that every industry is now governed by an entertainment imperative; every purchase is arbitrated by a need to keep the consumer entertained. This is part of a burgeoning world system which maintains a close link between entertainment and consumption, a beguiling axis of distraction to modern people.

Daphnephoria, Frederic Leighton, 1876

> Be suspicious of anything given a central location by the world, anything highlighted or promoted. Be suspicious of anything the world gives away liberally (like television content). There is usually an insidious motive.

First Corinthians 11:14 states that Satan masquerades as an angel of light. Thus, Satan plays with light, tosses it about in order to create shifting shadows (unlike God who does not change like the shifting shadows).[27] Satan co-opts light in order to induce error and confusion where God intended truth and clarity. That is, in a nutshell, the nature and intent of Hollywood, to whimsically play with light in order to deceive for Satan's purposes.

The media's chief propagandist, Hollywood, routinely creates visual allurements (such as movies) which might best be described as a kind of "collective sin projector." Movies project onto a screen the national ethos, the corporate *Zeitgeist*. The world's collective consciousness and conscience is exhibited and celebrated. That consciousness and conscience is thus affirmed and reinforced so that it becomes more thoroughly assimilated and "institutionalized" in society. Thus, society's collective sin is progressively petrified into individual hearts as it revels in the sin pictorial. Movies (and all visual media, for that matter), in a sense, recode the human moral "DNA" so that sin becomes normalized, routinized, and determinative.

The World's Cantata

---
[27] James 1:17

There is a theory that the highly influential Rockefeller family, working closely with media outlets in the 1950s, secretly promoted the widespread distribution of rock and roll music. The theory holds that rock and roll was seen as a way to pacify the masses, thus diverting attention from the rising social justice movements.

How does music inculcate the masses? It is not just the music lyrics, but the form of the music (its melody, beat, and timbre) which serenades with a particular worldview. That worldview either accords with, or opposes, the truth about reality. In this way, for example, there is an inherent superiority in classical music over rap. Classical music, in its very form, more closely accords with God's invested character in his creation. Even if one does not listen to the song lyrics, the music's form shapes the heart, calling it to repentance or greater rebellion.

> The theme of the world's music is "I want!"[28]

Music does not directly cause moral or immoral behavior, but it influences it, nudging it in a particular direction. The songs that fill one's heart are the counselors one will turn to in moments of indecision. When a person finds himself at a moral crossroads the music that fills his mind often encourages him to step in one direction or the other. Music does not force, it merely suggests, prods, or entices. While the counselor may not know a counselee's specific taste in music, he should be aware that the world's music, if it holds the counselee's attention, exerts a pronounced effect upon his heart. The medium is not neutral, and it does not invade without consequence.

The World's Legerdemain: Science

According to historian Stanley Jaki (1924-2009) author of *The Savior of Science*,[29] modern science was, from its advent, an eminently Christian endeavor, intimately tied to the knowledge of Jesus Christ. (This is an extensive argument requiring an entire book in itself.) The crux of Jaki's argument is that Aristotelian philosophy kept the Western world captive to a particular pre-scientific paradigm for 1,800 years. It was not until the 14th century that theologians at the Sorbonne, building upon the Bible's description of Jesus as *homoousios* (only begotten son of God), initiated the unraveling of the Aristotelian model. Jesus as "only begotten" proved to be the previously dormant truth which finally unlocked the concept of inertia (which would prove the breakthrough for Newton's classical mechanics).

As the Aristotelian model unwound, a worldview vacuum emerged which was quickly filled with proto-scientific theories and with the advent of experimentation. Thus,

---

[28] Edward Welch, Westminster Theological Seminary, Philadelphia, Pennsylvania
[29] Stanley L. Jaki, *The Savior of Science* (Wm. B. Eerdmans Publishing, 1988)

modern science was birthed from the chrysalis of a thoroughly Christian worldview. Jaki's thesis is that it was a specifically Christ-centered understanding of the universe which sparked the scientific revolution.

Ben Franklin Drawing Electricity from the Sky
Benjamin West, c. 1805

Science flourished for some five hundred years within a Christian milieu, until the rise of socialism. With the advent of the 20th century, science was loosened from its Christian moorings and co-opted for political expedience. Consider the way in which the world has taken science captive to its insidious agenda. Science has largely cast off its early days of sound investigation, having been hijacked to serve as a handmaiden of secular progressive liberalism.

> Stephen Hawking stated that cosmology is religion for intelligent atheists. Evidencing this atheistic agenda, science now hopes to uncover a single equation to explain the entire universe. That is the heart of scientism, seeking to make science function as the mind of God himself.

In short, science is now a weapon of the world's agenda wielded in the subjugation of humanity. Thus, so much of what masquerades as valid and verifiable science is nothing more than a sophisticated slight of hand, or a well-masked attempt to manipulate the created order for sinister ends. To my thinking there is no greater evidence of the world's power of persuasion than how effectively it mesmerizes by means of a scientific label. Thus, science has shifted from investigation to manipulation of the created order.

> "I wonder why Darwin occupies [a] position at the pinnacle of esteem. I can only imagine that he has been put there by a vast public relations exercise." (Dennis

Sewell)[30]

The World System: Intrusive Government[31]

Israel's demand for a king was an act of defiance toward God. They longed for a king, "such as all the other nations have,"[32] out of both envy and fear of surrounding nations. Kingship seemed to them a sure means of security, strength, and national pride. (The problem persisted in Jesus' time, as John 6:15 records, "Jesus, knowing that they [the Jewish crowds] intended to come and make him king by force…") In actuality, kingship would prove disastrous, leading to widespread poverty and abuse, as a centralized government soon exploited the people and siphoned off their earnings.[33]

Governments are always predatory when not held in check by Christian principles.[34] If not already in servitude to the holy God, a nation's subjects will be cast into servitude to the state, not through strong-armed tactics, but through winsome promises of relief from the curses of the nation's godlessness. Unrestrained government therefore seeks to advance subservience to the world system. Where relationship with the true God exists it is marginalized and subverted; where it does not exist it is never afforded an opportunity to germinate. By maintaining the hegemony of man-made systems of thought (most handily through popular psychology), the federal government keeps faith in Jesus Christ socially devalued. Government, when under the dictates of Marxist-based liberalism, seeks to insight class envy and subsequent class warfare so as to coax the populace from dependence upon a holy God (and the personal and corporate responsibility that entails). However, "freedom apart from God is just an illusion of pride."[35]

As each sinner is personally at war with God, he looks for allies in order to gain the upper-hand. Those allies can take many forms but the principle one is liberalism's masterful blame-shifting mechanism, converting personal failing into a supposed lack of adequate governmental oversight and provision. Liberalism ingeniously props up scapegoats for the very human degradation and foible that it often deliberately induces.[36] Because liberalism wields almost exclusive control of media and education, it can easily conjure, develop, and amplify new crises which it then blames upon

---

[30] Dennis Sewell, *The Political Gene: How Darwin's Ideas Changed Politics* (Picador, 2009)
[31] For a discussion of the government's role in maintaining psychology's power structure see the section, "Maintaining the Hegemony," in the first book in this series, *Ask for the Ancient Paths: From Art to Artifice to Arisen*, chapter 8: "What Has Jerusalem To Do With Vienna?: The Case Against Psychology"
[32] 1 Samuel 11:15
[33] 1 Samuel 8:10-18
[34] David Kupelian, *How Evil Works: Understanding and Overcoming the Destructive Forces That Are Transforming America* (New York: Threshold Editions, 2010) 1.
[35] David Kupelian, *How Evil Works: Understanding and Overcoming the Destructive Forces That Are Transforming America* (New York: Threshold Editions, 2010) 24.
[36] Adapted from David Kupelian, *How Evil Works: Understanding and Overcoming the Destructive Forces That Are Transforming America* (New York: Threshold Editions, 2010) 6.

political opponents or opposing worldviews. Such new crises, illuminated by the media and reinforced through education, serve to broaden the scope and tighten the grip of tyrannical government.

> Every government must create a plausible enemy if one does not exist. Every government needs an engaging target and a convenient scapegoat.

Liberal-minded government entices the populace to desire the things of the world, and it promises the attainment of those things as long as its subjects relinquish more of their labor, liberties, and will to the government with pledges of allegiance to its agenda. This is the impetus for Marxism, the promise of worldly prosperity, and ultimately utopia, as subjects surrender their independence, bowing in obeisance to the government's gods. (However, those who surrender their will to government control receive in spades the bitter fruit of its godlessness.) But the rise of tyrannical government is a symptom of a society rotting at its core, a society overrun by humanistic psychology, deluded by atheistic evolution, drunk with sexually depravity, plundered by the love of money, and unwilling to discipline its children.

> Even the encouragement of immorality – sexual promiscuity, abortion, and easy divorce – is all part and parcel of the socialist modus operandi, because dissolute, dysfunctional people who have crossed the moral line and thus become estranged from the laws of God now need the 'god' of socialist government.[37]

> "Rome wasn't built in a day, nor did it burn in a day." (Mark Steyn)

There is a theory that the United States federal government deliberately engineers economic downturns through carefully-crafted Federal Reserve policies in order to further its socialist agenda.[38] Every economic downturn is another opportunity to advance the lie that additional legislation and expanded government programs will prevent future recessions. Thus, downturns are by design to tighten government's stranglehold on the populace with delusive promises. This is termed the "Cloward-Piven Strategy" (inspired by radical thinker Saul Alinsky (1909–1972)), the deliberate orchestration of crises so that the government can offer a solution, the nature of which increases its size and control over the populace.[39] (As a side note, while lower tax rates have been proven to increase overall tax revenue, tax revenue is not the government's objective. The objective is to seize a greater *proportion* of each citizen's resources, so as to tighten control over the population.)

---

[37] David Kupelian, *How Evil Works: Understanding and Overcoming the Destructive Forces That Are Transforming America* (New York: Threshold Editions, 2010) 7.
[38] Adapted from David Kupelian, *How Evil Works: Understanding and Overcoming the Destructive Forces That Are Transforming America* (New York: Threshold Editions, 2010) 10.
[39] David Kupelian, *How Evil Works: Understanding and Overcoming the Destructive Forces That Are Transforming America* (New York: Threshold Editions, 2010) 16.

Liberalism's objective is to collapse the nation's economic system through massive governmental debt, the expansion of the welfare system, and the creation of an evermore bloated entitlement state so that the government is obliged to take control of, and nationalize, more of the nation's economy and institutions. The ultimate goal is to reduce all the nation's assets and productivity to commodities which the government alone controls and distributes according to its will. (Currently, land, food, and water supplies are increasingly subject to government control.[40]) Thus, there is no functional difference between liberalism and socialism and, of course, socialism is merely a hop-skip-and-a-jump from communism.

The Gare Montparnasse, Paris, 1895

> "We know that we are children of God, and that the whole world is under the control of the evil one." (1 John 5:19)

The Web of Lies Surrounding Government Intrusion: "Our Father, Which Art in Washington"[41]

In his 1925 autobiography, *Mein Kampf*, Adolf Hitler (1889–1945) explained the evil genius behind effective lies. Hitler understood that is there is a lacuna in the way people perceive lies. People are accustomed to routine small lies, but do not expect

---

[40] This is the directive behind the United Nation's "Agenda 21," that governments would assume greater control of vital natural resources so as to force the populace into subservience.
[41] This quote from Paul Harvey (1918-2009)

large-scale grandiose falsehoods. Therefore, in great lies there is a surprising ability to deceive the masses since they are unprepared for them. Generally, citizens cannot fathom that their admired leaders would impudently fabricate colossal untruths.[42] Thus, soaring "meta-lies" are particularly destructive because, even if successfully exposed and refuted, they have a lingering effect which cannot be blotted out. Further, if the one receiving the colossal lie can be made angry, confused, or fearful, the lie is more easily absorbed and internalized. Duress causes one to compulsively believe lies as one is drawn to any perceived relief from emotional pain.[43]

The exponential growth of governmental power throughout the world (with the concomitant rise of socialism), brings with it a causal rise of what might be termed "psychopathology." The rise of governmental power spawns a populace which refuses to take responsibility for its own moral failings (the psychopathology), instead laying blame upon the shoulders of economic or social systems, races, religions, ideologies, or genders, with the government as the perennially hailed and presumed savior. The prevailing blame-shifting game is to cast every perceived human need as somehow answered in a government policy. Couple this focus on government as savior with the modern obsession with self, and modern people are firmly ensconced within their sin in an ever-thickening shell of lies.

The glaring paradox is that as government becomes more liberal it exhibits more aggressive control. The reason is that as increasing segments of the population are viewed as victims (who do not need to take responsibility for themselves) this opens a portal for government to step-in and take responsibility. However, the government's sense of responsibility is to progressively remove rights and freedoms in the name of deliverance from various plights (plights that the government itself has engineered).

> One may question what this discussion of the world system has to do with counseling. The purpose of this discussion is to accurately appraise the milieu in which counselees now daily live and operate. Thus, such an analysis reveals the social mechanisms, and pressures to conformity, operative in modern people. The counselor should be equipped to counter those mechanisms and pressures with a cogent presentation of the gospel.

The Slavery Cycle

In 1888 Empress Do Wager Ci Xi (慈禧太后) used funds intended to build China's navy to construct her opulent summer palace in Beijing. In a mocking gesture, she built a stationary marble boat for tea parties. (In 1894 a highly-vulnerable China was

---

[42] David Kupelian, *How Evil Works: Understanding and Overcoming the Destructive Forces That Are Transforming America* (New York: Threshold Editions, 2010) 15.
[43] David Kupelian, *How Evil Works: Understanding and Overcoming the Destructive Forces That Are Transforming America* (New York: Threshold Editions, 2010) 16.

helplessly attacked by the Japanese navy.) In similar fashion, mankind squanders God's gifts for self-gratifying purpose. As he wallows in self-delusion, mankind makes himself evermore vulnerable to the world's lies, allowing himself to become its slave. Many believe that mankind, in his towering arrogance and defiance of God, is regressing into a highly-sophisticated form of slavery.

Israel in Egypt, Sir Edward John Poynter, 1867

The slavery cycle has six parts:

1. **Birth**

2. **Education.** Public education is increasingly calibrated to break down rational thinking and cognitive skills in order to force compliance to a humanistic worldview. The idea is to mold students to fit like cogs in the world system's gears (all the while causing them to believe that they are autonomous free-thinkers).

3. **Work.** Work has become a form of slavery to the corporate and financial system. Most work environments continue the plan initiated by public education to mold mere cogs. The continued rise of global corporations keeps the populace subject to a "commodification" of labor.

4. **Debt.** Consumerism entices people to overspend so as to assume debt. In some sense the world is now rigged to lure people into debt, and keep them mired in lifelong debt. They are induced to sacrifice more of their lives in acquiring material possessions and in servicing the resulting debt burden.

5. **Taxes.** As government reach increases, assuming more of an unchallenged socialist posture, so do taxes. As taxes rise the debt burden becomes a greater threat.

6. **Death**

This slavery cycle keeps the masses distracted, chasing, occupied, oppressed, and largely controllable. As long as they are functioning slaves to the world system they can be manipulated into acquiescing to an emerging New World Order. In line with this slavery cycle, to a large degree, rampant consumerism has replaced responsible capitalism. The modern consumer model recasts consumption as a virtuous pursuit, almost a civic duty for building community. Consumption keeps the entire populace shackled to one common goal, chasing the next sensual thrill. In fact, I might redefine the modern slavery cycle as a worldwide "toy grab." It would appear that the world's entire modus operandi is now to simply grab for other's toys, to out acquire one's global neighbors. There seems to be little other purpose.

> With the explosion of internet commerce, retailers, in order to attract customers, have reinvented malls to be more "experiential." Malls have evolved into more than just shopping venues. They now contain theme restaurants, stadium-seating theaters, children's rides, and luxury services such as salons, spas, and fitness clubs. One mall manager said, "We want to capture more of the shopper's time because if we capture their time we capture their money." This summarizes the world's agenda quite well, to keep humanity distracted and desirous so that it continually parts with its resources. This forms the nucleus of the slavery cycle.

Incidentally, the study of economics reduces economic activity to quantitative measures, assigning risk levels and probabilities to human activity. However, economics, built upon humanistic psychology, fails to recognize behaviors as motivated by worship mechanisms. Therefore, economics continually falls into grave error with regard to the potential peril of that activity. It also blindly builds upon the "false assumption that endless growth is possible in a finite world," crafting its metrics around the supposed sustainability of expansive consumption.[44] In this sense, economic theory is merely a handmaiden to the world's objective to keep people slaves to chasing meaningless things that can never satisfy them. This chasing is often the source of social unrest throughout the world.

> Matthew 6: 24 states, "No one can serve two masters. Either he will hate the one and love the other, or he will be devoted to the one and despise the other. You cannot serve both God and Money." It seems that those who most vigorously serve money are the ones who feel "small," a deathly emptiness, a throbbing inadequacy, a host of unrequited longings. They turn to money for deliverance, but only find the same smallness in greater measure.

In accord with the slavery cycle, the world's population is rapidly moving into cities. For example, 20 million Chinese farmers relocate into cities each year. This urban

---

[44] *Inc.* (February, 2011)

explosion is part of a master plan to control the populace, to homogenize lifestyles, to more easily inculcate, herd, and channel the masses for end times events. Cities function efficiently for the manipulation and subjugation of the masses. It is fascinating that, beginning in 1939, Nazi occupiers ordered Jews to move from the countryside into major cities so that they could be registered for the initial phase of "The Final Solution." Cities function as a form of population warehousing, facilitating government control.

> Rampant consumerism, now gaining momentum throughout the globe, is possibly the greatest enemy to the environment. The recent "green products" movement is just a clever disguise for maintaining high-consumption while imagining that one is protecting the environment in the process. Green products falsely assuage guilt over wanton waste and careless consumption (and in this way are a clever concoction of the world system).

Rain in an Oak Forest, Ivan Shishkin, 1891

With each passing year, the slavery cycle increasingly becomes a Hobson's choice as mankind either submits to the world's agenda or finds himself subject to its wrath. As the book of Revelation warns, a day approaches when those who refuse the mark of the beast (666) will be excluded from all commerce.[45] (As an intriguing sidelight, the number "666" is considered good luck in China.)

The Christian in the Context of the Slavery Cycle

---
[45] Revelation 13:16-18

Outside of my bedroom window, on a rolling hill, stand two Colorado Blue Spruce trees planted on the same day some three decades ago. The tree on the left, rooted in rich dark soil, shot up to the sky, exploding with full heavy bows. The tree on the right was rooted in red clay, its trunk now gnarled and twisted. It is barely half the height and girth of the left tree. In a sense, these two trees represent something of the Christian life in the context of the world. The faithful Christian, as he interacts with the world (but not necessarily all non-Christians), feels himself to be growing in clay, his spirit gnarled. The world system and the Christian clash, operate at cross-purposes, and feel a mutual nagging chafing. Whether in a social gathering, during a business transaction, or in an educational setting, I routinely feel out of place, awkward, embarrassed, and generally misplaced, like my spirit yearns for good soil but finds itself being knotted by nutrient deprivation. Thus, Hebrews 11:38a informs, "…the world was not worthy of them." As I look upon the world system, as I observe its obsessive chasing and futile striving, as I glimpse the reckless consequence of its slavery, my thought is that I was made for so much more than this.[46] My spirit yearns to shoot to the sky, heavily laden with bow-breaking good fruit.

The Triumvirate of Evil[47]

Satan deceived Adam and Eve with "one friendly conversation."[48] So, too, each sinner is easily deceived in this way. The world continually moves toward bringing to fruition Satan's lie to Adam and Eve, "You shall be as gods."[49] Satan's false promise is that mankind can, through his own effort, conquer death and defy God. World systems, orchestrated by Satan, dangle the promise that through mankind's own sinister plans he can achieve perfection and immortality (the modern day Promethean promise).

The world, the flesh, and the devil are intimately co-mingled, sinners living in a world of chicane under the tyranny of the great architect of sin, the Adversary. The world, the flesh, and the devil could be thought of as environment, motive, and mastermind. The world's environment is fertile ground for sin to germinate and grow. The flesh is the motive to disobey and depose God himself. The devil is the mastermind pulling the strings of a cosmic empire aligned against God. Satan seeks, at every turn, to direct human worship, to, through faulty worship, spawn sinful thought and behavior while people busy themselves largely unaware of his efforts.

> "Above all, you must understand that in the last days scoffers will come, scoffing

---

[46] Hebrews 11:40; 1 Peter 2:9
[47] For a discussion of the relationship between the world, the flesh, the devil, and suffering see "Suffering's Blueprint" in the third book in this series, *The Days of Reckoning Are at Hand: From Fig Leaf to Olive Branch to Laurel Wreath*, chapter 2: "Suffering: The Kintsugi Objective"
[48] Bruce Wilkinson, *The Prayer of Jabez: Breaking Through to the Blessed Life* (Sisters, Oregon: Multnomah Publishers, 2000) 69.
[49] This is called the Luciferian philosophy.

> and following their own evil desires. They will say, 'Where is this 'coming' he promised? Ever since our ancestors died, everything goes on as it has since the beginning of creation.'" (2 Peter 3:3, 4)

Under Satan's delusion most heinous sin is skillfully packaged as that which appears virtuous and noble. Consider the way in which ancient cultures surrounded their temples with prostitution, the sale of religious articles, extortion under the guise of superstition, and the consultation of mediums and spiritists for entertainment. These heinous displays of depravity were housed under supposed beneficent religious venues.

David Presents the Head of Goliath to King Saul
Rembrandt Harmensz van Rijn, 1627

"The Second Coming"[50] (excerpt)

Turning and turning in the widening gyre
The falcon cannot hear the falconer;
Things fall apart; the centre cannot hold;
Mere anarchy is loosed upon the world,
The blood-dimmed tide is loosed, and everywhere
The ceremony of innocence is drowned;
The best lack all conviction, while the worst

---

[50] William Butler Yeats, *The Dial* (Churchtown, Dundrum, Ireland: The Chuala Press, 1920) (the first eight lines only)

> Are full of passionate intensity.

Immerse a sinful heart in the world system, tempt it with Satan's lies, and one is left with a clear and present danger. One is powerless to resist evil unless he saved by Christ. Since the world is predatory by nature (a mirror of Satan's work and motives), the gospel also wields a kind of predatory quality. As with Lady Wisdom in the book of Proverbs, the gospel seeks and invites those who have been devastated by the world, those who have had their fill of its lonely, bitter, and enslaving existence.[51] Matthew 5:6 states, "Blessed are those who hunger and thirst for righteousness, for they will be filled."

> "For our struggle is not against flesh and blood, but against the rulers, against the authorities, against the powers of this dark world and against the spiritual forces of evil in the heavenly realms." (Ephesians 6:12)

Goliath's Weapons

> "David said to the Philistine, 'You come against me with sword and spear and javelin, but I come against you in the name of the LORD Almighty, the God of the armies of Israel, whom you have defied.'" (1 Samuel 17:45)

Goliath's Weapons	Purpose	Analogy
1. Sword	Close combat (arm's length)	The flesh
2. Spear	Near combat (several yards)	The world
3. Javelin	Distant combat ("faceless" combat)	Satan

One could think of the flesh, the world, and Satan in terms of Goliath's weapons. The flesh is the most intimate manifestation of evil, man's evil heart, and as such represents a form of "close combat" (as with a sword). The world, as a spear, is the proximate presence of evil, man's systems, surroundings, and daily interactions. Finally, Satan is a more distant and faceless evil, the long-flight combat of a javelin. God has specifically countered each form of evil in Jesus.

> "All those gathered here will know that it is not by sword or spear that the LORD saves; for the battle is the LORD's, and he will give all of you into our hands." (1 Samuel 17:47)

God defeated the flesh (the heart), the world (the environment), and the devil (the cosmic) with Jesus' death upon the cross. However, while that victory exists it is not yet fully realized. The world, the flesh, and the devil are alive and operative, despite the already achieved triumph. Through God's sanctifying work he continually reduces

---
[51] Luke 14:21-23

the effects of the flesh, seeks to change the world, and vigorously opposes Satan. The concepts of the world, the flesh, and the devil each receive varying degrees of emphasis throughout Scripture. At times the environment is mentioned (the world), at others the devil is the focus of God's attention. But God's overwhelming obsession is to destroy the flesh (the sin nature) within believers, to sanctify a people for himself. God seeks to remove that which is a host or receptacle for both the world and the devil, so that some would be holy.

The Devil Doesn't Dance in the Pale Moonlight; His Name is Not Mr. Scratch and He Doesn't Wear Prada®[52]

Satan Before the Lord
Corrado Giaquinto, c. 1750

Matthew 4:8, 9 states, "Again, the devil took him to a very high mountain and showed him all the kingdoms of the world and their splendor. 'All this I will give you,' he said, 'if you will bow down and worship me.'" However, Daniel 4:32 states that God is sovereign over the kingdoms of the world and gives them to anyone he wishes. Satan would not have control over the world unless God himself allowed this. Satan's authority is thus derivative, under the sovereignty of God.

> Satan's promise to bestow upon Jesus all the kingdoms of the world and their splendor serves as a metaphor of sin. Why would Jesus take this Faustian bargain? He is already in authority over the entire universe. Why would he grab for a grain of sand when the world's shores belong to him? However, the abject absurdity of

---

[52] The devil is referred to as "Mr. Scratch" in Stephen Vincent Benet's "The Devil and Daniel Webster" (Farrar and Rinehart, 1937)

> Satan's temptation is the same abject absurdity of sin itself. Why would the Christian settle for a godless existence when the God of the universe has invited him to participate in, and experience, eternal glory?
>
> Additionally, consider the fact that as the Father of Lies Satan never intended to give Jesus anything. He sought Jesus' worship but furtively planned to give nothing in return. This, too, is a picture of sin. In giving Satan his worship, mankind receives nothing in return. The kingdoms of the world and their splendor can never belong to man, and even if they did, they are mere dust pouring through his greedy fingers.

While Satan is under the confines of God's good sovereignty, many Christians functionally tend toward an ancient Manichean concept of God and Satan. They see the two as locked in a life and death struggle for supremacy, the outcome of which is uncertain. In reality, by means of the cross, God has already vanquished Satan.[53] The war is won; Satan has already been rendered a defeated foe.[54] However, that defeat is not yet fully realized. Satan is permitted to exist and continue his deception for a time as part of God's plan to differentiate the elect (those who are saved) from the reprobate (those who are lost). (Theologian John Murray (1898-1975) labeled this winnowing effect, initiated after Christ's vicarious atonement, the "playground of differentiation.")

Fallen mankind tends to wrongly ascribe God's qualities to Satan. For example, there is a tendency to make Satan omniscient, omnipresent, and omnipotent. In reality he is none of these; he is a created finite being, limited in every sense that the creation itself is limited. One should neither view Satan as more powerful than he is, nor underestimate his potential. The Bible offers the correct balance so that the Christian can live accordingly.

> C.S. Lewis' (1898-1963) classic work *The Great Divorce* (1945) includes a "ghost" influenced by a little red lizard perched upon its shoulder. Representing Satan, the lizard seeks to shape thoughts, words, and behavior. The ghost is both complicit in the lizard's schemes and at the same time longs to be free from them.

Mark 3:28, 29 states, "Truly I tell you, people can be forgiven all their sins and every slander they utter, but whoever blasphemes against the Holy Spirit will never be forgiven; they are guilty of an eternal sin." Additionally, Matthew 12:30-32 states:

> 'Whoever is not with me is against me, and whoever does not gather with me scatters. And so I tell you, every kind of sin and slander can be forgiven, but blasphemy against the Spirit will not be forgiven. Anyone who speaks a word

---

[53] Colossians 2:15
[54] Mark 3:27

against the Son of Man will be forgiven, but anyone who speaks against the Holy Spirit will not be forgiven, either in this age or in the age to come.'

Blasphemy against the Holy Spirit is attributing to the Holy Spirit that which is of Satan, and to Satan that which is of Holy Spirit. As the Holy Spirit moves the human spirit to repent and believe, if that work is resisted that is blasphemy. Such error strikes to the heart of one's deepest faith commitments. Also consider that what God gathers and concentrates, Satan scatters and dilutes. Thus, Satan seeks to diffuse God's power so that it has little impact. God works with sharp straight lines, but Satan blurs and bends those lines so as to make God's character and work appear largely the same as Satan's.

> As John 3:20 states, Satan and his followers love darkness, refusing to come into the light lest their evil deeds be exposed. Satan works best in the dark of night, in the umbra of the world system.[55] I find that Satan hews out a lair for himself in the bowels of every human institution. He emerges to strike out at the truth when there is no visible opposition, and then retreats in cowardly fear. Satan uses a contoured logic of lies to confuse, obfuscate, and cast doubt upon the truth, while being sure to never confront that truth head-on (lest his lies be exposed). Thus, Christians must be vigilant in recognizing that as soon as they sow seeds of the gospel, Satan will secretly emerge to subvert that effort, often snatching away the seed.[56]

It is intriguing that in Christian tradition Satan is often depicted with the cobbled physical attributes of animals, such as horns, wings, and cloven hooves. In the book of Genesis, Satan took the form of a snake, and later in the book of Revelation he appears as a giant beast. In line with this, the first page of *The Satanic Bible* (1969) by Anton LaVey (1930–1997) contains the statement: "Satan represents man as just another animal, sometimes better, more often worse than those that walk on all-fours. [Man because] of his 'divine spiritual and intellectual development' has become the most vicious animal of all!"[57]

> In John Milton's (1608–1674) *Paradise Lost* (1667) Satan said, "Hell is wherever I am."[58]

Ezekiel 28:17 is in tension with these ideas. "Your heart became proud on account of your beauty, and you corrupted your wisdom because of your splendor. So I threw you to the earth; I made a spectacle of you before kings." Satan, the guardian cherub, fell from heaven when, as this verse states, on account of his beauty he became proud and

---

[55] John 3:20
[56] Matthew 13:19
[57] Anton La Vey, *The Satanic Bible* (New York: Harper Collins, 1969) 1.
[58] Incidentally, this concept accords with the Bible's teaching that heaven is less about a *place* and more about a *person*, Jesus Christ. Thus, hell is wherever Satan is and heaven is wherever Jesus is.

corrupted his wisdom. Luke 10:18 states that Satan was cast from heaven like a bolt of lightning. Satan, as a created being subject to God's wrath, is derivative and dependent. He is never original but consigned to imitate God's work, perverting that work in order to subvert it.

> "Better to reign in hell than to serve in heaven." (Satan, *Paradise Lost*)

While Satan was once "beautiful" and filled with "splendor," he assumed animal forms out of hatred for God's image. Part of Satan's work as the Father of Lies and as the destroyer is to make humans believe that they are nothing more than animals. Satan effaces the image of God in man and replaces it with the image of created things such as animals. As Satan assumes an animal-like form, he seeks to replicate this in mankind. If Satan can convince humans that they are merely animals he has succeeded in *functionally* destroying the image of God within them, providing the rationale for mankind's continued denial, rebellion, and separation from God.

Satan Falls
Gustave Dore, 1866

> "Even as the words were on his lips, a voice came from heaven, 'This is what is decreed for you, King Nebuchadnezzar: Your royal authority has been taken from you. You will be driven away from people and will live with the wild animals; you will eat grass like the ox. Seven times will pass by for you until you acknowledge that the Most High is sovereign over all kingdoms on earth and gives them to anyone he wishes.'" (Daniel 4:31, 32)

The first sin to enter the universe was that of Satan's pride.[59] However, this sin did not have the cosmic effect that Adam's did because Satan was not God's image-bearer. Adam was made as God's vice-gerent, invested with the image and likeness of God, for the purpose of commanding and ruling the creation in God's place.[60] Thus, when

---
[59] Ezekiel 28:16, 17
[60] Douglas Green, "Old Testament History and Theology" class, Westminster Theological Seminary, Philadelphia, Pennsylvania

58 WHAT AGREEMENT IS THERE BETWEEN THE TEMPLE OF GOD AND IDOLS?

Adam fell he brought with him a cascade of evil and suffering, as the ambassadorial prophet, priest, and king had now fallen. This was the climactic event casting the universe into a state of evil.

> "Ingratitude is the daughter of pride and the mother of every vice." (French proverb)

Case Study: Balaam and Balak as Tropes of Satan[61]

Idol/Sin	Balak	Balaam
1. Fear of those who are stronger	Terrified, filled with dread over Israel[62]	
2. Love of money	Israel was too powerful; it would devour everything[63]	A seer/sorcerer but also a prophet; described God as "the Lord" his God.[64] It is likely that Balaam was once a true prophet who later gave himself over to sorcery in his love of money.[65]
3. To destroy those whom one fears	Pursued a curse on Israel, to defeat them and drive them out[66]	
4. To seek one with the ability to bring power, meaning, and blessing to oneself	Balak worshipped Balaam's ability because it suited his own purpose;[67] Balak ascribed to Balaam God's work.[68]	
5. To seek prestige through the will and acts of men	Pressured Balaam to comply with his wishes through exploiting the fear of man within him; sought more princes in order to appear more distinguished[69]	
6. Unmitigated	Ruthless and determined to	

Balaam and the Angel (detail)
Gustav Jaeger, 1836

---

[61] Numbers 22–25; For further discussion of Balaam see "Integrationism as Akin to Balaam's Error" in the first book in this series, *Ask for the Ancient Paths: From Art to Artifice to Arisen*, chapter 9: "Integrationism: The Modern Day Babylonian Captivity"
[62] Numbers 22:3
[63] Numbers 22:6
[64] Numbers 22:18
[65] Adam Clarke Commentary; Numbers 22:7, 8
[66] Numbers 22:6
[67] This "bless-bless, curse-curse" formula is from Genesis 12:3, used there to describe God's work.
[68] Numbers 22:6
[69] Numbers 22:15

The World, the Flesh, and the Devil 59

pursuit of one's own will	oppose God; no obstacle allowed[70]	
7. Manipulating another to effect one's own personal will	Balak obeyed Balaam as god and offered him a handsome reward; Balak resigned himself to do whatever Balaam said.[71]	
8. Fear of man, man pleasing		Balaam made Balak into an idol, as he inquired of the Lord a second time merely to placate Balak. Balaam should not have asked the Lord again, as it seems he merely wanted to find a way to gain money and receive the praises of men.[72]
9. Lustful desire		God gave Balaam over to his lust.[73]
10. Focused intent on one's own will		Balaam saddled his own donkey as a display of focused intent;[74] this revealed a very personal nature to the work ahead.[75]
11. Unrelenting intent to curse God's people		God was angry with Balaam as he knew the intentions of Balaam's heart.[76]
12. Reckless disregard for God's will	*Isaac's Servant Tying the Bracelet on Rebecca's Arm* (detail) Benjamin West, 1775	Balaam's path was reckless,[77] and so his donkey veered off the road.[78] The donkey moved between vineyards and crushed Balaam's foot against a wall.[79] The donkey then lay down in a narrow place.[80]
13. False piety and false repentance		Balaam bowed low and fell prostrate before the angel; he said that he had sinned, and if

---

[70] Numbers 22:16
[71] Numbers 22:17
[72] Numbers 22:19
[73] Numbers 22:20
[74] This seems reminiscent of Abraham saddling his own donkey as an act of humility (Genesis 22:3).
[75] Numbers 22:21
[76] Numbers 22:22
[77] Numbers 22:32
[78] Numbers 22:23
[79] Numbers 22:25
[80] Numbers 22:26

while still focused on self-serving gain		the angel was displeased he would go back.[81]
14. Eagerness to rush into sin	Balak impatiently waited for Balaam[82]	
15. False worship for the purpose of worldly gain	Balak sacrificed cattle and sheep to appease the gods;[83] he sought to gain the rewards of the world through opposing God's people.[84]	To appease Balak, Balaam instructed him to offer false sacrifices, making Balak think that he would receive a favorable outcome through his display of piety. Balaam accepted some of the sacrificed cattle and sheep offered by Balak as meat sacrificed to idols.[85] Balaam and Barak prepared seven altars and sacrificed bulls and rams on three separate peaks.[86]
16. Denial of the word of the Lord		Balaam clearly beheld a vision and heard the word of the Lord, yet denied it.[87]
17. Anger arising from not gaining one's idolatrous desire	Balak's anger burned against Balaam. Balak showed signs of a frustrated idol, one that he sought to guard and force into compliance with his will.[88]	
	Balak appealed to Balaam's loyalties, insinuating that misplaced loyalties impeded Balaam's financial gain. Balak asserted that the Lord had kept Balaam from being rewarded.[89]	
18. Laying a		Balaam found a way to placate

---

[81] Numbers 22:31, 34; the angel's sword was a prophetic indicator of how Balaam would eventually die – by Joshua's sword.
[82] Numbers 22:37
[83] Numbers 22:40
[84] This scene is reminiscent of Satan taking Jesus to a high place and tempting him with the kingdoms of the world (Matthew 4:8-10).
[85] Numbers 22:40
[86] Numbers 23:1,2, 14, 29, 30
[87] Numbers 24:3, 4
[88] Numbers 24:10
[89] Numbers 24:11

devious trap for God's people		Balak and gain the reward he sought. Balaam advised Balak to use Moabite women to seduce Israelite men.[90] Balaam caused the Israelites to curse themselves through sexual immorality and idol worship.[91]
19. Opposing God's work		Balaam represents the height of hypocrisy – one who had been privy to the Lord's will, yet was still intent on opposing it.

Consider 2 Corinthians 11:14, "And no wonder, for Satan himself masquerades as an angel of light." This verse offers a clue to the way in which Balaam operated. He could not oppose God's will directly. He could not verbally curse the Israelites, but Balaam did, nevertheless, find a way to temporarily thwart the Israelites. He instructed Balak to use Moabite women to seduce Israel's men. This is exactly how Satan works. He cannot curse God's people directly, but he can seduce them with images of pleasure, with the promise of immediate gratification.

Satan assumes the appearance of an angel so that he can beguile those who are not wise to his huggermugger. He puts forth an image of that which is desirable while concealing the deathtrap nestled within. This is often exactly how the church today is seduced. The church is charmed with the allure of psychology, the attraction of moralism, and the promise of experientialism and pragmatism, all made to appear beneficial and life-giving. Many, like Balaam, put on a form of godliness but merely for personal ambition.[92] They seek nothing more than monetary gain, prestige, or praise for their efforts. In the process, they bamboozle God's people with fine sounding arguments which ultimately lead to spiritual death.

The World's Singular Obsession: Destroy Faith in Jesus Christ

The world is a fluid concept, continually evolving and assuming various hues based on society's whims and machinations. Each person must interact with the world on some level, and each person either contributes to the world's degradation or functions as a purifying instrument. Without relationship with Christ one necessarily deepens the world's rebellion, intensifies its dereliction, and encourages its deviance and defiance.[93] Every word, every deed, either emboldens the world or confronts it. There is no neutrality.

---

[90] Numbers 31:16
[91] Jude 11-13
[92] 2 Timothy 3:5
[93] Matthew 12:30

Under the world's guile, the sinful heart seeks any means possible to deflect attention from itself. In compliance with the world, the church has fallen into this trap by offering sanctuary to sin. How does it do this? The church has largely redefined its existence and mission in worldly terms. In this way, the church is often complicit in the world's distortions of the gospel, externalizing and trivializing sin so as to siphon attention from the heart's depraved condition.

The Martyrdom of St. Bartholomew
Giovanni Battista Piazzetta, 1723

> In the context of evangelism, Christians are quick to state, "God has a plan for your life." While this is absolutely true, the implication is that God's plan revolves around something one is to *do*. Truer to the Bible, God's plan revolves around something one is to *be*. Thus, God's plan for one's life is that one would be sanctified in Christ, made holy for all eternity. Every action, every achievement, every undertaking is entirely secondary to this.

Ephesians 2:3 states "All of us also lived among them at one time, gratifying the cravings of our sinful nature and following its desires and thoughts. Like the rest, we were by nature objects of wrath." At one time each Christian was dead, captivated by his own desires, and worshipping in the church of the world. God called him out, set him apart, and brought him to life.

Consider the following analogy: a grey car is most likely to be in a traffic accident since it blends-in with the road surface and reflects light poorly. This makes it hard to see. Thus, just like a grey car on a similarly colored road surface, a Christian life which looks like that of the world, and poorly reflects the light of Christ, will soon find itself wrecked. However, the Christian, to the extent that he is faithful to God's Word, is set apart to function as the world's conscience.[94]

Thus, as each faithful Christian interacts with the world he continually either draws the world to repentance and faith or further confirms its eternal damnation. That is why Jesus warned that the world would hate Christians, just as it hates him.[95] The world cannot stand in the midst of Jesus or its followers; it must either submit in worship or else retreat in contumacious contempt. What is clear, however, is that the world operates under a singular obsession: to thwart faith in Jesus Christ. Either the world must die to itself, or else Jesus and his followers must die. The two, darkness and light, life and death, cannot peacefully coexist.[96]

Excursus: The Amish

Revelation 17 reads,

> There I saw a woman sitting on a scarlet beast…The woman was dressed in purple and scarlet, and was glittering with gold, precious stones, and pearls. She held a golden cup in her hand, filled with abominable things…The woman you saw is the great city that rules over the kings of the earth.[97]

The modern world is easily bedazzled by the allurements of wealth, pleasure, power, and achievement. It readily drinks from the "golden cup filled with abominable things," which is the greed, lust, hatred, arrogance, and gossip that fills the world.

The Amish recognize something of the inherent danger that lies in city life, technology, materialism, rapid transportation, and the media. They see that the modern world is on a path of destruction as it craves ever more enticing allurements, salvation through technology, greater wealth, faster travel, and more information to feed its pride and assuage its fears. Romans 1 speaks of the foolish hearts of men being darkened as they continually espouse futile and foolish thinking, filling themselves with wickedness, senselessness, and ruthlessness.[98]

The Amish rightly judge that much of the modern world is evil, that often technology only brings ungodliness and ready access to impure living. They seek a hedge against the world intruding upon their families, and suppose that simple living is the best means of remaining focused on, and committed to, God. Does this perspective implicitly neglect heart change so that a sanctified heart can interact with, and use,

---

[94] Harvie Conn (1933–1999), "Doctrine of the Church" class, Westminster Theological Seminary, Philadelphia, Pennsylvania
[95] John 15:18; 1 John 3:13
[96] 2 Corinthians 6:14; Ephesians 5:11
[97] Revelation 17:3, 4, 18
[98] Romans 1:21, 29, 31

technology for godly purposes? There is certainly a temptation to neglect heart issues with such an isolationist approach. However, there is also a piercing wisdom in the Amish perspective which rightly adjudges the frailty and limitations of the human spirit, even when highly-sanctified.

The Amish wisely plumb the perils of the heart; they understand something of its rhythms and reasons, its sickness and depravity. The Amish have taken the courageous step of separating themselves from that which only feeds and emboldens godlessness. They have chosen to forgo pleasures and wealth for the sake of community and for the sake of a lifestyle of worship to God. For this reason they are the unsung heroes of the modern world, truly a royal priesthood in the midst of a depraved generation.[99] They have without compromise put their faith and devotion into Jesus Christ, and in fact consider everything a loss compared to the greatness of knowing him who bore their sin.[100]

> The faithful are often difficult to find because they do not call attention to themselves. This is part of their beauty, that they are largely invisible to the world.

Jesus Has Overcome the World, the Flesh, and the Devil

Genesis 3:15, the first prophecy of Jesus' death on the cross, predicted that Jesus would crush the serpent's (Satan's) head. While Jesus' death did, in fact, strip Satan's power, he simultaneously disarmed the world and rendered the flesh inert. So, Jesus offered a competing system to that of the world, thus, breaking the world's monopoly on man's time and attention. In his perfect obedience, Jesus pierced the flesh's armament so that those in Christ can live in the Spirit's power. Jesus re-appropriated Satan's mantle so that the devil no longer holds sole authority over the human heart. Thus, in one final act, Jesus concurrently rendered the world, the flesh, and the devil inert entities, present but impotent, in existence but anachronistic.

Jesus is reckless in reaching those who have grown weary of the world, leery of themselves, cognizant of evil's power over them, and desperate for answers. Jesus seeks those who have reached the end of what the world has to offer and find themselves only more lost, afraid, empty, and longing than ever before. He invites those who no longer find comfort, security, meaning, and relationship in the world, who no longer plumb their own depths for answers. Those few who finally discover that the world is fractured, deceived, deceptive, ruthless, and in short, controlled by an evil being from whom they long for deliverance, are the ones to whom Jesus draws near. What's more, those who recognize that the world's constituents cannot live in safety within themselves, that they too are plagued by an inward evil whose grip is

---

[99] 1 Peter 2:9
[100] Philippians 3:8

beyond their comprehension or control are, as Jesus said, "not far from the kingdom."[101] Those who finally long for deliverance from the world, the flesh, and Satan, three entities of which they may have little real understanding but nevertheless feel their crushing presence, are the ones whom Jesus can ultimately reach and deliver.

---

[101] Mark 12:34

TOTAL DEPRAVITY:
This Imperiled Arcadia

Introduction

In Nathaniel Hawthorne's (1804-1864) short story "The Birth-Mark" (1843) eminent scientist Aylmer is entranced with his stunning new wife, Georgiana. Georgiana is flawless in appearance except for a hand-shaped red birthmark on her cheek, "a crimson stain upon the snow." Aylmer, though irretrievably infatuated with Georgiana, finds her birthmark repugnant. He grows ever more disquieted with it, so much so, that he recoils in disgust upon seeing this blemish. Aylmer opines:

Portrait of Lucretia Pickering Walker Morse
Samuel F.B. Morse, 1822

> It was the fatal flaw of humanity which Nature, in one shape or another, stamps ineffaceably on all her productions, either to imply that they are temporary and finite, or that their perfection must be wrought by toil and pain.[1]

Georgiana states that she would rather die than to continue living with the mark and Aylmer's disgust. One night Aylmer dreams of removing Georgiana's birthmark (which in his imagination continues all the way to her heart). To remove the stain, Aylmer finally concocts a potion which Georgiana lustily imbibes. Indicating that Aylmer has succeeded in creating perfection, the mark slowly fades, but tragically so does Georgiana, who soon dies. The moment physical perfection was achieved was the moment Georgiana entered into death.

Hawthorne has woven together a masterful allegory of the doctrine of original sin.

---
[1] Nathaniel Hawthorne, *Mosses from an Old Manse* (Wiley and Putnam, 1846)

The birthmark represents sin's pollution which taints God's perfect design, leaving it marred and mortal. Hawthorne implies that Georgiana's solitary, but pronounced, cosmetic imperfection serves as a reminder of a far deeper stain upon the heart. Thus, the birthmark is a symbol of the "liability to sin, sorrow, decay, and death."[2]

It is fascinating that on a more abstract level Hawthorne sought to draw attention to the danger of the scientific positivism of his day. Science (represented in Aylmer's concoction) sought to alter nature (represented in Georgiana's birthmark). While science appeared to offer some temporary results (the birthmark faded), it ultimately killed its subject, nature. Aylmer's attempt to achieve perfection in the body through science had become his religion. His attempts to undo that which only God can undo resulted in total loss. Thus, from a more theological perspective, science impertinently seeks to reverse the effects of the fall but cannot; the fall is not a cosmetic matter, but a failing of the human heart, and the heart is the provenance of God alone. The irony is that Aylmer, throughout his career, had known nothing but failure (even in his supposed scientific successes), and yet with Promethean bravado sought to perfect another.

Hawthorne's story, braiding together issues of original sin, false religion, idolatry of the heart, and humanity's impetuous and failed attempts to reverse the effects of the fall, forms a fitting prelude to the issue of total depravity.

The Root of Total Depravity

In Hungary's parliament building, under thick glass and guarded by twenty-four hour sentinel, is housed the Holy Crown of Hungary (The Crown of Saint Stephen) dating to the 12th century. At the crown's pinnacle is a gold cross bent at exactly a 23.5 degree angle. Some scholars believe that this was an homage to the earth's tilt, but upon careful inspection it is clear that the crown was dropped and the cross bent. This captures something of the human condition, a royal lineage fallen from grace so that the image of God within man is "bent." Some may explain away the bend as a design element (the 23.5 degree slant according with the earth's own orientation), but upon careful inspection it is clear that mankind is not as he was deigned to be.

> "I know that nothing good lives in me, that is, in regard to my sinful nature." (Romans 7:18)

In Leviticus 11:24, 27, and 39, the one who touched a dead animal was considered unclean for one day, while in Numbers 19:11 the one who touched a dead person was unclean for seven days.[3] Seven in the Bible is the number of completion. Therefore,

---

[2] Nathaniel Hawthorne, *Mosses from an Old Manse* (Wiley and Putnam, 1846)
[3] Adam Clark Commentary

the seven days mentioned here may symbolize the complete fall of mankind, or the utter corruption of mankind manifest in death. Thus, this passage may refer to either man's vastly more noble design in relation to animals, or to his inordinate sinfulness. Man, made in the image of God, fell with devastating cosmic consequence, a fall far greater than anything else in creation was capable of.

> While animals are subject to evil, they are not sinful. Thus, as one sees animals function, one sees beings acting and interacting without the taint of evil intent. Animals may be used by Satan to perpetrate evil,[4] but they do not willfully act out evil desire. Thus, in this regard, there is a categorical difference between mankind and animals. Only mankind is totally depraved, and only mankind willfully acts upon nefarious motive.

The Bunch of Lilacs
James Jacques Joseph Tissot, c. 1875

Adam and Eve grabbed for the forbidden fruit because they hated their finiteness. They longed to free themselves from their creature-hood, an existential state which rendered them limited and dependent on a holy God. They reasoned that if only they could gain the status of God himself, they could attain mastery over their own lives. Adam and Eve did not have a knowledge problem; they had sufficient knowledge to live holy lives. Adam and Eve had a submission problem; the same is true for mankind today. The greatest human need is for repentance, not knowledge; for deliverance, not mastery; for relationship, not independence. Seeking that which is only to its greater detriment, mankind's efforts always function in the opposite direction of God's.

> New York State produces an abundance of apples, so the natural conjecture that this is why New York City is nicknamed "The Big Apple." However, this is not true. The moniker comes from the city's sordid past. In the early 19th century a French noblewoman named "Evelyn" established an elite bordello near Wall Street.

---

[4] Matthew 13:4

> Neighbors called her "Eve" and her prostitutes "apples" because they tempted men. By the mid-19th century New York had more prostitutes per capita than any city in the world so it gained the ignominious sobriquet "The Big Apple."

Each sinner reinterprets God, the world, and himself through a sinful set of lenses. He invents an anthropocentric story and a godless universe in which he can be a god himself. Satan's theme lives in each sinner every moment of every day, "You shall be as gods,"[5] and this theme characterizes the fall. The fall brought a cascade of evil; the deception, the fear, the antagonism, the grabbing, the hiding, and the blame-shifting, that mar daily life, all began with a single act of the lust of the eyes, a lust to be God himself. The first rebellion was active and deliberate, it moved with purpose, it sought to destroy, it interpreted, it usurped, it exhibited lust, it sought freedom, it demanded, and finally it brought dire temporal and aeonian consequence.

Adam and Eve were beguiled because they wanted to be deceived; they were ensnared because they delivered themselves over to the trap; the lie was offered and they bought it, actively, willfully, deliberately, and in a heavy-handed manner. What is so tragic is that Adam and Eve had everything and lost it all. They were already basking in victory; their future was assured; their provision inexhaustible; they had the God of the universe as their friend and father; they just had to walk in obedience.

> Incidentally, Numbers 30:10-15, offers a blueprint of how Adam should have responded when Eve was tempted in the garden:
>
>> If a woman living with her husband makes a vow or obligates herself by a pledge under oath and her husband hears about it but says nothing to her and does not forbid her, then all her vows or the pledges by which she obligated herself will stand. But if her husband nullifies them when he hears about them, then none of the vows or pledges that came from her lips will stand. Her husband has nullified them, and the LORD will release her. Her husband may confirm or nullify any vow she makes or any sworn pledge to deny herself. But if her husband says nothing to her about it from day to day, then he confirms all her vows or the pledges binding on her. He confirms them by saying nothing to her when he hears about them. If, however, he nullifies them some time after he hears about them, then he must bear the consequences of her wrongdoing.
>
> Thus, Adam should have "nullified" Eve's "pledge" to Satan. Adam could have reversed the consequence of Eve's sin because he had final authority in the situation. However, because of Adam's silence, permissiveness, and participation, Eve's transgression stood, and Adam himself was counted fully culpable for it.

---

[5] Genesis 3:5

Satan deliberately attacked God's words ("Did God really say?"), and then sold Adam and Eve on a story. The story was that the victory was yet to come, that God's provision was not assured, that the universe was theirs for the taking. Satan offered the lie that the garden's main character was not God, but Adam and Eve themselves; they were to be the heroes. Satan's lie is that the plot is not God's perfect will but their own self-promoting wills. The outcome is not God's aeonian reign in glory, but Adam and Eve usurping and eclipsing God's glory. Adam and Eve had heard God's words, but chose to abandon them based on a deliverance they thought they saw.

Romans 11:36a states, "For from him [Christ] and through him and for him are all things..." Consider the three parts of Romans 11:36a:

1. From Christ
2. Through Christ
3. For Christ

All of creation was authored by Jesus,[6] redeemed through his life-giving act of salvation, and exists for his glory. Yet mankind usurps each of these roles setting up, what might be termed, an "inverted hermeneutic."[7] The inverted hermeneutic is an interpretation of life in which mankind lives under the delusion that all he has comes from himself, through his own reason and efforts (a functional form of salvation), and exists for his own glory. Mankind believes that his gifts exist to glorify himself, and he seeks to affect that glory through exploiting those gifts. Therefore, his gifts are used without and against God. The thrust of the inverted hermeneutic is that mankind makes God into the functional equivalent of Satan, liar, destroyer, and adversary against which he must battle.

> "I can calculate the movement of the stars, but not the madness of men." (Isaac Newton, in response to the South Sea Scheme of 1720)

A central feature of sin is the belief that one's root problem is his finiteness (intellectual, physical, social, etc.). To this end, mankind's activities are generally calculated to overcome this finiteness. However, man's greatest problem has nothing to do with finiteness; it has to do with his trenchant hatred of both God's infinitude and man's derivative status as creature. For this reason, mankind musters his gifts for his own glory in the futile attempt to attain the infinite, to finally perch god-like upon the creation. Therefore, if man possesses physical strength he exploits it to gain mastery through intimidation. If he is intelligent he applies this to outwit the world for his own betterment. If he is pulchritudinous he displays that beauty to beguile others

---
[6] Acts 3:15
[7] The term "inverted hermeneutic" from Joseph Schimmel, Pastor

and cultivate his sexual lust. Mankind refuses to countenance that these gifts were bestowed by God, to serve God's own aeonian purposes, to advance his heavenly kingdom.

> "But Jesus would not entrust himself to them, for he knew all people. He did not need any testimony about mankind, for he knew what was in each person." (John 2:24, 25)

Understanding the Nature of Depravity

Along the River During the Qing Ming Festival (清明上河图)
Zhang Ze Duan, 12th C.

The Legalists (5th - 3rd C. BC) were a group of officials and philosophers who established the first viable and coherent basis for Chinese government. They differed considerably from their predecessors, the Confucianists, in that they saw mankind as essentially evil, selfish, lazy, and greedy, while the Confucianists saw mankind as inherently good and noble. Under the Legalists, books were burned, rival philosophers were murdered, secret police used intimidation tactics, and neighbors were encouraged to spy on one another, all part of a draconian form of governance. Suspicion and fear pervaded China during that time. This divide between the Legalists and the Confucianists points to a central issue in the discussion of mankind's condition. Is mankind essentially good, with periodic lapses due to environmental factors, or is mankind essentially evil, with momentary displays of benevolence?

This dialectic between man's inherent goodness or evil has posed a contentious question throughout history. For example, Thomas Hobbes (1588-1679), like the Chinese Legalists, saw man as boorish, base, and brutal. To the opposite extreme, Platonic philosophy and Marxism see mankind as inherently good and destined for utopia. As a middling approach, one might sight Aristotelian and Lockean philosophy which both posit the *tablia rasa* theory, in which mankind is neither good nor evil but a blank slate upon which experience writes one's character.

> In his political treatise, *Leviathan* (1651), Thomas Hobbes theorized that human conflict arises from three fundamental sources: competition, diffidence (fear), and glory. Competition causes men to wage war for material gain; fear causes them to wage war for safety, and glory causes men to wage war so that their names are remembered.
>
> "Man is a rope stretched between the animal and the Superman – a rope over an abyss." (Friedrich Nietzsche)

Christians often seek to bridge this divide with the belief that man is a hybrid of good and evil. While this sounds reasonable (and unaided human experience might bear this out), there is not a scintilla of scriptural evidence for this. The Bible never presents mankind as an amalgam of good and evil. The Bible directly and deliberately presents mankind as originally innocent but decisively fallen into evil, an evil with distinctive contours.

> "For myself, though I am well aware of the incredible amount of destructive, cruel, malevolent behavior in today's world – from the threats of war to the senseless violence in the streets – I do not find that this evil is inherent in human nature." (Carl Rogers)[8]

The Bible's presentation of mankind's existential state offers the following descriptors of the psyche, a psyche consumed by:

1. The lust of the flesh[9]
2. Longings of the heart[10]
3. Loves/covetousness[11]
4. Warring idols[12]
5. Rulers of our minds[13]
6. Fears[14]

---

[8] Carl Rogers, *Journal of Humanistic Psychology*
[9] 1 John 2:16
[10] Ephesians 2:3; 1 John 2:17
[11] Hosea 2:12-17
[12] Romans 7:14-25
[13] Ephesians 2:3

74 WHAT AGREEMENT IS THERE BETWEEN THE TEMPLE OF GOD AND IDOLS?

7. Anxieties[15]
8. Controlling needs[16]
9. Demands[17]
10. Seeking covering/running/denying[18]

> "Television is the first truly democratic culture - available to everyone and entirely governed by what the people want. The most terrifying thing is what the people want." (Clive Barnes)

The Bible's presentation of human evil is properly couched in a creation-fall-redemption model. Thus, humanity's evil condition is not a design feature but a postlapsarian intrusion; it is not indelible, but can be eradicated through redemption. These nuances emphasize that evil is not imbedded in the human architecture, but rather is an alien element which humanity has willfully domesticated. Additionally, evil is not a permanent human element; Christ's death on the cross reverses and expunges evil through progressive growth in holiness.

The Interplay of Sin and Salvation

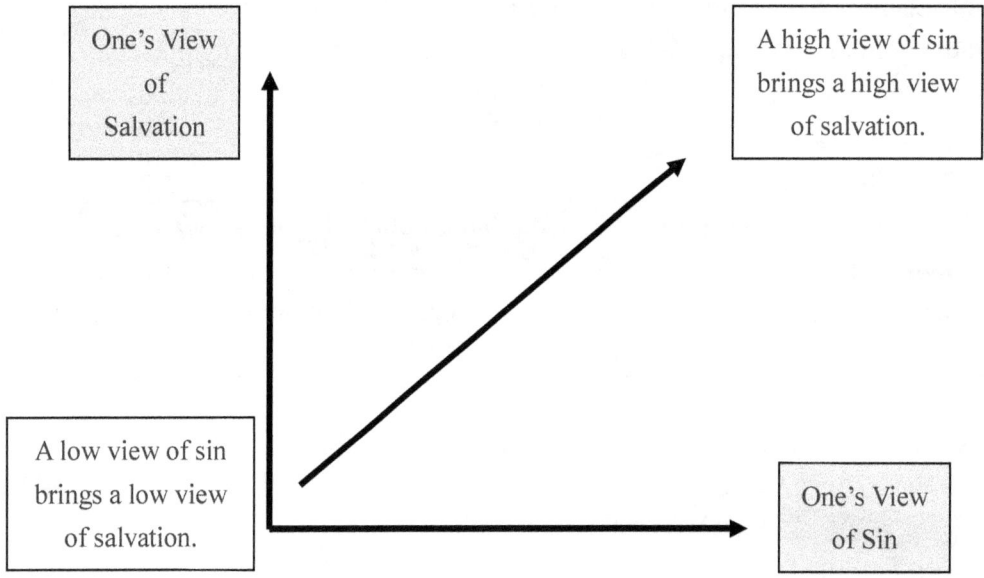

The assertion that the heart is evil (not by design, but as a consequence of the fall) must be ironclad in order to guard the import and power of the gospel. Without a thoroughly evil human condition the gospel losses its force and purpose. Put another way, a pale and weak view of human evil results in a pale and weak view of Jesus'

---

[14] Luke 12:4, 5
[15] Psalm 127:2; Philippians 4:6, 7
[16] Philippians 3:19
[17] Matthew 18:28-35; Luke 7:47
[18] Genesis 3:7

sacrifice. The erosion of a proper view of mankind is the first step in the abandonment of the gospel. Jesus himself hinted at this when, in Luke 7:47, he stated, "Therefore, I tell you, her many sins have been forgiven--as her great love has shown. But whoever has been forgiven little loves little." Jesus here implies that the repentant sinner rightly understands himself to have been forgiven far beyond his imagining, a degree of forgiveness which should result in boundless love for his Savior.

The Lament for Icarus, Herbert James Draper, 1898

One's view of sin and one's view of salvation are directly related. A glancing view of sin brings a glancing view of the cross, so that the one who believes he is only a slight sinner implicitly holds a low view of his salvation. However, recognition of the abject heinousness of one's sin brings overwhelming gratitude for the salvation Jesus wrought. If only one could understand the infinite depth of his sin, then he would appreciate the infinite price Jesus exacted to exculpate the sinner.

> Robert Oppenheimer (1904-1967), who oversaw the invention of the atomic bomb, after witnessing the devastation at Hiroshima and Nagaski said, "Now I am become Death, the destroyer of worlds."[19]

---

[19] Robert Oppenheimer quoted Vishnu in *The Bhagavad-Gita*.

The Bible presents the contours of the psyche with crystalline clarity. That psyche is in the grip of evil, but not irretrievably so. Additionally, mankind has surrendered himself to evil but, on account of God's common grace, he does not act upon evil to the fullest extent. Therefore, simply stating that mankind is inherently evil, and leaving it at that, does not capture the depth and richness of the Bible's teaching. While Hobbesian philosophy sees mankind as brutal, and irretrievably so, the Bible does not present humanity in this way. The Bible pinpoints the source of the problem (a root hatred of God), and offers a solution (submission to God through Jesus). So from the Bible's perspective mankind is under the restraining grace of a holy God at work to simultaneously initiate relationship with himself, and effect subsequent movement toward holiness.

> "When we remember that we are evil, the mysteries disappear and life stands explained." (Mark Twain)

If mankind is surrendered to evil how does one explain the myriad good that unbelievers routinely perpetrate? There are generally two explanations for this. The first is that which lends the appearance of arising from a good and noble heart actually arises from self-serving and self-glorifying intent. Sometimes man does good to win the praises of men, to gain some treasured outcome. Consider Luke 6:32, 33: "If you love those who love you, what credit is that to you? Even sinners love those who love them. And if you do good to those who are good to you, what credit is that to you? Even sinners do that." Jesus' point is that the sinner's love, even at its seeming pinnacle, is not genuine love at all. A further example, John 12:5, 6 recounts,

> 'Why wasn't this perfume sold and the money given to the poor? It was worth a year's wages.' [Judas] did not say this because he cared about the poor but because he was a thief; as keeper of the money bag, he used to help himself to what was put into it.

Judas' supposed concern for the poor was only a self-serving ruse, a well-camouflaged plot.

The second explanation for the good that unbelievers at times exhibit is that God, through his common grace,[20] restrains the evil within mankind so that he does not act out his heart's intentions to their full extent. Thus, God restrains the evil within man so that he may do good, not because of an inherent good within him, but in spite of the evil within him. On account of common grace, evil is mitigated so that the heart is guarded from itself to at times exhibit a shadowy good.[21]

---

[20] For a more complete explanation of common grace see chapter 1: "Deliver Us from Evil"
[21] Matthew 7:11

Consider Jesus' words in Matthew 7:11, "If you, then, though you are evil, know how to give good gifts to your children, how much more will your Father in heaven give good gifts to those who ask him!" What is the constitution of human evil if mankind still knows how to give good gifts? The answer is that human evil is firstly an intrinsic condition which does not always bear extrinsic manifestation. Human evil is a root defiance of God, an attempt to forge one's entire existence without God and against God. So Jesus' words reflect that internal condition while countenancing that even evil people may commit outwardly good acts. The paradox is that mankind's good acts in no way mitigate his evil nature, as that nature only darkens with time regardless of outward behavior.

> "Fear the goat from the front, the horse from the rear, and man from all sides." (Russian proverb)

The following diagram explains how the sinner may appear good when in reality he is ruled by self-serving, God-hating intent.

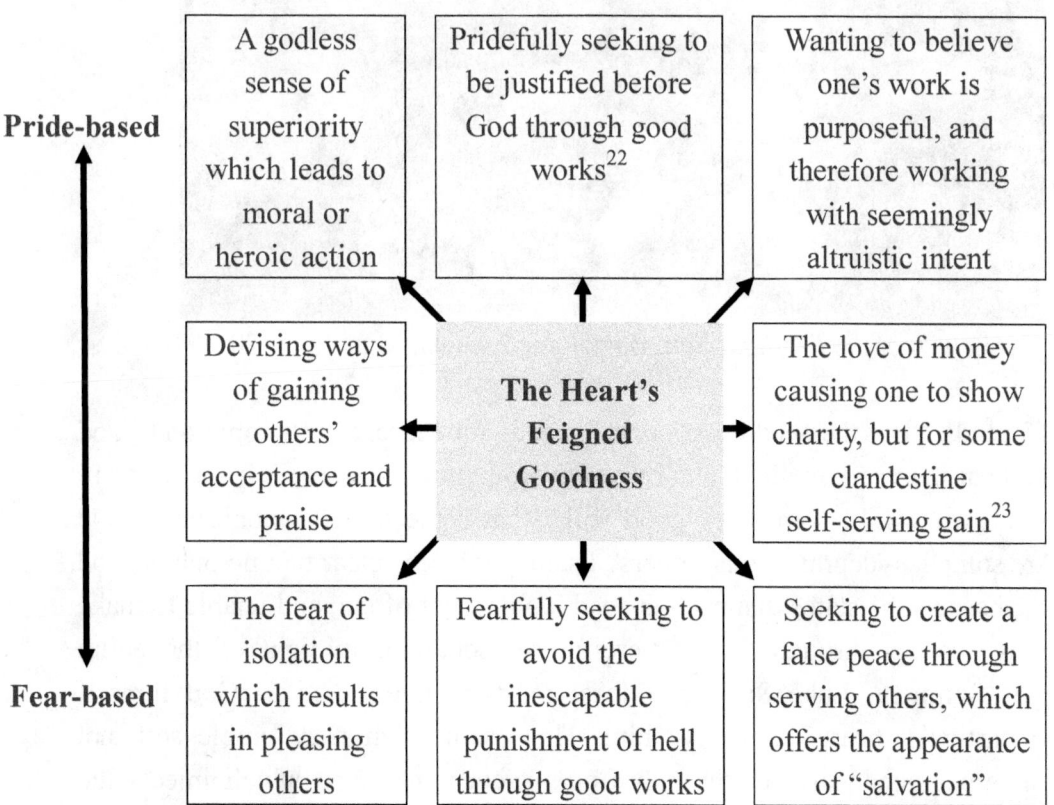

It is fascinating that even the vilest terrorist never describes his terror acts as "evil"; he always refers to them as "good." Rarely will people labor, much less sacrifice their lives, for what they believe to be evil purposes. Made in the image of a holy God, man instinctively wants to believe that he is good, and that his work advances a beneficent

---
[22] Ephesians 2:8, 9
[23] John 12:5, 6

cause.[24] If he cannot rationalize his work as good he usually will not act.

> "Men never commit evil so completely or joyfully as when they commit it from religious conviction." (Blaise Pascal)

Return of the Prodigal Son, Bartolome Esteban Murillo, 1670

Luke 8:15 reads, "But the seed on good soil stands for those with a noble and good heart, who hear the word, retain it, and by persevering produce a crop." It sounds as if, from Jesus' own words, some are "good soil," that some have "a noble and good heart." Are some less depraved than others? Psalm 14:2, 3, is clear that no one is good, not one. Ephesians 2:1 states that each is dead, on account of sin, and unable to make himself alive except through God's merciful resuscitation. In light of the entire teaching of Scripture, Luke 8:15, therefore, must be interpreted as God himself preparing particular hearts to receive him. Thus, some hearts are arable soil, not through inherent goodness, but through God's prevenient grace which injects the needed "nutrients and nitrates" to receive and prosper the seed of the gospel.

In the field of rhetoric there is an adage, "If one overstates an argument, he undermines the argument." In presenting the truth about the human condition one must be careful to assess it with the same balance and precision that the Bible offers.

---

[24] Tom Neven, *Do Fish Know They're Wet?: Living in the World Without Getting Hooked* (New York: Baker Books, 2005)

The Bible is clear that sinners are desperately depraved, that sin is a vastly greater affliction than anyone can fathom, a form of slavery to evil that inexorably shackles man's entire being. While the bad news of human depravity is beyond comprehension, the Bible does not see the human condition as irreparable. In fact, the Bible sees regeneration through Christ as wielding immense power, not just to reverse the effects of sin, but to produce within mankind a present and evident glory. The nature of this reversal is something too wonderful to fully comprehend. Thus, in summary, the human condition is a stygian darkness of immense evil; that's the bad news. Yet there is a brilliant glorious renewal, a soaring triumph made possible by Jesus' death on the cross; that's the good news.

> As a side note, temperocentrism is the belief that man has finally progressed past his primitive brutality, that humanity in modern times has reached a new level of civility and gentility. Thus, the belief is that man's Gargantua and Pantagruel days are merely a distant nightmare from which he has finally awoken. This is a complete fiction as the 20th century alone saw more people die at the hands of the state than in all previous centuries combined.[25] Mankind may have achieved a certain level of technological advancement, offering the appearance of heightened nobility, but he certainly has not evolved to a superior state which sheds his evil proclivities.

Total Depravity

> "Life is a maze in which we take the wrong turn before we have learnt to walk." (Cyril Connolly)

To understand the Bible's teaching on human evil one must understand the concept of total depravity. Total depravity asserts that every aspect of the image of God in man is fallen. This does not mean that mankind is as evil as he possibly could be. "Total" refers to comprehensive in scope, but not total in degree or measure. Total depravity, therefore, means that the image of God in man is fallen, damaged, faulty, marred and, from God's perspective, dysfunctional on account of sin. Thus, every aspect of man's being, while present, no longer functions as God intended.

Total depravity countenances that each sinner is equally inclined toward evil, but not all travel along that gradient to the same extent. Thus, each person is of the same ilk, equally predisposed toward evil, but each does not pursue that evil with equal vigor. It is crucial to note that while the Bible presents the doctrine of total depravity, it does not see mankind as absolutely or utterly depraved, as with Satan. Satan (and his rebel angels) is irredeemable, but mankind is redeemable. This is a significant distinction. As the Bible unfolds the stygian darkness within man, it never loses hope that that

---

[25] It is believed that approximately 160 million people died at the hands of government in the 20th century alone, the bloodiest century in the history of the world.

darkness can be brought to light, that mankind can be reconciled to God.[26] Thus, while Satan is irretrievably evil, mankind is *retrievably* evil. That is the whole point of Jesus' death on the cross; by his death he implemented the means to reverse and overcome the depravity within mankind, to progressively transform once wicked sinners into sanctified saints. The bad news is extraordinarily bad; the good news is unimaginably good.

Total Depravity: Physicality[27]

The human body was designed to live forever, to be gloried as the temple of the Holy Spirit.[28] However, on account of the fall that body is subject to decay and ultimately death.[29] The body is plagued by illness and often beset by injury, and it eventually fails in a fallen world which assails it with parasites, poisons, and pestilence.

Man's original sin brought disease and injury to the body, but ongoing sin may or may not be the cause of disease or injury. Christian counselors are careful not to draw a direct link between sin and specific physical maladies, unless such a link is clearly established. John 9:2, 3 reads,

> His disciples asked him, 'Rabbi, who sinned, this man or his parents, that he was born blind?' 'Neither this man nor his parents sinned,' said Jesus, 'but this happened so that the works of God might be displayed in him.'

Again in Luke 13:4, 5, Jesus stated,

> Or those eighteen who died when the tower in Siloam fell on them—do you think they were more guilty than all the others living in Jerusalem? I tell you, no! But unless you repent, you too will all perish.

Jesus was careful to distinguish between generally tragic events and personal sin. He pointed out that physical ailments or accidents can befall anyone and, as such, are not punishment for sin. However, there is clearly a direct link between certain individual sins and associated disease such as the link between promiscuity and AIDS, alcoholism and psoriasis of the liver, or years of smoking and lung cancer. The counselor must hold such links tenuously, reticent to identify moral failing unless the connection is evident, and then only for the purpose of helping the afflicted repent.

More often than not, disease and injury are simply the result of living in a fallen world

---

[26] 1 Timothy 1:15; Ephesians 3:8
[27] For additional discussion of this topic see the third book in this series, *The Days of Reckoning Are at Hand: From Fig Leaf to Olive Branch to Laurel Wreath*, chapter 2: "Suffering: The Kintsugi Objective"
[28] 1 Corinthians 6:19
[29] Genesis 3:19; Ecclesiastes 3:20

in which bodies are continually assaulted with destructive forces. Ecclesiastes 8:8 offers the sober reminder that no one has power over the day of his death since the world is afflicted with the pollution of a capricious evil that attacks anyone and everyone with wanton delight (while always under God's sovereignty).

The Stolen Kiss, Jean-Honoré Fragonard, c. 1789

Sin is eminently a worship disorder,[30] and as such, it infects, shapes, and directs man's inner life. That inner life, in turn, influences mankind's physical being. Thus, personal sin does carry with it a certain physical manifestation (although that may not always be apparent). For example, Psalm 32:3-5 states,

> When I kept silent, my bones wasted away through my groaning all day long. For day and night your hand was heavy on me; my strength was sapped as in the heat of summer. Then I acknowledged my sin to you and did not cover up my iniquity. I said, 'I will confess my transgressions to the Lord.' And you forgave the guilt of my sin.

Additionally, Proverbs 14:30 states, "A heart at peace gives life to the body, but envy

---

[30] Edward Welch, Westminster Theological Seminary, Philadelphia, Pennsylvania

rots the bones." Thus, there is clearly a somatic consequence to sin. Through the portal of the unrepentant heart, and its concomitant guilt, decay ravishes the body. Conversely, repentance, in some sense, reinvigorates and strengthens the body.[31]

Modern reductionistic thinking tends to attribute moral failing (as the Bible defines it) to physical factors (brain chemistry), societal pressures, situation, and other environmental influences. However, the force of the Bible's teaching is in the opposite direction. It is the moral failing which often drives the aforementioned factors, because that failing is actually a worship failing which infiltrates every aspect of the human existence. Sin's effect is like environmental pollution, widespread and pungent. Once unleashed, it cannot be contained nor eradicated through human agency. However, while the counselor is rightly timid and tenuous in drawing direct links between sin and specific bodily ailments, they frequently do exist, as the Bible states.

> Some claim that at the fall the structure of the human DNA was corrupted so that mankind would experience disabilities, disease, and ultimately death. Additionally, because of mankind's rebellion these same conditions would invade every corner of the earth so that each plant and animal would likewise be subject to them.[32] Is it possible that when one receives Christ, and is invested with his Holy Spirit, his DNA is in some sense progressively "corrected"? While the body may still be subject to disease and ultimately death, is its genetic code in the process of being subtly reprogrammed so that it gains a certain strength and resilience which it did not previously possess? This is purely speculative.

Total Depravity: Morality

Parents today pay great attention to automotive safety features in order to protect their children. While, of course, one applauds such efforts, there is a far greater problem which goes wholly unaddressed, the alarming neglect of safe driving practice, often in the parents themselves. This raises the question, "Is the greater danger outside the car or within it?" Is the greater peril that of an uncertain world or that of a heart that drives under the influence of the worship of false gods? It is tragic that today people focus such attention on the extrinsic while wholly blind to the intrinsic, a heart in which controlling idols are birthed and find a feathered nest. Certainly, the external world is fraught with dangers, but none like those within the heart.

> "The Lord saw how great man's wickedness on the earth had become, and that every inclination of the thoughts of his heart was only evil all the time." (Genesis 6:5)

---

[31] For additional discussion of this topic see the section on reductionism in the first book in this series, *Ask for the Ancient Paths: From Art to Artifice to Arisen*, chapter 8: "What Has Jerusalem To Do With Vienna?: The Case Against Psychology"

[32] Hosea 4:2, 3

> "Even though every inclination of his heart is evil from childhood." (Genesis 8:21)

Romans 7:18 states, "I know that nothing good lives in me, that is, in my sinful nature. For I have the desire to do what is good, but I cannot carry it out." Paul's assessment of his spiritual state is indicative of man's moral condition. Mankind is morally depraved, adrift on a sea of experience with no sense of where to find a safe harbor. Yet, on account of his image-bearing, man contains within him a moral compass so that even in his fallen condition, while morally depraved, he retains an innate sense of right and wrong. However, that sense is blunted, muted, darkened, and suppressed so that it does not function properly. While the compass' glass is shattered, one can still discern the movements of the needle below. However, the conscience, while present, is neither accurate nor active as God designed it. This means that it both wrongly excuses, and wrongly accuses, of sin.[33] It is silent when it should sound a cautionary alarm, and frequently alerting when there is no transgression.

> Mankind, aware of his sin, searches in desperation for a root cause. For example, the ancient Romans (as well as the Greek, Chinese, African, and Indian cultures), believed that a mirror had the power to confiscate part of the user's soul. If the user's image became distorted in any way, this could mean a corruption of his or her soul.[34]

For example, clearly the Bible ordains marriage as solely between a man and woman. Thus, homosexual marriage is an abomination and desecration of God's ordinance.[35] However, modern man, intoxicated with his own flawed sense of right and wrong, often makes gay marriage a civil right, and opposition to gay marriage hate-filled bigotry. Thus, the reprobate conscience often wrongly excuses a God-defined transgression (gay marriage), and wrongly convicts of a man-defined transgression (opposing gay marriage). The conscience, while in certain cases retaining some semblance of its original design, continually runs counter to accurate and active reflection, and compliance with, God's will.

> "We judge ourselves by our motives and others by their actions." (Dwight Morrow)

I have spent considerable time interacting with cultures throughout the world and have never encountered a culture that:

1. Was not depraved, to some extent, with regard to sexuality, alcohol, and the love of money

2. Was not immensely prideful

---

[33] David Powlison, Westminster Theological Seminary, Philadelphia, Pennsylvania
[34] Adapted from an unknown source
[35] Romans 1:26; 1 Corinthians 6:9

3. Did not place inordinate focus on the health and prosperity of its children (and conversely, often placed little value on its senior citizens)

The point is that there is a universal depravity to the heart which transcends culture or ethnicity (while not all cultures exhibit depravity to the same degree in all aspects of life). While some cultures have more fully given themselves to one form of rebellion, or have installed social contract mechanisms to restrain recognized dereliction, the unregenerate heart remains the same. That heart maintains the contours of its depravity despite its cultural overlays, even while some cultures seek to manage and mitigate recognized depravity, and others openly celebrating it.

> Judges 21:25 states that everyone did as he saw fit in his own eyes. This verse is a prescient look at the post-modern world where, likewise, everyone does as he sees fit with dire consequence.

Innocence
William Bouguereau, 1890

How dark can the conscience become? Can it be so obliterated that it ceases to work entirely? The conscience cannot be obliterated, so that even the most hardened and darkened sinner has a vague sense of his guilt before a holy God. To completely lose one's conscience would be to lose one's personhood as image-bearer. However, it is not clear to what extent the conscience can in fact become darkened. For example, Ephesians 2:3 says that fallen man gratifies "the cravings of the sinful nature...following its desires and thoughts." Additionally Ephesians 4:19 states, "Having lost all sensitivity, they have given themselves over to sensuality so as to indulge in every kind of impurity with a continual lust for more." What is clear is that to whatever extent the conscience can be darkened, mankind is entirely culpable for that.

> Henry Ford (1863-1947) worried about the implications of widespread automobile ownership. He speculated that the car could become an instrument of turpitude as

> young couples traveled far from their parents' watchful gaze. For this reason, Ford designed an exceptionally narrow backseat for the Model T.

Total Depravity: Relationships

Isaiah 59:2 states, "…But your iniquities have separated you from your God." This separation from God brings with it a parallel separation from one another. Mankind's social interaction is tainted by sin since he is separated from God both individually and corporately. Modern man, more so than ever before, lives in a fractured world so that every social environment resembles shards of relational glass.

> Teenagers often wrongly assume that the internet is an "iron curtain" shielding them from identification, reprisal, or prosecution. They often see social networking sites as beyond the gaze of their parents or the law, and have little sense that their online interactions can resurface. The internet allows them to assume various personalities which they would not dare show others, and provides a conduit for smoldering rage or bigotry. It seems that when people think others cannot uncover their actions, or link them to their actions, they are more likely to act immorally.
>
> "Give [a man] a mask and he will tell you the truth." (Oscar Wilde)

Total Depravity: Spirit

Mankind was made to interface with God's Spirit. However, man's spirit is dead as a result of his sin so that he cannot enjoy relationship with God.

Total Depravity: Reason

> "They can change my mind but they can't change me." (adapted from Jim Croce)[36]

Humanism carries with it the following three suppositions:

1. The ability of rational inquiry to investigate and solve every human problem

2. The ability to steer human destiny through mastery over the world

3. Science's (perceived to be the one unassailable front of human reason) inevitable conquest over the human plight

> The term "Dark Ages" was imposed by Enlightenment philosophers who considered

---

[36] Jim Croce, "I Got a Name" (1973)

> the dawn of the age of reason to be a welcomed advance over a dark millennium of Christian culture.[37]

The Questioner of the Sphinx, Elihu Vedder, 1863

Humanism essentially believes that mankind is born neutral and grows in goodness with time. In this way, humanism seeks to legitimize man's attempts at attaining deity within himself. Christianity states that mankind is born in sin and grows in his love for evil with time, so that that fundamental sinful state is enhanced and broadened.[38] Thus, humanism and Christianity could not possibly be more at odds.

> Adolf Hitler (1889-1945) was named *Time* magazine's "Man of the Year" in 1938, the same year many American college students named Hitler their greatest inspiration.

Man, as image-bearer, must, of necessity, assess everything into which he comes in contact. However, man continually evaluates every act, idea, person, event, or situation through a humanistic set of lenses. In this way, man is motivated to assign labels based on his own subjective evaluation, an evaluation based on his desire to ultimately be god. That which allows him ascent to a position of god, he regards as good; that which does not, he regards as evil. Man is also highly-motivated to view himself as good, and exhibits a universal desire to uphold the belief that he has met, and continues to meet, his moral obligations. Mankind's desperate quest to view

---

[37] Tom Neven, *Do Fish Know They're Wet?: Living in the World Without Getting Hooked* (New York: Baker Books, 2005)
[38] Romans 1:21

himself as good explains a great deal of human behavior.[39]

> "Courage is often just ignorance of the facts."

The idea that one sins against God in his *thinking* was utterly new to the ancient Greeks (as humanists) who saw the mind as divine like God himself. Therefore, the Christian concept that the mind is fallen was offensive to the Greeks. (Additionally, the Christian teaching on the resurrection of the body was also worrisome to Hellenistic people who longed to be free from the body, which they viewed as the seat of evil.) However, Jonah 4:11 states, "But Nineveh has more than 120,000 people who cannot tell their right hand from their left…" The result of sin is that mankind is blinded to the most basic truths about reality.

> "Never try to reason prejudice out of a man. It was not reasoned into him, and cannot be reasoned out." (Sydney Smith)

If, as the Greeks supposed, human reason is not fallen then truth can be ascertained outside of God's revelation. This opens the door for secular views of mankind (the chief being psychology) which ravage the biblical understanding. However, the Bible is clear that mankind's reason is fallen. Isaiah 5:20, 21 states, "Woe to those who call evil good and good evil, who put darkness for light and light for darkness, who put bitter for sweet and sweet for bitter. Woe to those who are wise in their own eyes and clever in their own sight." Since human reason is fallen it is incapable of arriving at truth on worldview questions. Mankind is trapped in a reasoning dialectic which swings from the rational to the irrational, and back again. This means that mankind engages in thought which pretends to be either omniscient (rationalism) or else resigned to incoherence (irrationalism). Only direct revelation from God provides a starting point for truth. (This is the theological concept of the epistemological integration point.)

> "You can only find truth with logic if you have already found truth without it." (G.K. Chesterton)

Depravity Through the Lens of Proverbs[40]

Concerning the issue of total depravity it is instructive to consider how the book of Proverbs describes people. There are essentially five types of people spoken of in Proverbs: the simple, the young, the fool, the mocker, and the wise.

---

[39] Jerome Kagan, "Three Pleasing Ideas," *American Psychologist* 51.9 (September, 1996): 905, 906.
[40] For additional discussion of this topic see the excursus "Intelligence versus Wisdom" in first book in this series, *Ask for the Ancient Paths: From Art to Artifice to Arisen*, chapter 5: "Redefining the Pygmalion Effect: Exploring the Image of God in Man."

The terms "simple" and "young" occupy the same semantic range, so they represent the same group. These are young people, those starting out in life, searching for answers, and eager to know how to direct their lives. According to Proverbs the simple and young are to be taught, encouraged, and given careful guidance. They are impressionable and, when faced with options, are willing to move in a host of different directions. Thus, Proverbs is directed specifically toward this group in the hope of winning them to relationship with Lady Wisdom, God himself.

The fool is confirmed in his rebellion; yet he is somewhat passive with regard to his way of life. He goes about life with little more purpose then to fill his stomach and satisfy his desire. The mocker is not just confirmed in his rebellion he instructs others, seeking to draw them into his hatred of God. The mocker is described in Matthew 7:15, "…watch out for false prophets. They come to you in sheep's clothing, but inwardly they are ferocious wolves." Additionally, 2 Corinthians 11:14, 15 states, "And no wonder, for Satan himself masquerades as an angel of light. It is not surprising, then, if his servants also masquerade as servants of righteousness. Their end will be what their actions deserve."

Commedia, Jacques Callot, d. 1635

The wise submits to God in obedience and grows in that relationship. The wise has been redeemed, changed, and prospers. Drawing Proverbs into the New Testament, the wise is the one redeemed by Christ.

It is important to note that the categories of simple/young, fool, mocker, and wise are not age dependent. While there may be age patterns, the categories are fluid. Thus, a young person could be a fool or even a mocker. An older person could be counted among the simple and young. Likewise, any aged person could find himself a member of the wise. Proverbs presents an idealized set of patterns for pedagogical purposes, but does not rigidly hold to categories.

It is crucial to point out that from the Bible's perspective there is no functional difference between unbelieving adults and children. Adults may possess a larger mental capacity, more developed verbal and physical abilities, and sophisticated social mechanisms for manipulating others, but at heart unregenerate adults and children are the same.

> "When I was a child, I talked like a child, I thought like a child, I reasoned like a child. When I became a man, I put the ways of childhood behind me." (1 Corinthians 13:11)

Observe people carefully and one sees the exact same cognitive and behavior patterns that resided in that person as a child. Whatever sinful state one was in as a child is the exact same state he will be in as an adult. In fact, that sin only intensifies with age, as the adult possesses more ability to cloak his depravity for self-serving purpose. A spoiled child will grow into an evermore spoiled adult, now more adept at manipulating or intimidating others to get what he desires. Additionally, the adult is increasingly more desirous and frustrated because his sin casts him into greater depravity and slavery to himself with each passing day. (This is why it is so vital to discipline children because discipline sets the stage for submission to God's authority and eventual repentance.[41])

One could view Proverbs in light of Matthew 13:1-23, the parable of the sower, which contains four types of soil, that which is,

1. Along the path
2. Along rocky places
3. Among the thorns
4. Good and noble[42]

To correctly interpret this parable one must see the first three types of soil as within one's own control. No one is innocent for being one of the first three types; each is culpable for the inhospitable "soil" of his own heart. The danger is to think that one is a victim of circumstance. Thus, in the context of the parable, one's heart creates the circumstance in which he finds himself. For example, as the soil along the path, one is not passive or innocent if "birds come" to steal the seed. However, there is an asymmetry, as the good and noble soil is not one's own work. It is the grace of God

---
[41] Proverbs 22:6
[42] Luke 8:15

which causes one to take on a humble posture which finally bears good fruit.

> A central paradox of the Christian faith is that each person is himself guilty for being born a sinner. How could one be guilty for the condition in which he was born? This is the mystery of original sin. Each is invariably born in sin, and at the same time willfully chooses to be born in that state, as one born in Adam.[43]

There is a saying, "With the same materials one man builds a palace and another a hovel." In God's common grace he extends to mankind the ability to fashion a world of his own choosing. Mankind can use his image-bearing to build a place of compassion, grace, justice, and truth or one of brutality, immorality, injustice, and falsehood. God has provided the framework, the revelation of himself, and the dictates of absolute morality within the conscience. It is up to mankind to do with it what he will; he has the ability and opportunity to erect a world of his own making. While God directs history toward a goal, he often does not interfere with man's plans unless invited to do so. This is the nature of mankind's freewill.

> "There is only cursing, lying and murder, stealing and adultery; they break all bounds, and bloodshed follows bloodshed. Because of this the land mourns, and all who live in it waste away; the beasts of the field and the birds of the air and the fish of the sea are dying." (Hosea 4:2, 3)

Excursus: Does Material Poverty Predispose One to Repentance and Faith?

Matthew 5:3 reads, "Blessed are the *poor in spirit*, for theirs is the kingdom of heaven." Luke 6:20b states, "Blessed are *you who are poor*, for yours is the kingdom of God." These two verses appear to be in tension as Matthew tends to spiritualize Jesus' teaching and Luke tends to temporalize it. Yet, both versions of Jesus' words are inerrant and infallible.

Commentators believe that Luke and Matthew record the same sermon. So how could the accounts differ in a key detail such as whether Jesus said "blessed are the poor" or "blessed are the poor in spirit"? One proposed solution is that when Jesus delivered his sermon he originally stated that the poor are blessed. However, possibly due to questions from more wealthy audience members, he clarified his statement to mean the poor in spirit. Therefore, some commentators believe the poor-in-spirit interpretation is more accurate to Jesus' intent.

Clearly, Jesus would have avoided the implication that material poverty, in and of itself, is blessed. Such a view is Marxist, linking indigence with virtue, prizing circumstance over inner-condition. Many throughout Scripture enjoyed a measure of

---

[43] 1 Corinthians 15:22

wealth, yet were counted righteous before God such as Abraham, Job, David, Solomon, Matthew, Nicodemus, the Roman Centurion, Zacchaeus, Joseph of Arimathea, Gamaliel, and Pricilla and Aquila. Yet, this does not overshadow the fact that by and large those who opposed Jesus' message where the religious and political leaders who were firstly powerful and incidentally wealthy.

Moving House, Viktor Vasnetsov, 1876

> Even in the most ordered and upstanding echelons of society there is a percolating depravity deep within the heart. Evil may be muted, but ever-present, in well-heeled members of society; it simply crouches behind a thin veneer of civilization.

Paul points out in 1 Corinthians 1:26, "Brothers and sisters, think of what you were when you were called. Not many of you were wise by human standards; not many were influential; not many were of noble birth." The implication is that some of those called were in fact influential, of noble birth, and presumably wealthy. Consider Acts 17:4, "Some of the Jews were persuaded and joined Paul and Silas, as did a large number of God-fearing Greeks and quite a few prominent women." Again in Acts 17:12, a number of prominent Greek women believed, and finally in Acts 17:34 some members of the Areopagus (the Greek intelligentsia) received Christ.

Yet, the majority of those who received the Christian message were the marginalized and the forgotten. Thus, one could conclude that those for whom the world's ways seem vacuous, and its pursuits prove unfruitful, hold a willingness to countenance a message that runs counter to the world.

It is not that riches in themselves are evil, but rather that the human heart so readily invests itself in them with delusional intent. Conversely, material poverty does not in any way reverse the condition of the heart. In other words, poverty does not modulate sinful proclivities; being materially poor does not make one inherently more godly, or even more inclined to godliness. The Bible is clear that one's desire for salvation is not driven by situation but rather by the heart's posture in the context of situation. Therefore, poverty, in and of itself, does not incline the heart to seek salvation.

> Money just magnifies what a person already is, and thus helps reveal who a person really is.

It is true that throughout Scripture God often condemns the rich, the powerful, and the noble,[44] but not on account of their wealth, power, or nobility. It is because they are easily tempted to exploit others. However, it is a logical fallacy to conclude that poverty is somehow a superior state. God recognizes that poverty is merely a more vulnerable condition, and God seeks to protect the vulnerable as a basic function of his common grace. Thus, poverty does not predispose one to special grace but only to common grace. As God seeks to sustain those who are subject to oppression and injustice, he never implies that the oppressed are somehow morally superior, or more inclined to faith, simply on account of their situation in life.

> "If absolute power corrupts absolutely, does absolute powerlessness make you pure?" (Harry Shearer)

Thus, from the Bible's perspective the issue of wealth and poverty is really a Morton's Fork, two lines of reasoning that lead to the same conclusion. Poverty lays bare one's acute need for answers, highlights one's glaring inability, reveals one's root vulnerability, and brings to the fore one's desperation. In this way the poor, if truly broken-hearted and searching for hope, may be more willing to listen to the gospel. Conversely, riches, as they increasingly prove themselves vacuous and burdensome, may equally drive one to search for hope in the arms of Jesus. So the mystery of the gospel is that it forms this Morton's Fork with regard to the world; those cast aside by the world often long for deliverance, as often do those exalted by the world.

> When one is hungry he craves just one morsel of bread.
> When one is lonely he longs for just one friend.
> When one is lost he searches for just one trail marker.
> When one is besieged by lies he clings to one steadfast truth.

Sin as Assault upon Mankind's "Very-Goodness"

---

[44] Matthew 11:8

Leviticus 21:16-23 states that any priest with a defect was not to offer sacrifices to God.

Priestly Defect	Common Meaning	Existential Meaning as Fallen Humanity	In Christ
1. Blind[45]	Blind	Blind to truth	Vision restored[46]
2. Lame[47]	Lame	Recalcitrant, "cistern-like"	Move with purpose[48]
3. Disfigured[49] (literally "a sunken or mutilated nose")	Ugly	The ugliness of sin	Inner beauty[50]
4. Deformed[51] (extra fingers, eyes disproportionate, ears misshapen, one leg too long)	Body not fully "created"	A misshapen spirit which does not find its home in God	Fullness of life as designed at the creation[52]
5. A crippled foot[53]	Labored or impaired movement	Dragging pride as a dead appendage	Impairments removed, to move with purpose[54]
6. A crippled hand[55]	Ponderous or impaired ability to work	Impaired work, frustrated and futile	Impairments removed, to work with purpose[56]
7. Hunchbacked[57]	Brought low through deformity	Sin "lowers" man, a kind of humiliation takes hold of the sinner, a certain pathetic, slovenly quality	Raised up to approach God with boldness[58]
8. Dwarfed[59]	Exceptionally	Small of stature, of	Ennobled as a

---

[45] Leviticus 21:18
[46] Psalm 36:9; John 9:6, 7
[47] Leviticus 21:18
[48] John 5:5-9; 8:36
[49] Leviticus 21:18
[50] Isaiah 52:7; 2 Corinthians 4:6
[51] Leviticus 21:18
[52] John 10:10b
[53] Leviticus 21:19
[54] Isaiah 35:6
[55] Leviticus 21:19
[56] Matthew 12:9-14; Colossians 3:23, 24
[57] Leviticus 21:20
[58] Hebrews 4:16
[59] Leviticus 21:20

	short	little consequence	royal priesthood[60]
9. An ocular defect[61]	Impaired vision	Impaired power of perception	Renewed and sharpened vision to see with the Bible's lenses[62]
10. Festering or running sores[63]	Externally visible illness	Sin makes the sinner ill, the illness is visible and degrading	Healing for the nations[64]
11. Damaged testicles[65]	One's masculinity and reproductive abilities are impaired	Sexuality defiled	Redeemed to be a pure and blameless bride[66]

Moses and Joshua in the Tabernacle, James Jacques Joseph Tissot, c. 1900

There are various levels on which to understand the defects mentioned in Leviticus 21:18-20. The first is as a practical matter; priests were to stand in front of the people to perform a function. Such a priest must be fit for service. He must be strong enough,

---

[60] As Luke 19:1-10 recounts, Zacchaeus, a chief tax collector, climbed a tree to get a glimpse of Jesus because he was a short man. Likely Zacchaeus felt that he was less than a man (which could explain his drive to gain wealth). Jesus dignified Zacchaeus by eating with him and by finally making him a disciple. Also see 1 Peter 2:9.
[61] Leviticus 21:20
[62] Matthew 7:5
[63] Leviticus 21:20
[64] Revelation 22:2
[65] Leviticus 21:20
[66] Ephesians 5:27

skilled enough, mobile enough, and tall enough to execute his duties. Secondly, the priests' physical appearance must not present a distraction to God's sacrificial work. The Israelites, like all sinners, had a trenchant tendency to judge based on appearances. They were quick to see physical appearance as indicative of spiritual health or value.[67] For example, they might associate external ugliness with moral turpitude. (The sinful heart is quick to make fallacious associations.) Additionally, God did not want the people to mock a priest, and in so doing belittle his work for the propitiation of sin.[68]

God created each plant, animal, and object as "good," but man as "very good."[69] In response, Satan masterminds the grotesque to mutilate and mock God's work. Thus, on a certain metaphysical level, there is something in physical defect which assails the creation itself, in some way detracting from the goodness of God's work. Such defect reveals the presence of evil, reminds the viewer of Adam's rebellion, of man's corporate guilt, and of Satan's assault upon the creation. Defects, especially those of priests dedicated to a sacrificial system for the propitiation of sin, were an affront to God's creative work.

Consider how people usually respond to one with a physical defect. There is something within them which is silently repulsed, wants to remain distant, and desires to overlook the problem. Conversely, what is the usual human response to unblemished beauty? People are drawn to pulchritude, feel a leap within the heart, and are often mesmerized by it. There is something in beauty which seems to capture the prelapsarian Edenic state, which seems to remind of the "very goodness" to which mankind was privileged. Conversely, the grotesque fills man with a nagging reminder of his collective sin, that something of God's "very good" design was maligned and obscured in the fall.

On a deeper more existential level, the defects listed in Leviticus 21:18-20 are possibly an extended metaphor for mankind himself. Mankind necessarily embodies all of these defects in his fallen spiritual state. With regard to God each is defective, grotesque, and misshapen on account of his sin. Only Christ heals and restores the design since Jesus took mankind's impairments upon himself. He willfully accepted and carried those varied states of "sub-humanity" in order to bring mankind to unblemished, fully-formed, and glorious humanity. Thus, in Jesus physical defects fade in their significance as the sinner is restored to that which is even greater than the original "very goodness." In Jesus, regardless of one's physical condition, there is a gathering glory, an azoth, a hidden beauty imparted, a dignity conferred.

Christ Reverses Man's Total Depravity

---

[67] 1 Samuel 16:7
[68] Matthew Henry Commentary, Bible Study Tools, 2012
[69] Genesis 1:31

> "Nothing disinfects like sunlight [the Son's light]."

The Christian's salvation, wrought in and through Christ, is assured. John 10:28, 29 states, "I give them eternal life, and they shall never perish; no one can snatch them out of my hand. My Father, who has given them to me, is greater than all; no one can snatch them out of my Father's hand." If the Christian can never be separated from Christ this means that God is committed to changing the Christian and will, in fact, accomplish that feat. Although Satan, the world, and the flesh may interfere with, and impede, God's work, that work cannot finally be thwarted. God will succeed in changing the Christian because he has already succeeded in raising him to new life in Christ.[70] This means that God is actively at work to reverse the effects of sin within the Christian, bringing total depravity into glorious renewal.

On account of the fact that the Christian is eternally anchored to Christ,[71] God fights for the Christian's sanctification. Isaiah 5:26-30 states,

> He lifts up a banner for the distant nations, he whistles for those at the ends of the earth. Here they come, swiftly and speedily! Not one of them grows tired or stumbles, not one slumbers or sleeps; not a belt is loosened at the waist, not a sandal thong is broken. Their arrows are sharp, all their bows are strung; their horses' hoofs seem like flint, their chariot wheels are a whirlwind. Their roar is like that of the lion, they roar like young lions; they growl as they seize their prey and carry it off with no one to rescue. In that day they will roar over it like the roaring of the sea. And if one looks at the land, he will see darkness and distress; even the light will be darkened by the clouds.

However, despite the Christian's eternal condition, redemption does not yet fully eradicate sin from the Christian's life. While sin still wages a battle within, two realities are assured: the Christian's salvation is secure, and God fights for the Christian's sanctification, a battle that will not cease until heaven.

Additionally, it is noteworthy that Christ's work on the cross also applies to the non-Christian through common grace. It is on account of Christ, and because of the Father's love for his Son, that he shows mercy to all mankind.[72] Through common grace, wrought through Jesus' death, God restrains mankind from "absolute" depravity so that mankind does not act out the fullness of the evil within himself. Common grace, in this sense, should offer a glimmer of salvation, the taste of fellowship with God.[73]

---

[70] Colossians 3:1
[71] Hebrews 6:19
[72] Luke 2:10
[73] Clair Davis, "Doctrine of Man" class, Westminster Theological Seminary, Philadelphia, Pennsylvania

One underlying motive of human depravity is seeking to make permanent that which is by design temporary, or making created things into ultimate things. Correctly related to Christ, the Christian recognizes that he is a sojourner in this world. This is not his kingdom and his reward is not in the here-and-now.[74] Since the Christian recognizes the temporal nature of this world, and its rapid dissolution, he lives in a kind of existential "tent" with regard to his earthly dealings.[75]

In Christ the Body Will Be Resurrected

Philippians 3:21 states, "...who, by the power that enables him to bring everything under his control, will transform our lowly bodies so that they will be like his glorious body." Christ transforms the Christian's lowly body so that it is already glorified (a transformation that will not be fully realized until heaven). There is a certain health, strength, and purpose in the Christian's renewed body. Additionally, the Christian's body will be raised from the dead because it has already been invested with the Holy Spirit.[76]

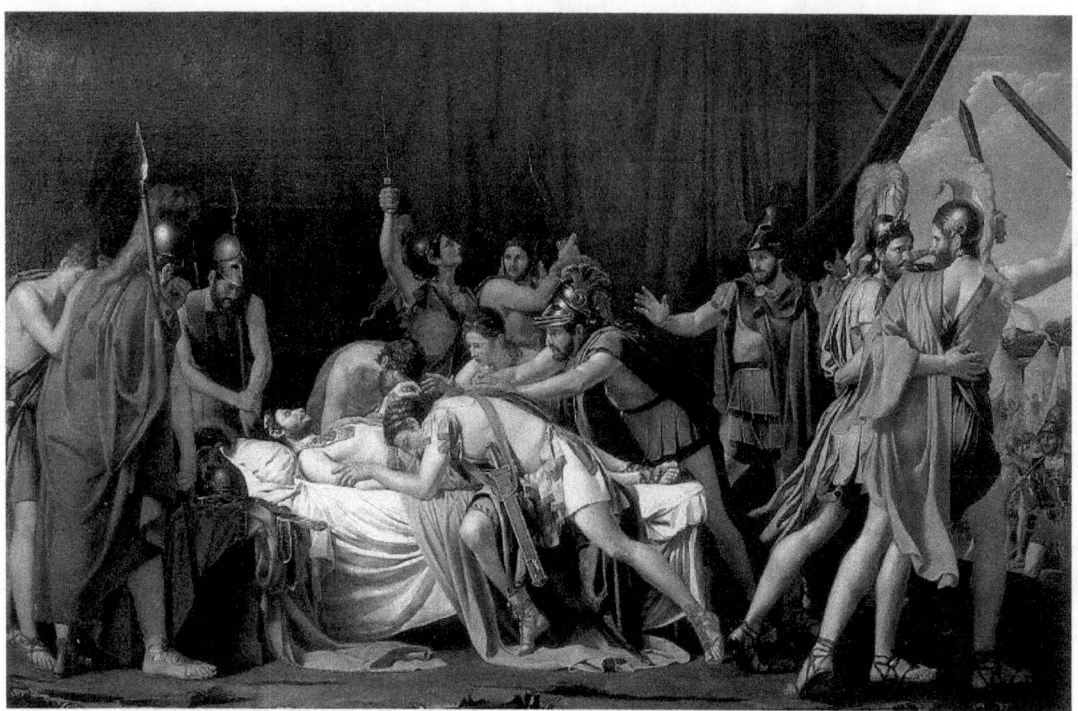

The Death of Viriathus, Jose de Madrazo, 1807

> So will it be with the resurrection of the dead. The body that is sown is perishable, it is raised imperishable; it is sown in dishonor, it is raised in glory; it is sown in weakness, it is raised in power; it is sown a natural body, it is raised a spiritual body.

---

[74] John 18:36
[75] Hebrews 11:38
[76] 2 Corinthians 1:22

If there is a natural body, there is also a spiritual body. So it is written: 'The first man Adam became a living being'; the last Adam, a life-giving spirit. The spiritual did not come first, but the natural, and after that the spiritual. The first man was of the dust of the earth; the second man is of heaven. As was the earthly man, so are those who are of the earth; and as is the heavenly man, so also are those who are of heaven. And just as we have borne the image of the earthly man, so shall we bear the image of the heavenly man.

I declare to you, brothers and sisters, that flesh and blood cannot inherit the kingdom of God, nor does the perishable inherit the imperishable. Listen, I tell you a mystery: We will not all sleep, but we will all be changed — in a flash, in the twinkling of an eye, at the last trumpet. For the trumpet will sound, the dead will be raised imperishable, and we will be changed. For the perishable must clothe itself with the imperishable, and the mortal with immortality. When the perishable has been clothed with the imperishable, and the mortal with immortality, then the saying that is written will come true: 'Death has been swallowed up in victory.'" (1 Corinthians 15:42-54)

In Christ the Conscience Is Revived

In Christ the conscience is made active and accurate, so as to function as God intended. It is alive and operative moment by moment to convict of sin. It is accurate to point out sin as God sees it, not as the world defines it. Romans 2:15 states, "…the requirements of the law are written on their hearts, their conscience also bearing witness, and their thoughts now accusing, now even defending them."

Hebrews 10:19-22 states,

Therefore, brothers, since we have confidence to enter the Most Holy Place by the blood of Jesus, by a new and living way opened to us through the living way opened for us through the curtain, that is, his body, and since we have a great priest over the house of God, let us draw near to God with a sincere heart in full assurance of faith, having our hearts sprinkled to cleanse us from a guilty conscience and having our bodies washed with pure water.

"Keep your conscience clear, then never fear."

In Christ There Is Relational Renewal

Wherever there is enmity toward God, relationships between people lie fractured and contentious. Yet, Isaiah 11:6 states, "The wolf will live with the lamb, the leopard will lie down with the goat, the calf and the lion…a little child will lead them." As relationship with God (the vertical) is restored, relationships between people (the horizontal) are likewise restored. This horizontal renewal is predicated on maintaining the vertical relationship. There is a peace between those in Christ, competition recedes, and other-centeredness takes hold. There is vibrant and growing faith which drives dynamic and energetic relationship. However, the Christian also experiences searing conflict with the world, as the world opposes his message and seeks to undermine his faith.

> "If the world hates you, keep in mind that it hated me first." (John 15:18)
>
> "You adulterous people, don't you know that friendship with the world means enmity against God? Therefore, anyone who chooses to be a friend of the world becomes an enemy of God." (James 4:4)

In Christ the Spirit Is Rekindled

Second Corinthians 5:17 states, "Therefore if anyone is in Christ he is a new creation, the old has gone, the new has come." The Christian's spirit is made alive so as to enjoy fellowship with God.

In Christ the Reason Is Realigned

On account of mankind's inherent deficiency with regard to reasoned thought, there must be an epistemological integration point (a starting point for knowledge) to break the vicious cycle of rationalism and irrationalism. That integration point is the Bible. It dethrones man's supposed omniscience, providing a coherent assertion of truth.

Isaiah 1:18 states, "'Come now, let us reason together,' says the Lord. 'Though your sins are like scarlet, they shall be as white as snow; though they are red as crimson, they shall be like wool.'" Additionally, Romans 12:2 states, "Do not conform to the pattern of this world, but be transformed by the renewing of your mind. Then you will be able to test and approve what God's will is—his good, pleasing and perfect will." God directs sound reason and invests it into sanctified Christians. The Christian, indwelled by the Holy Spirit, rightly assesses reality with a recalibrated reason. His reason, functioning under the auspices of Scripture, wisely judges and weighs matters to the extent that God has revealed them. Thus, the Christian's use of reason, when sanctified by Christ, is accurate and persuasive.

- 4 -

HAMARTIOLOGY:
Sin in All its Ignobility

Introduction

In *Amusing Ourselves to Death* (1986),[1] Neil Postman (1931–2003) states that there have been two perceived threats to modern society. One is the Big-brother theory of George Orwell's (1903–1950) *Nineteen Eighty-Four* (1949), the threat of totalitarianism, or the threat from "without." This is the fear that society's degeneration will come at the hands of both oppressive government and global corporate control of commerce, lifestyle, and eventually thought itself.

Destruction of the Temple in Jerusalem, Nicolas Poussin, c. 1640

The opposite threat is the Soma theory spoken of in Aldous Huxley's (1894–1963) *Brave New World* (1932).[2] Here the menace is from "within," the danger of unbridled freedom. In *Brave New World* the populace is led astray, not by propaganda, but by its

---

[1] Neil Postman, *Amusing Ourselves to Death*: *Public Discourse in the Age of Show Business* (New York: Penguin Books, 1986)
[2] It is ironic (or maybe fitting) that Aldous Huxley and John Fitzgerald Kennedy (1917–1963) died on the same day, November 22, 1963. JFK, in some ways, epitomized the dangers spoken about in Huxley's *Brave New World*.

own lust for excitement and escape. Rapacious autonomy leads to the loss of morality and sound reason. In this model it is that which one longs for, whatsoever gives him pleasure, which rots his soul.

So which theory correctly predicts the future – Big-brother or Soma? Neil Postman's thesis is that the latter has emerged as the greater threat and will prove to be the undoing of modern culture. In modern culture people are increasingly seen as victims of their own depravity and less as willful promoters of it. This blame-shifting runs to the heart of the Soma threat.

> Heaven's Mandate was devised by Confucius (551–479 BC). According to this theory, the emperor had to discern the moral order of the universe, and act in accordance with it, in order to maintain his mandate. Immorality undermined the mandate and would lead to the emperor's downfall, as would heavenly signs (such as comets) and natural disasters (such as earthquakes and floods).
>
> "Heaven-sent calamities you may stand up against, but you cannot survive those brought on by yourself." (Shu Qing)

The Bible's Handling of Sin[3]

The topic of sin is possibly the most unwelcomed in the Christian repertoire. However, without a profound understanding of sin the Christian life, and growth in sanctification, becomes moribund and delusional. In fact, the gospel is quickly stripped of its power whenever the issue of sin is marginalized and soft-pedaled. As Christianity increasingly sidelines this topic, Christ himself is rendered as little more than a spiritual snake-oil salesman. As sin is reduced to an incidental concern, or to a relatively minor offense, so too, salvation through Jesus is functionally reduced to a quaint folktale. I find that the issue of sin almost always separates faithful Christians from nominal Christians, those passionate about the gospel from those embarrassed by it. It is an accurate understanding, and honest handling, of sin which distinguishes disciples from mere saved people.

The Bible handles the issue of sin from two sides. It is both absolute (clearly defined in God's eternal Word) and under the dictates of a certain relativizing factor, God-directed earthly authorities. For example, it is absolutely wrong to murder in all places, at all times, for nearly all reasons (except in the case of demonstrable self-defense or justified military conflict).[4] This is God's eternal declared will. Sin is also a temporal concept since, as God says in Romans 13:1, each must submit to the

---

[3] For additional discussion of the topic of sin see "Resolving the Sin Rorschach" in the first book in this series, *Ask for the Ancient Paths: From Art to Artifice to Arisen*, chapter 10: "The Third-Way of Sanctification: From Abominable to Indomitable"

[4] Exodus 20:13

authorities above himself. It is sinful to disregard legitimate laws, to dodge properly imposed taxes, or to disobey a rightful authority's justified orders. Likewise, a child who disobeys his parents' warranted rules has sinned in God's eyes. In other words, sin is both absolute and defined by legitimate authorities ordained by God.

For example, 1 Samuel 2:25a states, "If one man sins against another, God may mediate for the offender; but if he sins against the LORD, who will intercede for him?" The idea is that there are two types of offenses – those directly against God's declared will, and those on account of the dictates of human authority and agency. There is sin directed specifically toward God, and sin directed toward others (which indirectly targets God).

> In 2014 the state of California experienced possibly the worst drought in its history. At the beginning of the drought homeowners were shamed (and often fined) for watering their lawns. Later as the drought sparked wildfires, homeowners were shamed for allowing their lawns to become so parched that they presented a fire hazard. It is fascinating to see the shift in public shame during that time and the ensuing sense of ethical confusion.
>
> This anecdote offers a window into the way in which public shame can vacillate and affect the psyche. Think about the fact that in biblical times for a father to neglect loving corporal punishment in the discipline of his children was a source of public shame. Today, for a father to exercise that same loving corporal punishment could receive gasps of horror from onlookers as well as an inquiry from the Department of Health and Human Services.

Case Study: Parents Picking-up Their Children[5]

> "When dealing with people remember that you are not dealing with creatures of logic, but with creatures of emotion, bursting with prejudice, and motivated by pride and vanity." (Dale Carnegie)

Day care centers experience a nagging problem: parents are often late picking up their children at the end of the day. A study was done to determine how to deal with this.

On average there were eight late pickups per week per center. So the centers imposed a fine of three-dollars upon any parent arriving more than ten minutes late. (Parents already pay an average of $380 per month per child for day care.) What was the result? The number of parents showing up late *increased* 150% to twenty per week. Parents found a way to feel exonerated for being late. They could pay for their lateness, as now it had become a commodity to be purchased.

---

[5] Adapted from Steven Levitt and Stephen Dubner, *Freakonomics* (New York: William Morrow Publishers, 2005)

Next the fine was eliminated altogether. The number of late pickups continued at the same level because parents viewed their lateness as a trivial matter – only worth three-dollars. Therefore, they no longer concerned themselves with it. In this case study one sees how parents were saddled with a social expectation which was lifted through the supposed ability to simply pay for an infraction. The payment option removed the sense of social responsibility and alleviated shame.

Christ in the House of His Parents, John Everett Millais, 1850

Exploring the Issue of Sin

Before continuing it is important to note that the Western world is saddled with a militant moral relativism making it socially treacherous to speak about moral judgments in the public arena. In other words, it is considered intolerant and bigoted to make absolute moral statements, to even speak the word "sin." The very notion of imposing standards, of any kind, is itself considered judgmental.[6] This discussion of sin is thus imperiled by moral relativism which will not countenance the concept of transgression before a holy God.

Moral relativism not withstanding, God's first statement after the fall was, "Where are you?"[7] This is an apt starting point for understanding the plight of man in his sin. Mankind is adrift in a cold dark lonely universe intended to be his home, but now lost to him, now a foreign land and a hostile nation. Mankind should be perfectly centered and grounded in his physical environment but rather he is a nomad to himself and his surroundings, a castaway searching for some touchstone. So the question, "Where are

---

[6] This observation from Rush Limbaugh, radio host
[7] Genesis 3:9

you?" captures mankind's desperate isolation, angst, loneliness, and blighted existence.

> Theologian Sinclair Ferguson said, "Why do we run from the very thing that would give us life?" This hints at the nature of sin. Sin is a running from the bosom of life into the clutches of death. Sin looks like a race into triumph; yet, it is a flight into oblivion.

Eve looked at the fruit, not in order to glorify God for his masterful design, nor to praise God for its brilliant color. She looked with eyes that grabbed for power without and against God; she craved blessing without and against God; she sought meaning without and against God. The original sin was pride, as Eve (and later Adam) believed that she could be like God. Eve had seen the fruit before and had trusted God's provision in her life. This time, however, she looked and thought God is not really God and he is not really good. I will take command of this garden. The creation will bow to me.

> Jim Croce (1943–1973) sang, "If it gets me nowhere, I'll go there proud."[8] This is the general posture of the sinner; he clings to his sin, even though it brings him to nothing, in the stubborn assertion of self-pride.

In Eve's mind the serpent was the liberator and God the enslaver.[9] The serpent's intervention promised to install Eve as god. Thus, she now looked at the fruit with eyes of longing, with a godless craving, with a faithless wanting and grabbing.

When exactly did the first sin occur?

1. Was it in listening to the serpent?
2. Was it in looking at the fruit with eyes of desire?
3. Was it in plucking the fruit from the tree?
4. Was it in eating the fruit?
5. Was it in giving that fruit to another to eat as well?

I believe that when Eve looked at the fruit with eyes of desire that functioned as a kind of "proto-sin," the precursor for sin. However, it was not until she actually ate the fruit that her sin was consummated. Eve's listening, looking, and plucking put her on a path that she finally confirmed as her own definitive will when the fruit entered her mouth.

What was Satan's role in the first rebellion? First he deceived Eve with his form,

---

[8] "I Got a Name," Jim Croce (1973)
[9] Joseph Schimmel, Fight the Good Fight ministries

disguising himself as a serpent. Then he questioned the Word of God, implanted doubt and, finally, outright lied. He told Adam and Eve that they would not die.[10] In fact, at the moment they ate they did die. Death entered their relationship with God as well as the entire creation.

1. Fellowship with God turned to fear and hiding. ("I heard you in the garden, and I was afraid because I was naked; so I hid."[11])

2. The man and woman's relationship to one another now became antagonistic. ("The woman you put here with me – she gave me some fruit from the tree and I ate it."[12])

3. Their relationship with creation was now hostile. ("The serpent deceived me, and I ate."[13])

The Expulsion of Adam and Eve from Paradise, Benjamin West, 1791

> "The eye is the lamp of the body. If your eyes are good, your whole body will be full of light. But if your eyes are bad, your whole body will be full of darkness." (Matthew 6:22, 23)

Adam and Eve lost the touchstone of their existence. They soon found themselves

---

[10] Genesis 3:4
[11] Genesis 3:10
[12] Genesis 3:12
[13] Genesis 3:13

between Scylla and Charybdis, barred from reentering paradise but trepid as they stepped into a haunted world. Cast from their garden home, Adam and Eve embarked upon an empty enterprise in a cursed universe. The fall brought with it a cascade of evil.[14] The deception, the fear, the antagonism, the hiding, the blame-shifting, all began with a single God-directed act of defiance, a willful exploration of the lust of the eyes. The first rebellion was active and deliberate. Adam and Eve were beguiled because they wanted to be deceived. They were ensnared because they delivered themselves over to the trap. The lie was offered for sale and they bought it, actively, willfully, deliberately, in a heavy-handed manner.

> Fyodor Dostoyevsky (1821-1881) wrote, "If God does not exist, everything is permitted." This is the posture of sin, the functional assertion that God does not exist.

The piercing tragedy in the fall is that Adam and Eve had *everything* and lost it all. They were already basking in victory. They were under God's covenant faithfulness; their future was assured; their provision inexhaustible. They had the suzerain of the universe as their friend and father; they just had to walk in obedience.

Satan sold Adam and Eve on a story. The story was that the victory was yet to come, that God's provision was not assured, that the universe was theirs for the taking. Satan peddled the lie that the garden's main character was not God, but Adam and Eve themselves; they were to be the heroes. The plot is not God's perfect will but their own self-promoting wills. The outcome is not God reigning for all eternity in glory but Adam and Eve eclipsing God's glory.[15] Satan deliberately attacked God's words with, "Did God really say?"[16] Adam and Eve had heard God's words but chose to abandon them based on something that they thought they saw. In what way does modern man keep falling into the same trap?

> "The bigger the lie, the more people will believe it." (Adolf Hitler)

One rightly views international terror organizations with justified horror and derision. Such organizations offer a glimpse into the heinous brutality of which the human heart is capable. However, what one does not often consider is that each person is, on account of his sin, equally a "terrorist" before a holy God. The terrorism played out on the world stage lives within each heart so that each is, in effect, subject to that which he abhors in others. Of course, few live out the fullness of the evil within their hearts, but all are capable of such evil, and if given the right opportunity might resort to

---

[14] This concept "cascade of evil" from Douglas Green, Westminster Theological Seminary, Philadelphia, Pennsylvania
[15] Some ideas in this paragraph from David and Sharon Covington, "Introduction to Biblical Counseling" notes, 2004
[16] Genesis 3:1

revolting behavior.

Pollice Verso, Jean-Léon Gérôme, 1872

> Just as mankind is not inherently good on account of sin, so too, children are not born innocent.[17] They desire to live out the same rebellion, hatred, and contempt as any other sinner.[18] Children do not need to be taught to lie, deceive, steal, or love themselves. This is the heart's most fundamental condition. Thus, the Bible's statements about the heart's heinousness are not limited to adults; they apply to children as well. However, children are underdeveloped ("underfunded") rebels without the means to fully perpetrate their sinful machinations. Children do not yet have the "equipment" at their disposal to fully act upon their heart's intent. This is not to say that every child will grow up to perpetrate horrendous evil, but it is to say that the same core evil disposition lives within every heart. It is a question of to what extent that disposition is tolerated, cultivated, embraced, and promoted or else rebuked and shepherded.

That being said, evil does not operate with equal persuasion and power in every heart. Some, more so than others, are more readily obsequious to and, therefore, more clearly influenced by, Satan. Thus, each person is eminently sinful while at the same time not equally "comfortable" with sin.[19] Each is of the same ilk while also somewhat heterogeneous in his cooperation with evil. Sin is hegemonic over the heart,

---

[17] Psalm 51:5; Isaiah 48:8
[18] 2 Timothy 2:22
[19] Term "being comfortable with sin" borrowed from Sharon Covington, Biblical counselor

but each person does not equally genuflect to this hegemony and, thus, does not equally surrender himself to evil. Sin, therefore, might best be described as "an inward tendency to evil" which reigns in man's being[20] (while he does not necessarily perpetrate evil to its fullest extent).

> Occam's razor states that the simplest explanation for any physical phenomenon is usually the correct one. This same concept might be applied to the Bible's understanding of people. Every true problem of the psyche is essentially a relationship with God problem, a simple truth offering a simple solution, which nevertheless is beyond the reach of even the most learned.[21]

Various Indicators That Each Is a Sinner

Over the course of many years I have interacted with dozens of churches in various parts of the world. I have encountered all manner of worship and custom, but the one universal feature is a stark blindness concerning the issue of sin. With almost eerie uniformity churches have abandoned the Bible's plenary counsel, often choosing to entertain chthonian voices.[22] The word "sin" may at times be mentioned, but almost always in man-centered terms (based on traditional or cultural standards) designed to tacitly exculpate the supposed sinner. The church has relinquished the Bible's understanding of sin because it is has largely vacated the gospel. With an anemic and misdirected view of sin, the gospel becomes functionally inert. Thus, most church interaction devolves into "caring pragmatism,"[23] of various stripes and colors, in order to somehow alleviate assumed human frailty, whether of design or situation.

Sin is the *lingua franca*, the modus operandi, of the unbeliever, and the anachronism of the believer (having been delivered from sin but persisting in it). Sin runs vastly deeper, and is immeasurably more pervasive, than one can possibly imagine. Thus, one of the first challenges in biblical counseling is simply convincing counselees of the full extent to which they are sinners.

What follows is a look at human depravity from various angles. The following list highlights the universally sinful inclinations of the heart, inclinations which spring up spontaneously given the right conduits and opportunities.

1. Anonymity

Anonymity changes how people think, speak, and act. Being able to hide one's identity does not just make one feel invisible, but lends a sense of invincibility.

---
[20] Charles. H. Spurgeon (1834-1892), sermon No. 1816 (January 1, 1885)
[21] 1 Corinthians 1:18-25
[22] 1 Timothy 4:1
[23] This term from David Powlison, Westminster Theological Seminary, Philadelphia, Pennsylvania

Consider the fact that in modern urban environments (where people are largely anonymous) immorality is generally higher than in small communities. Additionally, the internet's anonymity alters the tenor of interaction so that people are willing to post offensive statements that they would not dare utter in public.

> A study found the following:
>
> 1. 14% of emails contain lies.
> 2. 21% of instant messages contain lies.
> 3. 27% of face-to-face conversations involve lies.
> 4. 37% of phone calls involve lies.

The story of Judah and his daughter-in-law Tamar exposes the heart in the context of anonymity.[24] Judah traveled to Timnah where, unbeknownst to him, Tamar had disguised herself as a shrine prostitute. She accommodated Judah on condition that he send her one goat from his flock. In pledge, he gave her his seal, cord, and staff. Upon hearing that Tamar was pregnant as a result of prostitution, Judah ordered her to be immolated. However, after producing Judah's personal effects, proof of his guilt, Tamar was exonerated. Judah recanted his death threat, stating that Tamar was more righteous than himself. Under the cloak of anonymity Judah was willing to commit grave sin.

> "The human being who would not harm you on an individual, face-to-face basis, who is charitable, civic-minded, loving and devout, will wound or kill you from behind the corporate veil." (Morton Mintz)

2. Authority

I travel a great deal, regularly waiting on lines to get through customs. I notice that in the presence of customs agents, people seem more disciplined, quieter, and more attentive to their comportment. They stand a little straighter; they seem to adopt a more positive attitude. They are suddenly polite and responsive. There is something about this intensive authority structure which temporarily transforms each into an upstanding and honest citizen. However, think about what happens when authority is absent: property is vandalized, graffiti proliferates, and theft becomes common place. Even otherwise law-abiding citizens are deeply inclined to rebel against authority, and frequently do so to a degree proportional with its perceived absence.

> "Who then is the faithful and wise servant, whom the master has put in charge of the servants in his household to give them their food at the proper time? It will be good for that servant whose master finds him doing so when he returns. Truly I tell you, he

---

[24] Genesis 38:15-26

> will put him in charge of all his possessions. But suppose that servant is wicked and says to himself, 'My master is staying away a long time,' and he then begins to beat his fellow servants and to eat and drink with drunkards. The master of that servant will come on a day when he does not expect him and at an hour he is not aware of. He will cut him to pieces and assign him a place with the hypocrites, where there will be weeping and gnashing of teeth." (Matthew 24:45-51)

Each person, to one degree or another, hates the fact that others have authority over him and readily fabricates means to shield himself from that authority. Each person reflexively rebels against authority taking a defiant posture toward any imposed rules or expectations. When confronted by an authority each instinctively defends and excuses himself.

> The local police are often all that stands between civilization and anarchy.

Also consider that people often subjectively choose those laws that they will obey. For example, a housewife might responsibly dispose of litter at a local park but lie to a meter-maid to avoid a parking violation. A businessman might donate to a children's charity and then cheat on his taxes. A physician may offer caring advice to his patient but defraud an insurance company on the treatment plan. Rebellion against authority is neither uniformly applied nor rationally upheld. It follows its own twisted, degraded, and opportunistic path based on the idols ruling the heart.

> Consider the modern phenomenon of hypersensitivity with regard to child abuse. While much of this vigilance is desperately needed and heartily applauded, what about society's gross negligence with regard to the abuse of the opposite age group – elders? This is one of the most overlooked forms of abuse in the modern world. The willful abuse of seniors is another manifestation of the sinful heart's disregard for those who are weak and vulnerable.[25]

3. Charity

John 12:4-6 reads,

> But one of his disciples, Judas Iscariot, who was later to betray him, objected, 'Why wasn't this perfume sold and the money given to the poor? It was worth a year's wages.' He did not say this because he cared about the poor but because he was a thief; as keeper of the money bag, he used to help himself to what was put into it.

---

[25] This issue also points to society's lust for the young and beautiful so that those who are old and unattractive are largely considered worthless.

Much of what appears to be charity is actually coercive control. Those who are generous seek to manipulate the recipients of their generosity. Even worse they seek to leverage their generosity as a bargaining chip for acceptance before a holy God. Charity is, in some way, a fatuous attempt to gain an advantage in one's personal objectives. Consider, for example, that corporations routinely make charitable donations and then spend five times the donated amount to advertise their generosity to the public.[26]

St. Cecilia Distributing Alms to the Poor, Domenichino, 1615

> "In the same way, on the outside you appear to people as righteous but on the inside you are full of hypocrisy and wickedness." (Matthew 23:28)

Mankind continually worships at the altar of some god, sanitizing his worship as somehow virtuous and noble. For example, the desire to attend a top flight university may be a disguised love of money. The plan to become wealthy so as to assist the poor is often a cleverly concealed love of the praises of men. The heart cuts serpentine paths for self-worship, while cloaking such pursuits in imagined nobility.

---

[26] Kevin Trudeau, *Natural Cures "They" Don't Want You to Know About* (Alliance Publishing Group, Inc., 2004)

> "When it is a question of money, everybody is of the same religion." (Voltaire)

4. Friendship

Friendship usually lasts as long as there is an obvious benefit to both parties. However, when such benefits dissipate the friendship slowly dissolves. In this way, friendships are generally entered into for some self-advancement. Most choose friendships based on mutually perceived needs and, as those needs wane, so does the friendship. Remember that Jesus died completely alone, knowing that his closest friends had betrayed him, denied him, and forsook him.[27]

5. Gossip

Gossip is an outgrowth of one's pressing sense of guilt before God. As one is aware of his sin, and seeks alleviation from its guilt, he focuses on and feeds off of other's sin or misfortune. This is a masked attempt to exonerate the self, to quell the conscience's searing guilt.

> Gossip is a direct assault upon the gospel.[28]

In overhearing a conversation about others' failings most are far from grieved. Rather they are intrigued or even titillated (called *Schadenfreude*, literally "malicious joy," a secret pleasure in the tragedy visited upon others). Most privately relish other's shortcomings for two reasons. The first is that this makes one feel better about himself; there is a surge of self-righteousness. The second is that there is a certain excitement in sin, a certain mystery in it which attracts the human spirit. Fallen mankind loves the position of voyeur as drama unfolds in open rebellion against God. Upon hearing of others' sexual sin, for example, is one repulsed and sorrowful or is one secretly hungry for more detail so as to be entertained?

6. Gratitude

Acts of kindness are done more for self-aggrandizement than for the selfless service of others. The sinner's displays of love have implanted within them an agenda that others should shower thanks upon his head. Likewise, when others forsake gratitude one is immediately offended.

7. Humor

---

[27] In John 6:67 Jesus seemed to hint at this eventual abandonment by the Twelve.
[28] This idea from Jay Adams, *Ready to Restore: The Layman's Guide to Christian Counseling* (Phillipsburg, New Jersey: Presbyterian and Reformed Publishing Co., 1981)

Think about that which one finds humorous. Instead of being repulsed by coarse jocularity, the sinner is strangely attracted to it. Sinful man is strangely attracted to humor, especially that which is at the expense of others.[29]

However, "Many a truth is said in jest." Humor can be a window into the soul, as people routinely reveal their idols in their humor. Additionally, self-deprecating humor is a sign of pride (often indicating sought after compliments and assurances). Self-deprecating humor may also convey the impression that one can charitably concede ground to one's audience because he sees himself as superior.

> According to Augustine of Hippo (354-430), sinners are drawn to godless examples with no interest in examples for godly living. Men hold a penchant for, and exhilaration in, sinful living, seeking out models for how to make sin more comfortable to the soul, and more profitable in appeasing one's desires.

8. Being Insulted

Philip Dormer Stanhope (1694-1773) wrote, "An injury is much sooner forgotten than an insult." When the sinner is insulted he harbors plans for retaliation (in one form or another). Sinners will never permit contempt go unreprised in some fashion.

9. Losing

Mankind is often willing to lose in ways which do not matter to him, in a kind of mock-charity. However, each sinner feels that he must win at that which is linked to his idolatrous worship, so that in attempting to appease idols he will never accept defeat. When man loses at something which he deeply treasures, he devises careful plans for his eventual ascent.

10. Others' prosperity

"A friend is always happy about your success if it does not surpass his own." For example, in Numbers 12:1, 2 Miriam and Aaron expressed envy of Moses' station. "'Has the Lord spoken only through Moses?' they asked. 'Hasn't he also spoken through us?'" Honesty with ourselves reveals that we often more deeply relish others' disappointments and defeats than their successes (even those of close friends).

> A Christian friend contacted me; she had just enrolled in an overseas graduate school and found herself lonely and depressed. We talked about the causes for this. In the course of our conversation, I admitted that I, too, was at times lonely and depressed. She suddenly perked up, stating, "You sometimes feel depressed? I feel better now."

---

[29] Ephesians 5:4

> She then declared that her depression had departed and that she was once again joyful. I ended the conversation conflicted, thankful to help her, but unsettled that knowledge of my depression was the cure for hers.

11. Overstatement

There is a recalcitrant human tendency to overstate one's height, wealth, and accomplishments. Listen to most people carefully and a persistent theme resurfaces time and again, self-aggrandizement, often cleverly cloaked as humility.

The Trial of Strength of Yan Usmar, Grigoriy Ugryumov, 1799

12. Personal happiness

Instead of rejoicing with the truth,[30] the sinner is ambivalent to it, more concerned with immediate personal happiness. "We are more concerned with entertaining ourselves than with promoting what is good and true."[31]

In Numbers 11:18-20, the Israelites cried out for meat while expressing a longing to return to Egypt. This was a wailing for the things of the world and a longing to return to a state of slavery to it. The Lord's pronouncement was that the people would eat quail for a whole month – until it came out of their nostrils and they loathed it. This would happen because they had rejected the Lord in favor of that which would gratify

---

[30] 1 Corinthians 13:6
[31] R. C. Sproul, "Table Talk Day Calendar"

their sinful nature.

God often gives his people over to their derelict passions, letting them have their fill of that which lives in their hearts. This is similar to those who have everything the world can offer, fame, money, pleasure, and power. They have been given over to their passions to bloat themselves so that they would one day loathe the choices they have made. God's objective is that the things of the world would one day grow tiresome, burdensome, even loathsome to sinners, so that they would turn to God in repentance.

> How many modern heroes are self-sacrificial, focused on character-building, or encourage intellectual development? With noteworthy exception, heroes, instead, tend to be those who successfully gratify their sensual pleasures, dominate others, or project an image of leisure, all with impunity. This is the burning lust of the sinful nature, and man celebrates those who seem to have found a way to make rebellion against God rise, soar, and prosper.

13. Personal space

People easily lash out at anyone who invades their personal space (or that of their possessions). This points to the sinner's inflated sense of self.

14. Physical size and appearance

Sinners are quick to compare themselves to those around them. Men want to feel that they are taller and stronger than other men, and women want to feel that they are more beautiful.

> "Stop judging by mere appearances, but instead judge correctly." (John 7:24)

15. Rejection

What is the sinner's instinctual response to rejection, even an inconspicuous slight? The general response is, "How dare you! Do you have any idea who I am?"

> "There is only one thing in the world worse than being talked about, and that is not being talked about." (Oscar Wilde)

16. Relationships

An indicator of mankind's self-worship is the nature of his relationships. The sinner either surrounds himself with those who luxuriate in his presumed greatness, or with those in whose greatness he can luxuriate. Likewise, he flees from those who might think ill of him. We all want someone to love *us*, while neglecting how we might self-sacrificially love another. Sin causes one to look for the "best deal" that he can in every life situation, whether searching for a spouse or choosing friends and associates. Each instinctively wants others to herald his talents and accomplishments, to sing his praises, to laugh at his jokes. Those who serve the sinner in this way are rewarded with his presence, while those who seem ambivalent or critical are avoided.

> "Live in harmony with one another. Do not be proud, but be willing to associate with people of low position. Do not be conceited." (Romans 12:16)

17. Revenge[32]

Revenge comes naturally to fallen mankind. It is so ingrained in his sin nature that any transgression is met with some form of retribution. The human spirit feels a magnetic compunction to settle any score, and often devises create means for revenge. Yet, of course, revenge of any kind runs contrary to God's character.

> "Do not repay anyone evil for evil. Be careful to do what is right in the eyes of everyone. If it is possible, as far as it depends on you, live at peace with everyone. Do not take revenge, my dear friends, but leave room for God's wrath, for it is written: 'It is mine to avenge; I will repay,' says the Lord." (Romans 12:17-19)

Ajax
Henri Serrur, 1820

---

[32] For additional discussion of the issue of revenge see "The Transformative Power of Forgiveness" in the first book in this series, *Ask for the Ancient Paths: From Art to Artifice to Arisen,* chapter 4: "The Gospel as Inception Point: From Immorality to Immortality"

18. Respect

Each, when treated with respect, is secretly exhilarated. Does not something deep within one's being love being addressed as a superior, being listened to as important, meticulously served, or tirelessly accommodated? Sin causes people to crave respect from others. Consider Genesis 11:4 in which the Tower of Babel was constructed as part of a larger urban project through which the people would "make a name for themselves," and not be scattered over the face of the earth. Likewise, Luke 22:24 recounts a dispute among Jesus' disciples as to which of them was the greatest. The desire for respect is endemic to the sinful heart.

> "People seem to enjoy things more when they know a lot of other people have been left out of the pleasure." (Russell Baker)

> Our family has a tradition of dining at the Culinary Institute of America in Hyde Park, New York, for some special occasion each year. The Culinary Institute is unique in that it is staffed by students who wait on tables as part of their class evaluation. Being graded on performance makes for an exceptionally attentive wait staff. Wine is poured with the most delicate care. Water glasses are compulsively refilled. If a utensil is nudged out of place, a gloved hand reaches to straighten it. Dishes are served with a sense of showmanship, so that each course is a riot to the senses. There is a certain thrill in being waited on hand and foot, in knowing that someone is attentive to one's every dining need. And while there is nothing wrong with enjoying a fine meal, this experience offers a window into the heart's incline. The sin nature causes me to gravitate to, and delight in, experiences in which I am served, rather than those in which I am called to serve.

19. Self-absorption

"Those who praise others extravagantly desire to be praised themselves."[33] Each believes that he is the most important voice in his own life, and that others should also desire to listen to that voice. Each feels that he has some compelling reason that others should listen to him – advanced education, unique life experiences, or superior talent.

> "We all think we are exceptional, and are surprised to find ourselves criticized just like anyone else." (Comtesse Diane)
>
> "Speak to a man about himself and he will listen for hours."
>
> "It's not enough to succeed. Others must fail." (Gore Vidal)

---

[33] This quote from an unknown source

> Consider the way in which modern beauty pageants link themselves to charity. This is nothing more than a ruse allowing viewers to assuage a lust-plagued and guilt-ridden conscience. Neither the pageant's promoters, nor its contestants, care for a moment about others. Each cares only about garnering attention for her own beauty and talent. Yet, the heart, in all its lavish deception, fabricates a plausible means for placating the guilt of self-absorption.

20. Worry

While not always ostensible, mankind is paralyzed by worry. This takes on various forms and moods depending on the exigencies of the moment. For example, the poor are often consumed with worry about money. Yet, quite surprisingly, the wealthy are also (a Morton's Fork of the psyche). Worry is endemic to the human psyche since mankind habitually turns to himself for answers and invests hope in his own ability, always to his detriment.

> "Who of you by worrying can add a single hour to your life?" (Luke 12:25)

21. Being Wrong

How does one react when told he is wrong? Independent of the verity or speciousness of the statement, there is a reflexive hostility toward this.

The purpose of this section is to prove that each is a sinner. I would venture to say that every person struggles, to one degree or another, with each of the sins listed above. The evidence is clear: one habitually, spontaneously, instinctively, and without the slightest prodding or teaching, worships himself to the neglect of the worship of God.

Mankind's instinctual responses to the world, at every turn, reveal the tendencies of his heart. To correctly adjudge the evidence of sin, one must recognize that it entails motive as well as action, that it is as much an intrinsic event as an extrinsic one. Being counted a sinner is not just in the particular sins one commits, but in one's spontaneity to sin, in continually seeking to orient and define life without and against God. Further, as one considers the desires of his heart, he sees that his heart is prone to ever more wicked pursuits and evil ideations as he more fervently presses toward that which installs him as a god. As a short hand for glimpsing the heart, observe those who enjoy wealth, talent, opportunity, or power with few limitations. The fewer the constraints or checks on excess, the more one sees the heart emerge, as there is a feeling of impunity with regard to any sinful inclination.

> First John 1:10 states, "If we claim we have not sinned, we make him out to be a liar and his word is not in us." This idea of claiming that one has not sinned should be

> thought of more as a functional denial than as a propositional one. In other words, while Christians often propositionally state that they are sinners, they functionally consider themselves not to be. Thus, a disconnect exists between what Christians state and what they hold within their hearts.

As a final note on this section, it is vital that the wise counselor train himself to distill sin from mere personal idiosyncrasy in those he counsels. Sometimes Christians exhibit bad taste, poor timing, inarticulateness, or a lack of perception. Some may lack social grace, etiquette, or a sense of decorum, and may generally display the marks of poor upbringing. Often there is no sin involved in this (or there may be). The counselor must decant sin from surrounding peccadillos, keeping his personal sense of revulsion out of the assessment. While this can be a formidable challenge, for those who truly love God and others,[34] and who ask God for wisdom,[35] the salient sin issue can be elucidated in contrast to mere annoyances.[36]

Five Symbols of Sin

Reconstruction of the Temple of Jerusalem, William of Tyre, 15th C.

---

[34] Mark 12:30, 31
[35] James 1:5
[36] For additional discussion of this topic see "Counseling Threats: Stigmas and Stereotypes, Straw Men and Shibboleths" in the third book in this series, *The Days of Reckoning Are at Hand: From Fig Leaf to Olive Branch to Laurel Wreath*, chapter 8: "Diagnosis: Vanishing Secrets"

The book of Jeremiah offers five symbols of Israel's sin. These symbols are divided into three categories. The first is God's gifts turned into weapons against him, the second, overtly sinful pursuits which mimic God's work, and the last represents a world system which seeks strength in godlessness.

The book of Jeremiah condemns the nation of Judah's false sense of security in:

1. **The temple.** An edifice established by God for his worship, the temple quickly became an idol. Judah placed its trust in the temple's location, but not in the God inhabiting that location. This is analogous to institutions, sources of power, and societal structures in which one seeks false security.

> In ancient times people worshipped animals, now they idolize pop stars. Progress is nothing but an illusion; we just kneel at more sophisticated temple shrines.

2. **Sacred rituals.** God established rituals as sacrifices intended to glorify himself. However, Jeremiah 5:12 reads, "They have lied about the LORD; they said, 'He will do nothing! No harm will come to us; we will never see sword or famine.'" The people mistook God's mercy for his approval of their empty ritual, futile attempts to justify themselves before God (a practice which continues into the modern day).

3. **False prophets.** Those who opposed the truth and spread a false gospel, false prophets were welcomed because they suited the people's purposes.[37] This might be considered the conduits - media, psychology, or any source of falsehood - which seek to make the sinner comfortable in his sin.

4. **False gods.** Bowing before gods of their own making (such as Baal), the people then had the audacity to call on God for help.[38] These false gods are analogous to any object of worship in the modern world.

5. **Surrounding nations.** Seeking strength and protection in foreign allegiances (such as with Egypt), God warned Judah not to run to Egypt for refuge. However, because it would not listen, God decimated the nation while it was in exile. The surrounding nations are analogous to the unholy alliances forged to shield and justify rebellion against God.

In what way does each of these issues serve as a metaphor for sin? In what way does each draw out another aspect of sin? For example, the temple was built that God might receive the people's worship, but the temple became a locus of pride, an idol in

---

[37] Jeremiah 23:27
[38] Jeremiah 7:17-ff

itself. Sacred rituals were to serve as a reminder in the daily propitiation for sin. Yet, those rituals likewise became a source of pride, a faulty means of assuring salvation. These first two symbols represent using God's good gifts as weapons against him.

False prophets spread a message at odds with God's chosen prophets. Yet, the people readily turned to a message that either rationalized or overlooked their sin. Likewise, the people's false gods were cast in their own image to serve their own vanity. Thus, these second two symbols are overtly sinful sources of comfort, evil in themselves.

The strength of surrounding nations set the stage for Judah's false sense of security in unholy alliances. This is an example of friendship with the world which grows out of enmity toward God.[39] This last symbol represents turning to an evil system for protection, trusting in the enemies of God, in their resources and methods, rather than in God himself. In this way, through its five symbols, the book of Jeremiah offers a framework for understanding the Bible's teaching on sin.

The Jewish Money Lender
Auguste Charpentier, d. 1880

Fallen Man Believes Finiteness Is His Problem

Listen to most life stories of the rich and famous and one will probably hear a variation on the rags-to-riches theme. The reason is simple; presenting oneself as having overcome hardships serves many self-glorifying purposes. First, it diffuses criticism. If one struggled against, and defeated, opposition then one is cast as a victorious victim, not an imperialistic aggressor. Second, it offers a compelling narrative which invests meaning, even salvation, into one's wealth, so that wealth has delivered one from a life of misery. Lastly, a rags-to-riches narrative puts a face on one's wealth so that it is no longer a cold and imposing abstraction, but rather serves as the vehicle for a

---

[39] James 4:4

heart-warming human interest story.

A Russian proverb says, "When money speaks, the truth is silent." Most rags-to-riches stories are nothing more than a clever disguise for the love of money, an attempt to render that love beneficial and propitious. Such narratives often exonerate the sinner for frequent transgressions and justify Machiavellian tactics in the name of advancing an industry or providing employment to the underprivileged.

Man believes that his greatest problem is his finiteness and money seems like the ultimate answer. It seems to offer deliverance from one's experience of evil, from the brutality of the world, from the plebian concerns of the huddled masses, from man's timeless plight. Money seems like the answer to every sin-based need so that one's desire for money is directly related to the level of need that he feels. Money seems to offer everything that one demands of God and that he apparently fails to deliver. That is why money often wears the luster of a god.

This is an apt introduction to the issue of mankind's finiteness. Mankind believes that his greatest problem is not his sin but his finiteness. If only he can overcome his finiteness problem then he could become the towering triumphant hero that he knows he is capable of becoming.

On account of sin mankind instinctively hates God. Think about the number of times each day that you complain about your financial means, appearance, intelligence, or situation in life. This is a clenched fist raised against a holy God, a hatred of his work and plans, contempt for his love and provision. Each person seeks weapons in his war against God; this is the source of his uncontrollable cravings. Each hates his limitations, seeking to overleap and outrun his finiteness. But, in the end, this is all a futile grasping after the wind - vanity of vanities, all is vanity.[40]

Sin is the foolish notion that one's problem is his finiteness, rather than his separation from God. The following chart shows perceived finiteness needs:

Existential Station	**The Perceived Need**
1. The scholar	More knowledge
2. The one who loves security, pleasure, or the praise of the world	More money
3. The one in authority	More power
4. The lonely person	More companionship
5. The one who feels pressing emotional needs	More affirmation and acceptance from others

---

[40] Ecclesiastes 12:8

Mankind implicitly blames God for his limitations, feeling that if only God had not withheld his infinitude from human design then mankind would not be subject to a life of depravity and degradation. Thus, the vast majority of human effort is expended to overcome finiteness in the deluded hope that this will vanquish both man's intrinsic and extrinsic evil.

Departure Herald, Ming Dynasty, c. 1435

In light of this issue of finiteness, sin is routinely excused or explained away as the result of:

1. Deficiencies in the body or brain
2. Demons or Satan with supposed direct control of the will
3. Design flaws tacitly attributable to God
4. Emotions, which are presumed to be uncontrollable
5. Environment, which results in poor models for behavior
6. Ignorance, so that one is innocent in his neglect of the truth
7. Intelligence, a momentary lapse into "stupidity"
8. Low self-esteem, lacking a sufficiently high self-image
9. Maturity as simply lacking
10. Miscommunication
11. Negative thinking, a need for more positive thoughts
12. Past, the result of deterministic events in one's personal history
13. Situation, which drives one to unavoidable response mechanisms
14. Unmet emotional or physical needs

As is clear, mankind is a masterful blame-shifter, having perfected ever more elaborate schemes for exonerating himself through ascribing his sin to finiteness (of various forms). Thus, the quest to overcome finiteness grows out of mankind's nagging daily burden of sin. He flails against transgression for which he knows himself guilty by seeking, with ever greater fervor, to ascribe his guilt to a host of other factors which he supposes to be outside of his control.

For example, even as its economy soars, violent crime in China has risen in recent decades. Violence in China is popularly linked to frustration over the wealth gap which has only widened with its explosive economy. Sinologists claim that increased violence shows that China is paying the price for focusing on economic growth while ignoring social problems for more than three decades. There is a clever, albeit convincing, slight of hand in this analysis. Violence is excused as a somewhat unavoidable byproduct of economic growth, and the regrettable neglect of social concerns. This is full-flourished blame of finiteness (when reckless violence is willful hatred of the holy God).

> Sin is "like a virus that adapts in order to ensure its own survival and perpetuation, in this case by convincing its host it isn't there."[41]

Man's hatred of his finiteness is the impetus for his attempted exoneration from his sin. Because man makes himself his own reference point he deludes himself into believing that his finiteness is the source of his moral failing. He continually transfers the locus for his sin to plausibly culpable nodes within his design, or within the creation around him. As such, those nodes become the target of his hope for, not just acquittal before God,[42] but for his indictment of God himself.

Sinful man believes that his being itself, or his place in the outworking of history, or the creation's very design, are the perpetrators of his sin. This ultimately places the blame for sin squarely with God himself. For this reason, mankind seeks to repay evil for evil (a *lex talionis* of his own imagining), as he believes that an endemic evil was visited upon him through God's direct agency. Therefore, repaying evil for evil is an attempt to settle the score, a sought reversal of evil's curse both within and without the psyche. But, of course, such an effort is a fool's errand as there is not a scintilla of truth in this belief. (This repaying evil for evil is the linchpin for decoding all manifestations of insanity.)

Consider a husband and wife, brother and sister, or two friends, arguing about money concerns, entertainment choices, or fulfilling responsibilities. One way to handle this is to hand them money until they abandon their argument, give them unlimited personal entertainment until they fall into a cathartic stupor, or send them servants to attend to their every whim.

What is the outcome? They will still argue over the exact same issues! The problem was never the tangible object, the experience, or the situation. This was always about

---

[41] Adapted from Andrew O'Hehir; of course, with regard to sin, the virus metaphor must be handled gingerly so as not to tacitly remove culpability, as one would not be culpable for a viral infection.
[42] Cornelius Van Til, *Christian Apologetics* (Presbyterian and Reformed Press, 2003) 16.

control, wanting to feel loved, guarding against abandonment, craving respect, or demanding attention. The money, entertainment, and responsibilities are surface issues pointing to deeper heart ailments, worship alliances, fears, demands, and the quest for personal glory. In the final analysis, this is a with-regard-to-God problem (*coram Deo*).[43] This is a problem of hatred of one's own finiteness which at its root is hatred of the God who made mankind finite. Mankind's interpersonal conflict rides upon a blistering envy for God's infinitude. The point is that man's most rudimentary problem is not the strength of the gate, but the traitor behind the gate. The palace is lost because of man's own treachery, a treachery that keeps opening the gate to sin. Yet, man blindly continues to reinforce the gate.

Thus, fallen mankind shoulders two objectives with regard to sin. The first, redefine sin so that it can be managed through some human means and effort. For example, if sin can be recast as mental illness it can be conscribed to the failed mechanics of a feeble body and brain, delimited to a design flaw, and managed as any non-culpable disease would. Mankind's second objective is to minimize the power and depth of sin so that it is never seen as crucial and pressing. Most spend their entire lives engaged in these two pursuits, both redefining their sin and minimizing its effect.

> "To err is human, but to really cause a debacle you need a computer." The idea behind this statement is that mankind, when given more "tools," only furthers his error, expands his disastrous impact, and enhances his destructive capability. Mankind, as he seeks to overleap his finiteness, merely heightens the consequence of his rebellion.

Drawing Back the Veil on Moralism[44]

An early architect of Chinese culture, Confucius (551-479 BC) devised a system of morality that lent structure to society, government, and family life. He believed that virtue is the highest attainable quality as well as the mark of a good ruler. Confucianism purports that the heart is basically good, so that through properly reinforced behavior one can achieve this prized virtue. For the attainment of virtue there is a strict social hierarchy which should not be altered. Husbands rule over wives, fathers over sons, and kings over peasants. When this natural order is tampered with there are grave repercussions. By about 100 BC, Confucianism had unified the entire nation under one thought system, provided a basis for loyalty to the emperor, and legitimized the bureaucratic system.

---

[43] For a comprehensive discussion of the *coram Deo* concept see the first book in this series, *Ask for the Ancient Paths: From Art to Artifice to Arisen*, chapter 6: "Man Before the Face of God: The Imperium of the Psyche"

[44] For further discussion of this topic see "The Third-Way of Sanctification", "The Peril of Moralism" in the first book in this series, *Ask for the Ancient Paths: From Art to Artifice to Arisen*, chapter 10: "The Third-Way of Sanctification: From Abominable to Indomitable"

While Confucianism offered some limited temporal benefits for ordering society, it lacked power to fundamentally alter mankind's character. Nothing other than the chastening of God's Spirit leading to saving faith in Jesus can eradicate personal sin. Thus, any man-centered attempt to stifle sin only results in its expression in other ways, at other times. For example, military and athletic training seeks to instill discipline. A soldier or athlete may put forth a display of external discipline, but the heart below the uniform still beats with rebellion. Thus, those very same soldiers, when not in the presence of a disciplining force, will invariably follow the dictates of the indwelling sin nature. The sin nature has in no way been abrogated, only suppressed for a time until it can again gain unbridled expression.

Athletes and soldiers (or anyone subject to stringent standards of discipline) are notoriously sexually immoral. Could it be that external disciple offers the sinful heart a safe harbor, a means by which to go unchallenged as long as the proper behavior is maintained? Further, external discipline can serve as a ready source of arrogance as one becomes falsely confident in his own ability to resist temptation. In this way, a proud heart is shielded from its own debilitating depravity as long as external standards are meticulously maintained as a form of quasi-religious ritual.[45] (This, of course, was the crux of Jesus' confrontation with the Pharisees.[46])

> "The wise man looks for what is within, the fool for what is without." (Confucius)

Consider Matthew 12:43-45a,

> 'When an impure spirit comes out of a person, it goes through arid places seeking rest and does not find it. Then it says, 'I will return to the house I left.' When it arrives, it finds the house unoccupied, swept clean and put in order. Then it goes and takes with it seven other spirits more wicked than itself, and they go in and live there. And the final condition of that man is worse than the first…"

Notice that the exorcised house is "swept clean and put in order." This is the nature of moralism; it causes the unregenerate sinner to take on the appearance of cleanliness and order. However, the house is "unoccupied"; the Holy Spirit has not come in to fill the worship vacuum. Such a house is highly-vulnerable to an infestation of "seven other spirits more wicked." The idea is that moralism leaves the sinner evermore susceptive to evil under the false confidence that an unoccupied swept and orderly psyche is garrisoned against evil.

Most Christians don a Confucian set of lenses, seeing the human heart as

---
[45] Colossians 2:23
[46] Matthew 23:25, 26

fundamentally good and merely in need of a sound moral system to prompt the right behavior. The purpose of that moral system is simply that relationships assume proper structure and meaning. For most, Christianity's only purpose is to offer a persuasive pragmatism for maintaining relational order. Additionally, the godless pursuit of a distinctively Christian morality is often just another means of merely distinguishing oneself among others, just another form of human pride.

The Beijing Palace City Scroll (北京宫城图)
Ming Dynasty (c. 15th C.)

However, the Bible offers vastly more than morality. It recognizes that sin, as a result of the fall, influences all of mankind's "thinking and knowing; feeling and loving; doing and ethics."[47] In this regard, Mark 7:21-23 states, "For from within, out of men's hearts, come evil thoughts, sexual immorality, theft, murder, adultery, greed, malice, deceit, lewdness, envy, slander, arrogance, and folly. All these evils come from inside and make a man 'unclean.'" Sin is a comprehensive state of the heart, not just a cluster of forbidden behaviors to be eschewed in man's own strength. Thus, moralism is a paroxysm of human pride, compelling mankind to wander in a labyrinth of futility.

According to legend, Beijing's Forbidden City (which served as the emperor's palace from 1420 to 1912) contains 9,999 rooms. It was believed that this was one room fewer than the emperor's heavenly palace (containing 10,000 rooms). The belief was that perfection, while it could be approached, was not attainable on earth. The ancient Chinese, thus, longed for a perfected heavenly dwelling.

Case Study: Joseph's Naïvite

In Genesis 39:7 Potiphar's wife took notice of Joseph's virile appearance and sought

---
[47] David and Sharon Covington, "Introduction to Biblical Counseling" notes, 2004

to seduce him. Joseph spurned her advances time and again, day after day, and even refused to be in her presence.[48] However, one day, as Joseph entered the house to attend to his duties, and while the household servants were not present, Potiphar's wife, seizing the opportunity, caught Joseph by his cloak and propositioned him yet again. Joseph wisely fled. (However, Joseph's life took a turn for the worse as he ended up in prison for no fault of his own.)

Did Joseph handle this entire situation correctly? Is there something he could have done differently? In each episode of his young life Joseph seemed somewhat naïve concerning the heart's evil. While approaching his brothers in the desert, he seemed wholly unaware of their devious schemes. He was oblivious to the fact that his brothers loathed him.[49] Later, in dealing with Potiphar's wife, Joseph seemed unaware of the extent to which evil people will go to get what they desire. Joseph should have never put himself into a situation in which he could be seduced or slandered. He should have relinquished his duties, or ensured that trustworthy witnesses were always present. He likely should have alerted Potiphar to the potential dangers surrounding his position.

In like manner, Joseph did not reckon that Potiphar would so quickly cast a trusted servant into prison.[50] Joseph may have felt unduly secure in Potiphar's service. But as Joseph soon discovered, those in power are desperately insecure and seek to maintain control at any cost, regardless of whom they falsely accuse. Potiphar was more committed to expedience than justice, more focused on maintaining the status quo than uncovering the truth.

In prison Joseph naively hoped that Potiphar's cupbearer would remember to mention Joseph's faithful service.[51] Joseph, again, was sorely mistaken concerning human nature. It seems that time and again, Joseph was blindsided by the world around him because he lacked a sufficient understanding of the heinousness, persistence, and utter self-serving quality of sin.

Is it possible that Joseph made himself vulnerable out of self-pride? Genesis 39:9 recounts that Joseph told Potiphar's wife, "No one is greater in this house than I am..." Is it possible that Joseph allowed his high status to cloud his judgment, that he sought to maintain this status at all costs, even at the cost of putting himself at risk with a determined woman? Is it possible that Joseph made his position into an idol which caused him to take unnecessary risks in order to maintain its supposed blessing? Joseph might have avoided much pain and loss had he been more aware of the sin within his own heart, which in turn could have opened his eyes to the sin within

---

[48] Genesis 39:10
[49] Genesis 37:5
[50] Genesis 39:20
[51] Genesis 40:14, 15

others' hearts. Although this is somewhat speculative, there seems to have been a blind-spot within Joseph concerning the nature of sin.

> "Better to love God and die unknown, than to love the world and be a hero; better to be content with poverty than to live as a slave to wealth; better to have failed when serving God than to have succeeded when serving the devil. What a tragedy to climb the ladder of success only to discover that the ladder was leaning against the wrong wall." (Erwin W. Lutzer)

Society's Artificial Demarcation for Normal and Abnormal

Whalers Trapped by Arctic Ice, William Bradford, d. 1879

The book *Endurance: Shackleton's Incredible Expedition* (1959) describes the ship the *Endurance* commissioned to explore Antarctica in[52] 1914. *Endurance* measured forty-seven meters long by eight meters wide, outfitted with three sails and a steam engine. Its walls were a half-meter thick. The type of wood, greenheart, used to construct its hull is denser than iron and cannot be cut with ordinary saws. Despite its unparalleled strength, the *Endurance's* design was not right for traveling to Antarctica because its sides were too straight. When it was eventually stranded in the pack-ice the ice pushed in on its hull, crushing it. (Bowl-bottom ships must be used for navigating pack-ice because the hull gets pushed upward, not inward.) Possibly the sturdiest wooden ship ever built in Norway, *Endurance* snapped like a toothpick in the three-meter thick Antarctic ice.

---

[52] Alfred Lansing, *Endurance: Shackleton's Incredible Expedition* (Carroll and Graf Publishers, 1959)

Endurance serves as a fitting introduction to the issue of sin and society. Consider the *Endurance* as the human spirit, no matter how sturdy it's moral construction the design is all wrong for the forces leveled against it. Consider the pack-ice as sin which crushes even the sturdiest moral constitution with unrelenting force. The human heart cannot encounter evil without devastating consequence. Morality, no matter how resolutely construed, is no match for the pressing force of the world, the flesh, and the devil. Thus, the human spirit needs an entirely revamped design, one constructed by God himself, renewed by his Spirit, equipped to resist temptation and vanquish evil.

Cornelius Plantinga's, *Not the Way It is Supposed to Be: A Breviary of Sin* (1995),[53] speaks about society cultivating an artificial, manmade, and largely false understanding of wrong-doing, evil behavior, or sin. Society creates a false demarcation for what is considered acceptable and normal, as opposed to that which is unacceptable and abnormal. In this way society calls "normal" that which, from God's perspective, was always abnormal, aberrational and, in short, sinful. In labeling the sinful "normal" or "acceptable," society is then confused when that supposed normal behavior moves into deviant, destructive, criminal, or clearly aberrant behavior. Society is thus blind to the organic connection between the criminal or deviant and that which precedes it.

> "Crime is a sociopolitical artifact, not a natural phenomenon. We can have as much or as little crime as we please, depending on what we choose to count as criminal." (Herbert Packer)

Society's False Normal-Abnormal Delineation

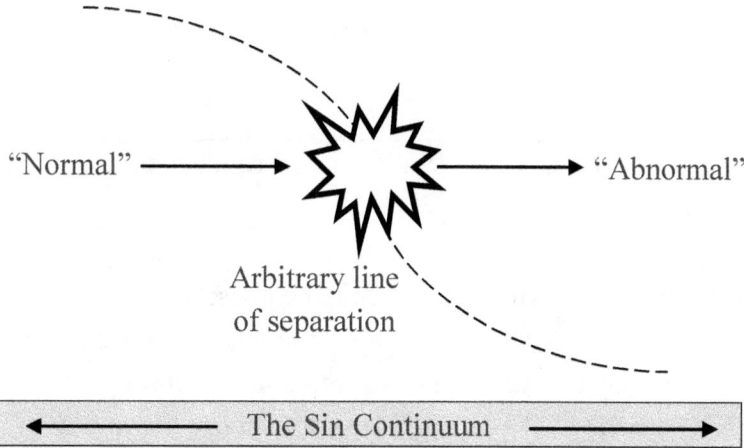

This is society's blindness, misplaced standards, and compliance to that which God calls evil. This blindness is often upheld by society's largest and most respected institutions, from healthcare, to government, to education, to entertainment, all of

---

[53] Cornelius Plantinga, *Not the Way It's Supposed to Be: A Breviary of Sin* (William B. Eerdmans Publishing Co., 1995)

which enable and embolden sin when it appears as mere normal behavior, while punishing it (in various ways) when society's imaginary "sin" line has been crossed.

> "Vice creeps into the heart under the guise of virtue." (Latin proverb)
>
> "All things truly wicked start from innocence." (Ernest Hemingway)

Behavior on one side of this imaginary sin line is socially acceptable, and even socially expected, but somehow crosses over to become deviant and condemned. However, this line never existed. It is merely a convenient means to tolerate that which society judges should be tolerated, and condemn that which society judges should be condemned. Society is perennially befuddled as to why abnormal, deviant, or criminal behavior arises because it has blinded itself with false categories of normal and abnormal. From society's perspective it is as if deviant behavior arises in a mysterious vacuum, when from God's perspective the connection could not be more clearly elucidated when one understands the nature of sin.

> "No man ever became wicked all at once." (Latin proverb)

Leviticus 18:30 warns the Israelites, "Keep my requirements and do not follow any of the detestable customs that were practiced before you came and do not defile yourselves with them. I am the Lord your God." These "detestable customs" are the culture of the surrounding nations. One of the most treacherous aspects of sin is how appealing it often looks to the outside world. Sin often stands behind socially acceptable practice, such practice functioning as a scatter-plate for the call to repentance.[54] Society may overlook, condone, promote, or praise sin at every turn, wholly unaware of what it really is, and its unparalleled ability to mold the heart into Satan's image.

> "How much of our culture makes sin look normal and righteousness look strange." (David F. Wells)

Consider the development of smoking in the United States. The Native Americans invented smoking as a means to blunt hunger pains and later embraced it as a means for social interaction. During the suffragette movement and throughout the 1920s cigarettes were called "torches of freedom," and touted as a symbol of cultural sophistication. In the 1940s physicians encouraged their patients to smoke as a supposed hedge against disease. During the 1950s smoking transitioned into a display of teenage rebellion, and as a means for social inclusion.

Today smoking tends to function as a relational shield behind which people cower out

---
[54] Matthew 12:30

of fear. Something in cigarette smoking connotes a means of managing stress and anxiety (while cigar smoking connotes an unrushed contemplative mind). The point is that cultural expressions, such as smoking, are co-opted to suit society's larger agenda.

Smoking, as a fixture in a societal décor scheme, sometimes blends harmoniously with the background agenda and at other times clashes garishly. However, without an understanding of the Bible it is never seen for what it really is, a rakish affront to the original Designer. This is why society displays such irrational vacillation with regard to activities such as smoking.

The Toreador
Mary Cassatt, 1873

One of the first issues to recognize is that society labels "behavioral" that which is worship in nature. Society is blind to the worship driver for all human behavior because it is blind to a holy God intimately and actively engaged with the psyche. The psyche is a with-regard-to-God entity and therefore either bows in supplication, or raises an angry fist of rebellion. All sin is directed toward God, so that there is a forceful, active, and deliberate quality to it. This is the reality behind all seemingly normal action which, from God's perspective, was always sinful when not committed to him.

The figmentary demarcation between normal and abnormal is the world's Procrustean bed, which though inviting to weary travelers, renders its subjects either tortured or maimed. Only Jesus Christ (the true Theseus) can free man from his blindness to forced and arbitrary standards, because from the perspective of the cross, a continuum exists between supposed normal and abnormal behaviors. That which is labeled "normal" is often based in sin, in rebellion, and in hatred toward a holy God, and therefore necessarily leads to that which is labeled "abnormal." From God's perspective the sinner receives the just consequences of sin as that sin continues its inevitable forward progress. An artificial social construct, the normal-abnormal demarcation shifts throughout history as society's standards shift. Additionally, society continually pushes the line of demarcation further out so that with each passing generation more is normalized, less is stigmatized, and that which was once called deviant is now considered an acceptable alternative.

> It is noteworthy that while society normalizes more human behavior, it operates a kind of clandestine pincer movement by means of psychiatry. Psychiatry increasingly medicates behavior and personality traits that are within the realm of the normal. So the category of normal is progressively expanded, while at the same time there is greater infiltration of psychotropic medication into that category. Thus, the modern phenomenon of cosmetic psychopharmacology seeks to sculpt the normal. Could it be that society is trapped in a grand contradiction? Since what it seeks to cast as normal is far from this, it must employ a pharmacological aid to make that normal seem manageable. The evidence points to a serious deficiency which psychiatry only exacerbates, the handiwork of scientifically-cloaked witchdoctors and shamans.

Examples of Society's Artificial Normal-Abnormal Demarcation

1. Aggression (generally in men)

It is fascinating that assault which, if perpetrated outside of an athletic environment would result in incarceration, when perpetrated within that environment is often accepted as part of the game (the most obvious example being North American ice hockey). Why should blatant assault be tolerated in any environment at anytime? Doesn't assault in one arena necessarily lead to it in others as well (such as domestic violence)?

Society wrongly asserts that in men certain natural aggression builds healthy self-image. It bandies about terms such as, "being a real man," "taking it like a man," or being "a man's man." These concepts seem to encourage a measure of aggression, as if it is a sign of virility and strength of character. However, as soon as that aggression crosses into violent behavior (directed against the vulnerable) the perpetrator is suddenly a criminal. From God's perspective the seed of aggression was always sin. It was a way to grab control from God, to gain power over others for selfish purposes. Thus, self-serving aggression which society labels as "natural" or "normal" God sees as sin, seeking control and mastery in God's place.

As described in his biography, *Unbroken: A World War II Story of Survival, Resilience, and Redemption* (2010),[55] World War II veteran, Louie Zamperini (1916-2014), exhibited the following pattern of behavior:

1. As a child, Louie was a neighborhood hellion, fighting, stealing, and causing

---

[55] Laura Hillenbrand, *Unbroken: A World War II Story of Survival, Resilience, and Redemption* (New York: Random House, 2010)

mischief.

2. As a teenager, Louie discovered a love for running, applying himself with such fervor that he eventually competed in the 1936 Berlin Olympics.

3. After returning home in October, 1945, following two years in Japanese POW camps, Zamperini sought to qualify for the Olympics again. However, due to a war injury, he was unable to compete.

Death of a Stag, Benjamin West, d. 1820

4. Louie then directed his attention toward returning to Japan to hunt down and murder his fugitive captor, Mutsuhiro Watanabe (1918-2003). ("Louie had found a quest to replace his lost Olympics. He was going to kill [Watanabe]."[56])

5. Unable to carry out his plot, Zamperini turned to alcohol, chain smoking, and pornography.

Louie's neighbors celebrated when, as a teenager, he turned from his rapscallion ways to compete in the Olympics. Nearly overnight, he transitioned from public menace to hometown hero. While to society, Louie was reformed, his idols were still operative, just redirected, given a socially acceptable goal. After returning home as a decorated war veteran, Louie again sought a socially lauded application for his root idolatry.

---

[56] Laura Hillenbrand, *Unbroken: A World War II Story of Survival, Resilience, and Redemption* (New York: Random House, 2010) 353.

When that plan failed, he redirected his energies toward carrying out premeditated murder. Again, striking up against obstacles, he applied himself to his vices.

The point is that even as an acclaimed athlete and war hero, Louie's root idolatry had never been broken. He was the same hellion, just wearing different clothes. From society's perspective, Louie's behavior underwent a metamorphosis from juvenile offender to war hero and back again to the criminal. Society is confused because it does not see the root God-hatred at the core of the heart. That hatred draped itself in ways which appeared virtuous, but never were. Louie's idolatry assumed various masks, some applauded, others derided, until liberation came in October, 1949, when Louis gave his life to Christ. Only then were the idols shattered and the storm stilled.

> Lord John Dalberg-Acton (1834–1902), British philosopher, wrote, "Power tends to corrupt, and absolute power corrupts absolutely." This statement assumes that it is the power, or the mere holding of a position of power, that corrupts the heart. In reality, there is a pre-existing corruption, sin. Human reason tends to externalize sin so as to deny the true corruption central to man's existence. It is not through the exercise of power that corruption arises, but through the inclination of a depraved heart. The power structure merely provides a conduit through which the inclinations of the heart are manifest.

2. Ambition

Ecclesiastes 4:4 states: "And I saw that all toil and all achievement spring from one person's envy of another. This too is meaningless, a chasing after the wind." So much ambition is just envious desire masquerading as that which is noble. One's hard work can arise from a root hatred of God and others, as work is often an attempt to gain that which one feels God cannot, or will not, provide. Wrongly motivated, work can offer a ready means for a sense of superiority.

A salesman puts in long hours and is praised by his manager as a "go-getter." He is employee of the month and his picture hangs in the office. His manager encourages the salesman to reward himself with a car befitting his ability, and that if he keeps his focus, he will receive a promotion. Meanwhile the salesman's wife is contemplating divorce, and his children lack the guidance of a father. This work ambition, while praised by the world, slowly erodes relationships so that the man feels increasingly isolated, derelict in his responsibilities, easily angered, envious of his neighbors, prone to flights of fantasy, and clamoring for escapes from nagging fear of failure. (This man's seemingly benign curiosity and inquisitiveness are, from God's perspective, covetousness, looking at the world through desirous eyes.) Thus, ambition can wear an alluring mask, but the correct lenses reveal that there is something deleterious lurking within.

> "He who sacrifices his conscience to ambition burns a picture to obtain the ashes." (Chinese proverb)

3. Drug abuse

Coffee is considered a cornerstone of American productivity, the hub around which people fuel their ambition. Yet, the caffeine in coffee is addictive. The corporate executive who downs several cups of coffee a day is seen as simply an overachiever (within the realm of the normal), yet he has placed himself on an addictive path. Likewise, smoking, while often stigmatized as a nasty habit, is nevertheless counted within the realm of normal activity. The teenager who occasionally enjoys a smoke with his buddies is considered a typical teenager. However, both caffeine and nicotine are gateways to greater abuses (whether of substance or other ilk) which can shipwreck a young life.

Even occasional alcohol abuse is considered part of the normal flow of life. The popular college student is praised for being able to "hold his liquor." Drunken binges are considered nothing more than a rite of passage, a display of youthful exuberance, healthy experimentation, and humorous fodder for college reunions. However, the young man who crosses the line into alcoholism has now become a social liability. Likewise, if the abuser ventures into illegal drug use he is condemned as a criminal. That which started out as socially acceptable crossed into the realm of a criminal offense. Why was any abusive activity, no matter how seemingly innocuous, ever socially acceptable?

A sample of the progression of drug abuse:

Activity	"What I would never do…"
I need a little boost, to fit in with the crowd, a quick escape.	Smoke
First puff of a cigarette	Smoke an entire cigarette
Smoke an entire cigarette	Smoke an entire pack
Smoke an entire pack	Smoke marijuana
Smoke marijuana	Snort cocaine
Snort cocaine	Snort heroine
Snort heroine	Inject heroine
Inject heroine	Steal to buy heroine
Steal to buy heroine	

> "The fault is not in our start but that in ourselves we are unsuccessful." (William Shakespeare)

4. Prioritizing one's social group

The Bridesmaid
James Jacques Joseph Tissot, c. 1885

A small town football star is a "real team player." He is "one of the guys" and won't "whine" or "cry." This athlete prizes inclusion on the team above all else, and upholds the team's religious fanaticism. He abides by the football culture's "ten commandments," the first of which is to never admit that one is injured. This young man sustains a concussion while on the field and is told to "walk it off." After lying about the extent of his injury, he is cleared to continue playing. Tragically, he ends up with permanent neurological damage. The team's cult mentality led to dangerous actions which cost this young man his livelihood. His future bouts with depression, anger, and possibly even suicide, are the curse of his willingness to risk his health for a man-centered, man-fearing standard, and for the love of the praises of men.

5. Seeking the "good life"

A state lottery advertises images of the good life in order to promote a sanitized form of gambling. The lottery justifies itself by stating that the funds support public education. This form of state-run gambling is legal, but the addiction it often spawns can easily carry over into illegal forms of gambling. When a gambling pool is uncovered in a corporate office the participants are arrested for illegal gambling.

> In trying to create heaven on earth mankind invariably produces hell. (adapted from Karl Popper)

6. Sexual suggestion (generally in women)

In society women are encouraged to flaunt their sexuality, to be sexually suggestive, or provocative with men. This has become a modern sickness in which women are told that this flaunting is a form of empowerment, and that it promotes a healthy self-image. In this regard, with each successive generation girls are being sexualized or sexually desensitized at a younger age. Advertising now routinely portrays young girls proudly showcasing themselves. From God's perspective this is an abomination on par with parents sacrificing their children to the god Molech.[57] Society seems utterly confused about the connection between flaunting sexuality and the searing concupiscence which now rends the very fabric of society. Society fails to see a connection between sexualized behavior and the loss of relationship, the instability in family life, widespread disease, and systemic depression. As women increasingly use sexuality to manipulate men's emotions they find themselves only more estranged from relationships.

> One of the most perplexing and disconcerting facets of modern society is its rank intolerance concerning establishing standards for moral conduct, especially sexual standards. In 2014 the United Nations hosted a conference in New York City on the growing global problem of teenage pregnancy. The conference addressed options for enlisting and mobilizing resources for these young mothers. Yet, not a word was permitted concerning abstinence programs. This is the modern trend; tremendous energy is exerted in trying to fix a problem after the fact, while those who offer moral solutions before the fact are branded as intolerant bigots.

7. Voyeurism

A "healthy red-blooded" all-American boy is expected to engage in mild voyeuristic fantasy. This is seen as a sign that he is emotionally healthy and displays what psychology would label "properly functioning" sexual desire. However, this voyeurism is based in sin from God's perspective, quickly leading down a derelict path. A supposed innocent voyeur may see his desire multiply to the point that it crosses into a criminal act. Additionally, his voyeurism, if pornographic, rapidly erodes respect for women, dehumanizing them to the point that he may callously beat a girlfriend or wife. What, from society's point of view, started out as normal and natural behavior becomes criminal when it crosses a line that society artificially marks out. The behavior from the very start was heinous and abhorrent to a holy God.

> "A single ant can destroy a whole dam." (Chinese proverb)

8. White lies

---

[57] Leviticus 18:21

From society's perspective lying falls on a continuum from seemingly beneficent, to innocuous, to inconvenient, to heinous and grievous. It is considered socially acceptable, even polite, to perpetrate white lies (the beneficent or innocuous type). These are not considered real lies but rather a way to maintain an assumed social order of kindness and respect. Of course, white lies are lies nevertheless (no less so because of the perceived benefit which accrues from them). Lying may be tacitly condoned, even encouraged, in one context, but when a lie is perpetrated on a tax return, or in a courtroom, it is criminal.

> "The measure of a man's character is what he would do if he knew he would never be found out." (Lord Macaulay)

In each example outlined above, false standards were established which euphemize or sanitize what is fundamentally sinful, cloaking it as socially acceptable behavior. The activities mentioned were sinful from the very start, and thus necessarily spiraled into greater loss when unrestrained by God's grace. When unchecked, sin results in grave loss, even criminal acts (as society defines them). (However, on account of God's common grace not all sin progresses to its logical terminus.)

Society seems blind to the causal connection between that which is deemed innocent, normal, and socially acceptable and later criminal or deviant behavior. On one side of the line behavior is labeled as "normal," on the other side, "abnormal." The supposed line demarking the two never existed. It was always a figment of society's imagination, a convenient way to sanction actions which from God's perspective were always already sinful, and therefore abnormal. Thus, destructive consequence should never come as a surprise.

> Modern culture does not deal in consequences anymore.[58] There is little or no outrage over immorality, corruption, or impropriety. There is no moral compass to correctly adjudge right from wrong, beneficial from derelict behavior. This points to a deeper sickness within the human spirit, an ever-growing separation from God himself.

Sin starts as an acquaintance who then enters as an invited guest. The guest soon transforms into the host and later the master of the house. The master of the house is quickly a tyrant demanding complete subservience.[59] One does not wake up one day and think, "Today I will become a pedophile, perpetrate fraud, commit adultery, or commit murder." Sin starts as small deviations which, if unresolved, metastasize like a cancer until they have enveloped one's life.

---

[58] Dennis Miller, "The O'Reilly Factor," May 6, 2013
[59] This concept from an unknown source

> "Blessed is the man who does not walk in the counsel of the wicked or stand in the way of sinners or sit in the seat of mockers." (Psalm 1:1)

Apotheosis of Homer, Jean Auguste Dominique Ingres, 1827

In their highly-controversial work, *The Bell Curve: Intelligence and Class Structure in American Life* (1994),[60] Richard Herrnstein (1930-1994) and Charles Murray present evidence that criminals tend to be about ten percent less intelligent than the general population. This finding tends to mirror the public perception that criminals are unintelligent, and that immoral behavior generally accrues from poor education. The conventional wisdom is that criminals do not think through the consequences of their actions, or else they would not commit crime. Thus, crime is reduced to some form of cognitive dissonance.

While there may be a correlation between low IQ and certain types of crime, it is fallacious to link low IQ and sin. Crime is often sin (but certainly not always), but sin is often not crime. In other words, sin is a wholly unique concept, a *sui generis*, and therefore should not be tacitly conflated with actions that resemble crime. Likewise, sin does not negatively correlate with intelligence, but rather with foolishness. Often the faulty logic goes that if one would just think more effectively then he would not sin. That is far from the Bible's perspective, one which never sees sin as arising from

---

[60] Richard Herrnstein and Charles Murray, *The Bell Curve: Intelligence and Class Structure in American Life* (Free Press, 1994)

a lapse in sound reason. Just as there is a mental hurdle in separating the concept of sin from that of criminality, likewise there is a hurdle in decoupling sin from intelligence.

Sin as Comprehensive State of the Heart

Western tradition holds that the heart is subject to seven deadly sins: anger, avarice, envy, gluttony, lust, pride, and sloth. In some medieval paintings these sins are symbolized with animals: anger – lion; avarice – frog; envy – snake; gluttony – pig; lust – goat; pride – peacock; sloth – snail. This represents one of Satan's most effective decoys: to externalize sin, to symbolize it, to make it appear to be a string of iterative events.[61] In reducing sin to discrete units of behavior, the attempt is to excuse and rationalize it through a focus on circumstance. The misguided objective is to make sin into discernable nodes of transgression rather than a comprehensive state of the heart,[62] a continual warlike stance toward the person of God himself.

Christians erroneously tend toward a seven-deadly-sins approach, reducing sin to dramatic iterative events such as: envy, gluttony, greed, lust, pride, sloth, and wrath. Thus, the logic goes that as long as one avoids obvious offenses one is living a somewhat virtuous life. However, sin cannot be distilled down to distinct nuggets of wrongdoing, as it is more akin to a sludge which wends its way through the chambers of the heart or a vapor embalming the soul.

> Bible describes the heart as proud,[63] insane,[64] arrogant,[65] rebellious,[66] wicked,[67] weak,[68] foolish,[69] and evil.[70]

A superficial view of sin reduces it to "deliberate volitional acts" so that sin is erroneously conflated with discrete moments of action or inaction,[71] thought or non-thought. Conversely, a holistic understanding of sin sees it as foundational to fallen human existence so that it is understood that the non-Christian can only sin.[72] Since sin is not merely iterative events, not just discrete moments of transgression to be distilled out, the Bible conceptually addresses the issue of "sin" (singular) rather

---

[61] It is fascinating that Buddhism also lists 108 specific sins. Thus, the attempt to quantify sin, to enumerate it, is a common feature of all false religion.
[62] This concept "comprehensive state of the heart" borrowed from David and Sharon Covington, Biblical Counselors
[63] Proverbs 21:4
[64] Ecclesiastes 9:3
[65] Isaiah 10:12
[66] Jeremiah 5:23
[67] Jeremiah 17:9
[68] Ezekiel 16:30
[69] Romans 1:21
[70] Hebrews 3:12
[71] Michael Bobick, *From Slavery to Sonship: A Biblical Psychology for Pastoral Counseling* (1995) 43. (class notes)
[72] Augustine of Hippo (354–430)

than "sins" (plural). Being a worship condition and a comprehensive state of the heart, sin is not a series of burn marks (thoughts, words, actions) on an otherwise pure background. Therefore, a weak view of sin isolates it to deviant behavior alone. The implication is that if one simply changes the behavior the sin has been eradicated (but, of course, it is not). Sin's back-story is a hatred for, disobedience toward, and rebellion against, the holy Creator God.

> In writing this chapter I had a "grammatical epiphany." Describing sin using a passive grammatical voice implicitly shifts blame. To capture the Bible's teaching on sin I would principally need to traffic in the active voice.

Sin is not a passive condition. It is not a semi-dormant state of a heart which occasionally wakes from its slumber. Like Satan, its chief architect, sin is active. It desires a particular outcome and pursues that outcome with relentless intent. Sin holds a death grip on unregenerate hearts and minds, dictating how they apply themselves.

> The movie monster Godzilla fed off of electricity. He sought out a power plant and simply walked through it, allowing the electricity to course through his reptilian body. The more current he received the stronger he became. This offers insight into the way that sin works. Sin increases in time as the flesh seeks out and encounters the world, and its mastermind, the devil. With each exposure to the world, sin only grows stronger.

A summary of man's sinful state:

1. Obsessed with himself, man cultivates and celebrates a magnified sense of self.

2. Darkened concerning the truth, man foolishly assesses the value of the creation, himself, and God.

3. Lacking discernment, man cannot correctly weigh matters.

4. Loving falsehood, man only embraces truth if it accords with cherished desires.

5. Living through his eyes, man often forsakes truth for a fantasy or an illusion.

6. Distracted, man cannot focus on matters of eternal consequence.

7. Fickle, man chases immediate, or at least pressing, desires.

8. Grabbing, man lusts for power over the creation.

9. Seeking immediate gratification, man lacks long-term vision as he feeds his base appetites.

Cleopatra Testing Poisons on Condemned Prisoners, Alexandre Cabanel, 1887

10. Seeking pleasure, man craves emotional stimulation.

11. Prideful and easily offended, man assumes some insult in each perceived disadvantage or loss.

12. Seeking revenge, man harbors resentment and finds forgiveness a monumental task.

All sin is, at its root, a posture of revenge, revenge simultaneously against God and his creation. Whether through open hostility, passive aggression, promiscuity, self-righteousness, greed, or fear of man, man seeks revenge against God for man's own finite condition, and against others for their perceived exacerbation of the finiteness curse.

What is the solution? God wants the Christian to thoroughly hate his sin, not just the consequence of his sin. Therefore, the solution is comprehensive, life-long, rehabilitation far more radical, powerful, revolutionizing than one could ever imagine. A sober understanding of, and regret for, one's sin should drive one to the feet of Jesus with piercing sorrow. In this way, any discussion of sin always starts with the sinner and ends with Christ.

> "God made him who had no sin to be sin for us, so that in him we might become the

> righteousness of God." (2 Corinthians 5:21)
>
> "Those who belong to Christ Jesus have crucified the sinful nature with its passions and desires." (Galatians 5:24)

The fact that Jesus admonished his listeners to love the Lord their God with all their heart, soul, strength, and mind,[73] presumes that mankind naturally does not. Rather, under the dictates of sin, mankind is consumed with a root hatred of God, a hatred that applies itself with all of one's heart, soul, strength, and mind. Jesus' second great command to love one's neighbor as oneself, again presumes that mankind naturally does not love others in the way that he already loves himself. Sin drives self-love. Thus, hatred of God and love for oneself are the heart's Scylla and Charybdis, complementary perils.

> "The acts of the sinful nature are obvious: sexual immorality, impurity and debauchery; idolatry and witchcraft; hatred, discord, jealousy, fits of rage, selfish ambition, dissensions, factions, and envy, drunkenness, orgies, and the like." (Galatians 5:19–21)

Vital Truths Regarding Sin

In the United States consumers will not purchase blemished fruit or fruit marred with insect bites. So in order to make the fruit look perfect, growers coat it with heavy insecticides during the growing process. Thus, imperfect fruit is actually healthier since fewer chemicals were used on it. There is something in this which explains sin within the heart; it is often invisible, yet insidious and poisonous. However, all the while, one deludes himself that since he appears upstanding, his psyche must be pure and healthy.

In order to draw out sin's hidden qualities, the following are some vital truths regarding sin:

1. Since mankind was designed to worship, sin derives from one's worshipping center.[74] Sin is fundamentally and inextricably a worship-driven event. Therefore, the sinner has a worship disorder.[75] Each person is a tangled knot of conflicting worship and dysfunctional desires.

2. Sin is anything outside of Christ, without Christ, against Christ, any substitute for Christ, that which forces Christ to the position of less than a savior. Sin is an entirely anti-Christ motive, action, and outcome.

---

[73] Luke 10:27
[74] This concept from Jay Adams, Biblical Counselor
[75] This concept from Edward Welch, Westminster Theological Seminary, Philadelphia, Pennsylvania

146 WHAT AGREEMENT IS THERE BETWEEN THE TEMPLE OF GOD AND IDOLS?

The Feast of Herodes, Peter Paul Rubens, d. 1640

> Your problem is infinitely worse than you think; yet the solution is infinitely greater than you ever imagined.

3. The non-Christian can only sin.[76] It is impossible for one outside of Christ to do anything but sin in every moment of every day, in every thought, word, and action. This does not mean that every thought, word, and action is demonstrably evil, but that the heart refuses to bow to God in all things.

> While the unbeliever possesses no declarative understanding of sin, the Christian often does not take sin seriously. Sin is possibly the most neglected, most misunderstood, and most reviled doctrine in the Christian repertoire. For this reason, grace, extended on account of Jesus Christ, is often cheapened and taken for granted. As the problem it solves is viewed as relatively minor, grace is debased and devalued.

---

[76] This concept from Augustine of Hippo (354–430)

4. Jeremiah 17:9 states, "The heart is deceitful above all things and beyond cure who can understand it?" Sin, at its root, is not logical or rational, and at times does not follow predictable patterns. There is something unwieldy and chaotic about sin, something twisted and insane, which warps the sinner's perspective.

> "I can calculate the movement of the stars, but not the madness of men." (Isaac Newton, in response to the South Sea Scheme of 1720)

Consider Acts 5:1-11,

> Now a man named Ananias, together with his wife Sapphira, also sold a piece of property. With his wife's full knowledge he kept back part of the money for himself, but brought the rest and put it at the apostles' feet.
>
> Then Peter said, 'Ananias, how is it that Satan has so filled your heart that you have lied to the Holy Spirit and have kept for yourself some of the money you received for the land? Didn't it belong to you before it was sold? And after it was sold, wasn't the money at your disposal? What made you think of doing such a thing? You have not lied just to human beings but to God.'
>
> When Ananias heard this, he fell down and died. And great fear seized all who heard what had happened. Then some young men came forward, wrapped up his body, and carried him out and buried him.
>
> About three hours later his wife came in, not knowing what had happened. Peter asked her, 'Tell me, is this the price you and Ananias got for the land?'
>
> 'Yes,' she said, 'that is the price.'
>
> Peter said to her, 'How could you conspire to test the Spirit of the Lord? Listen! The feet of the men who buried your husband are at the door, and they will carry you out also.'
>
> At that moment she fell down at his feet and died. Then the young men came in and, finding her dead, carried her out and buried her beside her husband. Great fear seized the whole church and all who heard about these events.

The point of this vignette is to highlight just how seriously God takes sin. He often brings his wrath directly upon those who feign godliness but lack integrity. While God is longsuffering and forbearing, he also hates the sin within his people and is consumed with burning anger to free them from that which stands between them and him.

5. Sin comes easily, spontaneously, and habitually to fallen man.

6. Every day God confronts the sinner with the sin in his heart. Every interaction, situation, and problem is part of God's plan to affect repentance. If one misses God's sanctifying work, he will experience the same problems and testing time and again, until God's work has been accomplished.

7. An Ethiopian proverb states, "When spider webs unite, they can tie up a lion." Sin always starts inconspicuously and seemingly innocuously. Sin arose as Eve looked at the forbidden fruit recognizing it to be pleasing to the eye and good for food.[77] Just a moment's rebellion led Eve to pick the fruit, eat it, and share it with Adam. Subsequently, the entire universe was cast into a darkened and deadened state. Eve's sin served as the spark, catalyst, and prototype for all subsequent sin, so that each individual sinner retraces and follows the pattern set by Eve.

> During the early 1990s New York City experienced a renaissance as crime diminished rapidly. One theory for this sudden change was the removal of graffiti in public places. The thought is that graffiti spawns malfeasance, prompting reluctant criminals to act as they otherwise might not. Graffiti creates the expectation of crime, and with its removal the atmosphere improves dramatically. Sometimes a sweeping transformation rapidly follows seemingly trivial changes.[78]

James 1:13-15 states,

> When tempted, no one should say, 'God is tempting me.' For God cannot be tempted by evil, nor does he tempt anyone; but each person is tempted when he is dragged away by their own evil desire and enticed. Then, after desire has conceived, it gives birth to sin; and sin, when it is full-grown, gives birth to death.

Thus, James 1:14 is clear, situation is not the culprit; evil desire, living within the heart, drives sin. There is also a progression to sin; it invariably intensifies and in so doing ossifies the soul, finally ravishing the sinner.

8. There is a vicious cycle to sin. Sinful desire often spawns a craving for pragmatic solutions which in turn produce more desire. The sinful desire for autonomy fosters existentialism making one a slave to the world. This in turn further exacerbates one's initial desire for autonomy. Consider another example. The lust for power causes one

---

[77] Genesis 3:6
[78] Malcolm Gladwell, *Tipping Point: How Little Things Can Make a Big Difference* (New York: Little, Brown and Company, 2002)

to pander to the dictates of men. This in turn renders one weak-willed and complicit, causing one to desire more power. Continuing in sin begets more entrenched sin.

9. The greater one's comfort level with sin, the greater one's emotional pain, frustration, futility, emptiness, weakness, feeling of being cursed, guilt, and sense of burden. Sin brings dire consequence of one form or another. The more deeply it is imbibed the more lethal its poison.

> Consider the tragic irony of thirsting to death on the ocean, to be completely surrounded by water yet that water, if drunk, would bring fatal dehydration. That is a picture of sin. Sin is like saltwater which only worsens spiritual thirst. One feels as though sin will satisfy; it is so available, convenient, and seemingly so ready to meet one's deepest yearnings. Yet, the more deeply one drinks of it, the more thoroughly one is rendered functionally dead in his rebellion.

The Street Enters the House
Umberto Boccioni, 1911

10. Sin has a certain dulling quality on the mind and the senses so that they do not function as intended.[79]

11. In Romans 6:1, 2, Paul is clear that there is never any net benefit from sin. Therefore, it is vital to point out that the Bible never presents sin as holding any disguised blessing for man. Sin is an unmitigated loss. However, God leverages sin's effect on the psyche to drive the sinner to Christ. Thus, God often brings good out of a seemingly irredeemable evil.

---

[79] 2 Corinthians 3:14

12. There is a saying, "Cease to struggle and you cease to live." As the Christian is raised to life in Christ there should ensue a subsequent daily struggle with his own sin. The Christian should expect this battle and engage it, all the while recognizing that victory is assured. The Christian struggles, not in his own strength, but rather in the Holy Spirit. This is the source of his joy and the basis for his assurance.

The Broken Window Theory on Sin

> "Watch the little things; a small leak will sink a great ship." (Benjamin Franklin)

In the 1960s American cities succumb to urban blight such as violent crime, graffiti, arson, and narcotics trafficking. By the 1990s, however, much of this malfeasance had faded. The reason may be explained in the broken window theory.

Suppose a window breaks in an urban neighborhood. If that window remains unrepaired it sends a message that residents are apathetic, even callous, toward their environment. That broken window indicates that no one cares for the neighborhood's well-being, rendering it vulnerable to crime. The neighborhood is soon plagued by vandalism, robbery, or arson. Crime escalates rapidly from just a single broken window.

The broken window theory, developed by criminologists James Wilson (1931–2012) and George Kelling, posits that crime propagates from the perception of disorder. Disorder is communicated in seemingly trivial nuisances such as graffiti, litter, a dilapidated fence, or a defaced sign. These marks of urban blight embolden would-be criminals who reason that if a neighborhood cannot, or will not, correct minor transgressions it will certainly cower in the face of more substantive crimes. Thus, crime metastasizes like a cancer.[80]

> "After one vice, a greater follows." (Spanish proverb)

This theory could apply to society as a whole. As explored previously, society routinely overlooks seemingly minor transgressions, making them appear trivial and inconsequential. The result is that deviant behavior grows on a logarithmic scale. This macro-theory could also be applied to the micro, the human heart. Sin within the reprobate quickly multiplies and grows, when unchecked by God's common grace. Mankind falls deeper into his sin as he continues to live in it, taking deeper root within the heart as it is indulged day-by-day. Thus, mankind must more vigorously suppress his conscience as it grows ever more disquieted. Even seemingly trivial sin spirals into greater darkness, the sinner continually suppressing his guilt, so that that

---
[80] Malcolm Gladwell, *Tipping Point: How Little Things Can Make a Big Difference* (New York: Little, Brown and Company, 2002) 141, 142.

sin flourishes unopposed.

> "Small crimes always precede great ones. Never have we seen innocence suddenly turn to destructive actions." (Jean Baptiste Racine)

Consider the following example. Two children grab for a lone ice cream cone in the kitchen freezer. While both grab for it, only one can have it, so they argue and tussle. Mother, hearing the commotion, runs to the kitchen and pleads with the children to stop bickering. However, she has a solution to the problem. From a second home freezer she pulls out an additional ice cream cone and hands it to the children. Now each child has what he desires and the arguing abates. From a pragmatic perspective the problem seems to be solved, the children are pacified and peace is restored. However, unbeknownst to the mother, there is an insidious threat which has just sunk its claws more deeply into the children. There is a far greater evil lurking in hidden places which will soon visit this home. Let's analyze the situation:

1. The children were acting out of self-centered hearts, demanding the desires of those hearts.

2. The situation was carefully orchestrated by God to reveal those hearts. It is not coincidental that the freezer contained only one ice cream cone on that particular day. To miss this is to miss the God uncovering the intentions of the heart.

3. The mother's actions, while appearing altruistic and wise, where actually the height of foolishness. In placating the children's demands she further instituted the idols of their hearts. She strengthened those idols, offering further evidence that those idols can, with the right techniques, gain what they desire.

4. Idols of the heart, now fortified, grow more determined and more effective at achieving their desires. In this episode idols have just grown more brazen and more defiant.

5. This home, having achieved a momentary détente, will soon erupt in another even more explosive argument in the next clash of agendas. Ultimately, the placation game will not work.

6. God will not let this home rest; he will not allow idolatrous harmony to rule. He will again orchestrate events to uncover heart worship for the purpose of repentance. God will continue to reveal hearts, at every turn and in every situation, until the cause of repentance is effected. This is his supreme goodness and mercy.

152 WHAT AGREEMENT IS THERE BETWEEN THE TEMPLE OF GOD AND IDOLS?

7. The situation exposes heart idols; heart idols expose self-worship. Self-worship is based in hatred of God's sovereignty and authority. God's objective is always to bring the sinner to repentance, to submission to his authority. As the mother placates she operates as a functional enemy of God's cause, as an emissary of Satan. Only when she disciplines her children, exposing to them their rogue agendas, and calling them to repentance in Christ, will she begin to function for God's purposes.

Hylas and the Nymphs, John William Waterhouse, 1896

Sin's Downward Spiral

If one thinks about it, buttons are laborious to uncinch and cinch, but zippers make removing clothing almost effortless. The proliferation of clothing zippers in the 1960s contributed to the sexual revolution. The speed with which people could undress and dress again made promiscuity more convenient. When coupled with sin, innovation often leads to undesirable consequences. There is something in this slice of trivia which offers a window into the human heart.

In Genesis 4:7 God warned Cain that "sin is crouching at your door." James 1:15 also speaks about "…sin, when it is full-grown." Like Cain and Abel in the field, away from their parents' protective gaze, often just a seemingly insignificant opportunity, provides the needed conduit for the heart's heinous rebellion to rise up. Once the table has been set the heart's sinful feast begins, so that as some speak of "a crime of opportunity," the Bible might describe "a sin of opportunity," given the right setting sin often flourishes and blossoms.

There is a "double-helix" quality to sin.[81] Sin springs from heart worship which results in thoughts, words, and actions. Those thoughts, words, and actions in turn prod, shape, and invigorate heart worship. Idols of the heart calcify as they are upheld and exonerated through lifestyle (i.e.: thoughts, words, and actions). Likewise, idols propel lifestyle by often celebrating the depraved nature, justifying it, excusing it, and giving it plausible outlets in a blindly tolerant world.

> "For Want of a Nail"[82]
>
> For want of a nail the shoe was lost.
> For want of a shoe the horse was lost.
> For want of a horse the rider was lost.
> For want of a rider the message was lost.
> For want of a message the battle was lost.
> For want of a battle the kingdom was lost.
> And all for the want of a horseshoe nail.

Psalm 1:1-3 hints at a certain downward regression to sin as some become more accustomed and acculturated, more comfortable and confirmed, in their hatred of God.

> Blessed is the man who does not walk in step with the wicked or stand in the way that sinners take or sit in the company of mockers, but whose delight is in the law of the LORD, and who meditates on his law day and night. That man is like a tree planted by streams of water, which yields its fruit in season and whose leaf does not wither—whatever he does prospers.

In this pericope "walk," "stand," and "sit" represent a steady regression into greater sin. Thus, the one who walks with the wicked acknowledges the wicked as a viable partner. The one who stands with the sinner seeks to learn more about sinful ways, and the one who sits in the company of mockers has now cast his lot with the rebellious. This is a picture of increased comfort with sin. From birth, the heart is inclined toward, and loves, sin. That inclination and love deepens, becomes more sophisticated, more embedded and emboldened, with continued practice.

Thus, the conscience eventually molds itself to accommodate the contours of one's sin. Consider John 16:2: "They will put you out of the synagogue; in fact, a time is coming when anyone who kills you will think he is offering a service to God." Those who commit heinous acts, murderous acts directed against God himself, can

---

[81] The concept "double-helix" from David Covington, Biblical Counselor
[82] Although this poem appears in many versions, one early rendition was composed upon the death of King Richard III at the Battle of Bosworth Field on August 22, 1485.

suppress and contort their own consciences to such a degree that they believe they are actually serving God.

> The grand delusion behind all sin is that, while it causes insanity, it appears to function as a remedy, a remedy that in increasing doses will finally deliver a cure.

The sinner may appear more socially respectable as he grows older, but he regresses into greater sin with each passing year. Romans 1:21-32 vividly captures this regression:

1. Thinking became futile (1:21)
2. Foolish hearts were darkened (1:21)
3. Became fools (1:22)
4. Exchanged the glory of God (1:22)
5. Sexual impurity (1:24)
6. Degrading their bodies (1:24)
7. Exchanged the truth for a lie (1:25)

Vanity
Jan Sanders van Hemessen, c. 1540

8. Worshipped and served created things (1:25)
9. Shameful lusts (1:26)
10. Exchanged natural relations for unnatural ones (1:26)
11. Inflamed with lust for one another (1:27)
12. Received in themselves the due penalty for their perversion (1:27)
13. Depraved mind (1:28)
14. Filled with every kind of wickedness, evil, greed, and depravity (1:29)
15. Full of envy, murder, strife, deceit, and malice (1:29)
16. Gossips (1:29)

17. Slanderers, God-haters, insolent, arrogant and boastful (1:30)
18. Invent ways of doing evil (1:30)
19. Disobey their parents (1:30)
20. Senseless, faithless, heartless, and ruthless (1:31)
21. Approving of those who practice the same (1:32)

> Petrified wood is produced when a fallen tree lies in stagnant low-standing mineral-rich water. The water slowly removes the particles of wood, replacing them with minerals. Petrified wood, therefore, looks exactly like the original wood but is now a rock-hard mineral. This is an effective metaphor for sin. Sin functions to remove the godliness in one's design and replace it with foreign objects which take on the appearance of living matter but are in fact, stone-cold and recalcitrant. In time, the heart becomes like petrified wood, solidified in sin. The process is painstakingly slow, purposeful, and deadly.

Traditionally, sin is categorized in terms of sins of commission and sins of omission. The implication is that certain sins are wrongly committed acts, while others are wrongly neglected acts. A sin of commission might be murder while a sin of omission might be failing to stop murder which one had the power to stop. While the terms, as they are traditionally construed, are biblical, there is something in the term "sin of omission" which seems to implicitly exonerate the sinner. It is as if one merely experienced a memory lapse. The implication is that sins of omission are somehow more passive expressions of sin. It is crucial to underscore that sins of omission are equally active and deliberate, and in this regard, as equally heinous as sins of commission.

Related to this issue is the common phrase that one "fell into sin," which often functions as a tacit form of exoneration. Just as one cannot stop himself from falling (being under the dictates of force outside of his control), so too, most use fell into sin to mean that one is a victim of forces outside of his control. The implication is that one is not culpable for his sin, just as one would not be culpable for the effects of gravity. While the concept of falling into sin does exist in the Bible, it is always closely associated with personal responsibility and culpability. For example, James 1:14 speaks about being enticed and dragged away by one's own sinful desire. One is responsible for his own experience of sin (being enticed and dragged).

Satan's Devices for Minimizing the Severity of Sin[83]

> "The coming of the lawless one will be in accordance with the work of Satan displayed in all kinds of counterfeit miracles, signs and wonders, and in every sort of

---
[83] Adapted from Thomas Brooks, *Precious Remedies Against Satan's Devices* (CreateSpace Independent Publishing Platform, 2013)

156 WHAT AGREEMENT IS THERE BETWEEN THE TEMPLE OF GOD AND IDOLS?

> evil that deceives those who are perishing. They perished because they refused to love the truth and so be saved. For this reason God sends them a powerful delusion so that they will believe the lie and so that all will be condemned who have not believed the truth but have delighted in wickedness." (2 Thessalonians 2:9-12)

1. Satan pollutes the mind with error in biblical doctrine so that it incorrectly weighs matters pertaining to absolute morality.

2. Satan presents God as only loving and merciful and therefore blind toward, or at least lenient on, sin.

3. Satan propagates the lie that one can, through his own efforts, extenuate the severity of sin's consequences.

4. Satan convinces sinners that repentance is effortless, or not even required.

The Melun Diptych
Jean Fouquet, c. 1450

5. Satan dangles attractive bait in which is hidden a deadly hook to make sin look virtuous, or at least innocuous.

6. Satan makes sinners foolishly self-confident and bold when the occasion for sin is near.

7. Satan sets up self-serving comparisons with those considered more sinful so as to excuse sin.

8. In order to placate one's guilty conscience, Satan highlights the moral failings of virtuous men while concealing their heavy sorrow, searing regret, and life-long repentance.

9. Satan makes holiness look weak, sorrowful, painful, and marked by loss.

Case Study: The Contours of Blame-Shifting and Hypochondriacal Sin

A young Christian woman, "Stacy," made deliberately hurtful statements to me. Her older friend, "Betty," said that Stacy did not mean to be hurtful but just needs encouragement. Later, when questioned, Stacy said her statements were merely the result of "having a bad day." When pressed further, Stacy told me that she "repented of her anger."

Consider the need for encouragement, the excuse of a bad day, and repentance of one's anger. Each statement is fundamentally a carefully constructed lie, a fraudulent perversion of the gospel. The excuse that sinful words are the result of a lack of encouragement shifts the blame to other people, or even to the victim himself. The lie is that if others had met Stacy's perceived needs she would not sin. Since they had not, she is justified to act with belligerence. The excuse of simply needing encouragement is a clever ploy to exonerate Stacy, while accusing those around her of negligent wrong-doing. If others had simply loved Stacy more, she would act in a godly manner.

The second excuse of experiencing a bad day, shifts blame to God himself who made the day which drove Stacy to sin. According to Stacy's logic, had God not placed her in this supposed bad day she would not have sinned. She is merely a victim of circumstance. As innocent as her excuse sounds, she implicitly accuses God of wrongdoing and holds him accountable for her sin.

The third excuse is in many ways the most insidious because it appears to be the most godly. Stacy repented, but not of the idol which gave rise to her sinful words. She did not repent of the heart which apotheosizes herself and seeks her own glory. She merely repented of her behavior, conspicuously leaving her heart unchanged. In reality Stacy had not repented at all because asking forgiveness for behavior is not the nature of repentance, but rather a perversion of repentance. She never repented of the cunning and wickedness of her heart. Thus, her mock-repentance was deliberately designed as a smokescreen, a red herring tactic to manipulate the unsuspecting. Her false repentance did nothing more than further entrench the idols of her heart. In her placating false repentance she had just proven to herself that her idolatrous heart could remain untouched, while simultaneously hoodwinking others into thinking that repentance had occurred. This pattern of blame-shifting followed by mock-repentance is a caustic formula for ever-deepening sin within the heart.

As a tangent, a somewhat bizarre counterbalance to this issue of blame-shifting is what might be termed "hypochondriacal sin." (Hypochondriasis is the imagining of fictitious illness.) Although not common, hypochondriacal counselees may fabricate fictitious sin from which they seek to continually repent. The counselor should be vigilant in recognizing certain imagined sins. (It should be noted that what I term hypochondriacal sin is of a more entrenched and intentioned nature than the classic overactive conscience.) While it is true that an aspect of sanctification is to renew the conscience so that it is properly active and accurate, hypochondiacal sin may be more of a deliberate smokescreen cloaking the true intentions of the heart. (In this way it may have more of an obsessive quality in functioning as a red herring.)

I coined the term hypochondriacal sin in dealing with a young Christian woman who frequently told me of her need to repent. As I listened carefully to her supposed sins, I soon picked up that these were not sins at all. She repented of encouraging a friend to attend seminary (which she later determined was not a good fit), of sending the wrong address in an email, of not having time to read a book she promised to read. While on the surface her desire to repent seemed to be an act of faith, over the course of several such episodes, I surmised that she almost concocted imaginary sin so that she could once again repent. Repentance, in effect, became its own idolatry. It was as if repentance, of anything and everything, had become a certain source of comfort (likely based in pride). I sensed that in her repentance there was a certain feeling of renewal, a faux-cleansing, all under-girded by an ill-defined sense of superiority. This idolatrous repentance may serve as a form of social deflection, drawing attention to phantom sin so as to keep true sin safely shielded.

Is There a Hierarchy of Sin?

Is some sin worse than others? All transgression is abhorrent in God's sight, no matter how trivial it may appear. However, the Bible singles out sexual sin as particularly destructive and heinous. In fact, God's chastisement often uses sexual metaphors, such as prostitution and adultery, to capture the severity of false worship. Conversely, sanctification is also described in sexual terms such as God presenting his church as a pure virgin of Christ.[84]

> "But I tell you that anyone who looks at a woman lustfully has already committed adultery with her in his heart." (Matthew 5:28)
>
> "Flee from sexual immorality. All other sins a man commits are outside his body, but he who sins sexually sins against his own body but he who sins sexually sins against his own body." (1 Corinthians 6:18)

There is a uniform guilt from sin, but not a uniform effect from sin.[85] For example, 1 John 5:16, 17 reads,

> If you see any brother or sister commit a sin that does not lead to death, you should pray and God will give them life. I refer to those whose sin does not

---
[84] 2 Corinthians 11:2
[85] David Covington, Biblical Counselor

lead to death. There is a sin that leads to death. I am not saying that you should pray about that. All wrongdoing is sin, and there is sin that does not lead to death.

What is the sin that leads to death, as opposed to that which does not? It would appear that John highlights a contrast between a repentant spirit which grieves for sin (desiring to be free from it), and a spirit which maintains an attitude of unrepentance. So the focus in this passage is on one's disposition with regard to repentance.

It is also noteworthy that blasphemy against the Holy Spirit, the "unpardonable sin" (mentioned in Matthew 12:31, 32), will not be forgiven, because it is an attack upon God's justifying, and later sanctifying, work

Charon Carries Souls Across the River Styx (detail)
Alexander Litovchenko, d. 1890

through his Spirit. In other words, it is through the direct work of the Holy Spirit that the sinner is brought to faith. If the Holy Spirit's work is blasphemed and opposed there is no further recourse except to be delivered to perdition.

The Clench and Conflict of Sin

Years ago our family owned a wonderful poodle named "Wesley." Once we gave Wesley a steak bone which he gnawed with relish. As he whittled the bone down, it soon became a dangerous spindle in his mouth. The dog began struggling, his tongue writhing. The bone had become lodged across his upper dental arcade, a crossbeam stuck fast along the roof of his mouth. Sensing what had happened, I attempted to dislodge the bone. However, Wesley snarled and clenched his teeth not allowing me to enter his mouth. Yet the dog had a terrified look on his face, his fear so intense that he even released his bladder. He was desperate to free the bone, but his instinct to guard food made him hostile to any attempt to remove it. Paradoxically, he contumaciously held fast to that which had the potential to kill him. He seemed to sense this but, at that moment, his conflicted canine instinct left him a confused mess. (All ended well as I used a wooden spoon to pry the bone loose and confiscate it.)

This story offers some insight into the nature of sin. Like Wesley, each sinner has a wedged intrusion in his design, something which harangues him to the point of intense fear. He recognizes that he must extract this vexing entity before it kills him. However, he inexplicably holds fast to this intrusion with mortal valor. Instinctively believing that this entity is his very life and sustenance, the sinner clenches down on that which is killing him, while flailing for deliverance from it. He knows that he is powerless to save himself, that he is doomed without outside intervention, yet he lashes out against the hand of salvation, salvation offered through the cross of Jesus Christ.

There is a tension in Scripture concerning how sin affects the unrepentant. On the one hand, as one ages, while he bears a greater burden for a life of sin, his specific sin often becomes less egregious to him. He increasingly develops greater comfort with a life outside of Christ, without Christ, and against Christ, having anesthetized himself to his particular form of rebellion.[86] In this regard, God, in his mercy, continually seeks to make the comfortable uncomfortable so that they never find rest outside of Christ.

In Psalm 73 David questioned why the wicked prosper. What David did not see is that the wicked are harangued, even tortured, by their sin (as David himself was, as evidenced in Psalm 51). This is the other side of the tension. Sin sits as a millstone upon the neck of the wicked, weighs upon his soul, keeping him continually searching for covering, comfort, escape, and finally, vindication. The wicked is haunted by his sin, and despite his "compulsive washing" (various methods to placate his conscience) he can never remove the bloodstains from his hands. While often not admitting it, the wicked is desperate for a savior of his own making and choosing, anything or anyone to relieve the trenchant pestilence of sin. Thus, there is an often forgotten aspect to sin, the intense psychic pain that routinely accompanies it.

The sinner, as he is exposed, is tossed by undulating waves of emotional angst, some mere surface swells, others cresting whitecaps (depending on the degree of his resignation to his rebellion). Sin casts one into a living torture chamber as he seeks to mitigate the daily consequence of hatred toward his Creator. The pain of unrepentance grows year by year, steadily consuming the psyche, from a glowing ember of regret, to a flame of loss, to a raging fire of existential angst. Sin leaves a burn-mark on the

---

[86] Psalm 1:1-3; Romans 1:28, 29

soul which only Jesus himself can remove.[87]

Sin Harangues the Sinner

Macbeth Seeing the Ghost of Banquo, Théodore Chassériau, 1854

Classic literature is replete with examples of the human desperation for freedom from sin.[88] For example, Sophocles' (c. 497 – c. 406 BC) Oedipus Rex put his eyes out rather than look upon the murder and incest he committed. Shakespeare's (1564-1616) Macbeth could not purge the blood from his murderous hands. Edgar Allen Poe's (1809–1849) short story "The Tell Tale Heart" (1843) recounts the torturous beating sound within a murderer's head as he was unable to muffle the sound of his victim's heart. Fyodor Dostoyevsky's (1821–1881) *Crime and Punishment* (1866) revolves around the perfect crime for which the perpetrator, Roskolnikov, could not find peace.

Classic literature contains stirring accounts of sinners haunted by their sin, tortured to the point of burning insanity. This is a picture of man's sinful state; it drives him to lunacy (in various forms) as he desperately seeks to alleviate the anguish of his personal transgression before a holy God (a transgression not just against abstract absolute standards but perpetrated against the person of God himself). That being said, one's sin-related emotional pain is directly related to the depth of one's depravity. As

---

[87] Isaiah 1:18

[88] For additional discussion of the topic of literature and counseling see the third book in this series, *The Days of Reckoning Are at Hand: From Fig Leaf to Olive Branch to Laurel Wreath*, chapter 6: "The Basic Plotlines Which Emerge in Counseling"

stated previously, all are not equally comfortable with sin as all have not acted upon their Adamic nature with equal profundity. Therefore, not all are equally tortured by their sin. Although to a degree each sinner is insane, not all are equally insane.

The Bible's entire teaching on sin could be summarized with the statement, "Your biggest problem lives within you." Sin curses, plagues, and harangues the heart, mind, and emotions, every moment of every day. The sinner carries around in his being a continual burden for his sin. His guilty conscience seeks comfort at every turn. He seeks justification through his good works. He longs to feel that he is good and deserving of salvation; this is the motivation for his charity and generosity. He seeks to numb the pain of his sin through somehow dismissing it. This partially accounts for the modern day obsession with psychology which is a grand rationalizing mechanism for sin. Mankind seeks escape from his sin through a host of addictions. Any distraction is welcomed in order to divert his attention from his throbbing conscience. This could account for the modern obsession with entertainment as a convenient psychic anesthetic. Mankind seeks to silence the "still small voice" of God within him through continually filling his spirit with some form of worldly static.

In Acts 7, as the Sanhedrin raised stones to pummel the deacon Stephen, he proclaimed Jesus to be sitting on the throne of heaven. Acts 7:57 records, "At this they covered their ears and, yelling at the top of their voices, they all rushed at him." The recalcitrant sinner cannot bear to hear the truth about God. Likewise, he cannot bear solitude or silence which magnifies that still small voice of God confronting him. Therefore, he seeks to fill his mind with the clang and clatter of futile thought, to fill his days with restless chasing and distraction. (Often this is the motive for pulsing music, a coffee klatch, or a city environment.) The sinner seeks some diversion, some interaction, some sound (no matter how banal), to divert his attention from his throbbing culpability before a holy God.

Sin as Pillaging Visigoths

People display a curious trait; they often build themselves up only to tear themselves down. Through words, appearance, associations, and possessions mankind is often self-infatuated; he then uses these very same means to abase himself. Why? People are fundamentally "schizophrenic" as a result of sin, living in a fantasy world in which they are apotheosized while continually abutting with the reality that they are mere mortals. As each lives out his deluded god fantasy he often denigrates himself in self-loathing disgust. This points to a "pillaging Visigoth" within the psyche, that is sin.

If one's life were in imminent danger he would expend every ounce of energy, exhaust every resource, focus every thought, to nullify that threat. This is how one should deal with his sin, as though his very life depended on defeating it. Matthew 18:8, 9 states,

> If your hand or foot causes you to sin cut it off and throw it away. It is better for you to enter life maimed or crippled than to have two hands or two feet and be thrown into eternal fire. And if your eye causes you to sin, gouge it out and throw it away. It is better for you to enter life with one eye than to have two eyes and be thrown into the fire of hell.

With this passage I am reminded of a brutal time millennia ago in which maiming ravaging razing plundering invaders terrorized civilizations. This is a fitting metaphor for sin. With the same violence that sin attacks man's being, man should seek to obliterate the sin within himself. This endeavor is a take-no-prisoners form of warfare (called "*herem* warfare" in the Old Testament and "total warfare" in modern times). God expects his people to do violence to their sin, not violence to themselves or others, but to their sin. They should be willing to take measures so drastic that they would be tantamount to cutting off one's own hand or foot. Just as Romans 6:23 warns, "The wages of sin are death," so too, one should treat sin as a life-and-death struggle, far more urgent than even meeting immediate physical needs. However, the key to the Christian life is that this warfare is waged by God himself. Thus, sin is obliterated, not in man's strength, but in God's, a victory appropriated through dwelling in the Spirit.

Hebrews 10:26-31 issues a dire warning:

> If we deliberately keep on sinning after we have received the knowledge of the truth, no sacrifice for sins is left, but only a fearful expectation of judgment and of raging fire that will consume the enemies of God. Anyone who rejected the law of Moses died without mercy on the testimony of two or three witnesses. How much more severely do you think someone deserves to be punished who has trampled the Son of God underfoot, who has treated as an unholy thing the blood of the covenant that sanctified them, and who has insulted the Spirit of grace? For we know him who said, 'It is mine to avenge; I will repay,' and again, 'The Lord will judge his people.' It is a dreadful thing to fall into the hands of the living God.

> Mankind may at times prune leaves and branches from his sinful behavior, but without an unregenerate heart he never pulls up the roots of sin because he fears that nothing will ever grow again. That is precisely the intent of God's work – that nothing of the sin nature should ever grow again within the heart, to cultivate an environment of faith so antiseptic to sin that sin can not even germinate.

Sin's Great Ravishment: Insanity[89]

R. D. Laing (1927–1989) wrote, "Insanity: a perfectly rational adjustment to the insane world." He, thus, makes insanity an innocent and expected response to outside stimuli. However, from the Bible's perspective insanity is birthed in sin directed against God himself. In Daniel 4:28-37, King Nebuchadnezzar II (c. 634–562 BC) arrogated to himself the glory of God and was cursed. God removed him from authority so that he lived among wild animals and ate grass like cattle. He became insane and even took on the appearance of an animal. By God's decree, Nebuchadnezzar was reduced to the appearance and mannerisms of an animal as a result of his brazen pride. This was the curse of his vaunting sin. It was not until Nebuchadnezzar acknowledged and glorified God that his position and sanity were restored.

> We are all born insane; some remain so. (adapted from Samuel Beckett)

The Last Judgment (detail - Damned Man)
Michelangelo Buonarroti, 1541

Sin darkens, deadens, frustrates, nags, ravages, robs, starves, and tires. Over the course of time this breeds insanity (to various degrees and in various forms); therefore each sinner is insane. Despite his relative level of insanity, on account of God's common grace, the sinner usually functions in society. However, when he can no longer function, society labels him "insane," ascribing various descriptors to that insanity in order to pardon it with a fictive narrative (errant brain chemistry, past abuse, unmet needs, etc.). But insanity does not arise in a vacuum, nor is it based in a somatic cause. Insanity exists on a continuum which, from the moment of birth, festers, advances, and ravishes until it finally debilitates (whether partially or completely). There is only one solution for insanity: repentance, on account of the fact that the insanity is actually sin perpetrated with regard to God. Repentance first

---

[89] For additional discussion of this topic see "Insanity's Inception" in the first book in this series, *Ask for the Ancient Paths: From Art to Artifice to Arisen*, chapter 8: "What Has Jerusalem To Do With Vienna?: The Case Against Psychology"

removes the penalty for sin and then progressively removes its power. As sin's power is removed, so too, is its concomitant insanity.

> "For God has bound all men over to disobedience so that he may have mercy on them all." (Romans 11:32)

Often when human evil shows itself in the most heinous atrocities, some are quick to describe the perpetrator as an animal (the label of "animal" somehow tacitly exonerating mankind). This marginalizes sin as mankind is seen as merely retracing his inchoate evolutionary past and, as such, represents a gross misconception. Animals do not perpetrate evil of their own will. They do not wantonly destroy life, and do not act out of malice to instill fear or visit destruction upon others. This is the hallmark of humanity, having entered into covenant relationship with Satan. In this regard, as man perpetrates evil, he makes himself *lower than* animals, not even worthy to live among that which is innocent of sin. Therefore, one must be careful not to associate the evil within Nebuchadnezzar's heart with the condition of an animal, as if the heart's evil is somehow a throwback to a primitive state.

> "To insult someone we call him 'bestial.' For deliberate cruelty and nature, 'human' might be the greater insult." (Isaac Asimov)

Sin Bears a Lifetime of Regret

First John 1:9 states, "If we confess our sins, he is faithful and just and will forgive us our sins and purify us from all unrighteousness." While the Christian's sin, individually and collectively, is forgiven by the shed blood of Jesus Christ, it often leaves ugly scars upon the soul which may not fully heal until death. There is often, for the Christian, a struggle with lasting freedom from the regret of grave sin. While the Christian recognizes that his sin is forgiven, and bears no aeonian consequence, there is a lingering pain that one's mind, heart, soul, strength, and body were once used as weapons against God, were once objects under wrath, were once the temple of Satan. David echoed this regret when he penned Psalm 51:3, "For I know my transgressions, and my sin is always before me." Paul, in 1 Timothy 1:15, also described himself as the worst of sinners.

Grievous sin (generally sexual sin) often hangs on the soul like barnacles on a ship's hull, and just as barnacles slow a ships progress, so too, the regret of sin slows the Christian's growth in Christ. Many of those whom I counsel are burdened with the nagging sting of sexual sin. They cannot seem to get out from under its crushing presence. It seems that such sin has written itself in indelible ink on the soul, haranguing the sinner like a pestilence. Sexual sin, like no other, seems to harass the soul with dogged resilience. Understandably, those who have committed sexual sin seem especially eager to confess their sin, as they seek some balm of absolution, some spiritual release.

Imagine folding a pristine piece of paper. If the fold is just a gentle bend, the paper remains uncreased and can resume its flattened shape. But when that fold is firmly pressed down there is a permanent crease. That paper can be opened and flattened, but the evidence of that crease remains, and will always remain. That seems to be the effect of grave sin, even upon forgiven Christians. While forgiveness through Jesus can straighten out the folds of sin, there are certain sins which leave a particularly deep and lasting crease, one which will not be fully removed until heaven.

The Death of Francesca da Rimini and Paolo Malatesta, Alexandre Cabanel, 1870

Sin, of all kinds, has a corrosive effect upon the soul, an effect that recedes as one drinks deeply and richly from Christ's forgiveness. But there is never a complete sense of freedom from that which seems etched into the soul. While in Christ indelible sin has, in fact, been erased, during one's earthly existence there is often lingering vexation.

Razing the Strongholds of Sin

"Search me, O God, and know my heart; test me and know my anxious thoughts. See if there is any offensive way in me, and lead me in the way everlasting." (Psalm 139:23, 24)

A Christian axiom is that God loves sinners but hates sin.[90] Most Christians emphasize the former to the neglect of the latter - quick to point out God's love, mercy, longsuffering, grace, and forgiveness, while neglecting his wrath upon sin, and his unwavering battle to decouple the Christian from it. Never underestimate just how atramentous sin is. It was our sin (your sin and mine) which drove Jesus to the cross. That puts sin in perspective, offering a window into just how unspeakably evil it is in God's sight.

A brother in Christ recently quoted 1 Peter 4:8, "Above all, love each other deeply, because love covers over a multitude of sins." He used this verse as an implicit polemic against the identification and confrontation of sin. However, this verse must be understood in context and in light of the entire corpus of Scripture. Peter wrote his epistles to severely persecuted Christians, offering them a blueprint for dealing with evil. It was against this background that Peter called for Christian unity. Therefore, Peter was intent on emphasizing and promoting a sense of solidarity, Christian standing with Christian in the face of opposition. This verse does not soften God's passionate and burning hatred of sin, nor his desire to eradicate it. Thus, love among Christians does not blindly overlook sin, but merely refuses to allow it to become a source of dissension, unnecessary division, and pharisaical pride.

In fact, to neglect an in-depth understanding of sin is to marginalize, trivialize, and undermine all other aspects of God's work and being. To soft-petal the gravity of sin is to fall into the trap of "easy grace" (a dangerous trend in the modern church). God's love seeks to free the sinner from his sin. God's mercy seeks, to not simply cover over or overlook sin, but to remove its presence as a canker on the human soul. God's longsuffering is neither permissive nor passive, but rather has built within it a mechanism to persistently call the sinner from his sin, to steadily persuade him to abandon his rebellion. The supreme payment Jesus wrought for sin should drive the sinner to increasingly seek to renounce sin, to eschew it as he would death itself. Thus, while justification removes the consequence of sin, God goes further than that; he effects sanctification to remove sin's vile and devastating influence upon lives. If one does not understand how much God hates sin, and longs to free one from it, he will never understand what God is doing in his life.

Each person with each passing day either grows into the image of God or into the image of Satan; there is no other option. Each person either moves forward in sanctification or moves backward into darker depravity; there is no neutral position. If one is not being sanctified through faith in Jesus Christ then he is progressively becoming more worldly, more comfortable with the evil within himself and others.

The point is that while God has already removed sin's power in the Christian, he is

---

[90] Augustine of Hippo (354-430)

equally passionate about removing sin's presence. God works with precision in believers' hearts to target and extricate that which keeps them from intimate relationship with himself. To this end, he pursues holiness within his people with unrelenting persistence. God does not rest until the sin within his people has been expunged, so that they fully enjoy the freedom Jesus earned for them.

- 5 -

METAPHORS FOR SIN

Introduction[1]

The Bible describes sin using vivid metaphor, in some instances graphic and repulsive. The biblical counselor ought to master the Bible's descriptions so as to rightly assess and label evidence of the heart's intentions. The counselor must eschew those metaphors, generally derived from psychology, which impinge upon a sound understanding of the psyche. (For example, the Bible does not describe sin as a mental illness.) As the biblical counselor describes sin he is careful to draw his explanations back to the Bible's own calibrated, and often unflattering, language. This guards against falling into specious descriptors which often serve as traps trivializing and mischaracterizing sin.

A catalogue of biblically-derived metaphors for sin:

Metaphor for Sin	Answer in Christ
1. Misdirected worship	Redirected worship
2. Inverting creation and Creator	The Creator-creature distinction restored
3. Slavery to evil	Slavery to righteousness
4. Addiction to self-worship	God-worship
5. Prostitution to false gods	Marriage to Christ
6. Lust of the flesh	Life in the Spirit
7. Rebellion and hatred of God	Submission to God
8. Demand and war toward God	Supplication and peace with God
9. Seeking gift over Giver	Seeking Giver over gift
10. A state of exile	Reconciliation, arriving home
11. Building one's own kingdom	Participating in the kingdom of God
12. Defacing the temple	Restoring the temple
13. Making God "small"	Making God "big"
14. Seeking covering	The righteous robe of Christ
15. False authority	Under God's authority
16. False rest	Lasting peace
17. Inverted sense of reality	A corrected sense of reality
18. Foolishness	Wisdom
19. Friendship with the world	Friendship with God

---

[1] This chapter could be studied in conjunction with "The Bible's Metaphors for Sanctification" in the first book in this series, *Ask for the Ancient Paths: From Art to Artifice to Arisen,* chapter 10: "The Third-Way of Sanctification: From Abominable to Indomitable"

170 WHAT AGREEMENT IS THERE BETWEEN THE TEMPLE OF GOD AND IDOLS?

20. Pollution	Purity
21. A man-centered set of lenses	Corrective lenses
22. Being a people of the eye	People of the ear

> "Sin has many tools, but a lie is a handle that fits them all." (Oliver Wendell Holmes)

1. Sin as misdirected worship

Matthew 5:27, 28 states, "You have heard that it was said, 'Do not commit adultery.' But I tell you that anyone who looks at a woman lustfully has already committed adultery with her in his heart." Jesus transferred the discussion of sin from the realm of action to the realm of the worshipping core. He called the Christian to focus on the root of sin and not on the trunk (thoughts) or branches (words, actions). Jesus targeted the heart for reform that not just thoughts, words, or actions would be changed, but the entire person.

The Idolatry of Solomon, Frans Francken II, 1622

Matthew 15:19 states, "For out of the heart come evil thoughts, murder, adultery, sexual immorality, theft, false testimony, slander." Mankind entertains evil thoughts because he harbors and nurtures an evil heart. Man's problem is not just erroneous thinking; his thinking is more driven, directed, and focused than that. The heart was designed to worship and, in fact, must worship. It either worships the true God or a false god. Thus, sin is a with-regard-to-God condition, meaning it is actively directed against God's very person. There is no one, and nothing, that is neutral. Fallen man is not simply guilty of not knowing the right answer. All error with regard to the central truth of the gospel is a deliberate attempt to usurp God's authority and make oneself god.

Therefore, sin attempts to functionally make oneself into a god, to define life on one's own terms and for one's own purposes. Sin seeks the status, command, and control of God himself. Moral or character failings are not mere pathologies or syndromes; they are attacks against a person, the person of God himself.

> "Make sure there is no man or woman, clan or tribe among you today whose heart turns away from the LORD our God to go and worship the gods of those nations…" (Deuteronomy 29:18)

One tends to wrongly think of sin in terms of a momentary lapse of judgment in the midst of general wisdom - discrete units of error, an iteration of failure, an aberration, or a burn-mark against a neutral backdrop. This misses the worshipping quality of sin. Sin is not an occasional lapse in an otherwise disinterested setting. Sin is worship specifically directed against a person, perpetrated in defiance of a holy God. In this way, sin is active; it is pursued with a passion to oppose, circumvent, and outwit the God of the universe.

The sinner's deepest problems are not simply cognitive, behavioral, or the need for greater self-actualization. The sinner's deepest problem is dysfunctional worship. Thus, the Bible deals with the heart, the worshipping core, issues of belief, the object of faith, where one places his trust, and what one lives for. This is the environment in which each person lives. Each person worships, puts faith in something, and in this way is irrevocably religious. In fact, each person is no more or less religious than anyone else, since each equally places his faith in some god.

> **In Jesus**: True worship of the living God is restored.
>
> "God is spirit, and his worshipers must worship in the Spirit and in truth." (John 4:24)

2. Sin as inverting or blurring the Creator-creation distinction

The first year of the Chinese calendar is 2637 BC.[2] Legend holds that in that year an

---

[2] In the Chinese calendar a discrepancy of sixty years exists because of the disparity between the lunar and solar calendars.

evil monster, the *Nian* (年), was destroyed and peace reigned throughout the land. The story goes that Lord Buddha sent twelve animals (the mouse, ox, tiger, rabbit, dragon, snake, horse, sheep, monkey, chicken, dog, and pig) to earth to defend humans against twelve devils associated with the *Nian*. As these animals were martyred in their heroic work each is honored once every twelve years.

The point is that fallen mankind worships the creation over the Creator, ascribing to the creation the role of creator, sustainer, and ultimately savior. On account of the fact that fallen man refuses to view himself as an analog of God,[3] he routinely blurs the Creator-creature distinction. In this way, sin inverts the Creator and his creation, making the creation or creature into the Creator, and the Creator into the creation. Sin worships the creation, to the exclusion of worshipping God himself. In sin, the creation (such as twelve animals) becomes man's god.

> "A great number of mankind's miseries are brought about by falsely estimating the value of things." (Benjamin Franklin)

The first Earth Day was held April 22, 1970, marking the beginning of the worldwide environmental movement. While Earth Day brings needed attention to the scourge of wanton disregard for the Earth, it serves as a symbol for a broader religious movement, making the Earth into a god. Is the Earth rightly described in divine terms or in derivative terms?

It is curious that people speak about atrocities committed against the Earth or against Mother Earth. Society often deifies the Earth so that it becomes an object of worship in itself. Yet, why is society offended when one speaks of a Creator God who carefully designed the Earth to reveal his glory? Is this any less reasonable than ascribing personhood to the Earth itself?

Mankind seeks to deify the Earth because it seeks to reverse the role of creation and Creator, making the creation into a kind of god and reducing the true God to a man-made entity. In reality the Earth is a derivation pointing to the true God, an aspect of the creation intended to reveal God to mankind so that man would worship God.

Fallen mankind hates God, hates his creative ability, and hates his authority over his creation. Man wants to attribute to the creation the quality of personhood, while denying that a supreme person (God) actually created and has sovereignty over that creation. Thus, the concept "Mother Nature" is very deliberately a *female* abstraction so that any offense against nature is seen as tantamount to brutalizing a vulnerable woman, and not just any woman, one's own mother. Nature is personal because it

---

[3] Cornelius Van Til, *Christian Apologetics* (Presbyterian and Reformed Press, 2003) 16.

reflects and communicates a personal God. However, in his rebellion mankind ascribes to nature that which God intended to ascribe to himself, namely creative acts.

> "May the rolling hills caress you.
> May her lakes and rivers bless you.
> May the luck of the Earth enfold you.
> May her many blessings behold you." (adaptation of traditional Irish poem)

Consider *The Legend of King Arthur* in which Arthur was trained by the magician Merlin. In order to teach Arthur wisdom, Merlin transformed him into various animals. Arthur became a fish to learn authority, a hawk to see the world without borders, an ant to develop loyalty, a goose to treasure peace, and a badger to learn to love his home. The idea is that, through the animal kingdom, Arthur became not just a man, but the zenith of humanity, a benevolent king. Merlin's objective was that civilization and genuine humanity would be attained through lessons learned from animals.[4] While it is true that each animal (indeed, each element of the creation) reveals something of God's wonder and character, mankind was not designed to gain wisdom through the created order. Such a notion is a direct affront to the Creator God, the deification of the creation as a deliberate slight to God himself. (There is only one way to attain

The Christian Heroes Tapestry
(King Arthur as one of the Nine Worthies)
c. 1385

genuine humanity, and that is through direct and intimate relationship with God himself, attained through the vicarious atonement of Jesus upon the cross.)

> "...darkened in their understanding because of the ignorance that is in them, because of the hardness of their heart." (Ephesians 4:18)

---

[4] A good source for the Arthur legend is T. H. White, *The Once and Future King* (United Kingdom: Collins Publishing, 1958)

God is a *person* who created a personal universe reflecting his personal qualities. A central thrust of sin is to depersonalize the creation, to depersonalize God himself, and to depersonalize mankind. Every time the world institutes a blind and impersonal principle it advances the cause of depersonalizing humanity. Every time a Christian holds to blind ritual without recognizing the heart of sin he depersonalizes the Christian life. When a Christian quotes Scripture to prove a self-serving argument, he has depersonalized Scripture, reducing it to an internally discordant amalgam of sayings, separated from their integration point in God himself. The point is that mankind seeks to "absolutize" the creation to make it ultimate, autonomous, and authoritative.[5] Mankind continually makes God into either a distant and impersonal being or into a pixilated abstraction so that God is reduced to one of his qualities such as "love" or "wisdom."

> "I urge you, brothers and sisters, to watch out for those who cause divisions and put obstacles in your way that are contrary to the teaching you have learned. Keep away from them. For such people are not serving our Lord Christ, but their own appetites. By smooth talk and flattery they deceive the minds of naive people." (Romans 16:17, 18)

> **In Jesus**: The Creator-creature distinction is rightly realigned so that mankind worships the Creator in all things.

3. Sin as slavery to evil.

Evil is embodied in a person, Satan, and evil is perpetrated by complicit allies of Satan, fallen human beings. This is the nature of human slavery to sin; it is a compulsion to serve Satan and the world, in defiance of God. Even for those in Christ, redemption has not eradicated sin from their lives. The Christian thus makes a choice to either return as a slave to sin or to live in the freedom Jesus bought for him.

> "Jesus replied, 'I tell you the truth, everyone who sins is a slave to sin.'" (John 8:34)
>
> "Those who live according to the flesh have their minds set on what the flesh desires; but those who live in accordance with the Spirit have their minds set on what the Spirit desires. The mind governed by the flesh is death, but the mind governed by the Spirit is life and peace. The mind governed by the flesh is hostile to God; it does not submit to God's law, nor can it do so. Those who are in the realm of the flesh cannot please God." (Romans 8:5-8)

---

[5] This seeking to absolutize the creation is seen in a pervasive advertising campaign which puts the word "absolute" on just about every product and place. For example, I recently traveled to Budapest, Hungary where one might find an advertising campaign, "Absolute Budapest." I wonder if this use of the word "absolute" is an attempt to gain some bedrock experience in a world of continually shifting images and messages, like an attempt to gain some sense of permanence.

> "The Spirit you received does not make you slaves, so that you live in fear again; rather, the Spirit you received brought about your adoption to sonship. And by him we cry, '*Abba,* Father.'" (Romans 8:15)

The Slave Market, Gustave Clarence Rodolphe Boulanger, 1888

> **In Jesus:** Those held captive to sin have been set free to become "slaves to righteousness."
>
> "So if the Son sets you free, you will be free indeed." (John 8:36)
>
> "You have been set free from sin and have become slaves to righteousness." (Romans 6:18)
>
> "When he ascended on high, he took many captives and gave gifts to his people." (Ephesians 4:8)

4. Sin as addiction to self-worship[6]

The former Soviet Union showed a movie, "The Grapes of Wrath" (1940), about the American Dust Bowl in order to highlight the perils of capitalism. The audience only noticed that even America's indigent owned cars – something they did not have. This highlights the nature of addiction, a desperate and compulsive grabbing for life

---
[6] This concept from Edward Welch, Westminster Theological Seminary, Philadelphia, Pennsylvania

outside of God. Within man's heart there is an incessant feeling of "just one more," so that each person, in his sin nature, is like a raging fire of desire.[7] Fallen mankind continually grabs for that which he thinks will give him power, meaning, and blessing outside of God's provision. He is, in fact, addicted to gaining that which he feels will give him victory in his war against God. There is an insatiable quality to worshipping the creation.

> "I know that nothing good lives in me, that is in my sinful nature." (Romans 7:18)

In Numbers 11:34, the Lord sent quail to bury the Israelites since they craved meat more than obedience to God. That place was thus called Kibroth Hattavah meaning "graves of craving" since the people craved food other than that which God had graciously provided. The more one seeks to be filled by anything outside of God the more he finds himself empty. The sinful heart always craves more; yet the more one consumes the less he is satisfied. The heart is easily deceived into believing that just a little more of what it seeks and it will be filled.[8]

Psychology is the heart's cunning co-conspirator as it tacitly encourages mankind's addiction to sin by supplying him with a numbing narcotic for the psyche. Psychology helps one search for ways to get more – more love, more happiness, or more self-confidence. The truth is that this quest leaves one in the opposite state, more forlorn, more longing, more insecure.[9]

> "Having lost all sensitivity, they have given themselves over to sensuality so as to indulge in every kind of impurity with a continual lust for more." (Ephesians 4:19)

> **In Jesus:** There is freedom from addiction to self-worship so that one can worship God alone.

5. Sin as prostitution to false gods

Throughout its history Israel succumb to the worship of the goddess Asherah.[10] The Israelites learned this practice from the Canaanites who raised Asherah poles on high places. Asherah was often referred to as the moon goddess and consort of Baal, the sun god.[11] Asherah worship was attended by sensual dancing, prostitution, fortune-telling, and divination. (In addition to Asherah, two other ancient near eastern gods, Baal[12] and Bel (Marduk),[13] were closely linked to prostitution, the chief ritual

---

[7] This concept from Edward Welch, Westminster Theological Seminary, Philadelphia, Pennsylvania
[8] This concept from Edward Welch, Westminster Theological Seminary, Philadelphia, Pennsylvania
[9] For a comprehensive discussion of psychology see the first book in this series, *Ask for the Ancient Paths: From Art to Artifice to Arisen*, chapter 8: "What Has Jerusalem To Do With Vienna?: The Case Against Psychology"
[10] Judges 2:13; 1 Kings 18:19; 2 Kings 21:7
[11] Judges 3:7, 6:28, 10:6; 1 Samuel 7:4, 12:10
[12] 1 Kings 16:31

in worship of these gods.)

> If a man divorces his wife and she leaves him and marries another man, should he return to her again? Would not the land be completely defiled? But you have lived as a prostitute with many lovers – would you now return to me? Look up to the barren heights and see. Is there any place where you have not been ravished? By the roadside you sat waiting for lovers, sat like a nomad in the desert. You have defiled the land with your prostitution and wickedness. Therefore the showers have been withheld, and no spring rains have fallen. Yet you have the brazen look of a prostitute; you refuse to blush with shame. Have you not just called me: 'My Father, my friend from my youth, will you always be angry? Will your wrath continue forever?' This is how you talk, but you do all the evil you can. (Jeremiah 3:1-5)

> "The acts of the sinful nature are obvious: sexual immorality, impurity and debauchery, idolatry and witchcraft, hatred, discord, jealousy, fits of rage, selfish ambition, dissensions, factions…" (Galatians 5:19)
>
> "You adulterous people, don't you know that friendship with the world means enmity against God? Therefore, anyone who chooses to be a friend of the world becomes an enemy of God." (James 4:4)

Exodus 34:15, 16 states,

> Be careful not to make a treaty with those who live in the land; for when they prostitute themselves to their gods and sacrifice to them, they will invite you and you will eat their sacrifices. And when you choose some of their daughters as wives for your sons and those daughters prostitute themselves to their gods, they will lead your sons to do the same.

God repeatedly warned that foreign (unbelieving) women would lead Israel astray with sexual temptation. The reason is that these foreign women prostituted themselves to false gods and seduced men to do the same.

> "Things forbidden have a secret charm." (Greek proverb)

Throughout Scripture the concept of adultery occupies the same semantic range as the concept of idolatry so that the terms are used interchangeably. Idolatry is tantamount to spiritual adultery (covenant breaking) and prostitution (selling oneself to false lovers). Thus, the concept of idolatry is couched in the language of sexual transgression. It is noteworthy that the theme of sin as adultery to false gods finds a

---

[13] Isaiah 46:1; Jeremiah 50:2

178   WHAT AGREEMENT IS THERE BETWEEN THE TEMPLE OF GOD AND IDOLS?

certain cadence point in David's adultery with Bathsheba,[14] in that this illegitimate union initiated a steady descent for both David and the nation as a whole. David's sin adumbrates his own destruction and the nation's eventual downfall. Thus, later in the books of Ezekiel and Hosea, Israel is described as a faithless bride.

> **In Jesus:** The Christian is Christ's pure virgin bride, holy and blameless in his sight, without stain or wrinkle.[15]
>
> "Let us rejoice and be glad and give him glory! For the wedding of the Lamb has come, and his bride has made herself ready." (Revelation 19:7)

Case Study: Is There a Fundamental Gender Asymmetry with Regard to Sexuality?[16]

Society generally upholds the fallacy that men are more libidinous than women, that men are more inclined to promiscuity while women merely desire love. The myth is that men are far more willing to engage in illicit sex, and far less stigmatized or ostracized by licentiousness. The old adage goes that men use love to get sex and women use sex to get love.

The Babylonian Marriage Market, Edwin Long, 1875

These assumptions are driven by psychology and a feminism which seeks to denigrate

---

[14] 2 Samuel 11:4
[15] Ephesians 5:27
[16] For a more comprehensive discussion of the issue of gender see the first book in this series, *Ask for the Ancient Paths: From Art to Artifice to Arisen*, chapter 5: "Redefining the Pygmalion Effect: Exploring the Image of God in Man." Also see the case study, "Is Sexuality an Inherent Need as Part of Human Design?" in the first book in this series, chapter 7: "The Needs Imperative."

men as somehow more primitive, boorish, and ultimately contemptible. The objective is to vilify men while elevating women to a more noble status, that somehow women are more pure, more nurturing, and more virtuous in their design. When women do exhibit perverse behavior, the excuse offered is that they are subjugated victims to a male-dominated society that drives them to concupiscence. Sadly, these stereotypes are perpetuated by a Hollywood-driven media which seeks to undermine the truth.

The Bible does not present a fundamental gender asymmetry with regard to the perpetration of sexual sin. Therefore, this supposed asymmetry with regard to concupiscence and promiscuity is Satan's device to divert attention from the desperate depravity inherent in all of mankind, both men and women. Men and women are equally prone to lust, equally willing to display promiscuous behavior, equally pursue their own pleasure at others' expense, and equally adulterous when it suits their self-aggrandizing purposes.

The incidence of promiscuity and adultery is not gender-based. Men are not more libidinous than women, not more predisposed to eroticism, not more likely to seek polygamous liaisons, not more given to sexual addiction or obsession. Men and women are equally depraved, equally likely to pervert God's good gifts for self-seeking purposes. Remember the second curse pronounced upon Eve after the fall, "'Your desire will be for your husband, and he will rule over you.'"[17] This desire often makes women sexual aggressors, those consumed with lust.

Consider the following Biblical evidence:

> 1. "When the woman saw that the fruit of the tree was good for food and pleasing to the eye, and also desirable for gaining wisdom, she took some and ate it. She also gave some to her husband, who was with her, and he ate it." (Genesis 3:6)

> 2. Tamar deceived Judah into thinking she was a roadside prostitute and seduced him into adultery.[18]

> 3. "…and after a while his master's wife took notice of Joseph and said, 'Come to bed with me!' And though she spoke to Joseph day after day, he refused to go to bed with her or even be with her." (Genesis 39:7, 10)

> 4. "While Israel was staying in Shittim, the men began to indulge in sexual immorality with Moabite women, who invited them to the sacrifices to their gods. The people ate the sacrificial meal and bowed down before these gods." (Numbers 25:1, 2)

---

[17] Genesis 3:16
[18] Genesis 38:15

5. While David committed adultery with Bathsheba, Bathsheba likewise committed adultery against her husband.[19]

6. "This is the way of an adulteress: She eats and wipes her mouth and says, 'I've done nothing wrong.'" (Proverbs 30:20)

7. "I find more bitter than death the woman who is a snare, whose heart is a trap and whose hands are chains. The man who pleases God will escape her, but the sinner she will ensnare." (Ecclesiastes 7:26)

8. The Samaritan woman at the well had five husbands and was living with a sixth man. In another account, Jesus intervened when a woman was caught in adultery.[20]

9. "Now to the unmarried and the widows I say: It is good for them to stay unmarried, as I am. But if they cannot control themselves, they should marry, for it is better to marry than to *burn with passion*." (1 Corinthians 7:8, 9, emphasis added)

10. The harlot of Babylon seduces the inhabitants of the earth.[21]

6. Sin as lust of the flesh

John Calvin (1509–1564) wrote that one aspect of sin is wanting inordinately. This means that one's problem is less with what one wants and more with the fact that one wants it too much. Mankind has a tendency to let desire overrun and outrun trust in God for provision. In other words, is it necessarily wrong to want the good things of life? No, this is not wrong in and of itself, but the problem is that one wants them so much that he covets, envies, and hates those that have what he wants. Fallen man easily lets desire overrun the heart and mind, so that the object of his desire becomes his all-consuming god. In this way, the biblical concept of lust of the flesh does not just refer to sexual lust; it is any inordinate desire.

> **In Jesus:** Life in the Spirit brings discipline and self-control so that the Christian can faithfully obey God with his body and remain faithful within marriage.
>
> "...in order that the righteous requirement of the law might be fully met in us, who do not live according to the flesh but according to the Spirit." (Romans 8:4)

---

[19] 2 Samuel 11:4
[20] John 4:18; 8:4
[21] Revelation 17:2

Case Study: Sexuality Forbidden in Leviticus 18

God admonished Israel not to follow the practices of Egypt and Canaan. (18:3)[22]

Sexuality forbidden:

1. Not with a close relative (directed toward both men and women) (18:6)
2. Not with one's mother (18:7)
3. Not with one's father's wife (18:8; 20:11)
4. Not with a sister (18:9)
5. Not with a granddaughter (18:10)
6. Not with a sister (18:11; 20:17)
7. Not with an aunt (18:12, 13, 14; 20:19, 20)
8. Not with a daughter-in-law (18:15; 20:12)
9. Not with a sister-in-law (18:16; 20:21)
10. Not with a woman and her daughter (18:17; 20:14)
11. Not with a woman and her granddaughter (18:17)
12. Do not take one's wife's sister as a rival wife (18:18)
13. Not during a woman's uncleanness (18:19; 20:18)
14. Not with one's neighbor's wife (18:20)
15. *Do not sacrifice one's children to Molech* (18:21)
16. Not between men (18:22; 20:13)
17. Not with an animal (directed toward men and women) (18:23; 20:15, 16)
18. Adultery forbidden (20:10)

The Flight of Moloch
William Blake, 1809

---

[22] Nearly all the prohibitions are only directed toward men except the first two and the last two, which are directed toward men and women alike.

Why is the admonition not to sacrifice children to Molech included in this section on sexual standards?[23] The Israelites often followed the practices of the surrounding nations, sacrificing their children to the sun god, Molech. In each family one child was sacrificed in the hope of bringing prosperity to his siblings. Sometimes this child was burned alive, and at other times made to serve Molech by jumping through fire or by passing between areas of fire.

Yahweh commanded the Israelites to sacrifice animals (goats, doves, bulls, rams, lambs, and the like); yet some Israelites insisted on sacrificing their children to false gods. God described this practice as "prostituting" themselves to Molech.[24] (This shows the inordinately greater fear and attraction associated with idolatry. The people sacrificed their livestock in appeasement to the Lord but their children to loathsome idols.[25])

Again in Leviticus 20:2-5, God warned that Israelites (and aliens) who sacrificed their children to Molech would be put to death. In 20:4 God further warned that if the community closed its eyes when a man dedicated one of his children to Molech, and failed to put that man to death, God would cut that community off from the nation. The admonition to end this abomination was a community affair as everyone was held responsible, and failure to act desecrated God's sanctuary and name.

Is this admonition against sacrificing children included among unlawful sexual relations because the result of illicit sexuality is children who are hated or neglected, and treated only as a sacrifice to appease false gods? Is it because illicit sexuality results in heinous idolatry which destroys one's children?

It seems that heinous sexual sin results in the neglect and abuse of one's children. While this was true more than 3,000 years ago, it is equally true today. As society falls into greater sexual depravity it figuratively sacrifices its children to Molech, giving them over to false gods to be denigrated. Could this issue of sacrificing children be applied to giving children over to secular progressivism which destroys their hearts and minds? Could it also be linked to abortion or possibly to "prostituting" children with sexualized behavior and attire?

> Leviticus 18:18 commands that a man not marry his wife's sister as a rival wife. In Genesis 29:16-30 Jacob married Leah and then her younger sister Rachel. Assuming that God's decrees in Leviticus are eternal, did Jacob sin in marrying two sisters? Would Leviticus 18:18 seem to imply that Jacob married Rachel out of lust? Should he have been content with Leah alone? However, if one considers God's

---

[23] Leviticus 18:21
[24] Leviticus 20:5
[25] Matthew Henry Commentary, Bible Study Tools, 2012

> decrees to apply only at the time he issues them, can Jacob be exonerated from the dictates of Leviticus 18:18, since he predated the Mosaic law?

7. Sin as rebellion and hatred directed toward God

There are two fundamental lies. The first is human autonomy, the idea that each person is an independent creature. The second is self-sufficiency, the idea that each possesses within himself all he needs to achieve godlikeness. These two lies are summarized as, if each can only become the best he can be, then he will be what he is supposed to be.[26]

These lies drive hatred of God, who is assumed to stand in the way of human autonomy and self-sufficiency. Thus, sinners believe that God is the enemy of each becoming his best, that God deliberately subverts the greatness for which man was destined. (Of course, God's intervention at the Tower of Babel would seem to bear this out.[27]) Fallen mankind hates God's sovereignty out of envy and desires to usurp his throne. This hatred is directed not just against God's creative design, but against the person of God himself. However, "hatred is self-punishment" since mankind only furthers his searing loss and pain as he peddles and pursues his lies.

> "The mind set on the flesh is death...hostile toward God." (Romans 8:6)
>
> "Once you were alienated from God and were enemies in your minds because of your evil behavior." (Colossians 1:21)
>
> "Anyone who hates his brother is a murderer, and you know that no murderer has eternal life in him." (1 John 3:15)

Rebellion against God is best described as "covenantal treason."[28] This treason exists within each person the moment he is conceived. Thus, rebellion exists even in the child's heart and colors the way he interacts with his world. God invests something of his authority within parents, so that a child submits to authority as the groundwork for eventually reversing the covenantal treason (by means of a conscious decision to place saving faith in Christ).

> Isaiah 40:3 reads, "A voice of one calling: 'In the wilderness prepare the way for the LORD; make straight in the desert a highway for our God.'" The biblical concept of the highway connotes a means to facilitate communion with God, the idea of ushering God forward to effect salvation. It is fascinating to note the way in which

---

[26] This concept from Paul Tripp, Westminster Theological Seminary, Philadelphia, Pennsylvania
[27] Genesis 11:6-8
[28] Michael Bobick, *From Slavery to Sonship: A Biblical Psychology for Pastoral Counseling* (1995) 34. (class notes)

> the highway metaphor was co-opted in the American psyche so that it took on a spirit of rebellion, an escape from civilization, and a defiance of convention. The American psyche associates the highway with a measure of derelict freedom, an association that began in the 1960s with the completion of the interstate highway system (the largest construction project in the history of the world).[29]

> **In Jesus**: The covenantal treason finds acquittal so that the Christian enjoys covenantal relationship with God.
>
> "Submit yourselves, then, to God. Resist the devil, and he will flee from you." (James 4:7)

8. Sin as demand and war against God.

Manhattan Island is a solid block of granite, which has enabled buildings to rise higher than in most cities. In the early 20th century New York experienced a "building war," as each new building project vied to become the tallest in the world.[30] In 1889 the tallest was eighteen stories. In 1903, twenty-three stories; in 1908, forty-six stories; and in 1913 the tallest building was the sixty-story Woolworth building.

In one memorable competition of 1929, the building at 40 Wall Street and the Chrysler Building, simultaneously under construction, vied to outdo one another. Finally, the 40 Wall Street building appeared to be one story taller than the Chrysler Building. Then on October 23, 1929, under the cover of night, workers at the Chrysler Building raised a needle, secretly assembled in its center, and at dawn it was the world's tallest. This historical chapter on building wars captures a facet of mankind's sinful heart, a heart at war with God, at war with his creation, at war with one another, and at war within man himself. The warfare within the heart shows up in every interaction, pursuit, and desire. For example, there is an expression, "A man conquers the world to conquer a woman; a woman conquers a man to conquer the world."[31]

> Men have always been at war, even during times of supposed peace. During the Renaissance men waged war through art, in the Colonial period they tussled for land, during the Industrial Revolution they vied for labor, during the burgeoning of rapid transportation they schemed for land rights, and today they battle in cyberspace. The means and location of war has frequently changed, but the human heart is still the same. Each is at war with others because each is at war with God.

---

[29] The dissolution associated with the highway is possibly an extension of the "hell on wheels" dysphemism for railroads as they stretched across the continent in the late 19th century.
[30] It is fascinating to note that this concept of building wars was not isolated to New York. Even Hong Kong experiences *feng shui* (风水) building wars in which building designers try to deflect inauspicious *feng shui* toward competitors' buildings.
[31] This quote from Mark Hua

Each has been sinned against, and each has in turn developed sin patterns to deal with a precarious world. For this reason, sin has nestled within it a demanding quality, an active consumer mentality, an entrenched self-protective and self-directed demand with a continual desire for more. At every point, in every way, fallen mankind demands more (love from others, acceptance, control over his world, power, possessions, knowledge, etc.). The sinner demands that he himself be glorified at the expense of God's glory. This results in anger, "playing God," putting oneself in the position of God to be the bearer of judgment, condemnation, and wrath.[32]

Jupiter and Mercury Beside Philomen and Bacchus, Johann Karl Loth, 1659

All of God's dealings with Israel after the Exodus were as a suzerain to subjects. God even established a law covenant with his people so as to impress upon them that he himself was their only sovereign. However, Deuteronomy 17:14 is a prophecy that Israel would one day demand a king. (The prophecy was fulfilled in 1 Samuel 8:1-5.) Israel's demand for a king was an implicit denial of God himself as king, repudiation that God had successfully delivered Israel from the tyrannical Pharaoh. Nevertheless, God gave Israel over to its demand so that the nation might be humbled and seek repentance.

"Inferiors revolt in order that they may be equal, and equals that they may be

---

[32] For a comprehensive discussion of the topic of judgment see "The Question of Judgment" in the first book in this series, *Ask for the Ancient Paths: From Art to Artifice to Arisen*, chapter 2: "The Counseling Ambition"

> superior." (Aristotle)

The parable of the worthless servant captures the nature of this war with, and demand of, God.

> Therefore, the kingdom of heaven is like a king who wanted to settle accounts with his servants. As he began the settlement, a man who owed him ten thousand bags of gold was brought to him. Since he was not able to pay, the master ordered that he and his wife and his children and all that he had be sold to repay the debt.
>
> At this the servant fell on his knees before him. 'Be patient with me,' he begged, 'and I will pay back everything.' The servant's master took pity on him, canceled the debt and let him go.
>
> But when that servant went out, he found one of his fellow servants who owed him a hundred silver coins. He grabbed him and began to choke him. 'Pay back what you owe me!' he demanded.
>
> His fellow servant fell to his knees and begged him, 'Be patient with me, and I will pay it back.'
>
> But he refused. Instead, he went off and had the man thrown into prison until he could pay the debt. When the other servants saw what had happened, they were outraged and went and told their master everything that had happened.
>
> Then the master called the servant in. 'You wicked servant,' he said, 'I canceled all that debt of yours because you begged me to. Shouldn't you have had mercy on your fellow servant just as I had on you?' In anger his master handed him over to the jailers to be tortured, until he should pay back all he owed.
>
> 'This is how my heavenly Father will treat each of you unless you forgive your brother or sister from your heart.' (Matthew 18:23-35)

> **In Jesus:** There is supplication to, and peace with, God.
>
> "And the peace of God, which transcends all understanding, will guard your hearts and your minds in Christ Jesus." (Philippians 4:7)

9. Sin as seeking the gift over the Giver

The gravedigger thesis is the idea that Christianity historically set the stage for the development of modern science, democracy, and capitalism.[33] However, the very social institutions Christianity birthed later ushered in its destruction. This points to mankind's general posture toward God, the very gifts which God invests into man, man then uses to attack God. If one focuses on the gift over the Giver then life will tend to be characterized by seeking, getting, and holding. This means that when the gift is prioritized, the Giver becomes merely a cosmic abstraction as mankind focuses on the tangible over the unseen. Seeking the gifts over the Giver always results in anxiety as one becomes greedy for treasure that he can "bank."[34]

In Exodus 16:20, 27, some of the Israelites stored their manna until morning even after Moses had commanded them not to. Additionally, Moses commanded the Israelites not to gather manna on the Sabbath, which they disobeyed. This offers a window into sin, a desire for the gift over the Giver, a focus on the gift to the neglect of the Giver.

First Corinthians 1:22 admonishes, "Jews demand signs and Greeks look for wisdom…" In this regard, John 12:9, 10 states, "Meanwhile a large crowd of Jews found out that Jesus was there and came, not only because of him but also to see Lazarus, whom he had raised from the dead. So the chief priests made plans to kill Lazarus as well…" The Jews wanted to see the *evidence* of Jesus' miracle (Lazarus raised from the dead), but Jesus, himself, was an afterthought. They sought the thrill of the miracle without paying adequate attention to the miracle worker. The fact that the chief priests made plans to murder Lazarus, in addition to Jesus, indicates that Lazarus' resurrection had become a kind of circus sideshow among the crowds, a distraction to the religious establishment's control efforts. However, the evidence of Lazarus' resurrection never should have competed with the imperative to seek and worship Jesus alone.

> "He has given us himself and his all-sufficiency for our everlasting portion; what more can we desire? He will never drive us from his house. Never has our great Father disowned one of his sons."[35]

One's life will only be free to the extent of what he lives for, and focuses his attention upon. As one focuses on the Giver alone, his life is empowered to be one of freely giving. One is enabled to give himself away because he knows the Giver personally, and so recognizes that the Giver cannot be out-given. But when one merely focuses on the gift, then one's life becomes limited to the extent of the gift - isolated, bounded, self-protective, because one's vista is the limits of a finite entity. If one has the Giver,

---

[33] Os Guinness, *The Gravedigger File: Papers on the Subversion of the Modern Church*. (Downer's Grove: Intervarsity Press, 1983)
[34] David Powlison, Westminster Theological Seminary, Philadelphia, Pennsylvania
[35] Charles. H. Spurgeon (1834–1892) sermon No. 1816 (January 1, 1885)

however, he has been invested with the infinite and his horizon becomes vast and other-centered. In summary, focus on the gift results in a grabbing heart; focus on the Giver results in a giving heart as one comes to the realization that the gift only exists that one would discover the Giver himself as the true gift.

> **In Jesus:** The Christian seeks the Giver over the gift and, in so doing, discovers that the Giver was the gift all along.

10. Sin as a state of exile

After the fall, Adam and Eve were cast into exile from the garden.[36] This exile from the land pointed to a far greater exile from fellowship with God himself. In man's sin he lives in exile from the source of his sustenance, a castaway to right relationship with God. Man lives as a restless wander in a desert of his own making, searching for the touchstone of his existence.[37] First Timothy 6:10b captures this sense of exile. "Some people, eager for money, have wandered from the faith and pierced themselves with many griefs."

> "A man can stand almost anything except a succession of ordinary days." (Johann Goethe)

> **In Jesus:** The Christian is welcomed home, returns to the "land," to be reconciled with God.
>
> "For if, while we were God's enemies, we were reconciled to him through the death of his Son, how much more, having been reconciled, shall we be saved through his life!" (Romans 5:10)

11. Sin as building one's own kingdom

Why are cities expanding and flourishing throughout the world? People increasingly love cities because they seem to make rebellion against God appear safe and successful. Cities offer the mock-blessing of entertainment and convenience, the mock-power of wealth and prestige, and the mock-meaning of significance and being "somewhere." In reality cities are nothing more than an ingenious system for making rebellion against God, hatred of his morality, and denial of his truth, look advantageous, fruitful, and crowned with triumph.

Consider the amount of effort required to maintain just one automobile, one house, or one street. Multiply that by billions of units and one sees why cities are a bottomless

---

[36] Genesis 3:23
[37] The term "touchstone of one's existence" borrowed from Tobias Iaconis, Screenwriter

pit of need. A city's infrastructure, buildings, airports, roads, bridges, viaducts, telecommunications, electrical grid, water supply and sewage treatment are each tremendous maintenance burdens. This is why the growth of cities and the growth of socialism are intertwined.[38] As behemoths of ever-decaying infrastructure, the city siphons off immense amounts of human effort and, in the process, births a socialistic structure needed for the city's upkeep. City governments have no choice but to seek ever-expanding tax revenue as the millstone of their crumbling kingdoms grows exponentially.

Tower of Babel, Lucas van Valckenborch, 1594

> It is fascinating that Athena was the ancient Greek goddess of wisdom, cities, science, and war. There appears to be some connection between these four elements, mankind's presumed wisdom in his own eyes which results in the growth of cities and science. The city, as a manmade environment, gives rise to a manmade system of thought, science. This often culminates in war, as mankind's efforts at crafting his own thought and environment only feed his hatred of God and the nascent war within his heart.

The more one invests in cities, expands their reach and heightens their presence, the more one is a prisoner to serving them. In developing cities mankind has shackled himself to the nearly infinite upkeep of perishable structures and systems. Man is rendered a slave to depreciating and decaying objects. The burden in building an

---

[38] For further discussion of this topic see the section "City as Incubator of the World" in chapter 2: "The World, the Flesh, and the Devil: Assessing the Threat Matrix"

earthly kingdom (such as that of a city) serves as a fitting metaphor for the burden of building one's kingdom of self-worship.

Mankind, both corporately and individually, thinks of himself as the center of the universe, and functions accordingly. Genesis 11:4 refers to trying to "make a name for oneself," seeking not to be scattered among the nations by building one's own tower, and surrounding city, to reach to the heavens. Mankind is at work building his own personal kingdom which could be summarized as: Since God is not God and God is not good, then one is justified in seeking to draw all of creation into the service of oneself.[39] If God is not God and not good, then one seems justified in making himself into his own god. Thus, sin is a focus on self-promotion, self-indulgence, and personal happiness.

God does not allow worship of the creation to satisfy, and likewise does not allow mankind's kingdom building efforts to stand unopposed. God alone deserves worship so he continually frustrates idols and subverts man's self-glorifying kingdom building. Thus, God's affront to the Tower of Babel was a merciful act,[40] drawing mankind out of citadel construction so that he might worship God. While each may for a time erect his own "Tower of Babel," God does not allow such efforts to stand for a lifetime.

Mankind in his sin constructs a stronghold against God, a way to guard himself from the whim and vicissitude of life, without God and against God. God, however, besieges man's self-protective bulwarks and punctures his fortifications. In time God takes the fortress and topples the tower. However, in a shocking reversal of fortune, God then installs the besieged rebels as glorified and exalted sons in his kingdom. This is the incomparable gift that mankind is offered in Jesus, that once bellicose rebels are now honored sons.

> **In Jesus**: Mankind abandons his kingdom-building efforts to rest in the accomplished work of Jesus upon the cross, a work which inaugurates God's kingdom within the hearts of believers.
>
> "Once, on being asked by the Pharisees when the kingdom of God would come, Jesus replied, 'The coming of the kingdom of God is not something that can be observed, nor will people say, 'Here it is,' or 'There it is,' because the kingdom of God is in your midst.'" (Luke 17:20)

12. Sin as defacing the temple of one's body

One who is dissatisfied with his height is said to suffer from height dysphoria.

---

[39] From theologian Paul Tillich (1886-1965)
[40] Genesis 11:8

Psychologists claim that this is one of the few psychological disorders that cannot be cured by therapy and thus requires surgery. Annually, thousands now elect to receive height-augmenting surgery which involves cutting the femur bones and slowly stretching them as they heal (an intensely painful process).

A young man described feeling depressed about his slight stature. He reasoned that increasing his height would give him what he had lost in life, and so he successfully underwent surgery to extend his legs. After the surgery he gave himself the sobriquet "Apotheosis" (which means "approaching God," or to achieve divine status), because he now has confidence, ambition, and commands more respect.

Mankind desperately seeks to alter the image of God invested within him, wanting to alter his design to suit his desires. He longs to achieve that which he dreams of, to become an "apotheosis" to himself.

The creation in every facet is perfect. Anything taken from it, or added to it, brings dire consequence. Environmental destruction is, by and large, the result of abuse of God's creation, as mankind both hates God's work and seeks to improve upon it. Thus, exploitation of the earth is due to man's attempt to place himself in ultimate authority over creation. Wantonly destroying the environment defaces the evidence of God in his creation so that the knowledge of God can be more effectively suppressed.

For example, in the same way that a vandal defaces a public monument with graffiti, so too, a tattoo vandalizes the intended temple of God on earth.[41] A tattoo desecrates the image of God, defacing that which God intended to show forth his glory. This is part of the larger goal of obliterating the evidence of God in the creation, distracting from, and detracting from, God's self-revelation. If evidence of God can be eviscerated he can be more readily denied.

Animals inherently honor their design, living out what God made them to be. Mankind, however, desecrates his design, looting his high purpose and ransacking his noble heritage. Mankind seeks any means to deny that God exists, so he endeavors to obliterate any sign of God around him. This is true of the corporate polluter, the chain-smoker, or those who wear tattoos. They each deface the creation so that, as rebels, they can live under the delusion that they are their own gods.

> God created a magnificent tree which displays something of His character and glory. That tree "speaks" of a good and loving Creator.[42] Mankind cut the tree down, fashioned it into a cross, and crucified God upon it.[43]

---

[41] Leviticus 19:28; 1 Corinthians 3:16
[42] Isaiah 55:12
[43] This concept borrowed from an unknown source

192 WHAT AGREEMENT IS THERE BETWEEN THE TEMPLE OF GOD AND IDOLS?

In Jesus: The human temple is rebuilt, restored, and glorified to a condition far greater than ever before, so that the Holy Spirit now lives within the hearts of believers.

"Don't you know that you yourselves are God's temple and that God's Spirit dwells in your midst?" (1 Corinthians 3:16)

"Now it is God who makes both us and you stand firm in Christ. He anointed us, set his seal of ownership on us, and put his Spirit in our hearts as a deposit, guaranteeing what is to come." (2 Corinthians 1:21, 22)

13. Sin as making God "small" and people into giants[44]

The Confusion of Tongues, Gustave Dore, 1865

In Genesis 11:31 Abraham's father, Terah, set out from Ur of the Chaldeans to settle in Canaan. However, it is recorded that when Terah came to Haran he settled there. Why is this detail included? Is there a connection between Terah's son Haran and the place Haran, so that Terah settled merely on account of the name? Is it possible that God had directed Terah to settle in Canaan but he would not enter the land because it was inhabited, and presented some danger? This passage may point to a persistent problem Israel faced in taking the Promised Land, the sin of making people into giants and

---

[44] This concept borrowed from Edward Welch, Westminster Theological Seminary, Philadelphia, Pennsylvania

God small and insignificant.

Later, in Genesis 18:10-15, the Lord promised Abraham and Sarah a son. Yet, Sarah laughed as she considered herself too worn out to bear a child. The Lord asked why Sarah laughed. Sarah, afraid, lied in denying that she had laughed. In this way, Sarah made God's promise "small" and her and her husband's advanced age "big." She made her understanding of life superior to God's; that was her sin.

In Numbers 13:27, 28, Joshua's spies returned with a report that there were giants in the land. Their words struck fear in the people, who surmised that they could not trust God to bring them safely into the land. This, like the previous examples, was making people and their will determinative, and God and his will ineffectual.

First Samuel 9:2 recounts that Saul, a head taller than the others, was chosen as Israel's first king. However, Saul proved a negligent and divisive king. He was soon replaced by David, who, while smaller in stature, was more faithful.

There is a curse in making people into giants and God small in one's life. As the sinner places others on a pedestal he soon rips them down to be trampled upon. There is a cycle of exalting, and subsequently hating, those that one worships.[45] For example, Amnon worshipped his sister Tamar, but then loathed her after he had raped her.[46] Likewise, the focus on affirmation from another is never an attention to the other; it is a highly self-directed gaze. There is something utterly self-indulgent in one's fixation on people, and what they are capable of.[47]

> **In Jesus**: God takes his proper place as the only one whom the Christian fears. Likewise, people are rightly viewed as having no final power in regard to one's ultimate destiny.
>
> "What is mankind that you are mindful of him, human beings that you care for them?" (Psalm 8:4)
>
> "Do not be afraid of those who kill the body but cannot kill the soul. Rather, be afraid of the One who can destroy both soul and body in hell." (Matthew 10:28)
>
> "They came to him and said, 'Teacher, we know that you are a man of integrity. You aren't swayed by others, because you pay no attention to who they are; but you teach the way of God in accordance with the truth...'" (Mark 12:14)

Case Study: An Analysis of Abraham

---

[45] This concept from David Powlison, Westminster Theological Seminary, Philadelphia, Pennsylvania
[46] 2 Samuel 13:15
[47] This concept from Edward Welch, Westminster Theological Seminary, Philadelphia, Pennsylvania

Abraham, from the land of Ur of the Chaldeans, was a man of both towering faith and vexing idols. He offers both a vivid display of one who believed God's promises and was credited with righteousness, as well as one under the scourge of a besetting fear of man.[48] The following are some examples of Abraham's faithfulness:

1. Abraham obeyed God's command to leave his Father in Haran and travel to the land of Canaan. Abraham courageously traveled to an inhabited land filled with potentially hostile enemies.[49]

2. When his nephew Lot was abducted, Abraham led a band of 318 men into battle against the kings in the Valley of Siddim. Abraham showed valor and unflinching love for his relative.[50]

3. Abraham, unwilling to accept any gift from the king of Sodom,[51] showed a sense of integrity in his dealings with other men.

4. Abraham pled for the cities of Sodom and Gomorrah in a timeless display of tenacious compassion. Abraham negotiated with God in a humble, yet direct, manner to secure the safe deliverance of his nephew, Lot, and Lot's family.[52]

5. Abraham must have experienced searing existential angst at being commanded by God to sacrifice his promised heir, Isaac. However, Abraham stalwartly obeyed, resolutely trusting that God would be faithful to his promise.[53]

Despite these displays of faith, Abraham was an enigma, beset by a fatal flaw, that flaw being his willingness to be manipulated by his wife, and his moral weakness with regard to her beauty. On two occasions Abraham was willing to lie on account of his fear surrounding Sarah's beauty. He surmised that Sarah's beauty would get him murdered, so he also asked her to prevaricate, to play along as his sister.[54]

The first instance of Abraham's mendacity is so puzzling because it came directly after God had called him, promising to make Abraham into a great nation.[55] Abraham's calumny caused grave calamity in Egypt. Not only this, but Abraham was willing to accept gifts from the king of Egypt on account of Abraham's own failing.[56] This was a clear reversal from Abraham's statements in Genesis 14:22, 23, in which

---

[48] Genesis 15:6
[49] Genesis 12:1-5
[50] Genesis 14:14-16
[51] Genesis 14:22, 23
[52] Genesis 18:22-33
[53] Genesis 22:1-13; Hebrews 11:19
[54] Genesis 12:12, 13
[55] Genesis 12:2
[56] Genesis 12:16

he refused gifts so that no man could claim to have made him rich. It seems that Sarah's beauty clouded Abraham's judgment, causing him to compromise his integrity.

A second time Abraham lied about Sarah, again saying that she was his sister. This time Abimelech, king of Gerar, took Sarah as a wife, bringing ruin upon his house.[57] Abraham explained away his sin in Genesis 20:11, "I said to myself, 'There is surely no fear of God in this place, and they will kill me because of my wife.'" In reality it was Abraham who lapsed in his fear of God. Again, as before, Abraham accepted substantial gifts: sheep, cattle, male and female slaves, as well as a thousand shekels of silver. It appears that Abraham was again willing to compromise his conscience, accepting ill-gotten gain, when beguiled by the fear of man.

Abraham, Sarah, and the Angel
Jan Provost, d. 1520

Abraham was, more than once, willing to stifle his conscience in regard to family matters. In Genesis 15:4, and again in 15:18, God promised Abraham that his legitimate son would be the heir to a great nation. Even after receiving the Lord's assurance and establishing a covenant,[58] Abraham still forsook God's Word, cowering to Sarah's demand that he father a son in an adulterous relationship.[59] So at Sarah's behest, Abraham fathered a child through her maidservant, Hagar.[60] Yet, the Lord had specifically told Abraham that his descendent would not be a servant born in his house. It was because of this transgression that Abraham eventually brought upon his people unspeakable grief, as Hagar's son Ishmael would sire a hostile line of adversaries to Abraham's

---

[57] Genesis 20:2
[58] Genesis 15:18
[59] Genesis 16:2
[60] Genesis 16:3, 4

descendents.[61]

What's more, Abraham passively permitted Sarah to abuse her now pregnant maidservant, Hagar,[62] even though Abraham's conscience prodded him to intervene. In Genesis 21:10, 11, Sarah callously directed Abraham to exile Hagar and Ishmael to the desert. Abraham's conscience was piqued, but he inexplicably stood idly by (in the same way that Adam stood idly by as Eve rebelled).[63]

It would also appear that Abraham failed to discipline his son Ishmael, as Genesis 21:9 recounts that Ishmael mocked his younger brother Isaac. With regard to his wife, servant, and children, Abraham was morally feeble, unwilling to properly exercise his God-ordained role as faithful husband and disciplining father.

Abraham, like so many men, seemed courageous in the face of bold broad threats, but weak-willed with regard to his wife. As he lusted after her acceptance, his courage, faith, and willingness to exercise godly authority, seemed to wither in the desert sun. In the presence of his wife Abraham was complicit with obvious sin, willing to lie and excuse his lies, negligent with regard to parental discipline, unwilling to assert godly authority, and emotionally distant from those in whom he should have taken the keenest interest. It was as if the pith of his soul was stripped from him so that he abandoned his identity in the Lord.

> Horace (65–27 BC) wrote, "Habit is a cable; we weave a thread of it everyday, and at last we cannot break it." From the Christian perspective: *sin* is a cable and each sinner weaves a thread of it everyday. One either strengthens sin's cords with every thought, word, action, interaction, and desire, or else cuts those cords. Additionally, each moment of everyday each person offers implicit counsel on what is real, what a person is, what the purpose of life is, what man's problem is, and the solution to that problem. Likewise, this counsel either strengthens sin's cable or slowly severs it.

Abraham showed faith in moving from his homeland, going to battle for a relative, pleading on behalf of the innocent, and even sacrificing his promised son. However, Abraham echoed Adam, and foreshadowed David, Solomon, and others, in his willingness to forsake his inheritance for the momentary acceptance of a wife after whom he lusted. When it came to standing up against his headstrong wife, or disciplining his son, he quickly rendered himself a coward. In effect, Abraham found it easier to contend with and plead for (acts involving "gross-motor coordination") than to enter into the machinations of his own flesh with godly counsel. Yet, Genesis 26:5 records, "Abraham obeyed me and kept my requirements, my commands, my

---

[61] Genesis 16:12; 25:18
[62] Genesis 16:4-6
[63] Genesis 3:6

decrees and my laws." With regard to fathering an heir who would become a great nation, God clearly saw Abraham as finally submissive to his will.[64]

In what way does Jesus shed a new light on Abraham, his faith and his failings? In Jesus, the Christian is given a far greater faith and assurance than Abraham ever had. The Christian is offered the fulfillment of a promise of which Abraham only dreamt. In Jesus, the believer has seen God sacrifice his only son where Abraham was forbidden to do so. Additionally, just as Abraham pled on behalf of Sodom and Gomorrah,[65] Jesus pleads before the Father on behalf of the righteous. While Abraham failed to secure the city's deliverance, Jesus has succeeded in welcoming believers into the New Jerusalem, a pure bride prepared for her husband.[66] Jesus was willing to confront even the most powerful and persuasive in his midst, discipline the wayward, champion the orphan, and oppose the proud as Abraham never could.

14. Sin as hiding and seeking covering

Hosea 10:8 recounts, "The high places of wickedness will be destroyed – it is the sin of Israel. Thorns and thistles will grow up and cover their altars. Then they will say to the mountains, 'Cover us!' and to the hills, 'Fall on us!'" Luke 23:30 also reads, "They will say to the mountains, 'Fall on us!' and to the hills, 'Cover us!'" These verses are a picture of mankind's desperate, yet futile, attempt to seek covering from God's wrath. Hiding and seeking covering are the modus operandi of a terrified humanity seeking to deal with its naked guilt before a holy God. The sinner grabs for covering in any form, some way to feel justified, righteous, and above the condemnation of an all-seeing God.

People seek any plausible covering as a way to guard others from seeing their sin. Covering can be affected through anger, busyness, clothing, food, humor, work, or other means. For example, gluttony often arises from psychotic episodes in which one seeks covering as a form of protection. Overeating produces a shield of flesh in the misguided hope of being guarded from some *bête noire*.

There is a striking contrast between Genesis 3:7 and 3:21. Genesis 3:7 reads, "Then the eyes of both of them were opened, and they realized they were naked; so they sewed fig leaves together and made coverings for themselves." Genesis 3:21 states, "The LORD God made garments of skin for Adam and his wife and clothed them." In Genesis 3:7 Adam and Eve sought their own covering, a humanly-crafted means of dealing with shame. According to John Calvin (1509-1564) this was the first act of

---

[64] It appears that sadly Isaac adopted his father's sin. In Genesis 26:7, Isaac also called his wife Rebekah his sister out of fear that he would be murdered by King Abimelech on account of her beauty. (Again, Abimelech was deceived by Abraham's line.)
[65] Genesis 18:16-33
[66] Romans 8:34; Revelation 21:2

culture, the start of man dealing with his sin problem in his own way, for his own purposes. However, in Genesis 3:21 God crafted animal-skin garments for Adam and Eve. In this God graciously dealt with Adam and Eve's shame through his unmerited favor.

In the first instance, Adam and Eve used flimsy material, fig leaves, to affect their own covering. In the second instance, God provided animal skins as garments. This involved the shedding of blood, a proleptic indicator of Jesus who would shed his blood to cover his people's sin in garments of righteousness.[67] Later, in Numbers 20:22-29, the priest Aaron was stripped of his garments and led up Mount Hor. He died raised up on a high place, naked, and alone, punishment for his part in the golden calf fiasco. Aaron is a type of Christ, a prophetic indicator of how Christ would die, raised up, naked, and alone. Yet, while Aaron was guilty, Christ was innocent.

> In Deuteronomy 4:41-43, Moses set up cities of refuge for the Gadites and Reubenites. These cities were places of protection in the event that one had unintentionally committed murder. Thus, they would save the perpetrator's life, redolent of the city, generally, as a form of covering from God's wrath.

> **In Jesus**: Jesus experienced nakedness that he might cover those who put faith in him. In this way the righteous dalmatic of Christ covers believers' sin.
>
> "He wore cursing as his garment;
> it entered into his body like water,
> into his bones like oil.
> May it be like a cloak wrapped about him,
> like a belt tied forever around him.
> May this be the LORD's payment to my accusers,
> to those who speak evil of me." (Psalm 119: 18-20)
>
> "Then each of them was given a white robe, and they were told to wait a little longer, until the full number of their fellow servants, their brothers and sisters, were killed just as they had been." (Revelation 6:11)
>
> "Fine linen, bright and clean, was given her to wear." (Fine linen stands for the righteous acts of God's holy people.)" (Revelation 19:8)

Case Study: Technology as a Form of Covering[68]

Increasingly, modern people have no ability to be alone for a meaningful purpose,

---
[67] Isaiah 61:10; Revelation 6:11
[68] Many ideas in this section borrowed from Sherry Turkle, *Alone Together: Why We Expect More from Technology and Less from Each Other* (Basic Books, 2012)

namely to be alone with God. Loneliness, even for a few minutes, makes people anxious, so being alone feels like a problem that needs to be solved. Many even teeter on the precipice of depression unless they know that someone somewhere is focused on them. As people exhibit less capacity for constructive solitude they turn to a technological arbitrator to quell their anxiety. Yet, such arbitrators (such as the social media) only serve as a momentary thrill of perceived acceptance, so that most have abandoned a sense that others truly care for them or can relate to them. Thus, a bizarre and disturbing phenomenon is taking shape: people find themselves to be alone even while they are together.[69]

The Flying Carpet, Viktor Vasnetsov, 1880

Rene Descartes famously wrote, "I think therefore I am." One could recast this phrase in modern terms as "I text therefore I am." People, today, do not so much think, as instead they seek to achieve a seamless emotional experience. The hope is that through technology (such as texting) one will feel alive, stimulated, recognized, fulfilled, significant, and included. Previously, people thought, "I *have* a feeling; I want to make a call." Today this has become, "I *want to* have a feeling; I need to send a text." In the past it was the desire to share a feeling that generated the interaction. Today it is the desire to get a feeling which generates the interaction.

On account of sin, mankind lives behind relational walls which often results in painful loss of community, the erosion of meaningful interaction, and the tedium of superficial relationships. For example, consider cigarettes and cell phones as modern forms of relational covering. Smoking maintains a certain distance and raises a shield of supposed respect. The cell phone also maintains distance in the perceived

---

[69] For additional discussion of the topic of loneliness see the third book in this series, *The Days of Reckoning Are at Hand: From Fig Leaf to Olive Branch to Laurel Wreath*, chapter 3: "The Hobgoblin in the Inglenook: Assessing Loneliness"

preoccupation with a task. The cell phone, in particular, is used as a way to deflect social interaction, to remain behind a protective social Mylar.

> The automobile and the iPhone® are quickly altering their roles in society. In the past (and to some degree into the modern day) the car was "the carapace, the protective and aggressive shell, of urban and suburban man."[70] This metaphor of automobile as protective shell is rapidly shifting to handheld devices.

People seek covering in the midst of their interconnectedness, sheltered within a Faraday cage deflecting unwanted interactions. They want to be known but protected, recognized but guarded, enjoyed but from a distance, more museum-piece-under-glass than flesh-and-blood person. There is an imaginary social boundary at which each wants others located, close enough to luxuriate in one's good qualities, yet far enough away to be obscured from one's sin.[71] The modern obsession with others' validation and approval, while simultaneously minimizing relational risk, has become the driving theme of social media.

As people interact with media and mobile technology they are, with growing alarm, unable to interact with others in meaningful ways. For example, while present at social gatherings they want sole control over where they place their attention, only paying attention to that which offers emotional stimulation. For this reason, today people less frequently make eye contact or sit and listen to one another. They are often incapable of holding a sustained conversation, and when conversation does occur it is, more often than not, a self-obsessed encounter.

People increasingly turn to technology in the areas of their lives where they feel most vulnerable. For example, conversation, since it takes place in real time and one cannot precisely control what is said, is considered a vulnerability. It is far easier to text or email so that one maintains control over the dialogue. Where there is fear of judgment, failure, or rejection technology is seen as a kind of social and emotional savior. In this regard, technology offers three gratifying promises:

1. That one can place his attention wherever he wants to
2. That one will always be heard
3. That one will never be alone

In light of these three promises, people seek to customize their lives with various technologies which they prop up for relational deliverance.

---

[70] Marshall McLuhan (1911–1980)
[71] This concept from Dan Allender, Biblical Counselor. For additional discussion of this topic see the case study, "The Invisible Relational Circle," in the third book in this series, *The Days of Reckoning Are at Hand: From Fig Leaf to Olive Branch to Laurel Wreath*, chapter 3: "The Hobgoblin in the Inglenook: Assessing Loneliness"

Relationships are thorny, risky, demanding, fraught with emotional pain, and often disappointing. However, many sanitize or homogenize those relationships with technology. Technology reduces the relational viscosity by offering turn-key acceptance behind the cloak of a virtual medium. Interacting through media often poses no risk, and appears hopeful, ever vibrant, and surprising. It fills one with the illusions he desires, advances the story he longs to live out.

Through the social media people present a "second identity" (an informal avatar). They edit, delete, or retouch their personalities to create the personae they desire. Quickly people forget that they are interacting with actual people. In fact, many would prefer to dispense with real time interaction all together so as to mediate every relationship through a filtering medium.

> What is astounding is the ease and sophistication of modern telecommunication as juxtaposed with its often meaningless content.

The great paradox is that people today, despite unprecedented levels of connectivity, are deeply lonely, even in the midst of relationships. They are increasingly fearful of meaningful intimacy while craving it. Technology is often so attractive because it creates the illusion of companionship without the demands of friendship. Technology allows one to maintain a grand relational charade, to feel connected in a way that can be comfortably controlled.

Technology is used to manage the fear of loneliness, and to this end, has become an illusory friend to most. Devices now function as surrogate listeners. People imagine that their MP4s, cell phones, iPads®, and computers somehow care about them, that these devices relate to them. Modern people increasingly look to machines for empathy.

This obsession with being the center of attention, or advancing a personal experience, now decides the nature and duration of relationships. As soon as one's experiential needs are not center-stage, he resumes his search for new associations. This fosters slavery to gaining attention which only results in frustration and disappointment.

> Endemic to human depravity and foolishness is the peculiar phenomenon that that which one turns to as "savior" is so often the very source of one's depression and fear. Technology, increasingly used as a form of social covering, fosters greater isolation, and yet, is inexplicably relied upon for deliverance from one's fears.

The modern method of relating is nothing more than an obsessive search for the self, to be self-actualized (à la the Adler-Maslow pyramid of needs). This pyramid keeps each enslaved to an impossible quest to satisfy perceived needs. This needs-driven existence causes people to adjudge their success or failure based on feelings. Feelings are the final arbiter of whether one is loved, accepted, significant, respected, and whole. However, feelings last for a moment and quickly evaporate in the scorching sun of a frenetic world. As the feelings fade, so does the sense of validation. This is the source of isolation: communication and connection are no longer about meaningful interaction; they are about deriving a feeling and discarding that which does not serve one's emotional needs. Others have become little more than pawns manipulated to guard and aggrandize one's fragile sense of self.[72]

Disembarkation of Maria de Medici at Marseilles (detail), Peter Paul Rubens, 1625

The glaring blindness in this technological maelstrom is that isolation is often a God-given gift for introspection, a means to understand who one is and why he exists. As one studies himself more deeply, he should be driven to see his desperate need for a holy God who longs to heal him. Concerning what is one in need of healing? The trenchant obsession with oneself. Yet, modern people show a stalwart incapacity for dealing constructively with solitude. Solitude has become the great nemesis since it means listening to one's conscience, a conscience which whispers that one is a sinner before a holy God, that one is in perilous need of immediate worship rehabilitation.

"Be still and know that I am God." (Psalm 46:10)

---

[72] For further discussion of the modern sense of self see chapter 9: "Marauding Visigoths: The Autocratic Self"

As God dismantles the propped-up relational walls there is hope of restoration. This is the beginning of community healing, gaining an eternal sense of meaning, and experiencing life-changing relationship. When the façade comes down, the self-protective covering is pried back, and the customized fantasies are shattered, life takes its first step toward the purpose that God intended, relationship through Jesus Christ's shed blood on the cross, the ultimate polemic against technology-driven experience.

Countervailing Forces to Disruptive Technology: "Analogue Strikes Back"[73]

While technology tends to sanitize, dehumanize, and isolate modern people, there appear to be countervailing forces, some valuable, some destructive, which reestablish or reconstitute one's sense of connection, the visceral sense of being. The following are some countervailing forces which people use to reground themselves in a technology-infused world, or ways that they seek to "detoxify" their technology-sick souls:

1. Artwork – Art serves as a reconnection to a material, imaginative, or historical world.

2. Baseball – At a baseball game one sits, watches, thinks, and lets the hammock-like sway of the game soothe. (Football is of a fundamentally different texture - brash, pressured, sudden, and shocking. The sinewy somatic nature of football offers a sense of reconnection with flesh, blood, sweat, and the drama of purely physical conflict.)

3. Books and board games – Sometimes just the texture of paper, the touch of a wheel or buzzer, is cathartic to those who routinely immerse themselves in a virtual world where everything appears to exist, but does not. (Related to this might be the attraction of traditional calligraphy, since the ability to write beautiful cursive has largely been lost.)

4. "The Choking Game" ("Blackout") – This ritual, popular among adolescents, involves asphyxiating oneself or another in order to receive a rush of adrenaline. Technology-saturated teenagers are often desperate for a visceral experience, especially one involving a loss of control or momentary terror.

5. Conflict – Some seek to create drama as a way to feel alive, to feel related, to feel some emotional connection, even if for a negative purpose. Continually exposed to a virtual world, conflict makes one feel that he is once again a sentient being.

---

[73] The phrase "Analogue Strikes Back" borrowed from an advertisement in Prague, Czech Republic

6. Connection with nature – A tactile connection with the organic, with the physical world, such as handling soil and plants, offers soothing comfort. A sense of adventure and exploration offers a respite from the demands of cold and predictable technology.

7. Pets – Pets have become emotional partners, the promise of connection to an anthropopathic organism.

8. Religious ritual – On account of saturation with cold impassive technology, people are often drawn to religious ritual. Ritual offers something experiential and sensory, and even offers the appearance of purity and holiness in a world swirling with sensuality. Ritual is attractive to those who long for a mystical experience which fills the senses, and offers some perceived deliverance from a scientific world devoid of wonder.

The Baptism of Prince Vladimir (detail), Viktor Vasnetsov, d. 1926

9. Sexuality – Gratuitous sexuality has become a ready means to reconnect with the physical tactile world. As people increasingly live in artificial environments they crave some natural or sensory experience. (This may explain why sexual immorality tends to flourish in urban environments.) People deprived of the organic on account of their virtual digital manufactured worlds soon crave the tactile, the sensual. In the perversion of the human heart, this often morphs into a

lust for sexuality, a return to a perceived sense of the innate, albeit often perilous, pernicious, and perverted.

10. Tattoos – Tattoos are a way to experience something somatic, to draw attention to the body, to embolden and emphasize the body (while defacing it).

The more technology functions as an existential "centrifugal force" (scattering, outward-directed), the more people are drawn toward centripetal experiences (inward, focused, concentrated) which seem to re-center their identity as image-bearers. How does genuine faith in Jesus offer an antidote to the cold and dehumanizing experience of technology? In what way does the believer find within his faith a continual deliverance so that he does not seek out false saviors, many of which are derelict and depraved? How does faith in Jesus function is a relational gravitational force, drawing the Christian toward the restoration of, more than just his design, but fellowship with his Creator?

15. Sin as standing on a false authority

As a child, my grandparents wielded sizable influence over me. A grandparent's praise was a source of unceasing joy, while rebuke carried with it stinging remorse. One of the most perplexing developments of the modern world is the abdication of authority among seniors, in general. I notice that older people seldom, if ever, offer wise counsel, rebuke, or otherwise seek to curtail what has traditionally been understood as immoral behavior. I have at times seen young people brag about promiscuity, drunkenness, or drug abuse; dress in an inappropriate manner; or use foul language in the presence of a grandparent, with no response. This loss of respect for recognized authority, and the related neglect in wielding authority, seems to mark the modern world with scarring effect.

> Recently, while visiting a church, a mother took me aside. With concern in her voice, she disclosed that her seven year-old son told her that he no longer believes in God, that the idea of God seem foolish to him, that no one could be that powerful. In learning a little more about the parent's approach, it became clear to me that the boy is not learning submission to authority. His parents have wholly neglected to make their son accountable to them, instead seeking to make him feel like a friend or an equal. Without a manifest power structure to which he is held accountable, it becomes apparent why this boy fails to recognize the existence of God. Lacking parental discipline, he has never been subject to the fear of God.

The modern erosion of recognized authority is reminiscent of Judges 21:25, "In those days Israel had no king; everyone did as they saw fit." Sin is refusal to submit to God's ordained authorities, indication of an ultimate refusal to submit to God's direct authority. Thus, the absence of pervasive and persuasive human authority indicates a broader, more pernicious, absence of submission to God's authority. Living outside of God's authority brings anxiety as one is stripped of his moral and existential orientation.

> **In Jesus**: Submission to God's beneficent authority, knowing and abiding by his eternal will, brings a hedge of safety and a harvest of peace.
>
> "For this reason I did not even consider myself worthy to come to You, but just say the word, and my servant will be healed. 'For I also am a man placed under authority, with soldiers under me; and I say to this one, 'Go!' and he goes, and to another, 'Come!' and he comes, and to my slave, 'Do this!' and he does it.' Now when Jesus heard this, He marveled at him, and turned and said to the crowd that was following Him, 'I say to you, not even in Israel have I found such great faith.'" (Luke 7:7-9)
>
> "For I did not speak on my own, but the Father who sent me commanded me to say all that I have spoken." (John 12:49)

16. Sin as false rest and false peace in the things of the world

As evidenced by the popularity of Dan Brown's *The Da Vinci Code* (2003), some are obsessed with searching for hidden number patterns. Numerology is a means of ordering events so as to make sense of them. In a world that appears to be chaotic and out of control, people crave patterns because this offers predictability and comfort. Some seek a glimpse into the future, or hints concerning the end of the world, and number patterns seem to offer clues.

For example, many in the West believe that the triune God works in patterns of three, that when blessings or trials occur in triplicate this is a form of communication from God. However, people often discern patterns through seeing what they want to see, accepting or discarding information that fits their beliefs about God. If one seeks them out, one can concoct connections between events and numbers. This does not mean that God communicates through a secret code, or that order exists as one imagines it to.[74]

> "It is not what we don't know, but what we know that is false, that gets us into trouble." (Artemis Ward)

In defiance of God, the heart seeks false sources of rapprochement to assuage a guilty

---

[74] For example, the superstition of not walking under a ladder derives from the ancient panentheistic belief that God is found in any triangle. Walking under a ladder breaks the triangle, offending the Trinity.

conscience. This is the motivation behind idolatry, to find a proximate god which offers a sense of blessing and safety. Fallen mankind is an idol factory,[75] continually fashioning new idols to serve his every perceived need. This fascination with, and commitment to, raising up idols keeps mankind in a perpetual state of chasing but never resting, in slavery to himself but never finding freedom. God promises to "shake all the nations" so as to allow sin neither rest nor peace.[76] Psalm 95:11 states, "So I declared on oath in my anger, 'They shall never enter my rest.'" God unsettles the wayward sinner at every turn so that he would finally find rest in Jesus.

The Birth of the Milky Way, Peter Paul Rubens, 1636

In Jesus: Those in Jesus find rest for their souls and lasting peace since Jesus has conquered chaos and evil, so that those in him enjoy a Sabbath rest.[77]

"Are not two sparrows sold for a penny? Yet not one of them will fall to the ground outside your Father's care. And even the very hairs of your head are all numbered. So don't be afraid; you are worth more than many sparrows." (Matthew 10:29-31)

"Cast all your anxiety on him because he cares for you." (1 Peter 5:7)

---

[75] The concept of the idol factory from John Calvin (1509-1564)
[76] Haggai 2:7
[77] Matthew 11:28

17. Sin as an inverted sense of reality

> "But Nineveh has more than a hundred and twenty thousand people who cannot tell their right hand from their left, and many cattle as well. Should I not be concerned about that great city?" (Jonah 4:11)

Modern art distorts its subject into the grotesque. It is deliberately ugly and harsh to the eye so as to communicate that life cannot be understood, that everything is meaningless, that thought lies fractured. Modern art is contorted, disjointed and confusing so as to renounce God's created order. For example, a Cubist rendering of a cat shows it with angular lines, discordant colors, and constructed of a series of asymmetrical polygons. The cat has lost the form which God invested into it. Stripping it of its "cat-ness" is an affront to God's creative acts. Art should not seek to alter God's design but uphold it, highlight it, capture its dignity, and convey its infused meaning.

Genesis 1:1 describes the original matter as formless and void before God fashioned it into the universe. Satan's singular obsession is to reverse God's created order, to bring the creation back to "Day Zero,"[78] to deface the beauty of the creation, to render it inert, to strip it of its invested dignity. Satan seeks to obscure and confuse the knowledge of God, so that in peering at the creation one no longer glimpses evidence of the original artist.

Often functioning as Satan's handmaidens, modern artists produce a perversion of the human form or natural order. They show contempt for God's design, instead preferring to fashion their own derelict reality. In this way, modern art adopts Satan's objective to mutilate God's work. For example, Satan intermingles images to conjure that which is repulsive and degrading. Consider the grotesque images found in Daniel 7:2-7, an apocalyptic vision of four beasts. Two of these beasts are composed of parts from various animals.[79] Thus, Daniel envisioned animal hybrids, a mixture of parts used to fashion beasts. One beast, for example, resembled a lion with eagle's wings. At one point those wings were torn off and the lion was made to stand upright like a man. The notion of splicing together or stripping animal parts is repulsive because it is an affront to the created order. Thus, this Danielic vision captures Satan's desecration of the human form, an attempt to obliterate the image of God in man.[80]

> A beautiful glorious God sent his only Son to become a disfigured and mutilated sacrifice upon a cross so that fallen man might be redeemed from the ugliness of his sin. In this sense, "the cross screams against all the sensibilities of God's divine aesthetic." Yet, this was the only way redemption could be won:

---

[78] The concept "Day Zero" from Douglas Green, Westminster Theological Seminary, Philadelphia, Pennsylvania
[79] Daniel 7:4, 6
[80] Quite oddly, the vision of heavenly creatures in Ezekiel 1 offers a similar picture of sundry animal parts.

> Sin had brought ugliness and death into the world. In order to save his lost creation, God sent his Son right into that absurdity and alienation. There Jesus took our sin himself, dying to pay the price that justice demanded. It was such an ugly death that people had to turn away.
>
> But God transformed this ugliness into beauty through the resurrection, in which Christ was given a glorious and triumphant body. In light of this towering reality, "we should devote our skill to making art for the glory of God, and for the sake of his Son—our beautiful Savior..."[81]

Moving beyond modern art, all man-centered thinking profoundly shapes the sinner's questions and categories,[82] inverting his sense of reality. Sin keeps one fumbling in the dark; the good soon appears bad and the bad, good. That which has no value seems priceless, while the best seems pedestrian. What is senseless appears to have some sense in it, so that there is an increasingly facile rationalization for sin. Thus, sin leaves everything topsy-turvy. Consider the following examples of how sin inverts every truth of God:

Characteristics of Saving Faith	Sin's Inversion
1. What can one give?	What can one get?
2. God is one's refuge, strength, provider, and salvation.[83]	One must look out for himself because no one else will.
3. One is the chief of sinners,[84] a wretch, a man of unclean lips.[85]	One must feel good about himself.
4. One is a humble servant if one has only done what is required.[86]	God is not meeting one's needs.
5. God is one's portion, a very present help in time of trouble.[87]	One must resort to self-protection, defend himself against a brutal world.
6. God is faithful and just to forgive the repentant sinner.[88]	One refuses to forgive himself or others

> **In Jesus:** The faulty human perception of reality is corrected as that perception passes through the prism of the gospel which resolves it into a God-infused stream of light.

---

[81] All quotes in this section from the Douglas Groothuis' review of Philip Graham Ryken, *Art for God's Sake* (Denver Seminary) p. 55-58.
[82] David and Sharon Covington "Introduction to Biblical Counseling" notes, 2004
[83] Psalm 91:2
[84] 1 Timothy 1:15
[85] Isaiah 6:5
[86] Luke 17:10
[87] Psalm 46:1
[88] 1 John 1:9

> "For from him and through him and for him are all things. To him be the glory forever! Amen." (Romans 11:36)

18. Sin as foolishness

On Christmas Eve, 1776, George Washington (1732–1799) led his troops across the icy Delaware River to surprise the British army stationed on the other side. A British spy, glimpsing the Continental Army's approach, scribbled a note warning his commander. The commander, playing cards at the time, slipped the note into his pocket without reading it. Washington overwhelmed his adversary, seizing 900 soldiers without firing a single shot.[89]

Washington Crossing the Delaware, Emmanuel Leutze Gottlieb, 1851

The card-playing British commander committed a form of "de facto treason" as he delivered his army into the hands of the enemy through this dereliction of duty. Just as this commander foolishly neglected a "word" of warning, so too, mankind neglects the Word of God to his own peril. Mankind, in his supreme foolishness, likewise commits "covenantal treason" against God.[90] While the resources for faith are at his fingertips ("notes" scribbled on the creation all around), mankind continually overlooks them as one fumbling in the dark.

At some point in each person's past he experienced humiliation, loss, pain, regret, embarrassment, desire, lust, envy, and grabbing. In response he developed sinful patterns in order to deal with those feelings, experiences, and desires. At an early age

---

[89] It is poetically just that George Washington had forbidden card playing among his soldiers.
[90] Michael Bobick, *From Slavery to Sonship: A Biblical Psychology for Pastoral Counseling* (1995) 34. (class notes)

each developed a manner and means of manipulating and wrongly negotiating his world. That manner and means is a godless approach to dealing with life's perceived challenges and assumed needs; that is the heart of foolishness. Therefore, foolishness is fallen mankind's default position for thinking, categorizing, feeling, analyzing, assessing, interpreting, and responding.

> "…All strive to discredit what they do not excel in, while none strive to discredit what they do excel in. This is why there is chaos." (Zhuang Zi)

The source of man's foolishness is his attempt at gaining wisdom apart from God,[91] a kind of epistemological "alchemy." It is ontologically impossible for the sinner to gain wisdom on his own without God's self-revelation. Therefore, man's foolishness arises from both actual and functional atheism. The choking poison of atheism lives within each sinner so that he desires, and seeks out, that which is ultimately to his detriment. The sinner focuses on the wrong problem (usually his situation) and likewise pursues wrongly-directed solutions to that assumed problem. So, focused on the wrong problem, mankind leaves the true problem (errant heart worship) unchallenged.

> It's not the wrong answers, but the wrong questions, that really vex us.

> **In Jesus:** The wisdom of God is made manifest to the Christian as he knows and lives according to God's Word, spawning ever-greater relationship with Jesus.
>
> "It is because of him that you are in Christ Jesus, who has become for us wisdom from God--that is, our righteousness, holiness and redemption." (1 Corinthians 1:30)

19. Sin as friendship with the world[92]

James 4:4 is clear, "You adulterous people, don't you know that friendship with the world means enmity against God? Therefore, anyone who chooses to be a friend of the world becomes an enemy of God." Sin is love of the world and its wicked ways. The Christian rightly hates the world system while caring for lost individuals.

> **In Jesus**: The Christian is called God's friend on account of Jesus' death upon the cross.
>
> "You are my friends if you do what I command. I no longer call you servants, because a servant does not know his master's business. Instead, I have called you friends, for everything that I learned from my Father I have made known to you."

---

[91] Genesis 3:6
[92] For a more detailed description of the world system see chapter 2: "The World, the Flesh, and the Devil: Assessing the Threat Matrix"

(John 15:14, 15)

"May I never boast except in the cross of our Lord Jesus Christ, through which the world has been crucified to me, and I to the world." (Galatians 6:14)

20. Sin as pollution

Ophelia, John Everett Millais, 1852

The idea of sin as pollution takes on new meaning in a globe choking on air, water, and ground pollution. Sin, like environmental pollution, is absorbed each day harming one's vitality and longevity. Just as one is helplessly conscripted to live in some amount of environmental pollution, so too, the sinner is conscripted to his sin. No matter what he does, or where he goes, pollution is there robbing the sinner's life, to one degree or another. As insidious, and as deadly, as environmental pollution is, the pollution which infiltrates the human soul is vastly worse.

A Hollywood star, well-known for his promiscuous lifestyle, mentioned in an interview that he enjoys taking three or four showers a day. Under normal circumstances, one does not need more than one shower per day. Thus, it may be that this star, burdened with his guilt before God, feels "dirty." He may be trying to "wash away" his guilt.

"What a wretched man I am! Who will rescue me from this body of death?" (Romans 7:24)

Ezekiel 16:4-6 states,

> On the day you were born your cord was not cut, nor were you washed with water to make you clean, nor were you rubbed with salt or wrapped in cloths. No one looked on you with pity or had compassion enough to do any of these things for you. Rather, you were thrown out into the open field, for on the day you were born you were despised. Then I passed by and saw you kicking about in your blood, and as you lay there in your blood I said to you, 'Live!'

This image of an unwashed infant left to die captures something of the human condition polluted by sin. Each sinner is in a state of spiritual filth, unmanicured, unkempt, and kicking about in his own blood. The sinner is in desperate need of washing, cleansing, and purification.

> **In Jesus**: The Christian's heart is progressively washed clean and purified from sin through Jesus' shed blood.
>
> "Now that you have purified yourselves by obeying the truth so that you have sincere love for each other, love one another deeply, from the heart." (1 Peter 1:22)

21. Sin as a man-centered set of lenses

Sin sees with eyes that look at the world through a man-centered, man-glorifying set of lenses.

> "Son of man, you are living among a rebellious people. They have eyes to see but do not see and ears to hear but do not hear, for they are a rebellious people." (Ezekiel 12:2)
>
> "But I tell you that anyone who looks at a woman lustfully has already committed adultery with her in his heart." (Matthew 5:28)

> **In Jesus:** The Christian's vision is restored through corrective lenses which cause him to rightly assess reality.
>
> "Taste and see that the LORD is good; blessed is the one who takes refuge in him." (Psalm 34:8)

22. Sin as being a people of the eye[93]

---

[93] This concept from Bruce Waltke, "Christ Our Wisdom" seminar, Christian Counseling and Education Foundation, King of Prussia, Pennsylvania, 1999. For additional discussion of this topic see the case study,

> "Bel bows down, Nebo stoops low; their idols are borne by beasts of burden. The images that are carried about are burdensome, a burden for the weary. They stoop and bow down together; unable to rescue the burden, they themselves go off into captivity." (Isaiah 46:1, 2)

Modern day secular Scriptures, magazines, are a vanity fair of glossy airbrushed pictures that bring a moment's thrill and a harvest of lasting anxiety. Magazines are a kind of testament of here-and-now wealth, happiness, and dreams, a kind of mosaic of redemptive messages told in pictures that call for belief. In glossy pictorials magazines showcase alluring models and images of the "good life." It broadcasts a message, "This is what you should live for." "This is a goal worthy of your time and energy." "This is the abundant life you've always desired." Image implicitly tempts the viewer to devote his life to the pursuit of the image's supposed promises. But few are aware that magazines foist a cunning deception upon the voyeur since their images are not real; they are engineered, sculpted, and crafted for a driving purpose, to hold forth a highly-polished world of fantasy which appeals to human desire.

> "Listen to the cry of my people from a land far away: 'Is the LORD not in Zion? Is her King no longer there? Why have they aroused my anger with their images, with their worthless foreign idols?'" (Jeremiah 8:19)

A fashion magazine generally features a young sleek starlet on a glossy cover. The woman is dressed in the latest fashion and wears a confident alluring look. The cover does not display an innocent image; it presents a religion. Magazines often function as Satan's Bible since one of Satan's most effective weapons is image. The magazine asks viewers to worship beauty, wealth, and pleasure. It holds forth promises of satisfying desire, the ability to wield power, and freedom from fear. The world's images generally assault the heart so that every interaction launches another battle for the turf of human worship. These images exist to induce compliance to a man-centered, man-glorifying story over a God-centered, God-glorifying one. Therefore, every visual image shapes the heart, petitions the heart on what to worship.

> "The ear tends to be lazy, craves the familiar, and is shocked by the unexpected. The eye on the other hand, tends to be impatient, craves the novel, and is bored by repetition." (W. H. Auden)

A magazine cover seeks to dominate the mind, etching its image into the memory. In this sense, its images fill the viewer with an odd "schizophrenia." On the one hand the viewer finds such pictures enticing, inviting, and winsome, but on the other, anxiety-provoking. The viewer yearns for something that he desires, while simultaneously resigned to the fact that he can never receive that image's promise.

> "The disciples remarked how the temple was adorned with beautiful stones and gifts dedicated to God. But Jesus said, 'As for what you see here, the time will come when not one stone will be left on another; every one of them will be thrown down.'" (Luke 21:5, 6)

The obvious question is, Why would magazine editors deliberately seek to create anxiety in their readership? The answer is simple. Magazines are produced to showcase and sell products and services. The magazine's seductive images create a kind of background anxiety which seeks relief in the promise of purchasing. That is why advertising works; anxious empty longing people often seek to "purchase" salvation through some promising product. Advertisers want one to expend his life chasing meaningless things in the illusory belief that this will produce deliverance from one's deepest fears and concerns.[94]

The magazine's message to women is "become this"; the message to men is "get this." To the first there is the promise that "becoming" brings blessing, meaning, and power. To the second there is the same promise through "getting." Beauty's temptation is like a steel cable wound around the heart, marshaled as a weapon of economic war. Beauty dominates, controls, and manipulates. It is a force which promises to keep women in power, not so much over men, but over other women. In fact, the magazine cover makes women think that they hold a blueprint for gaining power (while they merely enslave themselves).[95]

> A man conquers the world to conquer a woman. A woman conquers a man to conquer the world.[96] Regardless of gender, the objective is the same – conquest, more specifically, conquest of God himself.

Image easily renders one a prisoner to chasing something that can never be attained, and even if it could be attained, can never be kept. If one were to somehow gain the life presented in magazines one would find himself pursuing a lost, empty, and meaningless existence, an existence centered around maintaining an image that ebbs away with each passing day, an existence that draws its life-blood from financial slavery to consumerism.

> "All things are wearisome, more than one can say. The eye never has enough of seeing, nor the ear its fill of hearing." (Ecclesiastes 1:8)

---

[94] For further discussion of advertising's methods see the first book in this series, *Ask for the Ancient Paths: From Art to Artifice to Arisen*, chapter 7: "The Needs Imperative"
[95] For further discussion of the topic of beauty see "'I'm a Nightmare Dressed like a Daydream': The Quest for Flawless Beauty" in the first book in this series, *Ask for the Ancient Paths: From Art to Artifice to Arisen*, chapter 5: "Redefining the Pygmalion Effect: Exploring the Image of God in Man"
[96] Mark Hua

When people lack a moral compass, when society has few categories for truth, and when there is no absolute standard, people easily succumb to the lust of the eye. Where there is no objective right and wrong, people quickly fall into the trap of judging right and wrong based on mere appearances.[97] (This was the trap into which Eve fell.) When there are no biblical categories for understanding sin, or the need for a savior, life is soon judged by one's personal perceptions and feelings. That which looks good is judged to be good, and that which does not is castoff. Incidentally, what often appears to be mere curiosity or inquisitiveness is actually covetous eyes filled with craving.

> Most mammals enjoy strong night vision because of a mirrored retina. This bounces light around the eye so that it is detected more than once for sharper vision. It is fascinating that humans have poorer visual acuity (although greater sensitivity to color) than most other mammals. Could this be a result of the fall? Is this God's mercy to mankind to cause him to rely less on sight and more on other senses? (This is purely a speculative issue.)

Genesis 3:6 reads, "When the woman saw that the fruit of the tree was good for food and pleasing to the eye, and also desirable for gaining wisdom, she took some and ate it. She also gave some to her husband, who was with her, and he ate it." The first sin involved three tightly interwoven actions: looking, taking, and eating. In defiance of God, Eve looked at, took hold of, and ate the forbidden fruit. However, the launching point for the fall was Eve looking at the fruit. This looking with sinful intent I might label the "pre-rebellion," as strictly speaking Eve did not sin until she ate the fruit.[98]

Romeo and Juliet
Ford Madox Brown, 1870

There are three aspects to Eve's "pre-rebellion." The fruit of the tree was:

---

[97] John 7:24
[98] It is fascinating that in Genesis 2:17 God commanded Adam not to eat from the tree in the middle of the garden, but in Genesis 3:3 Eve somewhat altered that command. Eve correctly stated that God had forbidden her and Adam from *eating* from the tree, but she then seemed to backtrack in stating that they must not *touch* the fruit.

1. Good for food (autonomy)
2. Pleasing to the eye (lust of the flesh)
3. Desirable for gaining wisdom (the reliance on unaided human reason)

Just as Eve's eyes deceived her and she rushed into sin, so too, fallen man is easily beguiled by the eyes. The eye is easily deceived because it is hardwired to the heart. (This is why God is so adamant about eschewing the enticements of the eye.) Numbers 15:39 states, "You will have these tassels to look at and so you will remember all the commands of the LORD, that you may obey them and not prostitute yourselves by going after the lusts of your own hearts and eyes." Those who judge with the eye, allowing it to lead them, will be ensnared. Eve's worldview was aligned by means of a treasured set of presuppositions that she appropriated by means of the eye. Thus, in line with Eve, each sinner apprehends the world through eyes which are perceptive because created, inaccurate because wrongly-directed, limited because hitched to ignorance, distorted because sinful, and ultimately only corrected through regeneration by the Holy Spirit.[99] The Bible emphasizes the lust of the eyes because the heart, to which the eyes are connected, is so prone to idolatrous longing.

> "I have made a covenant with my eyes not to look lustfully at a woman." (Job 31:1)
>
> "…but each person is tempted when he is dragged away by his own evil desire and enticed." (James 1:14)

Consider the following sections of Scripture concerning the perils of the eye:

1. Genesis 13:1-13 records that Abraham and Lot parted company on the plain near the Jordan. Lot chose a land that was pleasing to the eye, so the reader is left to assume that Abraham was conscribed to a lesser territory. However, as one soon discovers, Lot chose poorly as Jordan's plain was cursed by Sodom and Gomorrah's iniquity. Lot chose with his eyes and was deceived, while presumably Abraham, on faith, agreed to the less desirable location and was blessed.

2. In Exodus 29:20, Aaron and his sons were consecrated with the blood of a ram. The blood was placed on the ear, right thumb, and right big toe of each. Placing the blood on the ear was presumably to remind them to attune themselves to the Word of God.

3. In Numbers 16:14, Dathan and Abiram rhetorically asked Moses if he would gouge out the eyes of the rebellious Levites as a means of making them slaves or

---

[99] David Powlison, "Which Presuppositions? Secular Psychology and the Categories of Biblical Thought," *Journal of Psychology and Theology* 12.4 (Winter, 1984): 274.

in order to deceive them. Dathan and Abiram's comments imply that, as idolatrous community leaders, they used their eyes to adjudge the situation (that Moses had failed to usher them into the Promised Land). Dathan and Abiram, in effect, stated that they would not refuse the evidence gathered with their eyes. Thus, to their detriment, their insurrection was driven by reliance on the visual. This reveals a fascinating irony; while Dathan and Abiram implied that the gouging out of eyes was an illicit means of enslavement, it was actually the opposite. The presence of functioning eyes enslaved these rebels' hearts, as their eyes were the means by which they were deceived.

4. Numbers 33:52 is a command from God to drive out the inhabitants of Canaan, to destroy their carved images, their cast idols, and their high places. There is a progression from flat image, to statue, to physical location. It is fascinating that God mentioned these three forms of visual image (the flat, the raised, and the topographical) which were to be purged. He did not mention silencing pagan music or smashing pagan literature. God prioritized the visual image as the primary point of contact marked for destruction.

5. Deuteronomy 4:9 states, "Do not forget the things your eyes have seen or let them slip from your heart…" This is an implied link between eyes and heart; the heart worships that which the eyes take in.

6. Deuteronomy 4:12 records, "Then the Lord spoke to you out of fire. You heard the sound of words but saw no form; there was only voice." It is fascinating that this verse explicitly states that the Lord spoke in an audible voice but with no visual image - "there was only voice."

7. Deuteronomy 4:15-17 states,

> 'You saw no form of any kind the day the Lord spoke to you at Horeb out of the fire. Therefore, watch yourselves very carefully, so that you do not become corrupt and make for yourselves an idol, an image of any shape, whether formed like a man or a woman, or like any animal on earth or any bird that flies in the air.'

8. First Samuel 9:2 mentions Saul's exceptional stature in relation to his peers. The text includes this detail to show that the people chose Saul based purely on appearance, but had little understanding of what constituted a great king. On the other hand, David was somewhat unremarkable, yet he turned out to be a more capable king. The point is that worldly people use their eyes to judge and are easily deceived. However, those cultivating a godly heart judge according to inner character traits.

> The world is engaged in a quest for physical perfection. It desires outward beauty as supposed god-likeness. However, Jesus renews his people inwardly so that their character is being perfected. Jesus instills inner beauty which mirrors his own perfection.

9. Job 42:5, 6 states, "My ears have heard of you but now my eyes have seen you. Therefore I despise myself and repent in dust and ashes." Job seemed to despise himself all the more after having seen the Lord. He may have felt more blessed having merely heard the Lord, since after Job, in fact, saw God he was without excuse or rationale for his sharp questioning.

The Longshoremen's Noon, John George Brown, 1879

10. Proverbs 2:2 states, "Make your ear attentive to wisdom. Incline your heart to understanding." A connection exists between a heart inclined to God and the ear's attentiveness. The ear seems to be the principal conduit to a heart in submission to God.[100]

> **In Jesus**: Christians are called to turn from being a people of the eye to a people of ear, those who hear God's Word and respond to it in faith.

---

[100] An additional example is the analysis of Numbers 10:29-32 found in the section "Pocket of Atheism within the Heart," chapter 6: "Uncovering Idols of the Heart: Make Us Gods to Go Before Us"

> "He who has ears to hear, let him hear." (Mark 4:9b)
>
> "My sheep listen to my voice; I know them, and they follow me." (John 10:27)

Further Development of the Lust of the Eye

Throughout most of recorded history the spoken word carried compelling social persuasion. Orators were given center-stage to inform and entertain the masses. The Greeks, in particular, prized locution and viewed eloquence as sure evidence of truth. Even until the late 19th century interlocutors could command an audience for hours. People paid careful attention to oral and written arguments, closely following the logic involved.

> "Politics will eventually be replaced by imagery. The politician will be only too happy to abdicate in favor of his image, because the image will be much more powerful than he could ever be." (Marshall McLuhan)

Today, however, the spoken word carries little weight. The focus is now on the visual: appearance, image, and spectacle. In fact, a recent study found that when forming a first impression of another person only seven-percent of that impression is based on the actual content of what one says, the majority of the impression being formed by image. As modern culture becomes increasingly pagan, it is more readily ruled by the eye. Today, the world's razzle-dazzle easily entrances with the promise of pleasure. Just as the forbidden fruit's allure visited death upon mankind, so too, modern visual enticements produce an ongoing societal death.

> Movies and television generally perpetuate archaic thinking about beauty and moral character. Screen villains are often portrayed as pale, having a poor complexion, bald (or balding), and aging. Many have physical deformities or chronic illness. This fosters the false perception that moral turpitude results in ugliness and infirmity.

Just as Eve was deceived as she looked upon the forbidden fruit,[101] so too, people are easily led astray by beguiling images. Eve should have obeyed God's command, to trust what she had heard, but instead she allowed herself to be ruled by haughty eyes. Eve denied the truth that she heard in order to run after the lie that she saw. She abandoned the ear for the eye. Proverbs 6:16-18 possibly picks up on this. "There are six things the Lord hates, seven that are detestable to him: haughty eyes, a lying tongue, hands that shed innocent blood, a heart that devises wicked schemes, feet that are quick to rush into evil..." The first mention of what God hates - haughty, covetous eyes.

---

[101] Genesis 3:6

> The twenty-ninth entry of the renowned Chinese work *Thirty-Six Stratagems* reads "*Shu shang kai hua*" (树上开花) which is literally "tying artificial flowers on trees." This refers to dazzling the enemy with a display which makes dead things appear to be alive, or things of no value appear to be valuable.

The Second Commandment is clear. "You shall not make for yourself an idol in the form of anything in heaven above or on the earth beneath or in the waters below,"[102] a command designed to guard one from the dangers of visual allurements. Yet, Romans 1:25 reveals that the Second Commandment is routinely broken in sinful hearts. "They exchanged the truth of God for a lie, and worshipped and served created things rather than the Creator…"

> Chinese culture has historically espoused monism, the belief that the human being is only a material body without a soul. This focus on the body (to the neglect of the soul) tends to foster the lust of the eye and attention to superficial personal qualities. There is a propensity to denigrate the aged and unattractive. As a guilt-ridden counterbalance, Chinese culture has historically practiced ancestor worship, a way to repel the inherent threats of monism through deifying the dead.

Throughout the Bible pagans were admonished for being people of the eye; God's people, however, are people of the ear. God's people are commanded to hear the Word of God and respond in faith. It was when they turned to evil and unbelief that the Jews became a people of the eye. When God's people stopped listening, they became legionnaires of the golden calf, the apogeal outworking of the lust of the eye. Danger arises when God's people cease listening to his Word and instead rely upon, and assess life based upon, what they see. First Corinthians 1:22 recounts that as the Jews drifted further from God they demanded miraculous signs. Again Luke 11:29 states, "This is a wicked generation. It asks for a miraculous sign…"

> "The prudent man sees evil and hides himself but the naïve are punished." (Proverbs 22:3)

Those who seek miraculous signs not only test God but are in danger of being deceived. Satan plays upon the lust of the eye to chicane through dazzling miracles that mimic God. Satan easily transfixes those who crave such displays, and 2 Corinthians 11:14 warns, "Satan masquerades as an angel of light." Throughout the book of Revelation Satan imitates God's redemptive acts. In one scene the beast emerged from the sea with what appeared to be a fatal wound. He perpetrated a false resurrection in order to deceive mankind into believing that the beast possessed god-like qualities. Those who trust their eyes will be sorely deceived and will suffer grave loss.

---

[102] Exodus 20:4

> "The coming of the lawless one will be in accordance with the work of Satan displayed in all kinds of counterfeit miracles, signs and wonders, and in every sort of evil that deceives those who are perishing. They perished because they refused to love the truth and so be saved. For this reason God sends them a powerful delusion so that they will believe the lie and so that all will be condemned who have not believed the truth but have delighted in wickedness." (2 Thessalonians 2:9-12)

Her Eyes are with Thoughts and They are Far Away
Sir Lawrence Alma-Tadema, 1897

In John 10:27, Jesus said, "My sheep listen to my voice; I know them, and they follow me." And again in John 20:29, Jesus said, "Blessed are those who have not seen and still believe." Christians are commanded "to live by faith and not by sight,"[103] and reminded in Hebrews 11:1, "Now faith is confidence in what we hope for and assurance about what we do not see." The Christian assesses reality based on that which is invisible, since he lives in an unseen world of faith.

> "A wise man sees as much as he ought, not as much as he can." (Michel de Montaigne)

Incidentally, a television world couches its storytelling in the visible, framing its presentation of reality based on that which is seen. Thus, Christian faith and practice must be at odds with a television world. The point is that television is not a neutral medium holding forth an innocuous form of story-telling. It is profoundly heart-shaping merely in its form, and therefore serves as a conduit for worship

---
[103] 2 Corinthians 5:7

through the eyes.

Quite deliberately, the Bible does not contain pictures because God communicates with his people through listening to his voice. In this way, only the Bible offers true freedom from the lust of the eyes. Those who are wise flee the bewitching spells foisted upon the eyes, instead searching for, and finding, the living Word. For this reason 2 Corinthians 4:18 admonishes, "So we fix our eyes not on what is seen, but on what is unseen. For what is seen is temporary, but what is unseen is eternal."

The Heart-Eye Feedback System

Numbers 15:39 indicates that the eyes are hardwired into the heart. The images before the eyes are placed there on account of the idolatrous heart's false worship, and the heart is, in turn, shaped by the images placed before the eyes. The eyes feed the idols of the heart, and the idols of the heart direct the eyes. Thus, the eyes serve as the heart's periscope sent up to spy where the treasure trove of idols lay. The data is then transmitted back to, and takes up residence in, the heart which fashions itself after what it sees.

> "The heart soon forgets what the eye does not see."

There is a mosaic of functional false gods residing within the heart.[104] They show themselves as felt needs and desires, an "I want" demand. Each sinner is in the process of being molded into the image of the world because he wants to be molded into that image. There is a lie that the heart longs to believe so that it seeks out, and feeds off of, the depravity the world places in front of it.

> "We are all just prisoners here of our own device."[105]

The primeval heart craves the Vanity Fair paraded before it. The temptations that the media dangles in front of the sinner appeal to something already resident in his heart. What resides within the sinful heart? Cravings for control, freedom, happiness, image, intimacy, money, popularity, and power.

Television, for example, does not force one to believe its lies. Its images stir up the lies into which the sinner has already bought. The heart is naturally deceived, distracted, and depraved. Like a plug inserted into a wall socket, television plugs itself into the wall socket of the heart. The lies offered by the plug perfectly fit the heart's receptacle for lies. The heart naturally believes the world's lies, just as naturally as a plug fits a socket.

---

[104] This concept from David Powlison, Westminster Theological Seminary, Philadelphia, Pennsylvania
[105] "Hotel California," The Eagles, 1977

> "Wisdom will save you from the ways of wicked men, from men whose words are perverse, who leave the straight paths to walk in dark ways, who delight in doing wrong and rejoice in the perverseness of evil…" (Proverbs 2:12-14)

From the Bible's perspective there are two directives. First, as an act of repentance, remove the plug. (When Adam and Eve were tempted, what should they have done? They should have rebuked Satan and cast him from the garden.) Second, ask God to search and transform one's heart. Christians are called to do battle in both arenas, to separate from the world's lies, and to desire the heart's sanctification. Jesus longs to turn the socket around and upside-down, to change what one functionally worships so that the plug no longer fits the receptacle. Jesus breaks the slavery from both sides of the equation, to free the sinner from the external image and to deliver him from an idolatrous heart. Jesus died to give men the power to remove the plug, and he recasts the socket.

> "Elijah went before the people and said, 'How long will you waver between two opinions? If the Lord is God, follow him; but if Baal is God, follow him.' But the people said nothing." (1 Kings 18:21)

God longs to bring freedom from the lie, to make the Christian blossom in Christ, that he would be a sweet and visible fruit to the world around. The more one is free from the images that invade from the outside, and the more one is free from the idols within, the more one experiences unspeakable joy in Christ. In Matthew 6:22, 23, Jesus said, "The eye is the lamp of the body. If your eyes are good, your whole body will be full of light. But if your eyes are bad, your whole body will be full of darkness."

> "I will set before my eyes no vile thing. The deeds of faithless men I hate; they will not cling to me. Men of perverse heart shall be far from me; I will have nothing to do with evil." (Psalm 101:3, 4)

Psalm 119:36, 37 draws the pieces together. "Turn my heart toward your statutes and not toward selfish gain. Turn my eyes away from worthless things; preserve my life according to your word." Romans 16:19b adds, "…I want you to be wise about what is good, and innocent about what is evil."

> "And now here is my secret, a very simple secret: It is only with the heart that one can see rightly, what is essential is invisible to the eye." (Antoine de Saint-Exupery)

Uncovering Idols of the Heart:
Make Us Gods to Go Before Us[1]

Introduction

In Edgar Allen Poe's (1809-1849) short story, "The Oval Portrait,"[2] a weary traveler seeks shelter in an abandoned chateau where he discovers a chamber filled with fine works of art. One work in particular captures his imagination, so much so, that he gazes upon it for "an hour, perhaps." It is the portrait of a young woman painted by her artist husband. The traveler discovers a book which offers some background on the composition. It seems the artist had become so enthralled with his painting that he neglected the very subject of the art, his wife. As he continued to paint, he soon no longer even looked at his wife, so that the art became his sole obsession. Upon the portrait's completion, the artist exclaimed, "This indeed is Life, itself." He then turned to discover that his wife was dead.

Elizabeth Elliot Mount
Shepard Alonzo Mount, 1838

For Poe the greatest subject of literary tragedy is the death of a beautiful young woman. In this story it is finally the wife's pulchritude, and her inspiration for art, which sealed her fate. Poe lamented that art could become a parasite upon life ultimately destroying the life it was intended to celebrate. Thus, art can become an idolatrous substitute for life itself. In this way, Poe saw the very creation of art as a means of exposing the evils within the human heart.[3]

Unbeknownst to Poe, "The Oval Portrait" offers a fitting introduction to the study of idols of the heart. Like the artist who was transfixed by the exquisite beauty before

---

[1] Exodus 32:23
[2] Edgar Allen Poe, "The Oval Portrait" (originally published as "Life in Death," *Graham's Magazine*, 1842)
[3] Wikipedia essay, "The Oval Portrait"

him, so too, the human heart is irretrievably drawn to the objects of its desire. While the artist sought to memorialize his young wife though his art, he made the art itself into his consuming obsession, and in the process wholly neglected the subject, to her untimely death. The story's central metaphors could be applied to the heart's idolatrous worship, a worship which forsakes the love of God and the love of others, instead hoisting idols which captivate the worshipping imagination to one's own untimely death. In summary, one's greatest affection is often one's greatest affliction.

> "I think computer viruses should count as life. I think it says something about human nature that the only form of life we have created so far is purely destructive. We've created life in our own image." (Stephen Hawking)

The World Is Not Enough

Caesar Crossing the Rubicon, Adolphe Yvon, d. 1893

In 1976 just before Jean Paul Getty (1892–1976), founder of Getty Oil, died he was asked if he was pleased with his life. Getty replied that he was not. His interviewer asked what more he wanted in life. Getty responded, "More money." The interviewer then pointed out that Getty already had $2 billion. How much did he want? Getty responded, "One dollar more."[4]

---

[4] Getty famously said, "The meek shall inherit the earth, but not its mineral rights."

> "Ambition is never content even on the summit of greatness." (Napoleon Bonaparte)

The movie title "The World Is Not Enough" (1999) aptly encapsulates the concept of idolatry. In a flourish of pride, Adam and Eve decided the garden (the known world at that time) was not enough. This same theme inhabits each human heart. Ecclesiastes 6:7 states, "All man's efforts are for his mouth, yet his appetite is never satisfied." Man's appetite for food serves as a synecdoche for his appetite for the things of the world. Unlike food which satiates the pangs of physical hunger, the things of the world swell the idolatrous appetite the more it is fed.[5] Since idolatry holds forth the empty promise to abrogate any lack, to mollify any desire, those who feel they lack something, or who are consumed with desire, are highly motivated. This is the fertile ground from which idolatrous worship arises.

> "A tomb now suffices him for whom the whole world was not sufficient." (inscription on Alexander the Great's tomb)

The first mention of idolatry in the Bible is Genesis 31:19 in which Rachel stole her father's household gods. Later in Exodus 20:3, 4: "You shall have no other gods before me. You shall not make for yourself an idol in the form of anything in heaven above or on the earth beneath or in the waters below." Exodus 20:5 says that bowing before idols is hatred toward God. Throughout, the Bible highlights material idols as a manifestation of heart idols, so that the internal conceives and fashions the external. The Ten Commandments prioritize the worship of God, emphasizing this imperative with a subsequent ban on idol worship. The Ten Commandments recognize the heart's tendency toward aberrant worship, thus calling it to worship reform.

> "Man was born free and everywhere he is in shackles." (Jean-Jacques Rousseau)

The Heart as Living Rorschach Image

> "A chronicle of my good deeds is really an altar to my self-idolatry." (Edward Welch)

Unbeknownst to my students, as a teacher I observe everything. Once, one of my classes was attended by an exceptionally beautiful young woman. She was not just beautiful but demur and studious. It seemed that every young man in class sought her affections. It was as if the entire room was transfixed by, and revolved around, this

---

[5] An excellent example of the heart increasing its idolatrous desire the more it is fed is Hitler's (1889-1945) annexation of Czechoslovakia in 1939. When Hitler asserted that Czechoslovakia would be his final acquisition, Neville Chamberlain (1869-1940) blindly acquiesced to Hitler's demands. Shocked that he was handed Czechoslovakia without any concessions, Hitler was emboldened to invade Poland. The lesson is that idols are never appeased but seek ever expanding conquest.

young woman. Each young man seemed singularly focused on her, how she dressed, where she sat, whom she spoke to, and what made her laugh. It was fascinating to observe how each suitor adopted a particular modus operandi in order to gain her attention. One young man assumed the role of the loud-mouthed alpha male, striking other men with a playful but hard fist to the arm. He seemed to revel in displaying his physical mettle and reminding others of his prowess. Another young man became the class "nice guy," speaking about how much he appreciated his classmates and how excited he was to get to know them better. One young man played the brooding conflicted loner, speaking in philosophical language with enigmatic tones. Another played the downcast victim, sharing his plan to deliver his struggling parents.

Each young man assumed a well-crafted persona which seemed calculated to win this young woman's attention. The various tactics appeared precisely calibrated to win the prize, and if that prize was attained then the tactic was deemed successful and justified in the victor's mind. It occurred to me that

A Moor Presenting a Parrot to a Lady
Nicholaes Berchem, c. 1660

this young woman had become the class' golden calf, the raised idol. The class seemed to be defined and controlled by gaining the supposed blessing, meaning, and power that the idol promised. The idol, for these young men, defined truth and morality, purpose and reality. This offers a window into how idols work; they assume every role that God himself was meant to assume. The idol delineates the good and the right, defines proper conduct, and demarks ultimate reality. The idolater cannot see past, nor live past, the idol, so that, as such, it functions as a shielding agent keeping him from relationship with the true God.

> Idolatry causes one to make a Faustian bargain only to feel like Sisyphus laboring under the sword of Damocles in Dante's inferno.

The human heart is simultaneously extraordinarily complex,[6] and astonishingly simple.[7] The heart is both a labyrinth of evil, a contorted and twisted world of shifting alliances, and at the same time governed by a single theme. What governs the heart's tides and seasons? The singular focus on denying, defying, and suppressing the knowledge of its Creator. This objective pulls the strings of the heart's manifold machinations. Thus, chiaroscuro patterns emerge time and again, like a spiritual Rorschach test, that resolve into the twin objectives of denying God and promoting self. Whether the counselor comes at the issue of human depravity from the perspective of denied God or exalted self, this is functionally of little consequence, as they are two sides of the same coin.[8] That is the Rorschach.

> In Hellenistic terms the heart's motive could be summarized as the daily quest for both a Greek chorus and a Praetorian guard. The chorus sings of the heart's plight, announcing tragic misfortune, and in this way serves as a blame-shifting mechanism. The Praetorian guard shields the heart's idols so that they cannot be identified or confronted. Life tends to degenerate into a quest for louder chorus and more impenetrable shield.

Consider the picture Jeremiah 2:13-28 paints of idolatry:

> 'My people have committed two sins: They have forsaken me, the spring of living water, and have dug cisterns that cannot hold water. Is Israel a servant, a slave by birth? Why then has he become plunder? Lions have roared; they have growled at him. They have laid waste his land; his towns are burned and deserted.
>
> Have you not brought this on yourselves by forsaking the Lord your God when he led you in the way? Now why go to Egypt to drink water from the Shihor? And why go to Assyria to drink water from the River? Your wickedness will punish you; your backsliding will rebuke you. Consider then and realize how evil and bitter it is for you when you forsake the Lord your God and have no awe of me."
>
> Long ago you broke off your yoke and tore off your bonds; you said, 'I will not serve you!' Indeed, on every high hill and under every spreading tree you lay down as a prostitute. I had planted you like a choice vine of sound and reliable stock. How then did you turn against me into a corrupt, wild vine?

---

[6] Jeremiah 17:9
[7] Isaiah 53:6
[8] John Calvin (1509-1564) offered this point.

> Although you wash yourself with soda and use an abundance of soap, the stain of your guilt is still before me,'
>
> How can you say, 'I am not defiled; I have not run after the Baals'? See how you behaved in the valley; consider what you have done. You are a swift she-camel running here and there, a wild donkey accustomed to the desert, sniffing the wind in her craving- in her heat who can restrain her? Any males that pursue her need not tire themselves; at mating time they will find her. Do not run until your feet are bare and your throat is dry. But you said, "It is no use! I love foreign gods, and I must go after them.'
>
> As a thief is disgraced when he is caught, so the house of Israel is disgraced – they, their kings and their officials, their priests and their prophets. They say to wood, 'You are my father,' and to stone, 'You gave me birth.' They have turned their backs to me and not their faces; yet when they are in trouble, they say, 'Come and save us!' Where then are the gods you made for yourselves? Let them come if they can save you when you are in trouble! For you have as many gods as you have towns, O Judah.'

The passage uses twelve ways to describe the idolater: a slave, one who is laid waste, one who is burned, one who is deserted, a wicked being, one deserving punishment, a functional prostitute, one who is guilty, one who is defiled, one who is disgraced, one filled with craving, and one chasing foreign gods. The picture could not be any clearer. To summarize the idolater's posture toward God, the passage uses the word "forsake" three times.[9] For example, Jeremiah 2:13 highlights forsaking springs of living water to dig porous cisterns. Idolatry is analogous to forsaking life-giving water for the stagnant water of death.[10]

> "Wealth is like seawater – the more we drink, the thirstier we become, and the same is true of fame." (Arthur Schopenhauer)

Pockets of Atheism Within the Heart[11]

On July 4, 1776, the King of England, George III (1738-1820), wrote in his personal diary, "Nothing important happened today." (Of course, a global movement of unfathomable proportions had ignited on that day.) This is often the functional posture of the Christian with regard to his new found identity in Christ. He may be blind to the independence movement taking place within him, choosing instead to remain

---

[9] Jeremiah 2:13, 17, 19
[10] In John 4:10 Jesus described himself as "living water," and later in John 19:28 as Jesus hung on the cross he said, "I am thirsty." As the source of living water, Jesus made himself into a porous cistern, so as to enter into a state of spiritual death on man's behalf.
[11] This term "pockets of atheism within the heart" borrowed from David Powlison, Westminster Theological Seminary, Philadelphia, Pennsylvania

under the tyrannical rule of idols. While the Christian is justified before God, he has also entered into a lifelong process of being sanctified. Sanctification seeks to uncover and uproot those heart allegiances not surrendered to Christ. As this process progresses there are invariably remaining pockets of idolatry (holdouts of man-centered desire) and newly-minted pockets of faith (surrendered and victorious elements). The counselor's objective is to be used by God to shrink the pockets of idolatry and to expand the pockets of faith. This is God's work within the heart, with the counselor as an instrument in the process.

In Numbers 10:29-32 Moses informed his father-in-law Hobab, son of Reuel the Midianite, that the Israelites were setting out for the place about which the Lord had told them. Moses told Hobab that if he would come with them Moses would treat him well. However, Hobab refused to go. Moses then pleaded, telling him that Horab alone knew where Israel should camp, and that he could be their "eyes." Moses promised to share with Horab every good thing the Lord had in store for the Israelites.

Hobab was apparently neither an Israelite nor a God-fearer. Why then did Moses lavish such attention and promise upon him? Why did Moses feel that Hobab needed to show the Israelites where to camp? Was not God himself leading them by means of pillars of cloud and fire?[12] It would appear that Moses was mistaken in elevating Hobab to a privileged position, and should not have designated him as the people's eyes. Moses had previously listened to God's command, not trusting that which he beheld with his eyes. Moses had tasted God's provision and promises, but this time he seemed to depreciate his faith by trusting in the guidance of man. This is an illustration of a pocket of atheism within Moses' heart, a resorting to man-centered direction at the expense of God's. At times Moses displayed towering faith and at others he seemed to abandon that faith in favor of worldly concerns.[13]

Worship Patterns

According to legend, the ancient Greek, Milo of Croton (6th century BC), won the highest prize in wrestling at six separate Olympics from 540 to 516 BC. He also carried a one ton ox across the stadium and wrote a work entitled *Physica* on science and natural history.

However, Milo met his demise on account of his hubris. Alone in a forest, Milo spied a cleft tree trunk with a wedge in it. He tried to split the trunk with his bare hands, but when the wedge fell out his hands were caught fast. As night fell, wolves emerged and, despite a desperate fight, devoured Milo.[14]

---

[12] Numbers 9:15-23
[13] For further discussion of this topic see chapter 10: "A Nouthetic Analysis of Moses"
[14] Kevin McFarland, *Incredible But True!* (New York: Bell Publishing Co., 1976)

Worship patterns tend to follow the contours of one's giftedness. In areas in which one is most gifted, he tends to most easily succumb to false worship. The reason is very simple; in the areas of greatest giftedness one is most tempted to rely upon himself, to install himself as god. Additionally, areas of false worship tend to function as idol attractors, so that idolatry clusters around those worship nodes. Thus, giftedness tends to offer trail markers for idolatry. Generally speaking, look for the gifts and idols will not be far behind. Consider Ezekiel 28:11-17 which mentions Satan's former high position in heaven. That privileged position served as the opportunity for Satan's attempted *coup d'etat*, the failed effort to become God himself.

Milo of Croton
Joseph-Benoit Suvee, d. 1807

I am not particularly gifted in basketball so I tend not to fall into idolatrous worship in that context. In observing my play one would notice a lighthearted spirit, an attitude of joy, the willingness to extend grace, the ability to love others with friendly competition, and the desire to glorify God. It is easy for me to show faith in the midst of a basketball game because it is not an attractive idol to me. However, as a teacher I tend to struggle with idolatrous control in the classroom. My area of giftedness offers a predilection to idolatry. Therefore, God is vigilant with a refining fire to cultivate a heart-set which loves my students, while at the same time resting in him for the outcome of my effort.

> How does one discern between godly perseverance and idolatrous obsession? Perseverance is a God-centered God-glorifying tenacity to fulfill that which one believes to be God's will. When one is filled with desire to serve God, the task at hand is secondary to God's direction. Idolatrous obsession is a man-centered quest to

> live out a self-glorifying will. Obsession makes the task at hand primary to all else, so that God and others become handmaidens to one's goal.

Idols of the Heart and the Vanity Fair[15]

The American Colonists sometimes devised imaginative ways to defy the British crown. In the early 18th century, King George III issued a decree that all wide wooden boards had to be shipped to England for construction of the British navy. A New England Puritan pastor, Adonijah Bidwell (1716–1784), defied this command by inserting an exceptionally wide board into his home's paneled foyer. This was a signal to guests that Bidwell supported America's cause for independence.

This anecdote serves as a vignette for the gospel's power within the regenerate heart, the conspicuous presence of presiding defiance toward oppressive idolatry. Each person by design worships something, so that that worship, whether idolatrous or faithful, underlies all that he does, thinks, and says. In false worship there is a constant exchange of the glory of God for images made to look like mortal man and beasts,[16] so that the sinner readily exchanges God for some God-replacement.[17] Isaiah 44:13 states, "He shapes the idol in the form of man, of man in all his glory, that it may dwell in a shrine."

> "No sooner are we supplied with everything that nature can demand, than we sit down to contrive artificial appetites." (Samuel Johnson)

Each person assumes the image of that which he worships, becoming like his idols, so that as he continues in them he is more deeply conformed to them, darkened, and finally destroyed. True worship, on the other hand, does not besiege, but liberates, so that one's humanity is cultivated and developed as it was intended.

> "So long as man remains free he strives for nothing so incessantly and so painfully as to find someone to worship." (Fyodor Dostoyevsky)

The Heart's Fine and Gross Motor Movements

While highly-intelligent, arthropods (such as the squid and octopus), possess a primitive neurological system, called a "neural net." If the arthropod receives stimulation at any spot on its body the entire body contracts. The neural net cannot discern where on the body the stimulus occurs, so the entire body reacts in self-protection. This is similar to the way in which many, in sinful response to their

---

[15] This subtitle borrowed from David Powlison, *The Journal of Biblical Counseling*, (Glenside, Pennsylvania: The Christian Counseling and Education Foundation)
[16] Romans 1:23
[17] Paul Tripp, Westminster Theological Seminary, Philadelphia, Pennsylvania

world, deal with any annoyance, threat, or fear. Their whole being reacts; there is a single reflexive response which does not, and cannot, discern the true nature of the stimulus and thus, in effect, lashes out with an unrefined dismissive self-protective response.

As one identifies idols one comes into contact with the heart's landscape, visualizing its contours. In this way, idols lend a confused, dissipated, and dissolute heart a "pictorial" motivator. In the same way that the forbidden fruit (an actual object in space-time) made concrete Satan's lies, so too, idols make material or substantive the heart's treachery. Idols disambiguate the intentions of the heart so that those intentions take on a sharply-defined and manifest presence in space-time. Thus, idolatry moves sin from abstraction to quantifiable entity.

There are principally two levels on which to study the heart, the macroscopic and the microscopic. Thus, the counselor, to be effective, must show a concomitant awareness of big picture and granular detail. He must read the heart's metanarrative, its "mission statement," and parse its subtext, how that mission statement is implemented. The heart maintains a certain "global" position on the compass while pinpointing, with surgical precision, idols for select purposes.

Consider 1 Samuel 17:26, "David asked the men standing near him, 'What will be done for the man who kills this Philistine and removes this disgrace from Israel?'" While David, in stepping forward to challenge Goliath, displayed a consuming passion for God's glory, he also revealed, with this one query, a self-serving motive. Nestled within David's heart was a chamber of lust for the things of the world. That is why, on the way to honoring God's name and nation, David stopped to ask what was in it for him. It was this filament of worldliness which eventually wend its way through his heart leading him to adultery,[18] premeditated murder,[19] and a refusal to discipline his sons to their untimely deaths.[20]

> Those ruled by fear tend to crave power, to be surrounded by demonstrable power, to be ensconced in a power structure. Those ruled by pride tend to crave attention, to be the object of others' worship.

Paul Tripp, in his masterful work *Instruments in the Redeemer's Hands*,[21] offers the following analysis of the heart:

1. Desire turns into demand.

---

[18] 2 Samuel 11:4
[19] 2 Samuel 11:15
[20] Amnon and Absalom
[21] Paul Tripp, *Instruments in the Redeemer's Hands: People in Need of Change Helping People in Need of Change* (Presbyterian and Reformed Publishing, 2002)

2. Demand gets metamorphosed into need.
3. Need sets up expectations.
4. Expectations lead to disappointment.
5. Disappointments lead to inflicting punishment, striking-back, lashing out.

Solomon at His Throne, Andreas Brugger, 1777

The heart's wickedness hides behind the plausibility of its idolatry, so as to justify its inflicted punishment upon others. In this regard, Jesus first identified idols in those he sought to draw to faith, so that they would repent and renounce their faulty worship. Pinpointing the primary obstacle in the heart, Jesus sought to first remove it so that the way was prepared for faith. Sometimes Jesus dealt with the idol directly, and other times through indirect means (such as through miraculous healing or other signs). The objective, however, was always the same, to break the idol's stronghold. In the young rich ruler Jesus identified the idol of wealth,[22] and in the Samaritan women the idol of sexuality.[23] With the man born blind Jesus healed his blindness in order to remove any doubt of Jesus' identity, therein inducing faith.[24]

---

[22] Mark 10:17-27
[23] John 4:1-30
[24] John 9

While idolaters tend to traffic in grays, the gifted counselor, like Jesus, draws out the heart's idolatrous worship so as to clearly define it and illuminate it. The counselor distills out the idol from its surrounding life situation, revealing the heart's worship in chiaroscuro. In this way the counselor directly confronts the heart, while not meddling in incidentals that frequently serve as a distraction. Like Jesus, the counselor keeps a laser focus on the idol, not allowing it to dart into shadowy corners.

Consider Luke 21:5, 6 in which Jesus' disciples remarked on the temple's adornment with magnificent stones and gifts dedicated to God. Yet, Jesus responded, "As for what you see here, the time will come when not one stone will be left on another; every one of them will be thrown down." Jesus went after idols with surgical precision. He understood their ways and movements, their cunning and slight of hand. The disciples lusted after what they saw before them. In this they failed to realize that the temple had been transformed into nothing but a display of human vanity, one that God would soon bring low ("not one stone will be left upon another"). Jesus honed in on his disciples' lust of the eye and exposed it.

Idolatry and the Quest for Happiness

As I ran along a busy city street I saw two police officers, heads down and frowning, writing a citation for a man sitting on his motorcycle. What caught my attention was that the man was glowing, chatting with the offices like a proud father on his daughter's wedding day. He handed his license to the officer with a grin and eagerly made eye contact with passersby as if to record the moment. I wondered if the man was thrilled just to matter, to receive someone's focus (albeit negative), grateful to be counted important enough to warrant two police officers' attention and a blocked street lane. What idols ruled this man's heart?

Human desire could be thought of under the metaphor of being "east of Eden." Man finds himself east of Eden in many situations in life, and in each he longs to reenter the garden. Man seeks a home within a cursed creation, not through God's gracious provision, but through his own. He longs to craft a surrogate garden of his own making, all the while lamenting being east of his self-construed Eden.

> Here's a good test for discerning idols: Idols never say "no." (This is similar to the fact that the objects of one's fantasy never say "no" either.)[25]

Why is idolatry so attractive to sinners? The sinful heart craves a God-substitute at every turn and in every circumstance. The heart desires external displays, the pageantry of human drama, the victory of the human will. That is why idolatry carries

---

[25] This concept from Paul Tripp, *Instruments in the Redeemer's Hands: People in Need of Change Helping People in Need of Change* (Presbyterian and Reformed Publishing, 2002)

such allure. It makes the war against God appear to be winnable. The heart loves the lie that one can be his own god, that one can through his own efforts effect salvation.

> The magnetic compass was first constructed in China in 1119 of a loadstone spoon and bronze plate. *Feng shui* (风水) inspired the invention of the compass because, according to *feng shui* principles, positive energy flows from the south. Therefore, precisely locating the south is crucial. An analogy could be drawn with idolatry which tends to fashion needed accoutrements to serve that idolatry. Thus, the heart, in pursuit of precise "south" (salvation), crafts its own "compass" (a means to acquire salvation outside of Christ).

When one's perceived needs are met (even just for a moment) there is a sense of elation, peace, satisfaction, vindication, and victory. However, these are false "positives." An idol-driven illusory peace soon succumbs to anxiety as one realizes that his needs are never satisfied. Momentary elation quickly turns to bitter desire. Thus, the wise counselor is attentive to momentary happiness (as opposed to abiding joy). He does not fall into the trap of thinking that that happiness is anything other than the work of temporarily functioning idols. Idols always produce false fruit, and that fruit is revealed as such in time.

> Two-thirds of all corporate mergers and acquisitions fail. Often the underlying business model reveals nothing more than human lust for domination and personal vanity.

One's degree of happiness is a function of the degree to which one's actual existence and one's idealized existence (idolatry) are in conformity. This means that if one's actual life and the life which one worships are nearly identical, one is happy.[26] Unhappiness occurs when one's actual life and one's idealized life become incongruous.

> "I can live for two months on a good compliment." (Mark Twain)

It is rare that one's actual life and one's idealized life conform for long. In fact, in God's mercy he does not allow the two to conform, so that the idolater is not permitted to rest in his rebellion. The idolater strives to achieve his ideal, but this is just a fantasy world which quickly deteriorates and disassembles itself. As the idolater pursues self-glory, he may at times display false fruit, fruit which appears productive, meaningful, even godly. But in reality this fruit is a mere byproduct of an idol that functions well for the moment, but will soon curse and destroy the idolater. The

---

[26] Michael Bobick, *From Slavery to Sonship: A Biblical Psychology for Pastoral Counseling* (1995) 37. (class notes)

idolater's sense of peace is momentary and illusory.[27]

> "The mass of men lead lives of quiet desperation…" (Henry David Thoreau)

Consider that the Christian sect the Quakers were so named because they trembled at the very mention of God. Today, such a notion seems laughable to most as self-promotion and greed have largely replaced the fear of God. The self functions as a surrogate god which keeps people focused on the polestar of money, the ultimate promoter of human desire. Money can be a potent social driver, seemingly efficacious for maintaining social order. But sooner or later, all false gods turn to dust. Society puts forth an outward appearance of order and law-abiding, while it is really composed of hollow rotted husks of citizens deluded by false gods, gods which drive people to irrational and wicked behavior when those gods are threatened. While such an analysis may sound Hobbesian, it is not as one considers the abysmal nature of sin. But as stated time and again, sin and its consequence never have the last word, as a luminescent Savior has delivered mankind from the prison of himself (should man choose to avail himself of that gift).

Brothers Sell Joseph into Slavery, Konstantin Flavitsky, 1855

> Pay careful attention to the jokes one tells, to what he finds humorous. Humor reveals poignant truths about the heart, so that often one exposes his idols in his humor.

---

[27] Jeremiah 6:13, 14

Idolatry as Uncreation

Deuteronomy 4:16-20 states:

> So that you do not become corrupt and make for yourselves an idol, an image of any shape, whether formed like a man or a woman, or like any animal on earth or any bird that flies in the air, or like any creature that moves along the ground or any fish in the waters below. And when you look up to the sky and see the sun, the moon and the stars—all the heavenly array—do not be enticed into bowing down to them and worshiping things the Lord your God has apportioned to all the nations under heaven. But as for you, the Lord took you and brought you out of the iron-smelting furnace, out of Egypt, to be the people of his inheritance, as you now are.

Creation (Seven Days)	An Idol Made in the Image of…	…Is a Reversal of…
1. Light/darkness	Man or woman[28]	Day 6
2. Sky	Animals on the earth[29]	Day 6
3. Dry ground, vegetation	Birds[30]	Day 5
4. Sun, moon, stars	Ground creatures[31]	Day 6
5. Water creatures, birds	Fish[32]	Day 5
6. Land creatures, man	Sun, moon, stars[33]	Day 4
7. Rest	An iron-smelting furnace of Egypt[34]	Day 7

From Deuteronomy 4:16-20, on account of the people's idolatry, one sees the reversal of days four though seven in the original creation. Day seven, in particular, was intended to be a day of rest, but on account of idolatry it became an iron-smelting furnace in the land of Egypt (a land of slavery and death). The Lord offered an inheritance when he delivered his people from this Egyptian furnace. All idolatry, in effect, seeks to return the creation to "Day Zero,"[35] to reverse God's creative acts.

At the creation God defeated chaos, imposed order, and invested his goodness into his creative acts. However, the theory of evolution, for example, seeks to return to a pre-creation state. It attributes God's creative work to chaos, and in so doing glorifies

---

[28] Deuteronomy 4:16
[29] Deuteronomy 4:17
[30] Deuteronomy 4:17
[31] Deuteronomy 4:18
[32] Deuteronomy 4:18
[33] Deuteronomy 4:19
[34] Deuteronomy 4:20
[35] This concept from Douglas Green, Westminster Theological Seminary, Philadelphia, Pennsylvania

Satan for God's work under the banner of blind evolutionary chance. Evolution is thus an attempt to deify a state of "uncreation" (the state before God affected his creative acts). This is Satan's attempt to undermine and vanquish God out of vengeance for God's conquest of Satan at the creation.

> To my sensibility much of modern art is despicable. Most of what is termed "art" is contorted, grotesque, out of focus, improperly scaled, and dark. There are days, oddly enough, when that describes my life. My life often feels like a modern art painting, a disjointed experience of continually fractured relationships, awkward gaffes, humiliating failures, and dark episodes. There are days when my life looks like "uncreation." Yet, God brings order out of life's uncreation, redeeming it by means of his Son's sacrifice, so that even that which seems disordered bears the imprimatur of a good God.

Idolatry as Zoetrope

The zoetrope (literally "wheel of life") is a rapidly rotating cylinder with pictures in its interior. The viewer looks through slits in the side of the cylinder to see the pictures appear to come alive. Thus, the zoetrope creates the illusion of motion using static images. Although the first known zoetrope dates to China in the second century AD, the modern zoetrope was invented in 1833 by British mathematician William George Horner (1786-1837). He labeled the device the "daedalum" (based on the Greek myth of Daedalus, father of Icarus, who constructed wax wings for this son), while it was popularly referred to as "the wheel of the devil."

> The Chinese zoetrope, operated by means of rotating vanes turned by the convection currents of a flame, was invented by Ding Huan, who labeled his device "the cylinder that makes fantasies appear."

This is an apt means for describing a certain aspect of idolatry. Idols, like the images in a zoetrope's interior, are static, motionless, and dead. But as the idol cylinder (analogous to the world) is spun, through Satan's guile and craft, the images (idols) seem to leap into action. They seem to come alive, mimicking life through optical illusion. The faster the cylinder spins, the more fluidly the images dance. The more concerted Satan's effort, the more beguiling and mesmerizing the idolatry becomes.

> "What a man desires, he easily believes."

Physical idols merely display idols within the heart. Man constructs idols which represent that which he worships in his inner being. The Bible puts little focus on the physical idol and far more on the inward condition of idolatry. James 4:1 states, "What causes fights and quarrels among you? Don't they come from your desires that battle within you?" Warring desires battle within establishing themselves as the functional and effective rulers of the heart. Idols themselves are dead entities. It is the heart that props them up, animates them, and dispatches them for battle.

> "Some pour out gold from their bags and weigh out silver on the scales; they hire a goldsmith to make it into a god, and they bow down and worship it. They lift it to their shoulders and carry it; they set it up in its place, and there it stands. From that spot it cannot move. Even though someone cries out to it, it cannot answer; it cannot save them from their troubles." (Isaiah 46:6, 7)

A Christian man, crippled from childhood, regularly speaks about his dog as one who can run long distances, can fight off an entire pack of mongrels, and can perform feats of strength. He routinely describes the dog's physical abilities to the neglect of its intelligence, beauty, or disposition. This man lives vicariously through his dog's physicality, assigning to him almost superpower, in an effort to feel connected to that which he himself lacks. The man's descriptions of his dog reveal the longings of his own heart – to be attached to physical health and liberated from the limitations of the somatic.

> As a culture we increasingly worship fictional heroes. Even the stories we believe about our flesh-and-blood heroes are fanciful projections, a self-indulgent fable.

The Idolater as Covenant Maker

In his book, *The World is Flat* (2006), Thomas Friedman presents what he calls the "Dell theory of conflict prevention."[36] This is the idea that nations which participate in Dell Computer's supply chain are highly-unlikely to go to war with one another. Friedman's theory posits that developing countries are desperate to participate in the global supply chain, and once they are part of that chain, they guard it assiduously with assurances of political stability. For a country to lose its credibility as a business partner is to potentially risk billions in revenue and foreign investment, setting it back a decade or more.

Rogue nations such as Afghanistan, Iran, Iraq, and North Korea are not links in the global supply chain, and therefore have no vested interest in preserving peace with the West. In other words, since they derive no economic benefit from Western manufacturing partnerships they see little reason to pursue peace with the West. If, however, these nations could be given economic incentives for peace the entire geopolitical environment might change. The idea is that where there is a vested interest in maintaining peace (financial gain, international prestige, etc.) countries do

---

[36] Thomas Friedman, *The World is Flat: A Brief History of the Twenty-First Century* (New York: Farrar, Straus, and Giroux, 2006) 522.

so. These "peace lines" tend to follow the global supply chain which itself is a cleverly veiled love of money. Friedman's Dell theory reveals something about the nature of idolatry.

> The heart is an idol factory. (John Calvin)

All idolatry follows the contours of man's original design:[37]

1. **Prophet** – proclaiming meaning and purpose

2. **Priest** – bestowing blessing

3. **King** – exercising power[38]

Young Women Looking at Japanese Objects
James Jacques Joseph Tissot, 1869

These three aspects of man's design - prophet, priest, and king, operate in three "covenantal spheres."[39] Within these covenantal spheres one either strikes covenants with idols or with God. Fallen mankind makes covenants with idols in order to extract from them all that was lost in the fall, and these covenants, when threatened, drive people to irrational and wicked behavior. However, when the heart is subdued by God, mankind is given the opportunity, power, and means to recast and reconstitute these covenants.

> "Those who cling to worthless idols forfeit the grace that could be theirs." (Jonah

---

[37] For a discussion of man's original design see "The Image of God: Prophet, Priest, and King" in first book in this series, *Ask for the Ancient Paths: From Art to Artifice to Arisen*, chapter 5: "Redefining the Pygmalion Effect: Exploring the Image of God in Man."
[38] Michael Bobick, *From Slavery to Sonship: A Biblical Psychology for Pastoral Counseling* (1995) (class notes)
[39] Michael Bobick, *From Slavery to Sonship: A Biblical Psychology for Pastoral Counseling* (1995) 40. (class notes)

> 2:8)

The Dell theory of conflict prevention is actually not so much an economic theory as a revelation of covert covenants. As mankind strikes covenants with idols those covenants impel motive, an allegiance of loyalty in exchange for meaning, blessing, and power. In this way, the idol as "I-doll" is used to seek meaning, blessing, and power without (defensive) or against (offensive) God.[40] While Thomas Friedman envisions a supply chain means for global peace, the Bible has something far greater in mind, peace with one's Creator so that worthless covenants are abandoned and enslaving idols are cast off.

> "The LORD said to me, 'Go, show your love to your wife again, though she is loved by another man and is an adulteress. Love her as the LORD loves the Israelites, though they turn to other gods and love the sacred raisin cakes.'" (Hosea 3:1)

The Pantheon of Gods

As an intriguing historical anecdote, until 1860 Greek revival was called "national" style in the United States because it was the country's most popular architecture. Greek revival buildings showcased a vaulted portico and imposing columns to capture the spirit of the Athenian pantheon. The idea was that every American homeowner wanted to own his own little Greek temple.

> "We don't want our buildings merely to shelter us; we also want them to speak to us." (John Ruskin)

The ancient Greeks and Romans erected pantheons to their legions of gods. They named gods for various natural phenomena, professions, and rites of passage (such as marriage and childbearing). They included any plausible god in their temples, even raising an altar to "an unknown god" as Paul referenced.[41] These temples were in effect stone representations of the human psyche. In fact, 1 Corinthians 6:19, 20, sets up this analogy as it describes the human body as a temple specifically designed to house the Holy Spirit. Thus, the human being was designed to showcase, praise, glory in, and glorify the Holy Spirit alone. As Christians profess Jesus Christ to be the only true God and savior of the world, Jesus reigns supreme in bodily temples where he lives on account of the believer's faith, fashioning that temple into his own timeless image.

> Idolatries tend to be construed in the midst of perfectly acceptable social or

---

[40] Michael Bobick, *From Slavery to Sonship: A Biblical Psychology for Pastoral Counseling* (1995) 37. (class notes)
[41] Acts 17:23

> "religious" practice. In the midst of doing good one gives his heart away to other gods.[42]

However, for many who profess Christ, he is merely one god in a pantheon surrounded by scores of equally attractive gods. To call Jesus "Lord" means nothing if one also calls a host of other gods "Lord" as well. (Jesus even said that many who call him Lord, and perform miracles in his name, were unknown to him.[43]) Consider 2 Chronicles 28:24, 25, "Ahaz set up altars at every street corner in Jerusalem. In every town he built high places to burn sacrifices to other gods and provoked the Lord, the God of his fathers, to anger." Just as Ahaz, Israel's king, "set up altars at every street corner," so too, the Christian readily raises altars to false gods within his heart. A Christian often willingly furnishes Jesus a place in his heart as long as Jesus can peacefully coexist with other gods. Such a "double minded" Christian seeks the blessings of a pantheon (all gods).[44] In fact, such a Christian is confused by the notion that Jesus must be his exclusive God, that Jesus must stand alone in his heart, that Jesus cannot harmoniously coexist with other deities. This type of Christian is continually at war, within himself, with others, with the creation, and with God. This war intensifies the more such a Christian tries to achieve détente (the easing of tensions or strained relations, as by agreement, negotiation, or tacit understanding).

> "Fill your bowl to the brim and it will spill. Keep sharpening your knife and it will blunt. Chase after money and security and your heart will never unclench. Care about people's approval and you will be their prisoner." (Lao Zi)

In this regard, while it is correct to understand Jesus as prophet, priest, and king, sinners long to co-opt these titles for their own derelict purposes. Sinners long for a prophet who suits their own interpretation of the world, a priest who comforts them in their sin, and a king who confers worldly power. However, Jesus is firstly a savior. He died to save the sinner from himself, from his own faulty interpretation, from futile attempts to rest in his sin, and from wrongly-wielded power. In short, Jesus saves mankind from his man-centeredness.

The point is that tragically Christians often erect a pantheon to false gods among whom they have tenuously raised an altar to Christ. Christ competes with these other gods for the Christian's devotion, praise, and worship. How does one tear down the false gods one by one, systematically and decisively, in order to allow only Jesus to stand in one's temple? This is the object, focus, and directive of spiritual warfare in the battlefield of the heart.

---

[42] Paul Tripp, *Instruments in the Redeemer's Hands: People in Need of Change Helping People in Need of Change* (Presbyterian and Reformed Publishing, 2002)
[43] Matthew 7:21-23
[44] James 1:8

> One proof of the Bible's veracity is the fact that it at times levels scathing criticism upon God's people. The Bible is not varnished sentimentalism but direct confrontation, often roughly hewn. God frequently confronts his own people for their disobedience, greed, lust, rebellion, and treachery. At times in the past God's wrath burned with fatal consequence, and at others his mercy prevailed in preserving a remnant through which the savior, Jesus Christ, would arise.[45] On account of Jesus' death the Christian is no longer under wrath, but basks in unmerited favor.

The Idol's Allure

Frog Tsarevna (Princess), Viktor Vasnetsov, 1918

Idols could be compared to a fishing lure, nylon thread and wire with a cleverly concealed hook. To a fish the lure looks scintillating and promising, the nourishment it craves. But the lure only brings death. A fishing lure exists for one reason - to deceive, to capture, and to kill the quarry. While it looks like food, in reality it offers no nourishment. It deceives a fish with a promise of sustaining life, but brings death. At the very moment the fish thinks it has won, it has lost.

In the Garden of Eden, Eve noted that the forbidden fruit was good for food and desirable for gaining wisdom.[46] The fruit was neither; it brought choking poisoned

---
[45] Isaiah 11:1-3
[46] Genesis 3:6

death, darkened depraved foolishness, and finally insanity. As Eve saw that which was pleasing to the eye, she blinded herself to the hidden hook.

A fishing lure is perfectly designed for the type of quarry it seeks to catch. If one wants to catch a fish he dangles a fly. If one wants to catch a bear he dangles a fish. If one wants to catch a sinner he dangles promising images and messages of life outside of relationship with God. Just as a captured fish ends up powerless and paralyzed, incapacitated and dead, even more so, fallen mankind ends up cursed as he feeds on Satan's dangled bait.

Deianeira Abducted by the Centaur Nessus
Guido Reni, 1621

> "The chains of habit are too weak to be felt until they are too strong to be broken." (Samuel Johnson)

Just as Adam and Eve thought they could become God, could replace the God of the universe, so too, the allurements of idols offer something of this same promise. The promise is that one can be like God, enjoy the praises of men, fulfilled, blessed, and at peace, but not through relationship with God, through worship of the creation.

> "When tempted, no one should say, 'God is tempting me.' For God cannot be tempted by evil, nor does he tempt anyone; but each one is tempted when, by his own evil desire, he is dragged away and enticed. Then, after desire has conceived, it gives birth to sin; and sin, when it is full-grown, give birth to death." (James 1:13-15)

Whatever one worships occupies his entire range of attention. If one idolizes beauty he is particularly attuned to image. If he idolizes success he focuses attention on whoever has achieved it, and upon how to achieve it. Regardless of the particular bait, that bait entices because it promises acceptance, approval, control, fulfillment, happiness, meaning, pleasure, power, to become a particular image, or to be associated with a particular image. But the bait is never to blame (just as the forbidden fruit was not to blame) since, like Adam and Eve, each is tempted by his own evil desire which drags him away. Temptation is the seed that plants itself in the fertile soil of mankind's desire; that seed soon takes root and flowers into sin and death.

> "We are all just prisoners here of our own device."[47]

Illustrations of how idols often operate:

Purpose	Need (real or perceived)	Idol		Result
		...as manifestation of prideful superiority	...as manifestation of the failed-pride in inferiority	
1. Nourishment	Food	Gluttony	Self-serving denial	Food is used as an escape, or as a means of prideful self-denial.
2. Shelter	Housing	A temple	A hovel	Home becomes a prison, one way or another.
3. Covering	Clothing	Flaunted fashion	Disheveled appearance	Clothing becomes a protective cocoon.
4. Transportation	"Chariot"	A mobile means of respect	A mobile means of mock-humility	A chariot becomes a rolling obsession.
5. Companionship	Spouse	Serves personal vanity and lustful pleasure ("show pony")	Servanthood as a means of self-righteousness	Spouse's love becomes one's master; not a desire to love another, but the desire that another would serve one's purposes.

---

[47] "Hotel California," The Eagles, 1977

| 6. Knowledge | Education | A means of conceit | Anti-establishment, anti-intellectualism | Knowledge creates increased confusion. |
| 7. Hobbies | Recreation | A way to avoid work, project a life of leisure | A life of austerity, self-denial as a means of excuse and control over others | Relaxation as merely an escape and, therefore, as another source of tedium to one seeking relaxation from his guilt before a holy God. |

Idolatry turns an often legitimate need into an object of worship. While God showers mankind with gifts, mankind makes the gift into his god. This is the root motivation for idolatry. It reverses the Creator-creation distinction so that the creation is worshipped.[48] In this way, for the sinner the creation represents a worship liability, as each element of his world becomes another potential conduit through which to express deviant worship.

According to the examples listed above, idolatry works in two principle ways:

1. It functions to advance prideful superiority (a narcissistic desire for worship).

2. It functions to advance the failed-pride in inferiority (a self-righteous desire to be excused from God's standards).

Often the one who uses idols for the purpose of inferiority seeks a perverse nobility, a means of self-justification, or a conjured indignation, through some sustained deprivation. Whatever the motive for idolatry, the heart is a miasma of repugnant pride.

> In 1589 Galileo (1564-1642) performed some of the first known experiments when he dropped objects from the leaning tower of Pisa's upper galleries. In a sweeping upheaval of Aristotelian cosmology, Galileo discovered that objects fall at a uniform rate regardless of their mass. Applied to the issue of idolatry, it is not the "size" of the idol, but its hold upon the heart, that determines its destructive gravitas.

Typical Idols

---

[48] For additional discussion of the Creator-creature distinction see chapter 5: "Metaphors for Sin"

In his epic poem the *Odyssey*, Homer (c. 8th century BC) describes Odysseus navigating between the Scylla and Charybdis, two monsters dwelling on either side of the Strait of Messina separating Sicily from the mainland. It was thought to be impossible to pass through this strait without one of the monsters (represented by a rock on the one side and a whirlpool on the other) attacking and killing the unwitting traveler. Try as he might, Odysseus was forced to confront one of the monsters. This may be a fitting introduction to a catalogue of typical idols. Thus, like the stone and whirlpool, each seeking Odysseus' perdition, so too, idols could be thought of as taking on this "bipolarity."

Colossus of Rhodes, Maerten van Heemskerck, 1570

Modern people tend not to bow before physical statues, but rather give sanctuary to a thriving world of idols within the heart. Internal idols are exactly the same in spirit and intent as external ones. In fact, external idols merely demark where internal idols exist. Thus, the external functions as a type of mirror of the internal. Yet, it is through internal idolatry that the true transgression occurs, so this is the locus of God's attention, tearing down worship strongholds. While external idols are often easily identified (and therefore easily confronted), internal idols are far more insidious and conniving, simply because they so facilely masquerade as good and noble practice.

The following chart offers a catalogue of typical idols. Each idol begins with the statement, "Like only has meaning, I only have worth if…" This is the idol's core formula. Within that formula, offensively-postured idols are those which seek to aggressively take ground from God. These idols are usually straight-forward and more obvious. Defensively-postured idols, on the other hand, are stealthier in that they appear to occupy a position of loss or defeat. (It is worth noting that defensively-postured idols are just as active and aggressive as offensively-postured ones, even while wearing a passive mask.)

Idolatry's Core Formulation: "Life only has meaning, I only have worth if..."[49]	
Offensively-postured Idols	**Defensively-postured Idols**
1. **Acceptance**: One may crave acceptance as assurance that he will never be abandoned or alone.	**Rejection**: The desire to be rejected may dovetail with a personal narrative of superiority and self-righteousness, that the world is blind, corrupt, and foolish.
2. **Control**: Idolatrous control offers the illusion that the world is predictable and that people can be safely managed.	**Lack of all control**: Some want to be out of control either as a mock-form of freedom from all discipline, or as a form of pietism ("Let go and let God").
3. **Ideology**: If one's ideology is dominant and influential then one assumes that he stands on unassailable truth (this lends the feeling of omniscience)	**Irrationalism**: This is the assertion that there is no truth and one can know nothing, the objective being to abandon all sense of absolutes (and its attendant morality).
4. **Image**: One's a particular look or image, whether superior (a tailored Armani suit) or inferior (a disheveled grunge look), becomes his means of delineating the true and good.	
5. **Independence**: One seeks to be completely free of obligations and responsibilities.	**Dependence**: One seeks dependence upon others, or to maintain others' dependence upon oneself.
6. **Intelligence or knowledge**: One asserts himself as the most intelligent or knowledgeable in any circumstance, so that others continually seek him out for answers.	**Anti-intellectual**: One deliberately eschews intelligence and knowledge, casting these as enemies of passion and matters of the heart.
7. **Love**: One either craves to be loved by a particular person, or to have another crave one's love.	**Hatred**: One may relish hatred of another, or to be hated by another. Maintaining a state of war (ultimately

---

[49] Some of the following ideas from Hannibal Silver's Doctor of Ministry project, Westminster Theological Seminary, Philadelphia, Pennsylvania, 1995

		with God) deflects attention from one's lack of given or received love.
8.	**Pleasure**: Experiencing a particular kind of pleasure or quality of life may feel like a sign of victory.	**Suffering**: Suffering (whether physical or emotional) can be a way to draw attention to oneself, and keep others focused and guilty. Playing the "wounded animal" is a way to create distance (or closeness), covering, and immunity from criticism. If one is suffering and wounded, he cannot justifiably be assailed, obliged to love others, or expected to succeed.
9.	**Power**: Power and influence over people may bring with it the rush of a narcotic, the feeling of apotheosis.	**Weak and vulnerable**: Some use weakness and vulnerability as a weapon of control, to keep others continually focused on their well-being, and guilty for not providing adequate care. An external display of weakness can become a convenient excuse for moral failings.
10.	**Racial Ascent**: One believes in an inherent superiority to his race or ethnicity, and vies to make that race ascendant.	**Loathing one's race**: Some are filled with loathing for their own race or ethnicity on account of some real or imagined transgression, or on account of an innate hatred of one's own personal limitations.
11.	**Recognition**: One desires to be recognized for his accomplishments and to excel in his career.	**Forgotten and forsaken**: Some long to be forgotten and forsaken, to feed the personal narrative that one is a tragic hero, an unloved victim.
12.	**Relationship**: One's obsession is that a certain person remain in close relationship, and feel delight in this.	**Reclusive**: Some seek to be relationally isolated so as to feel entitled to self-righteous hatred or bitterness.
13.	**Religion**: One tenaciously upholds his religion's moral codes or rituals.	**Anti-religion**: One seeks to be free of all "religion" so he pursues a self-defined morality attended by subjective beliefs.
14.	**Respect**: One craves respect from others as a hedge against humiliation or irrelevance. This also seems like the antidote to the fears of failure, rejection, and judgment.	**Seeking to be disrespected**: If one can deliberately make himself the recipient of disrespect he can feed a simmering hatred and a brooding sense of entitlement.
15.	**Social Standing**: If one enjoys a certain level of wealth and status he feels a surge of euphoria.	**Shunned and downtrodden**: Some seek a position of low social standing possibly out of a self-righteous hatred of society.

	This could be a way to feel justified in light of one's sin, a way to feel that one has done his penance.
16. **Work**: If one is highly-productive and remains on-task, he feels valued and immune to criticism. Idolatrous productivity can offer a sense of pride and power.	**Leisure**: Some seek to be free form all work, living in perpetual leisure so as to project an image of superiority.

The first observation is that the object of one's idolatry is not necessarily evil in itself (although it certainly may be). Many of the items listed above are good gifts which the idolater metamorphoses into a worship obsession. Often idolatry conceals itself as seemingly noble pursuits such as acquiring knowledge, expressing love, or being devoted to work. Idols wear a mask of godliness, even salvation, wolves in sheep's clothing. For this reason, idolatry easily persists for years, even a lifetime, as it effectively camouflages itself. The greater its mimetic skill in appearing noble and godly, the longer it can thrive unassailed. Judas' supposed concern for the poor in John 12:4-6 is an excellent example.

> But one of his disciples, Judas Iscariot, who was later to betray him, objected, 'Why wasn't this perfume sold and the money given to the poor? It was worth a year's wages.' He did not say this because he cared about the poor but because he was a thief; as keeper of the money bag, he used to help himself to what was put into it.

Also consider John 9:21, 22, concerning the man born blind,

> 'But how he can see now, or who opened his eyes, we don't know. Ask him. He is of age; he will speak for himself.' His parents said this because they were afraid of the Jewish leaders, who already had decided that anyone who acknowledged that Jesus was the Messiah would be put out of the synagogue.

The parents' fear of man was given a plausible camouflage, as deferring to their son's age was made to look prudent and respectful. This was a cunning cloaking device summoned at will to serve their purpose. The fear of man drove them to place even their son in a perilous position. This is a hallmark of idolatry; when an idol is challenged the heart becomes creative, disloyal to all else, and highly-motivated to deflect any menace.

> A professional cartoonist who annually submits thousands of pieces to *The New Yorker* magazine once described the feeling of near incessant rejection. He stated that he had become addicted to rejection to the point that the rare moment of acceptance

> seemed foreign and threatening. He came to embrace rejection as a familiar and comfortable friend.

One who worships his intelligence may deliberately make that which is exoteric esoteric so as to maintain control over others, to continually keep himself at the focal point of discussion, to ensure that his knowledge is in vogue. Thus, the idol operates under the cloak of shadows, appearing needed and noble.

One might outwardly shun greed or sexual lust, and appear virtuous doing so, in order to indulge a lust for the praises of men. The heart, being wicked beyond all reckoning,[50] often knows how to cover sin with masterful deception. Unassailable morality can itself become an idol, which one raises as a clenched fist toward God. Thus, the idolater tries in desperation to make his idol (or stable of idols) appear socially acceptable, innocuous, a right, or even just a minor failing to be easily excused.

> "When people are free to do as they please, they usually imitate each other." (Eric Hoffer)

Idols often appear to be nothing more than healthy ambition, team spirit, zeal, a passion for results, a quiet spirit, a servant's heart, or a studious demeanor. Often that which is idolatrous masquerades as socially acceptable, even commendable, behavior. However, more often than not idolatry shows itself as aggression, anxiety, "buying friends,"[51] complaining, covetousness, cursing, demanding, escapes, fantasies, fear of people, feelings of inferiority and superiority, flattery, grumbling, lust for comfort, lying, manipulation, murder, obsessive control, pessimism, procrastination, self-pity, sexual immorality, slander, violence, and workaholism.

The Smorgasbord of Idols

Consider that the average sled dog can pull double its weight for 120 miles over icy terrain at an average speed of fifteen miles per hour in a single day, and repeat this task everyday for nine days. How is it able to accomplish such a feat? Under heavy exertion muscles sustain tiny tears which release cell plasma, weakening the surrounding muscle. Sled dogs also experience this, but their muscles appear to shift stresses away from damaged muscle fiber. While torn fibers are repaired, new areas of the muscle are exerted. The muscles continually rotate the use of fibers almost as if they are "reprogramming" themselves.

Just as a sled dog's muscles reprogram themselves by rotating healthy and damaged

---
[50] Jeremiah 17:9
[51] This concept from David Powlison, Westminster Theological Seminary, Philadelphia, Pennsylvania

fiber, so too, the heart rotates healthy and damaged (dysfunctional) idols. Idols can be any activity, substance, object, or person. They can be tangible or intangible, simple or complex. The sinner readily mixes and matches idols to accommodate the desires of the heart. Idols take on various hues and forms, shifting and morphing into that which the sinner seeks. In other words, the human heart, in its desperate quest, is undiscriminating in its choice of how to express its idolatry. It can summon any desire, and find any activity, through which to manifest that desire. It can marshal the services of any person or object which appears to be a promising ally in its war against God.

> A Shang Dynasty (1600–1046 BC) emperor once feared a public uprising so he had his army collect the people's metal implements, including their eating utensils. As a result the people invented chopsticks. This may serve as a fitting metaphor for the issues of shifting idols. As one idol is removed often another arises to replace it.

Excursus: The Rise of Gluttony

The King Drinks, Jacob Jordaens, c. 1640

In modern times there has been a progressive increase in the worldwide obesity rate. For example, the average American now consumes 500 more calories per day (2,700) than in 1970 (2,200). That is forty-four pounds more food consumed annually per person. Why has there been such a marked increase in food consumption? Food has become a surrogate psychotropic drug, a way to soothe depression and feelings of inadequacy. Food can also be marshaled to magnify a jubilant heart so that those who are celebratory eat. Likewise, those who seek escape and comfort eat. A growing pattern is that food has become a convenient sympatho-mimetic drug, an enhancer or suppressor of emotion. Food is also an accessible drug for those who cannot afford other escapes such as luxury cars, jewelry, or vacations, so that those in the lower socioeconomic strata may use gluttony as a drug of convenience.

> "Prosperity is only an instrument to be used, not a deity to be worshipped." (Calvin Coolidge)

Idols and the Array of Sins They Spawn

The Chinese classic *The Journey to the West* (西游记) (16th century) contains the story of the monkey king who can assume seventy-two different identities by donning various faces. The idea is that one can change his face and character at will. This, in some way, is a fitting introduction to the issue of how idols transform themselves, assuming various forms depending on the situation at hand. In other words, even with manifold extrinsic characteristics, sundry idols may actually share a common root.

The Bible's concepts of sin and idolatry tend to fall within the same semantic range (their use dictated by emphasis). The concept of sin tends to emphasize the worship condition, while idolatry emphasizes the tangible outworking of that worship. Sin is generally more abstract, idolatry, more concrete. Idols are vivid manifestations of the intentions of the heart, storytellers offering a narrative of the heart's worship. Uncovering idols exposes the heart, discloses its intentions, removes its cloaking devices, and upends its cunning machinations.

Idols create an "asymmetry of integrity" within the heart. Here is an example. A young Christian woman routinely opposed my teaching, searching for ways to discredit my witness for Christ. She was quick to point out seeming contradictions in my interpretation, and was hypersensitive to perceived doctrinal incongruities. However, once she listened to a lecture by a much older teacher under whom she would eventually study. She knew that this teacher would evaluate her as part of a certificate program. In the course of his lecture, this teacher taught obvious doctrinal error and clearly misinterpreted much of Scripture. Yet, this woman blindly acquiesced to his teaching.

Even when exposed to clearly unbiblical teaching, the woman resorted to quiet compliance and convenient ignorance. The point is that this woman upheld doctrinal purity and sound biblical teaching only to the extent that it served her purposes. Conversely, she was quick to search for error when it suited her desires and advanced her agenda. This points to the glaring asymmetry within the heart, a heart which bends and contorts itself to serve its idols, which blindly allows idols to rule its passions and pursuits. Behavior then becomes a confused and tangled web of serving tyrannical gods.

Case Study: Amnon and Tamar: Idolatry and Hatred[52]

What the world calls love is, more often than not, a euphemism and front for idolatrous lust. As with all idolatry, that which appears good and noble can easily serve as a thin veil for that which is depraved. Second Samuel 13 records that Amnon fell in love with his sister, Tamar. However, Amnon did not experience love but burning lust.

> The Chinese idiom *"Ai bu shi shou"* (爱不释手) means to love something so intensely that one is not willing to part with it.

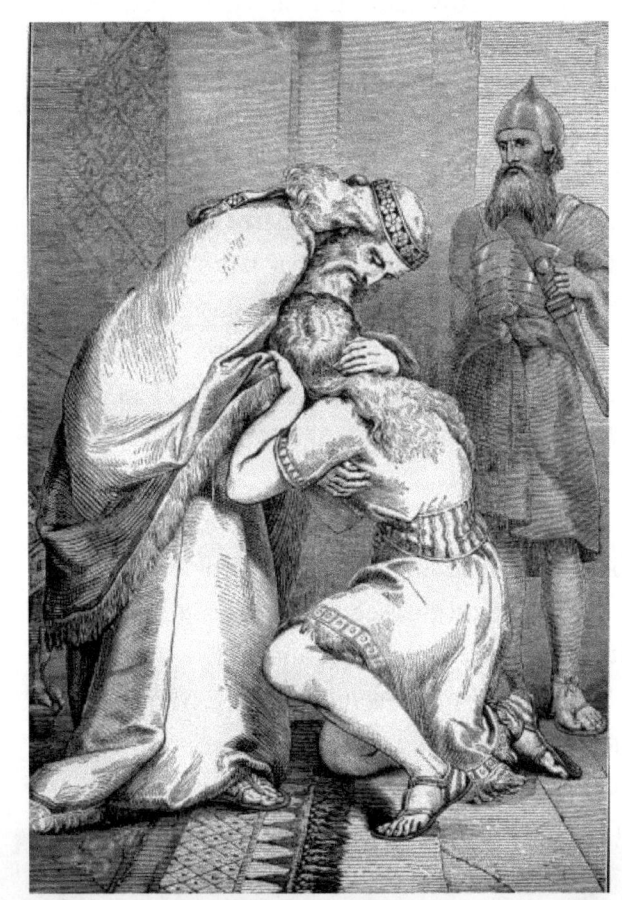

Absalom Pardoned
Cassell, c. 1880 (illustration from *The Child's Bible*)

Amnon became frustrated to the point of physical illness, so that his idolatry left him burdened, controlled, and without peace. He pretended to be ill in a devious plot to get his sister alone. Amnon was even willing to deceive his father, David.

Tamar pleaded with Amnon not to rape her, but he refused to listen. Amnon loved only himself in pursuing his desire. He cared nothing for his sister, since he had made her into an idol. Tamar's incisive cry, "What about me?" revealed that the idolater, Amnon, did not care about, nor remotely love, the object of his idolatry. His entire motive was desperately self-serving. Tamar's question struck to the heart of Amnon's self-obsession, since he cared nothing for her. Tamar then admonished, "And what about you?" warning that Amnon would end up a wicked fool. Amnon refused to listen, but instead only

---
[52] 2 Samuel 13:1-20

focused on satisfying his lust. Nothing else mattered at that moment.

In a shocking reversal, after the rape Amnon hated his sister intensely. The idolater hates that which he worships because he knows that it controls, enslaves, and dominates him. The idolater's recurring pattern is raising up idols and then tearing them down. The idolater deifies that which he desires, bowing to it in homage, only to soon loathe it. Amnon thought that violating his sister would satisfy his lust, but it did the opposite. It left him weaker, more frustrated, and more hopeless than ever before.

Finally, Tamar lived in her brother Absalom's house as a desolate woman, disgraced and forsaken. Two years later, in retribution, Absalom had Amnon murdered.[53]

The story of Amnon and Tamar follows a similar pattern to that found in Revelation 17:4-18, the harlot riding on the beast. The harlot is dressed in purple and scarlet, glittering with gold, precious stones, and pearls. The beast exalts the prostitute, honoring her among the nations. Yet, the beast finally hates the prostitute, bringing her to humiliating ruin. The beast tears her down, burns her, and eats her flesh. This is Satan's mark. He exalts in mock-glory, and then tears down in abject disgust.

> Idolatry is the limiting reagent in love. In other words, one's love for others is limited to the extent of his idolatry. One's love for others tends to accommodate itself to the contours of one's idolatry, so that one's love is delimited by, and under the dictates of, one's idolatry. The idolater cares for others only so long as his idols are not impinged upon.

Plumbing the Depths of the Idol Mine

How long is the British coastline? The answer depends upon the length of one's measuring device, the longer the measuring device the shorter the distance and conversely, the shorter the measuring device the longer the distance. As the measuring device's length approaches zero the length of the coastline

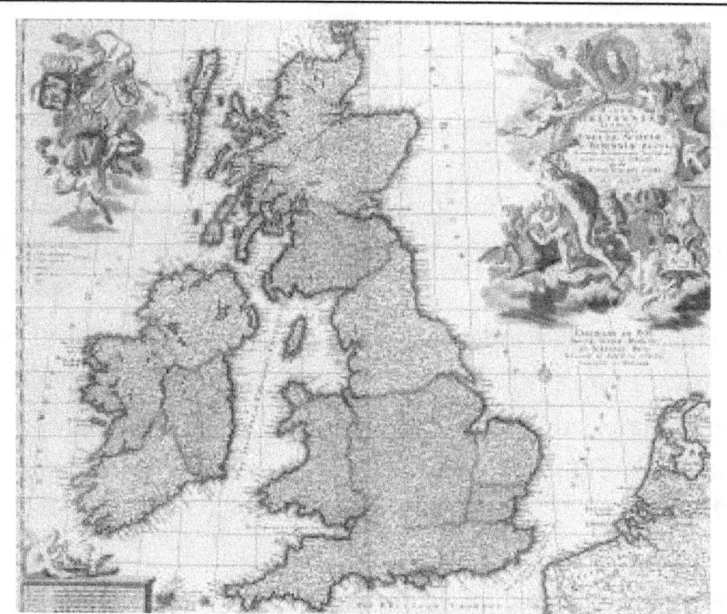

Composite Atlas of Great Britain
c. 1760

---

[53] 2 Samuel 13:29

approaches infinity. This phenomenon is known as the "Richardson Effect" after noted British mathematician Lewis Fry Richardson (1881-1953).[54]

The Richardson Effect could be used to explain heart idols. The more minutely one focuses on one's idols the more one becomes aware that they are infinite in both number and in degree. Additionally, the more refined one's "measuring device" (the intricacy of analysis), the more one uncovers within the heart.

> "The more you try to avoid suffering the more you suffer because smaller and more insignificant things begin to torture you in proportion to your fear of being hurt." (Thomas Merton)

One could organize the data surrounding idols in the following way:

1. Quest (desire)
2. Manifestation (activity/substance)
3. Enlisted allies (persons/objects)

Idols begin with a quest which manifests itself through some chosen means. That quest then enlists allies. Thus, the idol flourishes by means of invisible desire, outward manifestation, and a supporting cast.

> A Christian friend was scheduled to speak in front of a group. Just before he was to speak he told me that he felt "embarrassed." My immediate thought was to comfort him, to build up his confidence. However, I stopped myself. What if what he labels "embarrassment" is merely a euphemism for the fear of man? What if his embarrassment is based in a root distrust of God's goodness and provision? I did not want to merely buoy struggling pride. I did not want to placate an idol battling for his allegiance, or strengthen the fear of man by offering it a refuge in self-confidence. I love him too much to make seeking the praises of men simply work for him. I sought to uproot the idol and replace it with genuine faith.

It is crucial to emphasize that idols are often narrowly viewed from one perspective, that of forward thrusts of desire and obsessive pursuit. Idols must also be viewed from the reverse perspective, that which one fears, hates, eschews, and from which one seeks isolation. Thus, idols exhibit this "push-pull" quality, a magnetism toward the desired objective, and a repulsion from a reviled one.

Idols, thus, form a kind of Rorschach image within themselves. That which one desires also draws out that which he seeks to avoid. Idolatrous avoidance is an often forgotten aspect of dysfunctional worship, but is nevertheless a highly-insidious

---

[54] The Richardson effect not withstanding, most cartographers estimate the British coastline at 10,700 miles.

manipulator. That being said, it must be remembered that one always becomes like that which he worships, whether in the positive (pursuing) or negative (eschewing). Thus, the one who inordinately loves, and the one who inordinately hates, both end up in the same devastated condition.

> All that separates medicine from poison is dosage.[55]

A certain young Christian woman is not at peace in her heart; she is unsettled to her core. Her life is marked by warring idols raised in opposition to God, her relationships littered with conflict, her prayer tense and demanding, her study time chaotic and distracted. This woman often craves comfort, rest, and retreat from her war with God. She seeks out any interaction or situation that makes her feel better, and surrounds herself with those who make her idols function well for her. This woman feels most restful during moments of shielding herself from God, namely from his confrontation of her sin. However, these self-indulgent escapes later exacerbate her inner conflict, tension, and chaos.

Excursus: Barbie® in Iran: The Clash of Idols

Iran, now the world's third largest toy importer, has seen its markets inundated with smuggled Western toys (partly due to a dramatic rise in its consumer purchasing power driven by growing oil revenues). Capping a decade-long struggle to curtail the proliferation of what are considered subversive toys, a top Iranian official recently warned against the destructive cultural consequences of importing Barbie® dolls. While importing Barbie® is not necessarily illegal, the government discourages the practice as it seeks to protect Iranians from what it calls "the negative effects of Western culture."

> "The displays of personalities such as Barbie®, Batman®, Spiderman®, and Harry Potter® ... as well as the irregular importation of unsanctioned computer games and movies are all warning bells to officials in the cultural arena." (an Iranian official)

As far back as 1996, the head of an Iranian government agency labeled Barbie® a "Trojan horse" sneaking in Western influences such as makeup and revealing clothing. Barbie® wears swimsuits and miniskirts in a society where women must don headscarves in public, and where men and women are not allowed to swim together.

Beginning in 2002, authorities confiscated Barbie® dolls from toyshops, denouncing the dolls' anti-Islamic sensibilities. (But the campaign was eventually dropped.) Also in 2002, Iran introduced its own competing dolls, the twins Dara and Sara,[56] designed

---
[55] This concept from Michael Savage, radio host
[56] It is truly fascinating that an Islamic nation such as Iran, with strong ties and identification with Arab nations, would promote a doll named "Sara" since Sarah (c. 19th century BC) was the wife of Abraham and the mother of

to promote traditional Islamic values with their modest clothing and pro-family narratives. But the dolls proved unpopular.

Istanbul Boats, Amedeo Preziosi, d. 1882

The point is not whether Iran is right or wrong to ban Barbie®. What I find noteworthy is that the Iranian government developed competing dolls, Dara and Sara, which proved unpopular. There is something in the human heart, even in young girls, that craves the defiant, the dramatic, the *Verboten* (such as the arguably lustful display of a "Western" Barbie®). Girls, regardless of their culture, do not particularly want to play with dolls representing humility, responsibility, and family-devotion. Thus, Iranian girls, possibly influenced by a flood of Western media, are lured to an independent-minded, anti-authoritarian, and anti-conventional image. No amount of government intervention, no matter how draconian, can ever curtail the heart's idol worship.

Idols in Counterbalance[57]

"One meets his destruction often on the road he takes to avoid it."

The worldviews of naturalism (the basis for Darwinian evolution) and humanism are closely linked. However, if one considers each carefully, they are polar opposites.

Isaac, the progenitor of the Jews. Sarah and her son Isaac are considered the archenemies of Hagar and Ishmael, the ancestors of modern Arab (and Islamic) peoples (see Genesis 16).
[57] For a further discussion of this topic see "The Center Point Theory of Design" in the first book in this series, *Ask for the Ancient Paths*: *From Art to Artifice to Arisen*, chapter 5: "Redefining the Pygmalion Effect: Exploring the Image of God in Man"

Without entering into a lengthy analysis, evolution is built upon the premise that all life is the result of random chemical accidents. Thus, that which arises by accident is of no value. So according to naturalism, life has no inherent worth and therefore can be eliminated at will for any necessary, or unnecessary, purpose. Thus, the basis for Darwinian evolution, when taken to its logical conclusion, denigrates all life. Humans, therefore, are reduced to just another cosmic accident, a precipitous amalgamation of random elements and events with no value or purpose beyond the value and purpose of anything random. Naturalism, as a worldview, is only plausible through inordinate leaps of faith, and the willingness to accept its potentially disastrous consequences.

Humanism, on the other hand, deifies human life, assigning to it noble qualities so that mankind is somehow worthy of worship. Yet, such a belief makes no sense if not based in a God who creates human life, investing it with the noble. Humanism is an illogical outworking of naturalism; the two are incongruous.

The point is that in the modern world naturalism and humanism are inextricably linked, yet they bear no resemblance and no common mission (except to oppose Christianity). So, the question remains, "If they operate as diametric opposites, why then are they linked?"

The answer may lie in the nature of human idolatry. Idols may cohere as couplets, serving as counterbalances to one another. Where one idol seems to veer toward an extreme (rationalism), another seems to offer a corrective (irrationalism). Where one idol seems to belie its own frivolity, another may serve as a civilizing cover or camouflage. There seems to be this dyadic quality to idols, a kind of dialectic co-conspiracy.

However, the question arises, Does a single idol assert itself, and then recede based on the exigencies of the moment, or do partnering idols function simultaneously? This may be difficult to discern. The following example may (or may not) shed light on this.

A certain Christian woman tends toward a self-centered existence. She manipulates others for her own self-aggrandizement, and is insensitive and reckless with regard to other's feelings. She addresses others in a disrespectful way, often lacks basic social etiquette, and generally seems to pursue an undisciplined lifestyle. She focuses on her personal performance, as evidenced by anxiety when asked to meet any task. Speaking with her is often like speaking with a jittery contract attorney, as she makes certain to guard herself with every word. She is highly-critical of others, seeks to be right in every interaction, and uses her intellect to intimidate and control.

Yet, each week this woman attends a worship training class. In that seminar she has a towering emotional experience, an elevation of spirit, in an unfettered opportunity to sing in praise of God. While at the class she describes herself as completely focused on God, deeply repentant, and renewed. Oddly, soon after the worship seminar she returns to her self-centered existence, generally recommitting herself to self-indulgent pursuits.

This woman's experience of unbridled emotional release seems to serve as a counterbalance to her performance-oriented life. She seems to crave relief from her besetting sins and fatigue-inducing idols. More alarmingly, the worship experience seems to exonerate her, posing as counterfeit repentance. She stated that the worship seminar draws her out of her self-focus. While that may sound like a positive development, it is actually a tragic one, as she merely finds an ally for her self-worship, a convenient shield and sword against her God.

Her emotional excursus offers the look and feel of repentance (replete with raised hands, tears, joyful laughter, and loud fervent singing), but in reality is merely an escape from the spotlight on her heart, an artificial repentance that leaves core idols ensconced in their own nacre of God-hatred. Consider Jeremiah 3:4, 5: "Have you not just called to me: 'My Father, my friend from my youth, will you always be angry? Will your wrath continue forever?' This is how you talk, but you do all the evil you can."

This example highlights the need to understand the contours and customs of idols. It would appear that this woman is in covenant with powerful idols of prideful performance, but those idols weary her, beleaguer her, so that she escapes to idols of emotionalism and experientialism where she can find relief for a time. Her assertion of repentance during her worship experience is crafted to guard her core idols. While the worship experience offers sanctuary for this woman's idols, the wise counselor rightly seeks to lovingly undermine this refuge, so that Jesus himself can have supremacy in the heart.

Case Study: The Golden Calf: Idolatry in All Its Malevolent Glory[58]

At a college in a remote part of the world there exists a golden idol high atop a foothill in the heart of the campus. That idol bears a close resemblance to the Asherah poles spoken of in the Old Testament. An Asherah pole entices its beholders to sexual sin, a trenchant idolatry on that campus. While a physical idol is just a metal sculpture, its presence influences hearts. Therefore, my first day on campus, I rose before light and, carrying my Bible, ascended the mountain. I prayed and read Scripture as I

---

[58] Exodus 32:1 – 33:6; for further discussion of this topic see "Moses' Blindness to Foreign Gods Among the People" in chapter 10: "A Nouthetic Analysis of Moses"

circumscribed the six meter tall statue, asking God to bring down this abomination. My prayer was not just that the statue itself would topple, but that the heart idols it spawns would be cast down as well. (After three years of prayer the idol still stands.)

Adoration of the Golden Calf, Nicolas Poussin, 1634

The Israelites seemed magnetically attracted to falsehood, rebellion, and denial of God's goodness and provision. Time and again, the people were enticed from worship of the true God to the worship of idols. When false worship was attended by the attractions of wealth, pleasure and luxury, it naturally offered tremendous temptation for a "simple, restrained, agricultural people, whose worship and law demanded the greatest purity of heart and of life."[59] What follows is a summary of the raising of the golden calf:

1. As Moses met with God on Mount Sinai the Israelites grew impatient.[60] They forgot the deliverance that the Lord had just granted them, victory over the Egyptian army. They forgot the pillars of cloud and fire, and God's fearful display of power in speaking from Mount Sinai. The people craved an immediate god who would wait upon their biding.

2. Aaron instructed the people to relinquish their gold earrings.[61] This refers back to Genesis 35:4, in which Jacob instructed his family to stop worshipping foreign gods and to remove their earrings. (The Egyptians likely wore earrings associated

---

[59] Easton's Bible Dictionary (online version)
[60] Exodus 32:1
[61] Exodus 32:2

with their gods, and Jacob sought to purge this from the Israelites. Therefore, Jacob buried the earrings, and presumably the gods associated with them.) It would appear that on Aaron's watch, Israel, as evidenced by the people's earrings, had reverted back to a longstanding predilection for Egyptian deity worship.

> As a fascinating side note, in Exodus a slave whose ear was pierced with an awl belonged to his master for life.[62] There is some connection between having one's ear pierced and being in a state of slavery.

3. Aaron cast the gold earrings as a calf, and fashioned it with a tool.[63] (Previously, God had commanded Moses that, in building altars, they were not to hew rocks with a tool.)

4. The golden calf could have been the Egyptian god Apis (but some scholars question whether Apis worship existed in Israel at the time of the Exodus). Is it possible that Aaron offered a visual image of Yahweh? The calf may also have been considered a "seat" for Yahweh, as Egyptians gods were frequently pictured seated on animals.

5. Aaron declared, "These are your *gods*, O Israel, who brought you up out of Egypt."[64] Aaron specifically used the plural "gods," as likely the earrings were each considered gods themselves. The people reinterpreted their recent history so that it was not directed by Yahweh's gracious deliverance, but rather by the superstitious luck of their idols. They engaged in revisionist history because it conveniently served their self-centered purposes. They did not so much care which god they served as long as that god serviced their lust, desire, and quest for freedom from fear.

6. Aaron built an altar in front of the calf and announced, "Tomorrow there will be a festival to the Lord."[65] Did Aaron mean that the people were to worship Yahweh at the altar? Was Aaron delusional, now calling the calf the "Lord"?

7. The people rose early to offer sacrifices.[66] Then they ate, drank, and engaged in revelry. The Hebrew word for "revelry," *letsachek* (לְצַחֵק), literally meaning to "play," connotes fornication and adultery. (It is the same word used in Genesis 39:14 in which Potiphar's wife claimed that Joseph made "sport" of her.) Thus, from idolatrous worship was spun off secondary lusts.

---

[62] Exodus 21:6
[63] Exodus 32:4
[64] Exodus 32:4
[65] Exodus 32:5
[66] Exodus 32:6

> The licentious revelries and orgies which attended the worship of foreign gods seem to have been strong attractors for Israel. This points to an often nascent sexual component in idol worship. (However, on the flipside, sometimes idolatry brings with it a self-righteous chastity based in arrogance.)

8. The people offered acceptable sacrifices, but to the wrong god. Their sacrifices were essentially those that the Lord required, but they offered them in rebellion. That which was supposed to glorify God became an attack upon him. (Commentator Adam Clarke (c. 1761-1832) claims that the people illicitly ate the burnt offerings in rebellion.)

> Parties are collective validation. (Carl Jung)

9. God called the people "stiff-necked," a term used to describe oxen.[67] In the ancient Near East a farmer hitched two oxen to a plow and carried a thin rod with an attached metal spike. The farmer used the rod to tap an ox on its neck in order to direct it. An ox that refused to respond to the prod it was labeled "stiff-necked." The term refers to stubborn or intractable people who refuse not listen to God's instruction. It is fascinating that God used this term in referring to the people as they worshipped an ox idol. This seems to indicate that the people had become like that which they worshipped.

10. Moses pleaded with God not to be angry,[68] reminding the Lord of his real enemies, the Egyptians.[69] Moses did not want to afford God's enemies the opportunity to gloat, or to assign wrongdoing to God.

11. Moses reminded God of his covenant with Abraham, Isaac, and Israel,[70] mentioning that God swore by himself. It is crucial to remember that while the people had abandoned the blessings of knowing God, they were still under his covenant faithfulness, since that covenant is monergistic (established and maintained within God's own being). This means that the covenant's continuation is not based on the performance of the lesser party, but remains intact because of God's promise within himself.

12. The tablets Moses carried down from the mountain were the work of God.[71] The writing was God's writing. This is linked to God promise to write his laws into the hearts and minds of his people.[72] While Moses received the law on cold stone tablets, one day that law would be eternalized in living hearts.

---

[67] Exodus 32:9
[68] Exodus 32:11
[69] Exodus 32:12
[70] Exodus 32:13
[71] Exodus 32:16
[72] Jeremiah 31:33; 2 Corinthians 3:3; Hebrews 8:10

Upon descending the mountain, Joshua heard the people shouting. He said to Moses, "There is the sound of war in the camp."[73] Moses responded that it was the sound of singing.[74] As a result of its rebellion Israel, in effect, became a war ravished people. Likewise, the world, on account of idolatry, is at war with God and at war with itself. The world's singing is really the cry of warfare.

13. The tablets of the law had not even made it into the Israelite camp and already they had been grossly transgressed.[75] This indicates the nature of sin; it devastates God's law from the moment of one's conception. Like the people being birthed by means of God's law and rebelling against it, so too, a child is conceived a sinner and born a rebel.[76]

The Death of Moses, Alexandre Cabanel, 1850

14. The golden calf was subsequently burned, pulverized, scattered, and consumed.[77] This image of being ground into powder is the idea of reducing the idol to dust. Dust is the image of death in the Bible. To be pulverized into dust (albeit gold dust) is to be completely and utterly obliterated, so as to be blotted out from memory.

---

[73] Exodus 32:17
[74] Exodus 32:18
[75] Exodus 32:19
[76] Isaiah 48:8
[77] Exodus 32:20

Additionally, the Israelites were made to drink this pulverized gold as a form of punishment.[78]

Exodus 32 foreshadows the harlot of Revelation 17. The harlot is worshipped as she rides on the beast only to later be torn down, burned, and eaten by that same beast. This is the outcome of all idolatry. It ends in utter destruction for both the worshipper and for the object of worship.

However, there is a strange turn of events in the golden calf episode as it is fascinating that gold, a non-tarnishing precious metal, has for millennia been thought to have curative properties. For example, by the end of the third century B.C., Chinese royalty ingested gold as an elixir.[79] Later, Swiss physician, Paracelsus (1493–1541), found gold to possess astonishing medicinal qualities, so that ingesting gold particles suspended in a water solution was thought to heal chronic illness, restore body vitality, and fight depression.

If this medical knowledge is accurate, if gold really does possess health benefits, how does that nuance the interpretation of Exodus 32:20? Could this be a veiled reference to Christ? The people, while fully deserving death, rather than ingesting the cup of God's wrath (as they supposed), were given an elixir which brings healing. These rebels were extended a curative agent, as one day Jesus would drink the cup of God's wrath in their place.[80]

> At Jesus' trial the crowds cried, "Let his blood be upon us and our children."[81] While they intended this as confidence in their murderous actions, they unwittingly called down upon themselves both a curse and a blessing. The curse was that they were guilty of shedding the blood of God's Son; his blood was indeed upon their hands. The blessing was that through shedding that blood they might find eternal life. This bears some similarity to the idea of ingesting the gold of the pulverized idol, a simultaneous curse and blessing invariably pointing to Christ.

15. Aaron was as culpable as anyone for the "great sin" of the people.[82] Yet, he claimed that he merely threw the gold jewelry into the fire and the calf idol unexpectedly emerged.[83]

---

[78] Job 21:20
[79] The Chinese alchemical book *Great Secrets of Alchemy* (《太清丹经要诀》), dating from approximately AD 650, discusses in detail the creation of elixirs for immortality.
[80] Isaiah 53:5; Matthew 26:42
[81] Matthew 27:25
[82] Exodus 32:21
[83] Exodus 32:24

16. The people were running wild,[84] as their idolatry rendered them out of control. Moses interceded on behalf of the people, even requesting that he himself be anathematized rather than to see the people perish.[85]

17. The Lord told the people to remove their ornaments.[86] The people stripped off their ornaments (which were presumably of the same ilk as the earrings used in crafting the golden calf). The ornaments were symbols of Egyptian deities and showed that the people sympathized with, and syncretized their faith in Yahweh with, faith in other gods. The removal of the ornaments was an outward act symbolizing the renunciation of their heart idolatry.

Leviticus 17:4 states that any Israelite who sacrificed an ox, a lamb, or a goat in the camp, or outside of it, instead of bringing it to the entrance to the Tent of Meeting as an offering to the Lord in front of the tabernacle – that man shall be considered guilty of bloodshed. He has shed blood and must be cut off from his people. For the Israelites to offer idolatrous worship was tantamount to committing murder in the eyes of God.

Isaiah 66:3 states,

> But whoever sacrifices a bull is like one who kills a man, and whoever offers a lamb, like one who breaks a dog's neck; whoever makes a grain offering is like one who presents pig's blood, and whoever burns memorial incense, like one who worships an idol.

Therefore, false sacrifices were on par with murder. In this regard, Romans 8:20 states, "the creation was subject to frustration." This may be a muted reference to the practice of sacrificing animals to false gods, those animals therefore dying in vain for idolatrous worship.

> Since the Israelites prostituted themselves to goat idols (the translation could be "goat demons"), the Lord commanded the Israelites to offer all sacrifices at the Tent of Meeting. Leviticus 17:7 states, "They must no longer offer any of their sacrifices to the goat idols to whom they prostitute themselves. This is a lasting ordinance for them and for the generations to come." This may be the basis for the scapegoat mentioned in Leviticus 16:8. The reason for sacrificing a scapegoat may have been to highlight to the Israelites that they were worshipping false gods.

When the Israelites were placed in the midst of idolatrous worship they absorbed it like porous material absorbs smoke. They easily syncretized their worship of God

---

[84] Exodus 32:25
[85] Exodus 32:31, 32
[86] Exodus 33:5, 6

with the worship of idols. Therefore, one of the central lessons of this section is that sinners in the midst of idolatry seem to gravitate toward it. The heart naturally craves faulty worship, and is easily deluded by it.

Moses was partially to blame for the golden calf atrocity.[87] He undoubtedly saw the earrings in the people's ears and the ornaments on their clothing. Yet, while he witnessed the external trappings of idolatry he remained somewhat blind to the people's internal condition. From early on, he should have been counseling them instead of adjudicating civil cases. Sadly, as Joshua 24:14 indicates, the Israelites were not free from Egyptian idols even after their ordeal in the desert. "Now fear the LORD and serve him with all faithfulness. Throw away the gods your ancestors worshiped beyond the Euphrates River and in Egypt, and serve the LORD." Again, in Joshua 24:23, "'Now then,' said Joshua, 'throw away the foreign gods that are among you and yield your hearts to the LORD, the God of Israel.'"

---

[87] For further discussion of this issue see chapter 10: "A Nouthetic Analysis of Moses"

The Idolatry Doppler Shift

Imagine observing an ambulance racing through traffic with its siren blaring. As the ambulance approaches its siren becomes higher pitched, and as it speeds away the pitch deepens. This is the Doppler shift (or Doppler Effect), the shortening or lengthening of sound or light waves based on the relative speed of the object emitting them. The Doppler shift also offers evidence of the known expansion of the universe. As various heavenly bodies speed away from one another they emit light with a slight red cast because of the lengthening of light waves (red being the longest wavelength of light).

Starry Night Over the Rhone, Vincent Willem van Gogh, 1888

An analogy could be made to idolatry which induces a kind of Doppler shift to the human experience. Idolatry skews reality toward a certain "wavelength," causing one's perception to assume a particular cast, to adopt a distinct hue. Each idol could be thought of as a prism through which the world is refracted so that that which is good becomes evil, and evil becomes good. Additionally, sin takes on a transparency so that one is blind to it. Just as the faster the source the greater the Doppler shift, so too, the deeper the idolatrous worship the greater the damaging effect upon the psyche.

What Agreement Is There Between the Temple of God and Idols?

The Idolatry Doppler Shift	The Correction in Christ
1. Distracted	Alert
2. Disrupted	Peaceful
3. Dense	Pliable
4. Dull	Sharpened and perceptive
5. Dependent	Freed from perceived needs
6. Defenseless	Armored in the Holy Spirit
7. Deserted	Adopted
8. Desolate	Bearing abundant fruit
9. Disappointed	Resting in an eternal reward
10. Distressed	Settled
11. Depressed	Joyful
12. Divided/Divisive	Undivided devotion
13. Deceived	Discerning
14. Darkened	Brought to light
15. Demanding	Patient
16. Desperate	Secure
17. Desirous	Desiring only God himself
18. Delusional	In one's right mind
19. Defiant	Submissive
20. Deceitful	Trustworthy
21. Devious	Forthright
22. Debauched	Dignified
23. Defiled	Cleansed
24. Disgraced	Honored
25. Detestable	A fragrant offering
26. Damaged	Restored
27. Defeated	Victorious
28. Destroyed	Glorified
29. Devoured	Prosperous
30. Dead	Resurrected

The ways in which idolatry skews the human experience, or the perception of reality, so that the psyche becomes:

1. Distracted

Solomon's heart was not fully devoted to God, and so he was easily distracted by seducing idols. First Kings 11:2 states, "They were from nations about which the LORD had told the Israelites, 'You must not intermarry with them, because they will surely turn your hearts after their gods.' Nevertheless, Solomon held fast to them in love." Solomon's idolatrous desire for foreign women proved to be his undoing as he bowed in worship to their false gods.

> **In Jesus:** Those in Christ are alert, standing at the watchtower, so that they are prepared to combat evil.
>
> "And pray in the Spirit on all occasions with all kinds of prayers and requests. With this in mind, be alert and always keep on praying for all the Lord's people." (Ephesians 6:18)
>
> "Have nothing to do with godless myths and old wives' tales; rather, train yourself to be godly." (1 Timothy 4:7)

2. Disrupted

Upon descending Mount Sinai with the Ten Commandments, Moses and Joshua heard a commotion in the Israelite camp. "When Joshua heard the noise of the people shouting, he said to Moses, 'There is the sound of war in the camp.'"[1] At its core, idolatry is war with God and casts the world into interpersonal and intrapersonal conflict. The world, with its myriad contending idols, bears the look and feel of battle.

> "If anyone teaches otherwise and does not agree to the sound instruction of our Lord Jesus Christ and to godly teaching, they are conceited and understand nothing. They have an unhealthy interest in controversies and quarrels about words that result in envy, strife, malicious talk, evil suspicions and constant friction between people of corrupt mind, who have been robbed of the truth and who think that godliness is a means to financial gain." (1 Timothy 6:3-5)

> **In Jesus:** The Christian's life wades in an undercurrent of peace so that the Christian can focus upon his God, even in the midst of a turbulent world.
>
> "Do not be anxious about anything, but in every situation, by prayer and petition, with thanksgiving, present your requests to God. And the peace of God, which transcends all understanding, will guard your hearts and your minds in Christ Jesus." (Philippians 4:6, 7)

3. Dense

In idolatry the human spirit becomes fixated, recalcitrant, and obsessed with self-aggrandizing thoughts and behavior. For example, Jeremiah 25:5-7 states,

---
[1] Exodus 32:17

274 WHAT AGREEMENT IS THERE BETWEEN THE TEMPLE OF GOD AND IDOLS?

They said, 'Turn now, each of you, from your evil ways and your evil practices, and you can stay in the land the Lord gave to you and your ancestors for ever and ever. Do not follow other gods to serve and worship them; do not arouse my anger with what your hands have made. Then I will not harm you. But you did not listen to me,' declares the Lord, 'and you have aroused my anger with what your hands have made, and you have brought harm to yourselves.'

> **In Jesus:** The Christian's spirit is sensitive, pliable, and teachable.
>
> In Genesis 35:4, 5, Jacob gathered every foreign god that was found among his family and slaves. As he buried those gods, the fear of God fell upon the towns all around them so that no one pursued them. Turning from false gods brought victory to Jacob's household.
>
> In Jesus believers are given a malleable and teachable spirit which conforms to the need of every situation. Faith in Jesus lends one's spirit the agility to act, move, and think as God's analogue. The believer is freed from fixation with his own personality's modus operandi. He can display outrage, patience, encouragement and joy, all within a single social interaction, continually marshaling the proper response based on how God himself would respond.

The Chess Players, Adolphe Alexandre Lesrel, 1910

4. Dull

The IBM supercomputer "Watson" is rumored to possess artificial intelligence so advanced that it can actually reason. Watson is said to be a quantum leap forward in its ability to interpret paragraph-form writing, a first for a computer. It can process and understand 70 million pages per second, and answer complex questions with a high degree of confidence. Companies which manage risk (especially Wall Street money managers) clamor to employ Watson. (It seems that the lessons of the 2008 global economic crisis have already been forgotten as it was exactly this foolish reliance on blind computer models which primed the financial sector for a precipitous crash.)

Modernism is rife with hubris, the notion that models, metrics, and generated analysis can skillfully navigate a treacherous world of greed, deception, and wanton manipulation. Once again secular humanism is setting humanity up for horrific failure as it continues to hold forth the lie of conquest over human depravity through technology. Because modernist thinking holds no understanding of what generates depravity, it always fails to foresee the consequences of making technology into a savior. In this way, idolatry dulls the idolater as he wrongly analyzes each problem and the supposed solutions.

> "No one stops to think, no one has the knowledge or understanding to say, 'Half of it I used for fuel; I even baked bread over its coals, I roasted meat and I ate. Shall I make a detestable thing from what is left? Shall I bow down to a block of wood?'" (Isaiah 44:19)
>
> "...so that, 'they may be ever seeing but never perceiving, and ever hearing but never understanding; otherwise they might turn and be forgiven!'" (Mark 4:12)

> **In Jesus:** The Christian's mind is renewed, sharpened, and perceptive.
>
> "Whoever has ears, let them hear what the Spirit says to the churches." (Revelation 3:22)

5. Dependent

> "From the rest he makes a god, his idol; he bows down to it and worships. He prays to it and says, 'Save me! You are my god!'" (Isaiah 44:17)

The idolater finds himself dependent upon his idol to meet perceived needs for acceptance and validation. For example, Genesis 29:14 – 30:24 recounts Jacob's marriage to Leah and Rachel. Jacob's father-in-law, Laban, deceived him into marrying Laban's older daughter Leah, even though they had struck a deal for Rachel.

As it turned out, Jacob loved Rachel more than Leah.[2] In response, the Lord opened Leah's womb, but closed Rachel's.[3] Leah persisted in getting pregnant in the futile hope of eventually winning her husband's favor. With each son she thought, "Now at last my husband will become attracted to me...." Upon her fourth pregnancy, she finally resolved to stop seeking her husband's love as she stated, "This time I will praise the Lord."[4]

Meanwhile Rachel, who was barren, grew envious of her older sister. She eventually pleaded with Jacob, "Give me children, or I'll die!"[5] Rachel turned over to her husband her maidservant, Bilhah, in order to conceive a child. In response, Leah also gave Jacob her maidservant in order to bear a son.[6]

As each sister bore yet another son, she sought ascendant status in the eyes of both Jacob and the surrounding community.[7] With an air of victory, Leah stated, "This time my husband will treat me with honor, because I have borne him six sons."[8] Rachel, likewise, with the birth of her final son, Joseph, enthused, "God has taken away my disgrace."[9]

Each woman sought acceptance, love, superiority, and vindication through bearing children. Childbearing had become less about raising and caring for children, and more about a self-serving means to gain what they sought in their idolatry. Thus, the idol (seeking status and honor) kept them each dependent on a promised means of delivery from their fears. However, as with all false worship, the idol was never satisfied. It was not until Leah praised the Lord that she gained her first glimpse into freedom from idolatrous obsession.

> **In Jesus:** The Christian is no longer held captive to satisfying perceived needs.
>
> "Be devoted to one another in love. Honor one another above yourselves." (Romans 12:10)
>
> "It is for freedom that Christ has set us free. Stand firm, then, and do not let yourselves be burdened again by a yoke of slavery." (Galatians 5:1)

6. Defenseless

Exodus 32:25 reads, "Now when Moses saw that the people were out of control—for

---
[2] Genesis 29:30
[3] Genesis 29:31
[4] Genesis 29:35
[5] Genesis 30:1
[6] Genesis 30:9, 10
[7] Genesis 30:13
[8] Genesis 30:20
[9] Genesis 30:23

Aaron had let them get out of control to be a derision among their enemies—" Idolatry caused the Israelites to become gluttonous and sexually immoral. As the people grew undisciplined, they became vulnerable to their enemies. For example, Balaam, unable to curse Israel, exploited its glaring immorality for the sinister purposes of the Midianite king, Barak.[10]

> **In Jesus:** The Christian has been given indomitable armor to resist and defeat Satan's schemes. The Christian's defense is a pure heart which flees temptation under the guidance of God's Word.
>
> "Finally, be strong in the Lord and in his mighty power. Put on the full armor of God, so that you can take your stand against the devil's schemes. For our struggle is not against flesh and blood, but against the rulers, against the authorities, against the powers of this dark world and against the spiritual forces of evil in the heavenly realms. Therefore put on the full armor of God, so that when the day of evil comes, you may be able to stand your ground, and after you have done everything, to stand." (Ephesians 6:10-13)

Case Study: Contrasting Armor

Goliath Laughs at David, Ilya Repin, 1915

First Samuel 17 describes in vivid detail the contrast between Goliath, in full armor, and David, brandishing a mere slingshot. This foreshadows the armor-reversal offered to those in Christ.

---

[10] Numbers 31:16

Goliath	**David**	**Christ/Those in Christ**
A champion[11]	Youngest son,[12] tending his father's sheep in Bethlehem;[13] told Saul not to lose heart; promised to fight Goliath;[14] when a lion or bear carried off sheep, David struck it and killed it.[15]	"Be strong in the Lord and in his mighty power;"[16] put on the full armor of God; take one's stand against the devil's schemes;[17] the Christian's struggle is not against flesh and blood but against the world and evil.[18]
Stood nine feet tall[19]	A boy, ruddy and handsome[20]	Nothing in his appearance that one should desire him[21]
Wore a bronze helmet[22]	Rejected Saul's bronze helmet[23]	The Christian is given the helmet of salvation.[24]
		Wears the belt of truth[25]
Wore a bronze coat of scale armor (57 kg)[26]	Rejected Saul's coat of armor[27]	The Christian receives the breastplate of righteousness.[28]
Carried a sword[29]	Rejected Saul's sword[30]	The Christian brandishes the sword of the Spirit (the Word of God).[31]
Wore bronze greaves[32]		The Christian's feet are ready with the gospel of peace.[33]
Carried a bronze javelin[34]	Carried a shepherd's staff[35]	Christ carried his cross.[36]

[11] 1 Samuel 17:4
[12] 1 Samuel 17:14
[13] 1 Samuel 17:15
[14] 1 Samuel 17:32
[15] 1 Samuel 17:34, 35
[16] Ephesians 6:10
[17] Ephesians 6:11
[18] Ephesians 6:12
[19] 1 Samuel 17:4
[20] 1 Samuel 17:42
[21] Isaiah 53:2
[22] 1 Samuel 17:5
[23] 1 Samuel 17:38
[24] Ephesians 6:17
[25] Ephesians 6:14
[26] 1 Samuel 17:5
[27] 1 Samuel 17:38
[28] Ephesians 6:14
[29] 1 Samuel 17:51
[30] 1 Samuel 17:39
[31] Ephesians 6:17
[32] 1 Samuel 17:6
[33] Ephesians 6:15
[34] 1 Samuel 17:6

Carried a spear shaft like a weaver's rod with an iron point (7 kg)[37]	Placed five smooth stones from the stream in his shepherd's bag; carried a sling[38]	Upon Jesus' death his side was pierced with a spear so that blood and water flowed from his side.[39]
Sent a shield bearer ahead of him[40]		The Christian takes up the shield of faith to extinguish the flaming arrows of the evil one.[41]
Challenged any Israelite to fight[42]		"As a sheep before her shearers is silent…"[43]
Defiant for forty days[44]		The Christian is able to stand his ground;[45] Jesus fasted in the desert for forty days and remained submissive to the Father.[46]
Cursed David by his gods[47]	Stepped forward in the name of the Lord[48]	The Christian is called to pray in the Spirit[49]
	Triumphed with sling and stone[50]	
	Decapitated Goliath with Goliath's own sword[51]	Jesus crushed Satan's head to the Christian's aeonian benefit.[52]

7. Deserted

> "I will do this to recapture the hearts of the people of Israel, who have all deserted me for their idols." (Ezekiel 14:5)

Luke 15:13 states, "Not long after that, the younger son got together all he had, set off for a distant country and there squandered his wealth in wild living." The prodigal,

---

[35] 1 Samuel 17:40
[36] John 19:17
[37] 1 Samuel 17:7
[38] 1 Samuel 17:40
[39] John 19:34
[40] 1 Samuel 17:7
[41] Ephesians 6:16
[42] 1 Samuel 17:10
[43] Isaiah 53:7
[44] 1 Samuel 17:16
[45] Ephesians 6:13
[46] Matthew 4:1-11
[47] 1 Samuel 17:43
[48] 1 Samuel 17:45
[49] Luke 6:28; Ephesians 6:18
[50] 1 Samuel 17:50
[51] 1 Samuel 17:51
[52] Genesis 3:15

once he had in his possession all that he thought he needed, deserted his father. As a result of his idolatry, however, the prodigal would soon find himself deserted by those he had "purchased" as friends. That is the character of idolatry; it leaves the idolater deserted, parched, forgotten, and forlorn.

On the Desert, Jean-Léon Gérôme, c. 1867

> **In Jesus:** The Christian finds his home in God himself and, therefore, is never abandoned, never forsaken.[53]
>
> "You will seek me and find me when you seek me with all your heart." (Jeremiah 29:13)
>
> "Jesus replied, 'Anyone who loves me will obey my teaching. My Father will love them, and we will come to them and make our home with them.'" (John 14:23)

8. Desolate

Numbers 20:22-29 states that Moses' brother, Aaron, died in dishonor on Mount Hor. He was stripped naked and led up the mountain to die ashamed and alone. Aaron died

---

[53] Hebrews 13:5

a desolate and disgraced priest on account of his co-conspiracy at the waters of Meribah. Aaron's bitter end is a foretaste of Hosea 9:2-4:

> Threshing floors and winepresses will not feed the people;
>   the new wine will fail them.
> They will not remain in the LORD's land;
>   Ephraim will return to Egypt
>   and eat unclean food in Assyria.
> They will not pour out wine offerings to the LORD,
>   nor will their sacrifices please him.
> Such sacrifices will be to them like the bread of mourners;
>   all who eat them will be unclean.
> This food will be for themselves;
>   it will not come into the temple of the LORD.

Each begins life as a sinner and worsens his own plight with each passing day. Each becomes more deeply depraved as he continues in his self-constructed sinful "ecosystem." In this way the sinner's life irretrievably migrates toward greater desolation outside of Christ. As the outer man wastes away, this reflects the wasting away of the inner man with aeonian consequence.

> **In Jesus:** Jesus is the Christian's source of living water so that in him the Christian is no longer a desolate parched land but bears abundant fruit.
>
> "Others, like seed sown on good soil, hear the word, accept it, and produce a crop--some thirty, some sixty, some a hundred times what was sown." (Mark 4:20)
>
> "Jesus answered her, 'If you knew the gift of God and who it is that asks you for a drink, you would have asked him and he would have given you living water.'" (John 4:10)

9. Disappointed

I once had a neighbor who took on various hobbies to satisfy his restless spirit. His first hobby was showing dogs. He invested tremendous time and energy training and grooming his dogs. But they soon grew old, and he tired of the shows. He then took up woodworking, transforming his basement into a near professional workshop in which he constructed precision clocks, cabinets, and other furniture.

He soon tired of woodworking and adopted a passion for sports cars. Each of his cars seemed to meet with some tragedy, however. His first car was severely damaged in an ice storm. Another had vexing mechanical problems; still another was stolen. He was an unsettled motoring enthusiast, as his cars never seemed to satisfy his cravings.

Next he purchased the largest fish tank that his house could structurally sustain, filling it with thousands of dollars in exotic fish. Unwisely, he introduced a sand shark into the tank and one day discovered the shark alone. He later became certified in scuba diving and traveled throughout the world in search of thrilling underwater adventures.

He tired of diving and took up building and racing model airplanes. Eventually most of his handiwork ended up in splinters on the ground. He moved on to speedboats but the outcome was the same, a lost and lonely pursuit that never measured up to his expectations. Each hobby left him chronically disquieted.

I wish my neighbor had read the book of Ecclesiastes which traces the trajectory of a godless life to its logical terminus - searing angst. (He could have saved himself a tremendous amount of time and energy.) Like all who seek meaning outside of God, my neighbor found himself unsettled to his core. He searched the world for thrills and was left wanting. Each new hobby visited upon him a more embattled spirit, a flailing longing, an emptiness that never found satisfaction. In fact, this was God's supreme mercy to him so as to afford him no rest in the things of this world. This highlights the towering disappointment associated with idolatry, a disappointment which is God's hidden mechanism leading idolaters to faith in Jesus Christ.

> "Those who cling to worthless idols turn away from God's love for them." (Jonah 2:8)

> **In Jesus:** The Christian is confident in the hope that he will meet a satisfied conclusion in the eternal reward promised by his God.
>
> "Until now you have not asked for anything in my name. Ask and you will receive, and your joy will be complete." (John 16:24)
>
> "May the God of hope fill you with all joy and peace as you trust in him, so that you may overflow with hope by the power of the Holy Spirit." (Romans 15:13)

Excursus: The Growth of Personal Wealth and Dissatisfaction

Humanism brazenly touts the triumph of economic growth over material want, so that want is thought to be eliminated. In actuality, the world is witnessing the enslaving triumph of material want over humanity. Why? Material want is infinite and can never be conquered within the unregenerate human spirit. The exponential rise in global abundance brings with it heightened desire, envy, greed, and lust.

> God orchestrated American prosperity as a means to a gospel-centered end (to bring Christ to the world), but sadly that prosperity has become the end in itself, and for this reason it will end.

Yachting in the Mediterranean, Julius LeBlanc Stewart, 1896

A trend has emerged concerning the global explosion of personal wealth. As income increases, dissatisfaction with income increases far more sharply. Thus, the more one has the more one wants, to a disproportionate degree, so that one can never earn enough to slake the desire. This seems counterintuitive. Shouldn't burgeoning wealth bring greater contentment? The sinful heart is construed in such a way that envy increases exponentially as one's wealth increases, and there is no human cure for envy. Thus, even though wealth briefly boosts happiness, there is a magnetic pull to acquire even more wealth.

Consider this same argument with regard to any other form of idolatry such as lust for image, sexuality, power, or achievement. The more one has of idolatrous gain the greater one's thirst for it. For example, seeking to satisfy sexual lust breeds ever more sexual lust. Thus, the supposed sexual revolution (currently taking hold of the world) has produced quite the opposite, the subjugation of humanity to ever rising desire. The answer is not asceticism (which merely assumes a form of godliness, yet is powerless to transform the desiring heart). The answer is the total transformation of the heart through God's indwelling Spirit, the ability to quell the seemingly insatiable and replace it with empowerment to live in accordance with holiness.

284 WHAT AGREEMENT IS THERE BETWEEN THE TEMPLE OF GOD AND IDOLS?

10. Distressed

> "Whenever Israel went out to fight, the hand of the LORD was against them to defeat them, just as he had sworn to them. They were in great distress." (Judges 2:15)

In Jesus: The Christian is joyful and peaceful, even in affliction. He may be hard pressed, but does not despair.

"Be joyful in hope, patient in affliction, faithful in prayer." (Romans 12:2)

"We are hard pressed on every side, but not crushed; perplexed, but not in despair; persecuted, but not abandoned; struck down, but not destroyed. We always carry around in our body the death of Jesus, so that the life of Jesus may also be revealed in our body. For we who are alive are always being given over to death for Jesus' sake, so that his life may be revealed in our mortal body." (2 Corinthians 4:8-11)

11. Depressed

George Washington at Valley Forge, Thompkins H. Matteson, 1854

George Washington (1732–1799) was usually the tallest strongest man in a room. (He was so strong, in fact, that he could bend a horseshoe with his bare hands.) This lent him superlative confidence. However, as Washington aged he slowly lost his strength, triggering frequent bouts with depression.

George Washington, based his security, prestige, and meaning on physical prowess. This was the foundation on which he built his social status, and from which he maintained control, even tacitly, over others. As the idol of physical strength slowly waned, he became melancholic because he no longer felt that sense of control. With age, his idol was exposed as worthless, and with it his previous basis for negotiating the world.

> "When Jesus heard this, he said to him, 'You still lack one thing. Sell everything you have and give to the poor, and you will have treasure in heaven. Then come, follow me.' When he heard this, he became very sad, because he was very wealthy." (Luke 18:22, 23)

> **In Jesus:** The Christian experiences unceasing joy, regardless of circumstance, because his joy is built upon a solid rock that cannot be shaken.
>
> "However, as it is written: 'What no eye has seen, what no ear has heard, and what no human mind has conceived -- the things God has prepared for those who love him—'" (1 Corinthians 2:9)
>
> "Consider it pure joy, my brothers and sisters, whenever you face trials of many kinds," (James 1:2)
>
> "In all this you greatly rejoice, though now for a little while you may have had to suffer grief in all kinds of trials. These have come so that the proven genuineness of your faith—of greater worth than gold, which perishes even though refined by fire—may result in praise, glory and honor when Jesus Christ is revealed." (1 Peter 1:6, 7)

12. Divided/Divisive

Knowing full-well God's promise of a son through his wife Sarah, Abraham agreed to his wife's demands to father a child through her Egyptian maidservant, Hagar.[54] Why would Abraham abandon God's promise of an heir?[55] Remember, in Genesis 15:6, Abraham trusted God, and in 15:9–18, God established an eternal covenant with him. Yet, Abraham was quick to abandon God's provision in the burning sun of his wife's pressing demands.[56]

Abram showed an invidious weakness in blindly placating his wife, a weakness on

---

[54] Genesis 16:2
[55] Genesis 15:4
[56] See the case study "An Analysis of Abraham" in chapter 5: "Metaphors for Sin"

account of her beauty.[57] Abraham appeared to be so utterly hapless and helpless in the midst of his wife. He seemed to fall into Adam's transgression, allowing his wife to dictate the nature of the relationship, being passive and irenic when he should have stepped forward with wise command. For example, Abraham was complicit in Sarah's abuse of her maidservant Hagar, tacitly giving his wife authority to mistreat another.[58] This is the curse of idolatry, a divided heart which quickly turns away from recognized truth to placate the will of those one worships. Romans 7:21-23 echoes this as Paul stated that he wanted to do good but evil was right there with him, waging war against the law of his mind.

Hagar in the Wilderness
Giovanni Tiepolo, c. 1726

> "But when you ask, you must believe and not doubt, because the one who doubts is like a wave of the sea, blown and tossed by the wind." (James 1:6)

> **In Jesus:** The Christian can experience undivided devotion to Christ, a devotion that offers freedom from doubt.
>
> "Then we will no longer be infants, tossed back and forth by the waves, and blown here and there by every wind of teaching and by the cunning and craftiness of people in their deceitful scheming." (Ephesians 4:14)
>
> "And have you completely forgotten this word of encouragement that addresses you as a father addresses his son? It says, 'My son, do not make light of the Lord's discipline, and do not lose heart when he rebukes you, because the Lord disciplines the one he loves, and he chastens everyone he accepts as his son.' Endure hardship as

---

[57] Genesis 12:11
[58] Genesis 16:6

> discipline; God is treating you as his children. For what children are not disciplined by their father?" (Hebrews 12:5-7)

13. Deceived

Former president William Henry Harrison (1773–1841) was a decorated general in the Battle of Tippecanoe of 1811, and was later commended for a key victory in the War of 1812. At age sixty-eight Harrison was elected president, taking office on March 4, 1841. The day of his inauguration was cold and wet, yet Harrison refused to don a hat and overcoat. He wanted to project an image of toughness and resiliency as a former war hero. In addition, he insisted on delivering a two-hour speech.

At his inauguration, William Harrison caught pneumonia which did not show itself until three-weeks later. When the symptoms did arise, he desperately needed rest but refused himself repose, as he was busy negotiating with office-seekers flooding the White House. Harrison died thirty days after taking office.

The circumstances surrounding Harrison's death indicate something about the issue of idolatry. Harrison felt a need to project a particular image to his eventual demise. Possibly lusting for the praises of men, he also allowed himself to be harangued by visitors to the extent that he could not make a life-saving recovery.

> "For sin, seizing the opportunity afforded by the commandment, deceived me, and through the commandment put me to death." (Romans 7:11)

> **In Jesus:** The Christian is invested with life-altering wisdom and discernment.
>
> "He replied: 'Watch out that you are not deceived. For many will come in my name, claiming, 'I am he,' and, 'The time is near.' Do not follow them.'" (Luke 21:8)
>
> Acts 17:29, 30 states that God is not gold, silver, or stone; he is not an image of man's design and skill. In the past God overlooked such ignorance but now commands men everywhere to repent.
>
> "It is because of him that you are in Christ Jesus, who has become for us wisdom from God—that is, our righteousness, holiness and redemption. Therefore, as it is written: 'Let the one who boasts boast in the Lord.'" (1 Corinthians 1:30, 31)
>
> "See to it that no one takes you captive through hollow and deceptive philosophy, which depends on human tradition and the elemental spiritual forces of this world rather than on Christ." (Colossians 2:8)

14. Darkened

> "For although they knew God, they neither glorified him as God nor gave thanks to him, but their thinking became futile and their foolish hearts were darkened." (Romans 1:21)

With the rise of Adolf Hitler (1889-1945) in 1930s Germany, anti-Semitism was gaining ground. Jews were steadily being excluded from academia, politics, corporations, literary circles, journalism, and the practice of law. In an effort to stem the tide of anti-Semitism, Jews produced books and pamphlets highlighting Jewish contributions to German philosophy, literature, technology, jurisprudence, and the arts. The Jews hoped to persuade the Nazis that they were valuable and loyal citizens, not a liability as previously thought.

However, the plan tragically backfired. With greater understanding of Jewish achievements, the Nazis redoubled their efforts to purge the nation of its Jews. The Nazis interpreted Jewish contributions as an attempt to hijack German culture, and to transform Germany into a Jewish state. Aryan pride asserted itself with far greater vigor when faced with the prospect that Jews were rival thinkers and visionaries.

This ugly episode in world history reveals an insidious aspect of idolatry. It is not rational and cannot be logically reasoned out of the heart. German Jews wrongly sought in the Nazis an innate goodness and reasonability, to which they could appeal. They assumed that the Nazis would prize cultural contributions and, thus, abandon petty misanthropic prejudices. However, the Nazis prioritized their own cultural achievement and ethnic superiority above all else, railing against the notion that outsiders had contributed to building the nation. The idol of nationalism darkened the German soul so that it viewed Jews as sub-human intruders to be expunged. Thus, began the systemic extermination of the Jews.

> **In Jesus:** The Stygian darkness of the human soul is brought into the light so that it adjudges truth rightly. In fact, in Jesus, the believer becomes light itself.[59]
>
> "The eye is the lamp of the body. If your eyes are healthy, your whole body will be full of light. But if your eyes are unhealthy, your whole body will be full of darkness. If then the light within you is darkness, how great is that darkness!" (Matthew 6:22, 23)
>
> "In him was life, and that life was the light of all mankind." (John 1:4)
>
> "But if we walk in the light, as he is in the light, we have fellowship with one

---

[59] Matthew 5:14; John 12:36

> another, and the blood of Jesus, his Son, purifies us from all sin." (1 John 1:7)

15. Demanding

> "When the people saw that Moses was so long in coming down from the mountain, they gathered around Aaron and said, 'Come, make us gods who will go before us. As for this fellow Moses who brought us up out of Egypt, we don't know what has happened to him.'" (Exodus 32:1)

A "Napoleon complex" is the idea that men of small stature are overly aggressive as a way to compensate for their perceived loss of social respect. The idea is that men of diminutive stature become obsessively focused on gaining something that they feel they lost, seeking any means to draw attention to themselves. (It is odd that most musicians and billionaires tend to be of slight stature.) There is a certain craving of the heart, a non-descript demand of the soul, a seeking validation, which at its root is nothing more than human vanity in full flight.

The Coronation of Napoleon (detail), Jacques-Louis David, 1808

> **In Jesus:** The Christian patiently rests in God's provision recognizing that nothing he needs will ever be withheld from him.
>
> "…you anoint my head with oil; my cup overflows." (Psalm 23:5b)

> "Then some soldiers asked him, 'And what should we do?' He replied, 'Don't extort money and don't accuse people falsely--be content with your pay.'" (Luke 3:14)
>
> "Do not take revenge, my dear friends, but leave room for God's wrath, for it is written: 'It is mine to avenge; I will repay,' says the Lord." (Romans 12:19)

16. Desperate

In Genesis 31:14 Jacob ordered his wives Rachel and Leah to leave their father's country and flee to Canaan. The sisters questioned if they still had an inheritance in their father's estate. They worried that their father had squandered their dowry, and felt that the wealth God had taken from their father belonged to them. On impulse, before fleeing Rachel stole her father's household gods,[60] and eventually deceived her father concerning their whereabouts.[61] Rachel's actions seemed to be driven by a desperate love of wealth.

A later example, 2 Samuel 13:2, states that Amnon was frustrated to the point of illness on account of his sister Tamar, whom he claimed to love. Amnon soon orchestrated an evil plan to isolate his sister and rape her. Idolatry drives sinners to desperate acts which unravel in a downward spiral of deadly deception.

> **In Jesus:** The Christian has been given supreme confidence, security, and satisfaction in Christ. There is something strangely Quixotic about the Christian life, a participation in a grand and ever-evolving adventure that never grows wearisome.
>
> "Some trust in chariots and some in horses, but we trust in the name of the LORD our God." (Psalm 20:7)
>
> "So don't be afraid; you are worth more than many sparrows." (Matthew 10:31)
>
> "Do not let your hearts be troubled. You believe in God; believe also in me." (John 14:1)

17. Desirous

In his landmark work, *The Romantic Ethic and the Spirit of Modern Consumerism* (1987), Colin Campbell propounds the thesis that modern consumerism cunningly transformed itself into a template for moral superiority. The consumer who employs the latest technology, sports the finest clothing, and enjoys the highest living standard

---
[60] Genesis 31:19
[61] Genesis 31:35

is somehow viewed as morally upright, a better provider, and a sound manager of life.

The vigorous consumer is also viewed as supporting the economy and creating jobs. In fact, certain automobile advertisements in the 1950s encouraged sales by stating that each domestic car purchase put one American to work for three months. Thus, purchasing a car was a patriotic and altruistic way to provide others with jobs and a stable livelihood. After September 11, 2001, the mayor of New York, Rudolph Giuliani, encouraged New Yorkers to frequent local restaurants as a way to bolster the city's bruised economy. Those who patronized a restaurant were seen as bettering the plight of others, helping to maintain those who might be struggling. Likewise, then President Bush encouraged those receiving federal tax rebates to spend them as a patriotic gesture of confidence in the American economy.

In these seemingly sound justifications for a consumer culture one views the machinations of the sinful heart. The consumer machine writes a narrative which promises to disambiguate the love of pleasure and the love of others. The grand plan is to make purchasing a morally upright act so as to assuage the conscience, to make conspicuous consumption appear altruistic. However, one sees yet another facet of the idolatrous heart, a heart that desires inordinately, and relentlessly searches for moral justification for that desire.

Consider young David's two questions in 1 Samuel 17:26. "David asked the men standing near him, 'What will be done for the man who kills this Philistine and removes this disgrace from Israel? Who is this uncircumcised Philistine that he should defy the armies of the living God?'"

On account of his first question, it would appear that David desired something other than God's glory in his imminent battle with Goliath. Did he secretly crave power, wealth, prestige, respect, or the attention of women? One can only speculate. But his question about the benefit to the one who killed Goliath seems to belie his supposed faith (evidenced in the second question). Does one spy a kernel of rebellion in David that would take root and flower as he aged? Romans 1:24 offers a window into what eventually became of David's desire. "Therefore God gave them over in the sinful desires of their hearts to sexual impurity for the degrading of their bodies with one another."

> **In Jesus:** The Christian is given a new heart which shuns the things of the world and desires only God himself.
>
> "Peter answered him, 'We have left everything to follow you! What then will there be for us?'" (Matthew 19:27)

> "But if we have food and clothing, we will be content with that." (1 Timothy 6:8)
>
> "The world and its desires pass away, but whoever does the will of God lives forever." (1 John 2:17)

18. Delusional

In AD 79 the coastal city of Pompeii, Italy was suddenly blanketed in scorching ash from nearby Mount Vesuvius. The inhabitants were interred so quickly that there was no possibility of escape. Many remains have been unearthed perfectly intact, just as they were at the moment of death. One such corpse was found clenching a sword and standing next to a pile of gold. It appears that a wealthy merchant foolishly guarded his gold even at the moment of his death.

Pygmalion and Galatea
Louis Gauffier, 1797

Moses' brother Aaron fashioned the golden calf in the sight of the Israelites. Yet, Exodus 32:24 states, "'So I told them, 'Whoever has any gold jewelry, take it off.' Then they gave me the gold, and I threw it into the fire, and out came this calf!'"

> "No one recalls, nor is there knowledge or understanding to say, 'I have burned half of it in the fire and also have baked bread over its coals. I roast meat and eat it. Then I make the rest of it into an abomination, I fall down before a block of wood!' He feeds on ashes; a deceived heart has turned him aside. And he cannot deliver himself, nor say, 'Is there not a lie in my right hand?'" (Isaiah 44:19, 20)

> "They say to wood, 'You are my father,' and to stone, 'You gave me birth.' They have turned their backs to me and not their faces; yet when they are in trouble, they say, 'Come and save us!'" (Jeremiah 2:27)

Habakkuk 2:19 states, "Woe to him who says to wood, 'Come to life!' Or to lifeless stone, 'Wake up!' Can it give guidance? It is covered with gold and silver; there is no breath in it." The idolater invests life into the object of his idolatrous worship. As ridiculous as it may sound, the idolater seeks to make his inanimate idol come to life so that he can feel as though it relates to him, delivers him, and reinvigorates him with abundant life.

> **In Jesus:** The Christian lives in reality, having come to his senses, and having been restored to "his right mind" (the mind of Christ).[62]
>
> "When they came to Jesus, they saw the man who had been possessed by the legion of demons, sitting there, dressed and in his right mind; and they were afraid." (Mark 5:15)
>
> "When he came to his senses, he said, 'How many of my father's hired servants have food to spare, and here I am starving to death!'" (Luke 15:17)

Excursus: Delusional Idolatry

A renowned comedian owns one of the most prized private car collections in the world, more than 200 vintage and exotic cars. This comedian annually invests millions into purchasing, restoring, and maintaining his collection. He employs full-time mechanics and runs a sophisticated machine shop capable of complete auto restoration.

This man casts his passion for cars in noble terms. He makes car restoration appear to be a high-calling, so much so, that many throughout the world praise him for preserving yesteryear. He is looked to as an "automobile savior," one who restores and cares for cars that might otherwise remain abandoned in barns or fields. He is heralded as a true patriot for preserving cars of the golden age of American motoring. This man also specializes in caring for "orphaned" cars, those which were ahead of their times, but for which the motoring public was not prepared. All this makes his hobby appear virtuous and eminently altruistic. Thus, a well-crafted public relations narrative functions to lionize his man's work.

However, there is a delusional idol lurking in the depths, subtexts which emerge

---

[62] Mark 5:15

revealing the deeper, more insidious, nature of the human heart. This comedian sometimes mentions having been embarrassed as a teenager as he drove his parents' car (since he could not afford his own). He even spoke of his father once being humiliated when purchasing a car.

This comedian speaks about an early plan to become wealthy so that he could finally afford desirable cars, and so that he would in turn be desired by others. Certain flashpoints in his adolescent quest for an automobile reveal a lust for respect. He speaks about his early longing for a car that would command the attention of his peers, and most importantly, draw girls. The longing for female attention seems to have been a chief motivator; he even uses the epithet "pretty girls" to refer to his cars. He routinely jokes about a particular car's ability to "get girls." There is a consuming drive to finally acquire a car that would give him all he longs for, and all that he believes he was denied.

As an auto aficionado, this man can now feel included in an exclusive club among the desirables. In his mind he has "won." He has succeeded in the battle to be respected and admired, a "somebody," at least in the automotive world. The teenager who was left out, forgotten, looked down upon, and humiliated, has now exacted the revenge he always sought. He now owns cars that turn heads; he is the center of attention.

On occasion, this comedian has spoken about his car collection as a socially acceptable substitute for marital infidelity or drug abuse, keeping him out of trouble with his wife and the law. In reality, his car collection has become nothing more than a cleverly disguised form of infidelity and addiction, albeit one that society condones, even applauds.

Despite his outward success, this man remains a lost, empty, afraid, longing, and deluded idolater. He is still prisoner to the idolatrous heart that he has always had. Now he just has the wherewithal to live out that idolatry and bring it to full flower. From the Bible's perspective this man is in fact in a far worse condition than he ever was. His idolatry has progressively hardened his heart, ossified his spirit, and more deeply beguiled and enslaved him. In the final analysis, this man has rushed forward into error as he worships at the altar of his idol.

Thus, a common pattern with idolatry is that it leaves indelible marks upon the soul. One longs for something that he cannot get so he spends his life vying, striving, longing, grasping, chasing, and competing, always under the illusory promise that his prize lays just one step ahead. Each person wastes his life chasing that for which he lusted early on. The heart's cunning is to make that pursuit appear acceptable, noble, laudable, and socially admirable so that the idol remains firmly ensconced in plausible vindication.

> "Wrongs are often forgiven, but contempt never is. Our pride remembers it forever." (Lord Chesterfield)

19. Defiant

> "When the people of Ashdod rose early the next day, there was Dagon, fallen on his face on the ground before the ark of the LORD! They took Dagon and put him back in his place." (1 Samuel 5:3)
>
> "[King Nebuchadnezzar] said, 'Is not this the great Babylon I have built as the royal residence, by my mighty power and for the glory of my majesty?'" (Daniel 4:30)

The idolater maintains his pride and asserts his superiority even in sinfully abandoning his idols. He only relinquishes his worship commitments on his own terms, for his own purposes, to serve his own agenda, while making himself appear godly in the midst of supposed defeat. That becomes his secret victory. For example, one who must surrender his livelihood only does so in a manner that allows him to maintain his sense of moral integrity and dignity.

> **In Jesus**: Those in Christ are submissive to God.
>
> "…if my people, who are called by my name, will humble themselves and pray and seek my face and turn from their wicked ways, then I will hear from heaven, and I will forgive their sin and will heal their land." (2 Chronicles 7:14)
>
> "Submit yourselves, then, to God. Resist the devil, and he will flee from you." (James 4:7)

20. Deceitful

> "Their heart is deceitful, and now they must bear their guilt. The LORD will demolish their altars and destroy their sacred stones." (Hosea 10:2)

Saul exploited his own daughter in a plot to trap and control David. First Samuel 18:20-22 states,

> Now Saul's daughter Michal was in love with David, and when they told Saul about it, he was pleased. Saul thought, 'I will give her to him that she may become a snare to him, and that the hand of the Philistines may be against him.' Therefore Saul said to David, 'For a second time you may be my son-in-law today.' Then Saul commanded his servants, 'Speak to David

secretly, saying, 'Behold, the king delights in you, and all his servants love you; now therefore, become the king's son-in-law.'

Saul cared nothing for his daughter; she was an expendable pawn on the chessboard of his greater ambitions. Saul's idol was political control, and he was willing to sacrifice anyone and anything to that end.

> "All you need to say is simply 'Yes' or 'No'; anything beyond this comes from the evil one." (Matthew 5:37)

> **In Jesus:** A heart of deception is transformed into an honest and upright heart.
>
> "I am sending you out like sheep among wolves. Therefore be as shrewd as snakes and as innocent as doves." (Matthew 10:16)
>
> "Do not let any unwholesome talk come out of your mouths, but only what is helpful for building others up according to their needs, that it may benefit those who listen." (Ephesians 4:29)

David and Saul
Julius Kronberg, 1885

21. Devious

> "The Lord says:
> 'These people come near to me with their mouth
>   and honor me with their lips,
>   but their hearts are far from me.
> Their worship of me
>   is based on merely human rules they have been taught.
> Therefore once more I will astound these people
>   with wonder upon wonder;
> the wisdom of the wise will perish,
>   the intelligence of the intelligent will vanish.

> Woe to those who go to great depths
>   to hide their plans from the Lord,
> who do their work in darkness and think,
>   Who sees us? Who will know?'" (Isaiah 29:13-15)

Consider Genesis 12:11-13, in which Abram asked his wife Sarai to prevaricate so that Pharaoh might be duped into thinking that she was Abram's sister. Abram, fearing for his life, hatched a devious plot which brought grave calamity.

> **In Jesus:** Those in Christ are given his Spirit to be honest, forthright, and trustworthy in all things.
>
> "Do not let any unwholesome talk come out of your mouths, but only what is helpful for building others up according to their needs, that it may benefit those who listen." (Ephesians 4:29)
>
> "Now the overseer is to be above reproach, faithful to his wife, temperate, self-controlled, respectable, hospitable, able to teach," (1 Timothy 3:2)

22. Debauched

> "So the next day the people rose early and sacrificed burnt offerings and presented fellowship offerings. Afterward they sat down to eat and drink and got up to indulge in revelry." (Exodus 32:6)

> **In Jesus:** The heart is purified so that it hates sin. Additionally, the heart is invested with the discipline to maintain purity.
>
> "Blessed are the pure in heart, for they will see God." (Matthew 5:8)
>
> "Do not get drunk on wine, which leads to debauchery. Instead, be filled with the Spirit," (Ephesians 5:18)

23. Defiled

> "'If a man divorces his wife and she leaves him and marries another man, should he return to her again? Would not the land be completely defiled? But you have lived as a prostitute with many lovers-- would you now return to me?' declares the LORD." (Jeremiah 3:1)
>
> "I said to them, 'Cast away, each of you, the detestable things of his eyes, and do not defile yourselves with the idols of Egypt; I am the LORD your God.' But they

rebelled against Me and were not willing to listen to Me; they did not cast away the detestable things of their eyes, nor did they forsake the idols of Egypt." (Ezekiel 20:7, 8)

Snow Maiden
Viktor Vasnetsov, 1899

In Jesus: The Christian is purified, cleansed, raised up, and made holy.

"How much more, then, will the blood of Christ, who through the eternal Spirit offered himself unblemished to God, cleanse our consciences from acts that lead to death, so that we may serve the living God!" (Hebrews 9:14)

"Now that you have purified yourselves by obeying the truth so that you have sincere love for each other, love one another deeply, from the heart." (1 Peter 1:22)

24. Disgraced

"You burn with lust among the oaks, and under every spreading tree; you sacrifice your children in the ravines and under the overhanging crags. The idols among the smooth stones of the ravines are your portion; indeed, they are your lot. Yes, to them you have poured out drink offerings and offered grain offerings. In view of all this, should I relent?" (Isaiah 57:5, 6)

"For of this you can be sure: No immoral, impure or greedy person—such a person is an idolater—has any inheritance in the kingdom of Christ and of God." (Ephesians 5:5)

In Jesus: Those in Christ are honored sons and daughters.

"Who may ascend the mountain of the LORD?

> Who may stand in his holy place?
> The one who has clean hands and a pure heart,
>   who does not trust in an idol
>   or swear by a false god." (Psalm 24:3, 4)
>
> "Humble yourselves before the Lord, and he will lift you up." (James 4:10)

25. Detestable

There was a fascinating and chilling social regression in early first century Roman culture, so that by the second century AD the Romans had largely abandoned their temples in favor of the theater. The temple simply no longer wielded much social clout, while the theater increasingly became a focal point of social commentary and intellectual stimulation.

But the Romans slowly tired of theatrical dramas and tragedies. They soon craved armed conflict, carnage, and bloodshed for entertainment. They converted their ampitheaters into centers for mock naval battles, held in what were once the theatrical chorus areas (ironically, used for the expression of social inquiry and conscience), as well as for gladiator and animal carnage. As a symbol of how far Roman culture had fallen, the front theater seats, reserved for nobles, were removed to provide more room for tunnels to channel wild animals into the arena. The populace was reduced to a single surging mass hungry for bloodshed. This historical fragment offers a window into the world of idolatry, a world filled with all manner of detestable practice, practice often lauded by society.

Quite ironically, the world calls *God's* character and plans detestable. For example, in Exodus 8:26 Moses warned Pharaoh that the Israelite worship would be "detestable" to the Egyptians so that they would stone the Israelites. This again points to the desperate insanity of idolatrous worship, a labeling of the holy as abhorrent, and the accursed as laureate. (An example is the issue of abortion in which the world labels the pro-life stance a baseless encroachment, while the murder of the unborn is seen as a protected right.)

> "Because of all your detestable idols, I will do to you what I have never done before and will never do again." (Ezekiel 5:9)
>
> "Therefore say to the people of Israel, 'This is what the Sovereign LORD says: Repent! Turn from your idols and renounce all your detestable practices!'" (Ezekiel 14:6)

> **In Jesus:** Those in Christ are a royal priesthood, a fragrant offering to their God.

> "But thanks be to God, who always leads us as captives in Christ's triumphal procession and uses us to spread the aroma of the knowledge of him everywhere. For we are to God the pleasing aroma of Christ among those who are being saved and those who are perishing. To the one we are an aroma that brings death; to the other, an aroma that brings life. And who is equal to such a task?" (2 Corinthians 2:14-16)
>
> "…and walk in the way of love, just as Christ loved us and gave himself up for us as a fragrant offering and sacrifice to God." (Ephesians 5:2)
>
> "But you are a chosen people, a royal priesthood, a holy nation, God's special possession, that you may declare the praises of him who called you out of darkness into his wonderful light." (1 Peter 2:9)

26. Damaged

In 1 Kings 18:28, as the priests of Baal worshipped their god, they cut themselves with swords. Idolatry causes grave damage to the human soul (and at times, to the body). It is a caustic agent ravaging God-given design, and stripping human sensibilities, so that one is finally rendered a burned-out husk.

> **In Jesus:** The idolater's life can be restored and rebuilt to that which is far greater than ever existed in his original design. Faith in Jesus does not merely restore the sinner to the pre-fall state, it recasts him into that which is vastly more glorious.
>
> "The thief comes only to steal and kill and destroy; I have come that they may have life, and have it to the full." (John 10:10)

27. Defeated

> "Whenever Israel went out to fight, the hand of the LORD was against them to defeat them, just as he had sworn to them. They were in great distress." (Judges 2:15)

Robert Service (1874–1958) wrote, "It isn't the mountain ahead that wears you out. It is the grain of sand in your shoe." Idolatry is like a grain of sand in the shoe that wears down one's resistance, and ultimately ushers in one's demise. In the midst of his war with God, the idolater gambles that false gods will offer final victory, but they instead render one slowly defeated. Clinging to false gods always ends in tragic loss of a far greater nature than one ever imagined.

Marshall Ney at Retreat in Russia, Adolphe Yvon, d. 1893

> **In Jesus:** The Christian participates in an assured victory, despite not fully realizing that victory in this life.
>
> "I have told you these things, so that in me you may have peace. In this world you will have trouble. But take heart! I have overcome the world." (John 16:33)
>
> "No, in all these things we are more than conquerors through him who loved us." (Romans 8:37)
>
> "Everyone who competes in the games goes into strict training. They do it to get a crown that will not last, but we do it to get a crown that will last forever." (1 Corinthians 9:25)

28. Destroyed

Lou Lan Gu Cheng (楼兰古城) was a storied city along the Silk Road in modern day Xin Jiang Province, China. Legend holds that this opulent and decadent city, during a sunny day, was mysteriously buried in a sandstorm and obliterated from history. Its inhabitants, thought to be especially beautiful and proud, perished without warning. This legend offers a glimpse into the idolater's final condition - destruction.

> "But if your heart turns away and you are not obedient, and if you are drawn away to bow down to other gods and worship them, I declare to you this day that you will certainly be destroyed." (Deuteronomy 30:17, 18)
>
> "They set up kings without my consent; they choose princes without my approval. With their silver and gold they make idols for themselves to their own destruction." (Hosea 8:4)
>
> "Their destiny is destruction, their god is their stomach, and their glory is in their shame. Their mind is set on earthly things." (Philippians 3:19)

Everything thought, said, and done without glorifying Jesus is sin. This is the heart's insanity, that it would live for an illusory surrogate glory outside of Christ. The insanity arising through sin authors a man-centered man-directed and man-glorifying story, in which mankind reckons itself the victor over its desperate state. Like boarding boxcars to Birkenau, the story has a perilous ending, man's self-destruction through his own idolatrous worship. The insanity is thinking that any other outcome is possible.

> **In Jesus:** Those in Christ are already glorified and will one day be resurrected in full realization of that glory.
>
> "For as in Adam all die, so in Christ all will be made alive." (1 Corinthians 15:22)
>
> "And you also were included in Christ when you heard the message of truth, the gospel of your salvation. When you believed, you were marked in him with a seal, the promised Holy Spirit, who is a deposit guaranteeing our inheritance until the redemption of those who are God's possession—to the praise of his glory." (Ephesians 1:13, 14)

29. Devoured

> "You will perish among the nations; the land of your enemies will devour you." (Leviticus 26:38)

> **In Jesus:** The Christian is restored to abundant prosperity (not as the world defines prosperity), the prosperity of a contrite heart at peace with its God.
>
> "Humble yourselves, therefore, under God's mighty hand, that he may lift you up in due time. Cast all your anxiety on him because he cares for you." (1 Peter 5:6, 7)

30. Dead

Idolatry results in spiritual death so that the sinner is a walking corpse, an animated cadaver, merely going through the motions of his life on God's gracious life-support.

The Duel After the Masquerade, Jean-Léon Gérôme, c. 1859

"For when we were in the realm of the flesh, the sinful passions aroused by the law were at work in us, so that we bore fruit for death. But now, by dying to what once bound us, we have been released from the law so that we serve in the new way of the Spirit, and not in the old way of the written code." (Romans 7:5, 6)

In Jesus: The Christian has been raised from death to life in Christ, so that in this new life idols might finally die.

"But because of his great love for us, God, who is rich in mercy, made us alive with Christ even when we were dead in transgressions—it is by grace you have been saved. And God raised us up with Christ and seated us with him in the heavenly realms in Christ Jesus," (Ephesians 2:4-6)

Conclusion

Idolatry creates a kind of Doppler shift within the human psyche and experience. That shift affects each sinner every moment of every day, to varying degrees in various situations. The Doppler shift is the idea that the many facets of idolatry (outlined above) skew the psyche's function with disastrous consequence, consequence that may not be readily seen, but nevertheless works with perilous effect. Thus, the shift is pronounced, decisive, and ultimately indomitable outside of Christ.

Those in Christ, however, have entered a reality in which the idolatry Doppler shift is reversed, its effects negated, and its skewing influence corrected. It is not just that God applies a canceling effect (a blue shift to an idolatrous red shift, for example), but something far greater. Those in Christ experience a newness of life, free from the curse of enslaving idols, so as to live fruitfully and abundantly.

- 8 -

THE SEARCH FOR ELDORADO ENDS:
Repenting of Idols of the Heart

Saint Ignatius in Glory (America detail), Fra Andrea Pozzo, c. 1691

Uncovering Idols: Back to the Basics

"If you wish to learn the highest truths begin with the alphabet." (Japanese proverb)

Nineteenth century children learned the alphabet through the nursery rhyme, "The Tragical Death of A, Apple Pie, Who Was Cut in Pieces, and Eaten by Twenty-Six Gentlemen, With Whom All Little People Ought To Be Very Well Acquainted." This rhyme seems to capture much of the nature of idolatry as it reveals the various ways and means by which idols arise and manifest themselves. Each of the rhyme's action verbs represents a distinct manifestation of heart idols, so that one could reinterpret the rhyme from the perspective of uncovering idols.

---

[1] This chapter might contain the traditional theological concept of "adoption."

Action Verb	What Idolatry Manifests of the Heart	Answered in Christ
A was an apple pie		
B bit it	The heart longs to taste the supposed sweetness of the idol. "Food gained by fraud tastes sweet, but one ends up with a mouth full of gravel." (Proverbs 20:17) "I tell you, not one of those who were invited will get a taste of my banquet." (Luke 14:24)	"Taste and see that the LORD is good; blessed is the one who takes refuge in him." (Psalm 34:8)
C cut it	The idolatrous heart is divided. "Jesus knew their thoughts and said to them, 'Every kingdom divided against itself will be ruined, and every city or household divided against itself will not stand.'" (Matthew 12:25)	"I in them and you in me—so that they may be brought to complete unity. Then the world will know that you sent me and have loved them even as you have loved me." (John 17:23)
D dealt it	The idolatrous heart is filled with scheming. "…a heart that devises wicked schemes, feet that are quick to rush into evil," (Proverbs 6:18)	"Rather, we have renounced secret and shameful ways; we do not use deception, nor do we distort the word of God. On the contrary, by setting forth the truth plainly we commend ourselves to everyone's conscience in the sight of God." (2 Corinthians 4:2)
E eats it	The heart feeds on its idols. "The discerning heart seeks knowledge, but the mouth of a fool feeds on folly." (Proverbs 15:14)	"Whoever eats my flesh and drinks my blood has eternal life, and I will raise them up at the last day." (John 6:54)
F fought for it	The idolatrous heart is	"The LORD will fight for you;

	consumed with warring desires. "What causes fights and quarrels among you? Don't they come from your desires that battle within you?" (James 4:1)	you need only to be still." (Exodus 14:14)
G got it	The idolatrous heart grabs for life. "But when [Tamar] took it to [Amnon] to eat, he grabbed her and said, 'Come to bed with me, my sister.'" (2 Samuel 13:11)	"For I am the LORD your God who takes hold of your right hand and says to you, Do not fear; I will help you." (Isaiah 41:13)
H had it	The heart experiences loss and regret in its idolatry. "For I know my transgressions, and my sin is always before me." (Psalm 51:3)	"Godly sorrow brings repentance that leads to salvation and leaves no regret, but worldly sorrow brings death." (2 Corinthians 7:10)
I inspected it	The heart weighs ungodly gain. "…in whose hands are wicked schemes, whose right hands are full of bribes." (Psalm 26:10)	"I made a covenant with my eyes not to look lustfully at a young woman." (Job 31:1) "Everyone has heard about your obedience, so I rejoice because of you; but I want you to be wise about what is good, and innocent about what is evil." (Romans 16:19)
J jumped for it	There is often momentary, but fleeting, happiness associated with the idol. "Men worshiped the dragon because he had given authority to the beast, and they also worshiped the beast and asked, 'Who is like the beast? Who can make war against him?'"	"Rejoice in that day and leap for joy, because great is your reward in heaven. For that is how their ancestors treated the prophets." (Luke 6:23)

		(Revelation 13:4)
K kept it	The idolater hoards that which he desires. "And I'll say to myself, 'You have plenty of grain laid up for many years. Take life easy; eat, drink and be merry.' But God said to him, 'You fool! This very night your life will be demanded from you. Then who will get what you have prepared for yourself?' This is how it will be with whoever stores up things for themselves but is not rich toward God." (Luke 12:19-21)	"But store up for yourselves treasures in heaven, where moths and vermin do not destroy, and where thieves do not break in and steal." (Matthew 6:20)
L longed for it	Idolatry brings searing longing. "Among those nations you will find no repose, no resting place for the sole of your foot. There the Lord will give you an anxious mind, eyes weary with longing, and a despairing heart." (Deuteronomy 28:65) "The wicked will see and be vexed, they will gnash their teeth and waste away; the longings of the wicked will come to nothing." (Psalm 112:10)	"Meanwhile we groan, longing to be clothed instead with our heavenly dwelling, because when we are clothed, we will not be found naked." (2 Corinthians 5:2)
M mourned for it	The idolater is finally filled with grieving. "The roads to Zion mourn, for no one comes to her appointed festivals. All her gateways are desolate, her priests groan, her young women grieve, and she	"Nehemiah said, 'Go and enjoy choice food and sweet drinks, and send some to those who have nothing prepared. This day is holy to our Lord. Do not grieve, for the joy of the Lord is your strength.'" (Nehemiah 8:10)

		is in bitter anguish." (Lamentations 1:4)	"And do not grieve the Holy Spirit of God, with whom you were sealed for the day of redemption." (Ephesians 4:30)
N nodded at it		The idolater offers honor and obeisance to his idols. "'Do not make idols or set up an image or a sacred stone for yourselves, and do not place a carved stone in your land to bow down before it. I am the LORD your God.'" (Leviticus 26:1)	"Come, let us bow down in worship, let us kneel before the LORD our Maker..." (Psalm 95:6) "On coming to the house, they saw the child with his mother Mary, and they bowed down and worshiped him. Then they opened their treasures and presented him with gifts of gold, frankincense and myrrh." (Matthew 2:11)
O opened it		The heart invests itself into its idols.	"Jesus said to her, 'I am the resurrection and the life. The one who believes in me will live, even though he dies...'" (John 11:25)
P peeped in it		Idolatry nurtures the lust of the eye. "Do not lust in your heart after her beauty or let her captivate you with her eyes." (Proverbs 6:25)	"It was revealed to them that they were not serving themselves but you, when they spoke of the things that have now been told you by those who have preached the gospel to you by the Holy Spirit sent from heaven. Even angels long to look into these things." (1 Peter 1:12)
Q quartered it		The idol finally becomes an object of hatred to be destroyed. "The beast and the ten horns you saw will hate the prostitute. They will bring her to ruin and leave her naked; they will eat her flesh and burn	"'Therefore, I tell you, her many sins have been forgiven--as her great love has shown. But whoever has been forgiven little loves little.'" (Luke 7:47) "...save others by snatching them from the fire; to others

		her with fire." (Revelation 17:16)	show mercy, mixed with fear--hating even the clothing stained by corrupted flesh." (Jude 1:23)
R	ran for it	The idolater rushes into evil pursuits. "Their feet rush into sin; they are swift to shed innocent blood. Their thoughts are evil thoughts; ruin and destruction mark their ways." (Isaiah 59:7)	"But those who hope in the LORD will renew their strength. They will soar on wings like eagles; they will run and not grow weary, they will walk and not be faint." (Isaiah 40:31) "How beautiful on the mountains are the feet of those who bring good news, who proclaim peace, who bring good tidings, who proclaim salvation, who say to Zion, 'Your God reigns!'" (Isaiah 52:7)
S	stole it	Idolatry drives one to ill-gotten gain. "Such are the paths of all who go after ill-gotten gain; it takes away the life of those who get it." (Proverbs 1:19)	"Commit your way to the LORD; trust in him and he will do this: He will make your righteous reward shine like the dawn, your vindication like the noonday sun." (Psalm 37:5, 6) "Unlike so many, we do not peddle the word of God for profit. On the contrary, in Christ we speak before God with sincerity, as those sent from God." (2 Corinthians 2:17)
T	took it	The idolatrous heart is consumed with drawing all of creation into the service of itself. "'Come, let's drink deep of love till morning; let's enjoy ourselves with love!'"	"Give to everyone who asks you, and if anyone takes what belongs to you, do not demand it back." (Luke 6:30)

		(Proverbs 7:18)	
U upset it	Idolatry may experience peace for a brief moment, but that peace quickly takes flight. "But the wicked are like the tossing sea, which cannot rest, whose waves cast up mire and mud. 'There is no peace,' says my God, 'for the wicked.'" (Isaiah 57:20, 21)	"'I have seen their ways, but I will heal them; I will guide them and restore comfort to Israel's mourners, creating praise on their lips. Peace, peace, to those far and near,' says the LORD. 'And I will heal them.'" (Isaiah 57:18, 19)
V viewed it	The idolater loves to behold his idol, thinking that it is lasting beauty. "Do not love the world or anything in the world. If anyone loves the world, love for the Father is not in them." (1 John 2:15)	"For God, who said, 'Let light shine out of darkness,' made his light shine in our hearts to give us the light of the knowledge of God's glory displayed in the face of Christ." (2 Corinthians 4:6)
W wanted it	The idolater is consumed with burning desire. "They said to you, 'In the last times there will be scoffers who will follow their own ungodly desires.'" (Jude 1:18)	"Therefore, I urge you, brothers and sisters, in view of God's mercy, to offer your bodies as a living sacrifice, holy and pleasing to God--this is your true and proper worship." (Romans 12:1) "Flee the evil desires of youth and pursue righteousness, faith, love and peace, along with those who call on the Lord out of a pure heart." (2 Timothy 2:22)
X, Y and **Z** all wished for and had a piece in hand	Acting upon the object of its lust, the heart allows lust to fully flower. "Of what value is an idol carved by a craftsman? Or an image that teaches lies? For the one who makes it trusts in his	"Sanctify them by the truth; your word is truth. As you sent me into the world, I have sent them into the world. For them I sanctify myself, that they too may be truly sanctified." (John 17:17)

| | own creation; he makes idols that cannot speak." (Habakkuk 2:18) | |

The Idol's Circle of Safety

Some readers may remember the blockbuster movie, "Raiders of the Lost Ark" (1981) in which the hero Indiana Jones ventured into a Peruvian cave guarded by the Hovito tribe. Jones sought the tribe's golden idol. However, claiming this idol would prove a death-defying ordeal. In his quest Jones encountered gregarious tarantulas, a light-activated impaling gate, a yawning chasm, and poisonous blow darts. In the breath-taking climax Jones was chased by a rampaging boulder.[2] Layer upon layer of protection guarded the treasured god from intruders.

Consider the lengths to which the Hovito went to preserve their golden statue. Modern man guards his idols with equal vigor, not by means of poisonous darts, but through subterfuge, chicanery, intimidation and every other means at his disposal. Idols enjoy a thick circle of safety as the sinner props up shields to hide himself from God's confrontation. The sinner deliberately surrounds himself with those whom he believes will accept his idols, or at least not uncover them. (This accounts for the way in which one generally chooses his friends, those who somehow facilitate and compliment one's idolatry.)

When confronted with his idolatry, the idolater invariably clamors for protection. However, each attempted protective relationship, unless resting in God himself, is to some degree anxious, frustrated, and unsettled. This is by design so as to expose the heart. God, in his mercy, continually undermines attempts to rest in anything other than himself. The sinner will not experience peace until his spirit is broken, and his heart exhibits undivided faith. To this end, God deliberately brings people and circumstances into the idolater's life to expose his idols, a carefully orchestrated leverage of revealing relationships in the hope of eliciting lasting repentance.

> Numbers 34:3-12 presents the boundaries of the Promised Land:
>
> 1. Along the South: the Desert of Zin, the Salt Sea (the Dead Sea), the Wadi of Egypt
> 2. Along the West: the Great Sea (the Mediterranean Sea)
> 3. Along the North: the Great Sea to Mount Hor
> 4. Along the East: Hazar Enan to Shepham, along the Jordan to end at the Salt Sea

---

[2] Director Steven Spielberg admitted that in filming this scene he felt something was missing. He finally determined that the scene's climax would involve a boulder.

Some features of these boundaries:

1. They offer diverse scenery such as forests, deserts, and sea.

2. They provide natural protection, as certain boundaries function as a shield.

3. The land is bordered by Egypt to the south in order to serve as a continual reminder of Israel's deliverance from slavery in Egypt.

4. According to Deuteronomy 11:24, God promised to expand Israel's borders with its ongoing obedience.

It is noteworthy that this border description both begins and ends with the Salt Sea (the modern Dead Sea), since this sea was the former site of Sodom and Gomorrah. After the city was destroyed, the sea formed over the site. The Dead Sea supports no life and is essentially useless for travel because no wind moves across it. Israel bordered this sea as a constant reminder of God's hatred of sin. Ezekiel 16:49 states, however, that Israel fell into the sins of Sodom and Gomorrah, that it did not heed God's admonition. It was for its iniquity that Canaan was later reduced, not to a sea of salt, but to barren soil.[3]

Hanging of the Sigismund Bell at the Cathedral Tower in 1521 in Krakow
Jan Matejko, 1874

The Idolatry Bell Curve

---

[3] Matthew Henry Commentary, Bible Study Tools, 2012

314 What Agreement Is There Between the Temple of God and Idols?

> Warring desires establish themselves as the functional and effective rulers of the sinner's life:
>
> 1. Desire turns into demand.
> 2. Demand gets metamorphosed into need.
> 3. Needs set up expectations.
> 4. Expectations lead to disappointment.
> 5. Disappointments lead to punishment, striking-back, and lashing out.[4]

Idolatry within the Christian's heart could be thought of in terms of as a bell curve. The x-axis, from left to right, goes from a low to high level of idolatrous worship. The y-axis, from bottom to top, shows the intensity of conflict within the heart. The bottom of the y-axis is complete peace, while the top shows a raging internal battle of desires (total warfare).

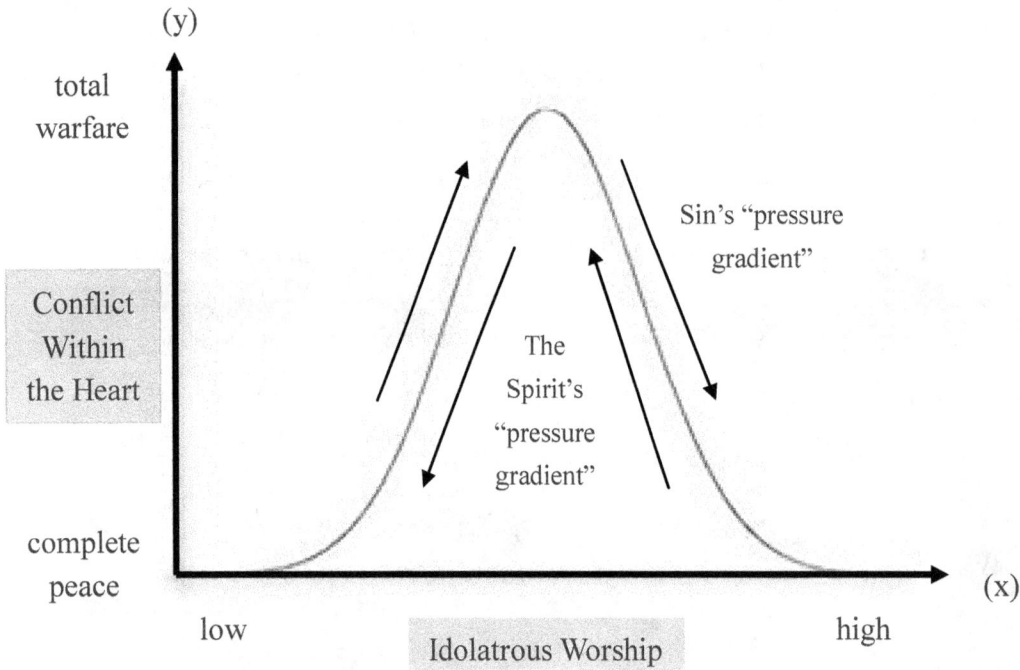

Understanding the graph:

1. When there are few idols within the heart (far left on the x-axis) there is also little battle within the heart (bottom of the y-axis). The heart is a subdued territory, claimed by Christ and basking in victory in Christ. (The complete absence of idolatry would bring complete peace.)

---

[4] Paul Tripp, *Instruments in the Redeemer's Hands: People in Need of Change Helping People in Need of Change* (Presbyterian and Reformed Publishing, 2002)

2. When the heart is equally split between idolatry and faith, in the middle region of the graph (middle of x-axis and top of the y-axis), the war within the heart is greatest. Warring idols grapple with the Holy Spirit for supremacy, and that battle is most intense (total warfare).

3. When the idols within the heart are legion (far right on the x-axis) there is again little war (bottom of the y-axis) because that heart has largely given itself to idolatrous worship. The Holy Spirit has nearly been quenched so that its power is muted, and its opposition to idolatry barely felt.[5] This is the severely compromised Christian who no longer walks in faith. There is diminished conflict within his heart because he has afforded his idols uncontested asylum. However, the sense of compete peace is momentary and false, as idols invariably frustrate and confound. (In God's love he never allows this situation to stand for long, as he will soon reignite the Spirit's war on the Christian's idols.)

4. Sin pushes the heart toward increased idolatry. This is sin's "pressure gradient" (a pressure toward the right of the graph). When the heart experiences peace in the Holy Spirit and low idolatrous worship (on the left side of the graph), sin seeks to push the heart toward increased conflict (toward the middle of the graph). Likewise, when the heart is at a peak of conflict (the Holy Spirit waging intense war against idols), sin seeks to push the heart toward greater idolatrous worship and reduced conflict.

5. God pushes the heart toward greater peace in the Spirit as idols are relinquished. This is the Spirit's "pressure gradient" (a pressure toward the left of the graph). When the heart experiences false peace in high idolatrous worship (on the right side of the graph), the Holy Spirit seeks to push the heart toward increased conflict (toward the middle of the graph). When the heart is at a peak of conflict (the Holy Spirit waging intense war against idols), the Spirit seeks to push the heart toward the renunciation of those idols and reduced conflict. (Thus both sin and the Holy Spirit ultimately seek to render the heart at peace, the former through the complete domination of idols, and the latter through the complete domination of the Holy Spirit itself.)

How Idols Masquerade as Sanctification

Idols often assume a good and noble appearance. They routinely mask themselves as that which is upstanding and righteous, beneficial and profitable. In fact, they are carefully crafted that way. Idolatry's greatest artifice is its chameleon quality, making itself appear as that which is both from God and glorifying to God. Idols can appear holy, as they are camouflaged by prayer, Bible study, and giving alms. The heart is

---

[5] 1 Thessalonians 5:19

skilled at transforming that which is holy into that which is self-serving. (Of course, the Pharisees performed "holy" acts for public display and for casuistry, the ultimate reward being to win the praise of men.[6]) The idolater's hope is that others will blindly accept his faux self-sacrifice, prayerfulness, and generosity.

Idolatry most loves to fashion itself as a kind of false sanctification. The idolater can exhibit the mere appearance of change, while in reality the idol remains firmly ensconced, nestled within a carapace of godliness, derisively denying God's power.[7] Mock-virtue can take on the appearance of the genuine article; faux humility and self-discipline are crafty coverings for self-righteousness. The heart is cunning and highly-skilled at fabricating a façade which appears good and noble, while concealing its true intentions.

> "The heart is deceitful above all things and beyond cure. Who can understand it?" (Jeremiah 17:9)

The world's kindness and graciousness are weak pale posturing. The world creates an artificial representation of truth, righteousness, and goodness, propped up by hollow words and acts. The world's mock-humility is designed to appeal to human pride, and self-aggrandizement. Thus, such humility poses in man-centered raiment for a man-centered objective.

> Idolatry always ends in purposelessness, cursing, and weakness. There is never a positive payoff for idolatry, only unmitigated loss.

Knowing that the heart is desperately wicked and depraved, the counselor is aware that the counselee readily seeks camouflage for his idolatry. The counselee scrambles for covering for his sin so as to perpetrate mock-repentance. For example, the one who displays fear of man may simply look for ways to avoid people so that this idol is rarely exposed. On the other hand, this same person may become aggressive and defiant in order to appear as though no longer fearful. In reality, the fear of man is still just as operative, but now it has been shrouded with a cloaking device. The heart has never been confronted; it still operates under the same deception, yet it wears the guise of sanctification. This is a common problem in the Christian walk – false fruit (that may even receive enthusiastic praise), or that which masquerades as change, concealing an underlying idol. Thus, God affects a continual process of revealing the secret intentions of the heart by placing that which is fake alongside the genuine, so that the fake is exposed.

The Herod Effect[8]

---

[6] John 12:43
[7] 2 Timothy 3:5
[8] For additional discussion of this topic see "What Christians Often Say and What They Mean" in the third book in

The Wise Men and Herod, James Jacques Joseph Tissot, c. 1894

Matthew 2:7, 8, 16 states,

> Then Herod called the Magi secretly and found out from them the exact time the star had appeared. He sent them to Bethlehem and said, 'Go and search carefully for the child. As soon as you find him, report to me, so that I too may go and worship him.'

> When Herod realized that he had been outwitted by the Magi, he was furious, and he gave orders to kill all the boys in Bethlehem and its vicinity who were two years old and under, in accordance with the time he had learned from the Magi.

Herod stated that, along with the Magi, he sought to worship Christ; but in reality he planned to murder him. As with Herod, there is often a glaring disconnect between the Christian's stated theology and his functional theology.[9] This phenomenon I term the "Herod Effect." Just as with Herod's stated plans, one's stated theology usually accords with sound biblical teaching. However, as with Herod's true intent, one's functional theology can be vastly different (functional theology being that by which the Christian daily lives). There can, of course, be numerous points of continuity

---

this series, *The Days of Reckoning Are at Hand: From Fig Leaf to Olive Branch to Laurel Wreath*, chapter 8: "Diagnosis: Vanishing Secrets"

[9] This concept of functional theology from David Powlison, Westminster Theological Seminary, Philadelphia, Pennsylvania

between stated and functional theology, but, especially as they pertain to idolatry, there is usually glaring discontinuity.

The Herod Effect scenarios:

	Stated Theology	Functional Theology
1. The undivided Christian	correct	correct
2. The hypocrite/false Christian	correct	incorrect
3. The young/simple/fool	incorrect	incorrect[10]

The Christian professes that God controls all things, working everything for His glory, and for the believer's ultimate good. He professes that God is his rock and refuge. He purports to worship God alone, to trust, love, and obey Him. However, in a moment of anxiety, escape, or ambition, that same Christian lives as if he must control all things, as if money, approval, success, health, avoiding conflict, or being in control, matter more than trusting and loving God. In this way, the Christian lives as if some temporal gain provides needed refuge, as if the world revolves around him and for him. Thus, the Christian's functional god competes with his professed God. While unbelievers are wholly owned by ungodly motives, true believers are often severely compromised, distracted, and divided.[11]

> "The Lord says, 'These people come near to me with their mouth and honor me with their lips, but their hearts are far from me. Their worship of me is made up only of rules taught by men.'" (Isaiah 29:13)
>
> "They say to wood, 'You are my father,'
>   and to stone, 'You gave me birth.'
> They have turned their backs to me
>   and not their faces;
> yet when they are in trouble, they say,
>   'Come and save us!'" (Jeremiah 2:27)

Matthew 20:20-22 reads,

> Then the mother of Zebedee's sons came to Jesus with her sons and, kneeling down, asked a favor of him.
>
> 'What is it you want?' he asked.

---

[10] Note that it is generally not possible for one's stated theology to be incorrect and one's functional theology to be correct (although there may be examples of this happening).

[11] David Powlison, "Dynamics of Biblical Change" class, Westminster Theological Seminary, Philadelphia, Pennsylvania

> She said, 'Grant that one of these two sons of mine may sit at your right and the other at your left in your kingdom.'
>
> 'You don't know what you are asking,' Jesus said to them. 'Can you drink the cup I am going to drink?'
>
> 'We can,' they answered.

Notice that this mother knelt to ask Jesus a favor. She took on a posture of submission and reverence, but her request was self-serving and prideful. She sought that Jesus serve her desire for prestige, to honor her through her sons. This clearly illustrates the difference between stated and functional theology. Her stated (or "demonstrated" theology) was to honor Jesus, but her functional theology was to seek self-honor. She appeared submissive to Jesus' will, but sought that he should submit to hers.

> "…having a form of godliness but denying its power. Have nothing to do with them." (2 Timothy 3:5)

John 9:24 states, "A second time they [the Jews] summoned the man who had been blind. 'Give glory to God,' they said. 'We know this man is a sinner.'" The Jew's stated theology was to "give glory to God," but their functional theology was to undermine Jesus so as to glorify themselves. Their stated and functional theologies were discordant.

> "A man [who] speaks the truth is always at ease." (Persian proverb)

John 12:4-6 reads,

> But one of his disciples, Judas Iscariot, who was later to betray him, objected, 'Why wasn't this perfume sold and the money given to the poor? It was worth a year's wages.' He did not say this because he cared about the poor but because he was a thief; as keeper of the money bag, he used to help himself to what was put into it.

Judas' stated and functional theologies were highly-discordant.

Becoming Vulnerable to the Truth[12]

The truth of God is in the very air that one breathes. The sinner deliberately and actively resists, runs from, and reacts to, a holy God. He is not a neutral being. Each,

---

[12] William Edgar, "Without Apology: Why I am a Presuppositionalist" *Westminster Theological Journal* 58 (1996): 26. (I have adapted the idea of being "vulnerable to the truth.")

in his sin, is a willful, deliberate God hater.[13] This shows up in even the most seemingly trivial actions, thoughts, and attitudes about life. Life lived, through one's own means, for one's own purposes, in one's own way, for one's own glory. Thus, the idols which attend this God-hatred do not arise in a vacuum. They arise in a God-infused environment as a deliberate and demonstrable rebuttal against the person of God himself.[14] Idols demand uncompromised allegiance and will not rest until sated.

The Last Day of Pompeii, Karl Bryullov, 1827

As one fills his heart with false gods and increases his rebellion against God, he must continually manufacture lies to suppress the truth,[15] a truth that daily arises like the sun itself. The heart must maintain its binge of lies so as to keep the truth distant and concealed. Without this diet, the heart's calumny is vulnerable to being exposed.

> In college I played on a sports team. Our coach was a brazen philanderer who frequently bragged about his exploits. Whenever he saw a beautiful woman, he blurted out an odd expression, "Have mercy!" Clearly, he meant this as a mockery of

---

[13] Proverbs 8:36
[14] For a comprehensive discussion of this topic see the first book in this series, *Ask for the Ancient Paths: From Art to Artifice to Arisen*, chapter 6: "Man Before the Face of God: The Imperium of the Psyche"
[15] David Kupelian, *How Evil Works: Understanding and Overcoming the Destructive Forces That Are Transforming America* (New York: Threshold Editions, 2010) 13.

> God, but I wondered if something of a suppressed truth routinely surfaced in this man. It was as if his spirit cried out for mercy under the weight of an oppressive idol, as if each cry was the pleading of a soul in bondage.[16]

One of the biblical counselor's prime objectives is to make those he counsels vulnerable to the truth. To this end, the counselor functions as an intruder into lives. He does not sit back quietly waiting for opportunities, but rather, breaks into lives as God himself does in order to spark a desperate need for God. The counselor reveals the tilt of reality in God's direction so that the counselee will hurtle toward that reality. That was Jesus' objective in every conversation, to set up the need for the gospel through exposing his subject's sin as a fictive belief system. (The counselor will often be persecuted for this as Jesus himself was.[17])

It is the accumulation of subtle sin, allowed to enter through fallacious worship that has a slow and insidious poisoning effect. The counselor seeks to challenge, tear down, and recast the counselee's fundamental allegiances so that the counselee is made aware of, and on-guard toward, sin, even when inconspicuous. But to merely root out sin leaves a vacuum in the heart. The counselor's ultimate objective is to replace idols with the person of Jesus himself.

> "The chains of habit are too weak to be felt until they are too strong to be broken." (Samuel Johnson)

When an idol is challenged the scene is often explosive. There can be rage to guard that idol at all costs. Idolatrous people are hurting people, and hurting people often cry out loudly with unholy anger. As an idol is exposed the idolater either becomes enraged, or otherwise masterfully manipulative to maintain control of, and submission to, that idol. Observe this sudden change of personality carefully, that impassioned moment when a counselee flails and spars to keep an intruder at bay. Idols are both the root (source) and driver (motive) in this pathology.

Idols tend to form "cold welds" with the heart, so that they remain stubbornly entrenched and resistant to exposure. Like the old adage that a politician spews his bafflegab most loudly when he is about to be exposed as a fraud, so too, those who see their idols under assault immediately cry that they are being hurt. But once the idol's cold weld is broken it tends to unwind quickly. Once "the man behind the curtain" is revealed as a phony wizard, the idol's charade disjoints and unfolds.

> Jacob harbored a trenchant fear of man until he wrestled with God (or an angel).[18]

---

[16] Some in the Bible cried out for mercy and God heard their plea. Consider Psalm 51:1 and Luke 18:13.
[17] Matthew 10:22
[18] Genesis 32:22-32

> After this, his fear of man receded to the extent that he was able to meet face-to-face with his nemesis and brother, Esau.[19] It is vital to note that Jacob's deific wrestling match immediately preceded his long-awaited encounter with Esau. Jacob in effect had to wrestle with God, to be subdued by God, to be "afflicted" by God, in order that he might be recast to wrestle rightly with men. He needed his gods realigned and redefined.
>
> Jacob's hip socket was touched so that he limped at sunrise.[20] At the very next moment "Jacob looked up and there was Esau..."[21] As Jacob discovered, life is planned in such a way that it will never work, nor make sense, without God. Life is a riddle one cannot solve without God's direct input; that is by design, and it is God's mercy to those he longs to save.

The counselor does not take an atomistic view of idolatry. His objective in exposing idols is not simply to search for and label each as a distinct entity, like identifying and extracting malignant tumors. Instead the counselor engineers a comprehensive reconstruction, reorientation, and rehabilitation of the heart. He seeks to craft his confrontation so that Jesus himself is invited to shape that heart. Thus, as idols are identified and removed, they are replaced with living worship of the true God. This fills the worship vacuum ensuring that harassing idols are not permitted to return.[22]

> "When any of the Israelites or any foreigner residing in Israel separate themselves from me and set up idols in their hearts and put a wicked stumbling block before their faces and then go to a prophet to inquire of me, I the LORD will answer them myself." (Ezekiel 14:7)

The "Heisenberg Uncertainty Principle" of Biblical Counseling[23]

The Heisenberg Uncertainty Principle concerns the limitation on studying subatomic particles so that an observer can either know a particle's position or its velocity, but not both at the same time. Oddly, in the process of measuring that particle, one invariably alters its position and velocity. Therefore, the measuring process influences the subject of one's measurement (known as the observer effect[24]). So, at a discrete moment in the past one may know a particle's position or velocity, but never its *current* position or velocity.

---

[19] Genesis 33:3
[20] Genesis 32:31
[21] Genesis 33:1
[22] Matthew 12:43-45
[23] For additional discussion of this topic see "The Search for Themes and Patterns: Data Gathering" in the third book in this series, *The Days of Reckoning Are at Hand: From Fig Leaf to Olive Branch to Laurel Wreath*, chapter 8: "Diagnosis: Vanishing Secrets"
[24] "The Heisenberg Uncertainty Principle" article, Wikipedia

This principle might be applied to biblical counseling. As the counselor seeks to uncover a counselee's idols (the "subatomic particles"), the heart is operative to thwart that effort. Thus, the counselee's idols are active in the counseling process itself,[25] so that, as the counselor pinpoints them, he often alerts the heart to more effectively cloak itself, to act to blend those idols in with their background. This is the observer effect, a warning to the heart that its idols must either seek greater self-protection, or else surrender to Christ. Thus, shedding light on idols tends to in some way alter their "position" (their rank within the heart) and "velocity" (their degree of mobility or level of activity) so that one is not entirely sure what characteristics they assume in disguising themselves.

What is the antidote to the Heisenberg Uncertainty Principle of biblical counseling? The counselor must not allow idols a refuge. This means identifying an idol, exposing it, pursuing it, and seeking to replace it by living faith. Remember that nature abhors a vacuum, so any time idols are extracted they must be replaced by Jesus himself, lest other idols rush in to fill the worship void.

Pinpointing Idols for Extraction

Deuteronomy 20 contains the first mention of *herem* warfare (similar to the modern concept of "total war"). *Herem* warfare is the idea that everything associated with an enemy must be decimated. God wanted no record or reminder of the enemy. All the massacred enemy's livestock was to be slaughtered, all buildings razed, and all women and children put to death. *Herem* warfare is a picture of the utter annihilation which God effects (and accomplished through the cross of Jesus Christ) toward his enemies – the world, sin, and Satan. God's objective within believers is that sin would be annihilated so that there is no record of it. This is what Jesus died to effect, and he longs to make that a daily actuality in his people.

> Once, as I sat in a tenth-story apartment with floor-to-ceiling sliding glass doors, a violent windstorm arose. As the wind gusted to some fifty miles per hour, I watched the glass panels perilously bend inward. I placed my hand on the door frame and felt tremendous pressure. Thinking quickly, I pushed heavy furniture against the doors, and placed spacers on the frames, so that the furniture's weight produced an even back-pressure. As the storm raged, the inward pressure upon the glass was countered by the outward pressure of the propped furniture.
>
> In some sense I see this as a metaphor for the Christian life. As I place my hands upon the glass of my heart, I feel a terrifying primeval force pushing with unrelenting intent. However, there is a counterforce, someone, not myself, pushing back with a carefully applied back-pressure. The pressure of sin and evil is

---

[25] This concept from Paul Tripp, Westminster Theological Seminary, Philadelphia, Pennsylvania

> formidable (like rapacious winds), but this is countered by the Holy Spirit, so that God himself fights to take ground within my heart. Thus, there is a roaring inner battle, but I am not fighting it. God himself wages the war, and that is the source of my indomitable confidence in a final victory.

Watson and the Shark, John Singleton Copley, 1778

Often idolatry is so bound up with the idolater himself that to challenge idols is viewed as a personal affront. How does the counselor tactically launch a surgical strike while leaving the healthy tissue of faith untouched? This is only accomplished as God himself guides the counselor's surgical hand. God himself dictates the terms of the confrontation. He himself is the person meeting people. In the needed confrontation of idols, an abiding focus on Jesus guards the discussion from devolving into what might otherwise appear to be a personal attack. The engagement of idols is never to be seen as criticism, but as God's own tearing down and rebuilding process. Thus, the encounter with idols is a focus on a pyretic intrusion which, alien to the sinner, is broken down and extracted through God's own means. In God's masterful work, he does not merely remove the offending idol, but simultaneously replaces errant worship with a quickening faith in the living Jesus. Thus, the confrontation with idols is never a personal attack, but it is a personal work.

> A good rule of thumb for identifying idols is this: anything one is unwilling to sacrifice for Jesus is an idol.

Just as a tumor resides *within* a patient but is not *of* the patient (not intrinsic to his original design), so too, idolatry lives within the sinner but only as a welcomed intruder, non-original to the sinner's psyche. Thus, the skilled counselor, like a dexterous surgeon, must be clear about that which is the healthy tissue of the psyche, and that which is the intrusion. The counselor must know the psyche's anatomy, and how it works. Then he can be used by God to perform life-saving heart surgery, without imperiling the healthy tissue of faith. In actuality, God himself must perform the surgery, with the counselor as a willing instrument.

> "It is easier to detect error than to find truth. Error lies on the surface and is easily seen, while the truth is at a great depth where few are willing to search for it." (Johann Goethe)

Laying Siege to Buttressed Idols

On the one hand, one is right to explore and apply his own personal design characteristics in God's kingdom building efforts. On the other, he is to renounce and cast off those personality features which arise through sin. Thus, mankind suffers with a bizarre spiritual elephantitis – design to be celebrated, sin to be extricated. How does the counselor help the counselee to be the "real" him? What is the real him?[26]

Many Christians view the call for repentance, the call to admit one's sinfulness and renounce one's self-directed life, as somehow hurtful. The only thing that is ever hurt in repentance is human pride. That is the entire point; God seeks to remove that which stands between him and those he created. Sometimes that extrication process is painful because the heart clenches its idols for fear dear life. When repentance is neglected or avoided the result is more deeply entrenched, more assertively buttressed, idols which, when unchallenged, leave the idolater in an ever-accelerating death spiral.

> "Wounds from a friend can be trusted, but an enemy multiplies kisses." (Proverbs 27:6)

I have never once seen any Christian immediately thankful for confrontation with his sin (myself included). In even the most mature Christians, there is an instinctual self-protection which repels any affront to the heart. I have, on rare occasion, after some civil tussle, seen a Christian thank me for the confrontation, finally coming to his senses that he had just received a gift. (I have done the same to others, as well.) But the heart instinctively guards its idolatry at all costs, with vehement protestations when idols are wrangled.

---

[26] For further discussion of this topic see chapter 9: "Marauding Visigoths: The Autocratic Self"

> "Even if I caused you sorrow by my letter, I do not regret it. Though I did regret it—I see that my letter hurt you, but only for a little while—" (2 Corinthians 7:8)

Matthew 19:16–22 reads,

> Now a man came up to Jesus and asked, 'Teacher, what good thing must I do to get eternal life?'
>
> 'Why do you ask me about what is good?' Jesus replied. 'There is only One who is good. If you want to enter life, obey the commandments.'
>
> 'Which ones?' the man inquired.
>
> Jesus replied, 'Do not murder, do not commit adultery, do not steal, do not give false testimony, honor your father and mother, and 'love your neighbor as yourself.'
>
> 'All these I have kept,' the young man said, 'What do I still lack?'
>
> Jesus answered, 'If you want to be perfect, go sell your possessions and give to the poor, and you will have treasure in heaven. Then come, follow me.'
>
> When the young man heard this, he went away sad, because he had great wealth.

Jesus recognized that this man, though outwardly virtuous, was inwardly self-righteousness. He considered himself good and his wealth a deserved reward. His idol of self-righteousness manifest itself in a self-justifying love of money. Yet, Jesus did not permit the idol peace. He went after it with lethal intent, not to harm the sinner, but to extricate the sin.

> "The first test of a truly great man is his humility." (John Ruskin)

A young Christian woman exhibited unforgiveness, self-centeredness, manipulation, and a lifestyle of lies. I offered counsel with a gentle and calm demeanor using sensitive and respectful words. In applying Scripture to the issues which surfaced, I pressed her to repent, to effect an abject renunciation of her sin before the face of God. Yet, she derided the call to repentance as "attacking and hurtful." She recounted her suffering, the pain of her father's criticism, her attempted suicide while in college, and a former fiancé who reneged. Her attitude was, "How dare I ask her to repent in light of all that had happened to her!" At issue was not what had happened to her, but how she responded to what happened to her. That is the source of her ongoing suffering and her sin against others, a daily maintenance of her defiant siege-works. This woman's unforgiving heart is the iron-maiden into which she has locked herself.

> "These people honor me with their lips, but their hearts are far from me. They worship me in vain; their teachings are but rules taught by men." (Matthew 15:8, 9)

I raise this example to point out a crucial issue in biblical counseling. As the counselor confronts false worship, exposes sin, and harangues idols, he will be vehemently opposed. In the eyes of many Christians, these are by definition bellicose acts, since the counselor confronts that which the Christian often most loves and lives for. The counselor must be clear about what is in fact hurtful and what is not, that which lovingly confronts and that which unlovingly burdens. The counselor speaks truth tempered with love, and he must not waiver from the task God puts before him, regardless of obstacles strewn along the tracks seeking to derail his mission.

Dismantling the Pantheon One God at a Time

The Bible uses two principle metaphors for idolatry – adultery and prostitution.[27] Adultery is being disloyal to one's spouse, breaking the marriage covenant; prostitution is selling one's body for some perceived gain. Both images are deliberately sexual, alluding to the extreme and vile nature of idolatry, an assault against one's most intimate commitment (that which is to God himself), and an implicit attack upon one's very being.[28]

> "What causes fights and quarrels among you? Don't they come from your desires that battle within you? You want something but don't get it. You kill and covet, but you cannot have what you want. You quarrel and fight. You do not have, because you do not ask God. When you ask, you do not receive, because you ask with wrong motives, that you may spend what you get on your pleasures. You adulterous people, don't you know that friendship with the world is hatred toward God? Anyone who chooses to be a friend of the world becomes an enemy of God." (James 4:1-4)

It is because idolatry is such an extreme form of worship, tantamount to adultery and prostitution, that God must deal with it by means of the most drastic measures. Galatians 5:24 states, "Those who belong to Christ Jesus have crucified the sinful nature with its passions and desires." The Bible addresses sin in the strongest possible terms; it seeks to *crucify* the sinful nature, the most violent and brutal handling of the flesh. For those who rest in Jesus' crucifixion, the crucifixion of their own flesh is not only a possibility, but a living reality.

---

[27] For further explanation of these concepts, see chapter 5: "Metaphors for Sin"
[28] 1 Corinthians 6:18

A Roman Art Lover, Lawrence Alma-Tadema, 1868

To simply tell a sinner to desist from certain action leaves the heart unconfronted. To leave worship untouched is to leave behavior enslaved to the same internal forces.[29] Thus, the Bible never focuses on morality, principles, methods, standards, applying a psychic salve, or merely increasing endorphin levels. It always speaks about the heart, what one worships, what one lives for, what one must have, the object of one's focus, what one's "planet" orbits around. The Bible focuses on hearts riddled with idolatry seeking to transform them into strongholds of faith. Deuteronomy 30:17, 18, states, "But if your heart turns away and you are not obedient, and if you are drawn away to bow down to other gods and worship them, I declare to you this day that you will certainly be destroyed."

> "'Are you still so dull?' Jesus asked them. 'Don't you see that whatever enters the mouth goes into the stomach and then out of the body? But the things that come out of the mouth come from the heart, and these make a man 'unclean.' For out of the heart come evil thoughts, murder, adultery, sexual immorality, theft, false testimony, slander.'" (Matthew 15:16-19)

---

[29] Jay Adams, *How to Overcome Evil* (Presbyterian and Reformed Publishing, 2010) 49.

As the counselor confronts the counselee with false gods, as he calls him to worship Christ alone, tearing down the high places within the heart, the counselor always receives strong opposition (of one form or another); the Christian is often content to merely afford Jesus a niche in his pantheon of serviceable deities, but not an exclusive position. To put all of one's hope in one God, Jesus alone, is to assume what feels like a life-threatening risk. The defective logic behind this is that there is safety and wisdom in allowing many gods to occupy one's temple. Thus, if one god fails he can turn to others for deliverance. If one god proves incapable of providing meaning, power, and blessing, another can be summoned to accomplish the purposes of a derelict heart.

Consider 1 Samuel 5:3, 4 in which the Philistines captured the Ark of the Covenant and subsequently housed it in Dagon's temple. The first morning in the Ark's presence Dagon fell on its face before the Ark. The second morning Dagon was found decapitated and missing its hands. This is a picture of God dismembering and humiliating idols. That which is raised in defiance of God, God will, in time, bring low and render impotent.

> "You looked, O king, and there before you stood a large statue – an enormous, dazzling statue, awesome in appearance. The head of the statue was made of pure gold, its chest and arms of silver, its belly and thighs of bronze, its legs of iron, its feet partly of iron and partly of baked clay. While you were watching, a rock was cut out, but not by human hands. It struck the statue on its feet or iron and clay and smashed them. In the time of those kings, the God of heaven will set up a kingdom that will never be destroyed, nor will it be left to another people. It will crush all those kingdoms and bring them to an end, but it will itself endure forever. This is the meaning of the vision of the rock cut out of a mountain, but not by human hands – a rock that broke the iron, the bronze, the clay, the silver and the gold to pieces." (Daniel 2:31-34, 44, 45)

The good news is that Jesus never tolerates a mere niche in the pantheon of competing gods. He must either reign supreme or he will not reign at all. He must vanquish competing gods, waging war every moment of everyday to achieve victory (although there can be moments of false peace). In each Christian, Jesus must win this war or Jesus was never present in the first place. The wise counselor, aware of the heart's pantheon, cognizant of the ravages and scars of warring idols, labors to champion Jesus' cause. Like Jesus, the counselor does not rest until the battle has been won for Christ.

One of the many paradoxes in the Christian faith is that surrender to Jesus, submission to his will, is the greatest source and display of strength that any human being could ever exhibit. Ongoing submission to Christ forges in the Christian a tempered steel resolve, able to resist and repel evil, able to renounce and turn from sin. This submission results in a majestic display of other-centeredness of which mankind is simply incapable in his own strength through his own means. Thus, the Christian understands that surrender is victory.

A Tree Metaphor for Idolatry[30]

Part	Meaning	Explanation
1. Sun, sky	Common grace	God constructs a life-giving environment (sunshine and rain) for the tree in the hope that it will change its nature (the godly and ungodly alike).
2. Sand	The source from which one seeks life (performance, works, etc.)	The sand starves the tree to death. Its effect is felt even when the idolater is not actively engaged in his idolatry.
3. Roots	A history of fear (guilt, rejection, failure)	One defines and derives his life from the roots of fear. This is a set of lenses through which fallen man views the source of his life – the sand. The roots grow to different sizes based upon how one views his history.
4. Trunk	Slavery to a covenant with idols	The trunk connects the roots (history) and the branches (behavior), offering a sense of stability. However, that stability is actually slavery to a treasonous covenant with idols.
5. Sap	Lust	Sap is unseen and unperceived, but is the tree's life-blood. In the same way, the psyche is driven by a "sap" of lust. (While the term "lust" usually connotes sexual sin, from the Bible's perspective it is an all-encompassing term meaning any demand, desire, or love outside of God.[31])
6. Branches	Control – extension into the visible environment	Control can be any form of behavior which seeks to manage one's fear problem.
7. False fruit	False peace	The condition of the tree's fruit reveals the condition of the entire tree. False fruit is the curse of covenant treason which falls to the ground and poisons the sand. The sand is thus re-injected with poison, which in turn

---

[30] Michael Bobick, *From Slavery to Sonship: A Biblical Psychology for Pastoral Counseling* (1995) 39-42. (class notes)
[31] Titus 3:3; Philippians 3:19

| | | produces more false fruit. (A flock of birds which feasts on the false fruit, or an ice storm which withers the fruit, may be God's mercy to prevent the fruit from re-poisoning the sand.) |

| "If you will return, O Israel, return to me. If you put your detestable idols out of my sight and no longer go astray, and if in a truthful, just and righteous way you swear, 'As surely as the Lord lives, then the nations will be blessed by him and in him they will glory.' This is what the Lord says to the men of Judah and to Jerusalem: 'Break up your unplowed ground and do not sow among thorns. Circumcise yourselves to the Lord, circumcise your hearts, you men of Judah and people of Jerusalem, or my wrath will break out and burn like fire because of the evil you have done – burn with no one to quench it.'" (Jeremiah 4:1-4) |

Farmers Nooning, William Sidney Mount, 1836

A Tree Metaphor for Redemption[32]

Part	Meaning	Explanation
1. Sun, sky	Special grace	God brings a life-giving environment (sunshine and rain) to the tree because it is his own.

---

[32] Michael Bobick, *From Slavery to Sonship: A Biblical Psychology for Pastoral Counseling* (1995) 42-44. (class notes)

2. Soil	The source from which one seeks life (God's promises, grace)	The soil feeds the tree with life. This could be summarized as righteousness in Christ, acceptance in Christ, and holiness in Christ. God's promises and grace operate even when the Christian is not aware of them.
3. Roots	A history of righteousness in Christ (justified, acceptance, faithfulness)	One defines and derives his life from the roots of Christ. This is a like a set of lenses through which regenerate man views the source of his life – the soil.
4. Trunk	Sonship under a covenant with God	The trunk is the connection between the roots (history) and the branches (behavior). The trunk offers a sense of stability based upon covenant relationship with God.[33]
5. Sap	God's Spirit	Sap, unseen and unperceived, is the tree's life-blood. This is analogous to the way that regenerate man is renewed and enlivened by the Spirit.[34]
6. Branches	Servanthood – extension into the visible environment	Servanthood is a heart-set which seeks to glorify Christ, while forgetting about oneself.[35] This heart-set results in good works.
7. Fruit	Life-giving, peaceful	The fruit is the blessing of covenant relationship with God. The fruit's condition manifests the condition of the entire tree. The fruit falls to the ground continually giving life to the soil. The soil is thus re-injected with nutrients from the fruit, which in turn produces more good fruit. Thus, good fruit falls to the ground, dies, and produces more good trees.[36]

Fallen man can only be the tree of idolatry, while the Christian can live as either tree, depending upon whether he lives in the Spirit or in the flesh.

Case Study: Applying the Tree Metaphor

A young Christian man is committed to his church, regularly participating in various functions with a spirit of joy. However, there is a perplexing quality to him. In his mannerisms he moves at a very slow pace (he likes to "take his sweet time"). He often

---

[33] Romans 6:17-23
[34] Colossians 1:27
[35] Luke 6:27-38
[36] John 12:24

speaks slowly, walks slowly, and does everything slowly. While normally not a problem, there are times and situations when speed is called for, a split-second decision to hop a bus, the reflexes to catch a falling vase, a response to a friend's greeting. This issue of his chronic slowness, while not ostensibly sinful, is an object of concern since it seems to at times impede love of God and love of others.[37] I have wondered if it is an intelligence issue, but his IQ seems to be about average or a few ticks over. Is this possibly linked to hypothyroidism since he complains about sensitivity to cold and the inability to keep his weight down? That may be a factor, but there is more going on.

Sleeping Venus
Simon Vouet, c. 1640

I asked this man about his slowness in the context of drawing his attention to what I believe is sinful passivity. He responded that this is the way God made him. (Whenever I hear that response I am skeptical because it so conveniently acts as justification for sin.) I would simply label the problem "laziness," but there is something more to be uncovered. His slowness has nestled within it a rebellious quality. It seems to be grounded in either a smoldering anger or in a martyr complex. (For example, with a certain victimized tone, he once recounted that a supermarket checkout clerk snapped at him for taking too long to complete the transaction.)

There are likely one or more idols at the root of this problem:

---

[37] Luke 10:27

1. Possibly an idol of control (he seeks to dictate the pace of interactions)

2. Possibly a seeking revenge for having been pushed in the past (an angry fist that no one will ever push him again)

3. Possibly an effective means to gain attention (albeit negative), as he is often the one others are waiting for

Slowness can be a convenient way to play the wounded victim (and when others react angrily that plays right into the self-righteous objective). Regardless of the specific idol, in what way is this man called to bring himself face-to-face with Jesus? How is he called to relinquish his stubborn spirit so that his heart becomes pliable, able to respond in accordance with the dictates of the situation? How is he called to surrender his right to slowness in the larger calling to love God and others?

Using the Tree Metaphor to Analyze this Man's Idolatry

Part	Meaning	Explanation
1. Sun, sky	Common grace	This man is a Christian so he is under special grace.
2. Sand	The source from which one seeks life (performance, works, etc.)	This man seeks to derive life from maintaining control of his emotions (*sang-froid*), and over the pace of his life (refusing to cede control to others). Maintaining control may be a way to keep others at a distance, so as to manage potential threats.
3. Roots	A history of fear (guilt, rejection, failure)	This man's personal history has demonstrated that people are aggressive and nefarious. He feels fearful when either pushed to perform or manipulated to act. An impassive exterior seems to maintain a sense of stability and control. He remains guarded to future manipulation in keeping his "martyrdom cocoon" at the ready.
4. Trunk	Slavery to a covenant with idols	Stability is found in being his own protector. He only feels safe when he maintains an impassive demeanor, regardless of situations which might dictate acting differently.
5. Sap	Lust	The sap is a lust for control or respect, a demand to be his own god, living life at his own pace.
6. Branches	Control – extension into the visible	When others are rude or critical the man retreats into a victim's carapace; isolation only furthers a victim mentality.

		environment
7. False fruit	False peace	The false fruit is acting in a slow manner so as to gain a measure of control over others, or respect for one's own timetable. As others sense this man's deliberate slowness, they may become impatient and speak in a curt manner which furthers his desire for respect. The heart is consumed with self, and its false fruit continues to poison the heart.

Using the Tree Metaphor to Analyze this Man's Sanctification

Part	Meaning	Explanation
1. Sun, sky	Special grace	God has planned this man's life for good purposes. God seeks to prosper him as his own, so that all that comes to pass is part of his good and perfect will.
2. Soil	The source from which one seeks life (God's promise, grace)	Jesus is this man's holiness, provision, protector, and source of acceptance. It does not matter what others do (although that may at times be hurtful) because Jesus himself is his promise of future prosperity (as he is sanctified). Since Jesus is his source of strength, this man can release his self-protective desire for control over his world.
3. Roots	History of righteousness in Christ (justified, acceptance, success)	Even though others have at times been hurtful, this man's history belongs to Christ, who has cared for him and has led him on a path to Jesus himself. The soil of his life is nurturing, and will continue to be so, as he trusts in Jesus for all things.
4. Trunk	Sonship under a covenant with God	This man is a son of God in covenant relationship, so that he can, therefore, show wisdom and joy in the midst of any situation. Regardless of his past, he can still be at peace, even when he feels threatened.
5. Sap	God's Spirit	The Holy Spirit can work in this man to no longer fear aggression or criticism. He can deal graciously with rude or curt people through a means that glorifies God. His strength is the Holy Spirit within him and not in the supposed safety of the martyrdom cocoon.
6. Branches	Servanthood – extension into the visible	Servanthood means speaking and acting in a way that most loves others in any given situation. Jesus can cause this man to forget about himself so

	environment	as to enter into other's lives for good purpose. In interacting with others he can trust Jesus' protection.
7. Fruit	Life-giving, peaceful	There are times when speaking and acting slowly is most loving toward others, and other times when one is called to speak and act more quickly out of love. The good fruit is acting in a way that serves others without regard for self-protection. Since this man is in covenant relationship with God, he can be at peace as he relates with others.

The Christian Martyrs Last Prayer, Jean Léon Gérôme, 1883

A crucial application of this model is that those rooted in Jesus Christ (and not rooted in the world) maintain a stability and a resilience which those of the world lack. The Christian is not thrown by every grievance, is not tossed by every offense. He maintains a certain navigable quality, a certain sense of identity that, while it may be assaulted, cannot be shaken. While the world is fundamentally shallow-rooted, the Christian maintains an iron resolve concerning matters of eternity. Thus, the Christian can display grace regardless of the enemy surrounding him.

The Call to Repentance

In 1876 President Rutherford Hayes (1822–1893) placed the first long distance phone call from Washington, D.C. to Philadelphia. After the call Hayes commented, "An amazing invention – but who would ever want to use one?" The telephone would go on to revolutionize the world, but at the time few saw its value. This anecdote serves as a fitting introduction to the call to repentance, a call that revolutionizes the Christian life, but few ever want to receive.

Idolatry is slavery, and God, with the full force of his being, seeks to liberate slaves from their captivity.[38] The archetype for liberation is Moses leading Israel out of their Egyptian servitude. This serves as a foreshadowing of Christ leading his people out of, not a physical slavery to men, but slavery of worship. Repentance is the gateway to this liberation, revolutionizing the Christian's life.

> "Changed by the Bible a man can eliminate his prejudices, not just recognize them."

However, the vast majority of Christians rarely repent (or call others to do so), assuming this to be the vestige of a Byzantine form of repressive guilt. In fact, today any attempt to draw out another's guilt before a holy God is seen as an act of aggression and hostility, a personal attack and an egregious affront. This is why talk of sin is vociferously scuttled and so vigorously suppressed. The thought of imposing, or merely exposing, guilt is intolerable. (This, incidentally, is one among many reasons parents refuse to discipline their children. They fear imposing some guilt upon the child, which they view as a crippling hindrance to self-expression and self-esteem.) Guilt before a holy God is the locus of the unregenerate human existence, and yet it is the most feared and reviled topic.

> "I am so full of niceness I have no sense of right and wrong, no outrage, no passion." (Garrison Keillor)

Repentance is invariably the glaring omission in the Christian's life, keeping him chronically hobbled by self-obsession, separated from God, and joyless. Yet, in ancient Israel the call to repentance was a revitalizing community event, one which has largely been lost in the modern church.

> On the twenty-fourth day of the same month, the Israelites gathered together, fasting and wearing sackcloth and putting dust on their heads. Those of Israelite descent had separated themselves from all foreigners. They stood in their places and confessed their sins and the sins of their ancestors. They stood where they were and read from the Book of the Law of the LORD their God for a quarter of the day, and spent another quarter in confession and in worshiping the LORD their God. (Nehemiah 9:1-3)

> Those who routinely mention that everything is by grace frequently do so in order to neglect the need for ongoing repentance. Easy grace allows the sinful heart to go

---

[38] Ephesians 4:8

> unchallenged, resulting in stunted growth in Christ and increased depravity. Thus, easy grace wrongly assumes that God's grace excludes the requirement of repentance from sin.

Repentance Explored

> "To err and not reform, this may indeed be called error." (Confucius)

Viruses routinely assail computers in the form of adware, malware, spybots, trojans, trolls, and worms. They often appear as harmless advertisements, or helpful warnings, even infiltrating a computer completely undetected. Such viruses can bore into nested files, becoming vexatious to ferret out and destroy.

In the same way that viruses sabotage a computer, idols, which appear harmless, even beneficent, assail the unsuspecting heart. Like their electronic counterparts, idols burrow their way into the depths of the heart, taking up residence, infecting self-image, relationships, and work. As these idols fester and multiply, the unregenerate heart becomes a cesspool of desire, an angry fist raised against a holy God.

> "Because they have forsaken me and burned incense to other gods and provoked me to anger by all the idols their hands have made, my anger will burn against this place and will not be quenched." (2 Kings 22:17)
>
> "Because your heart was responsive and you humbled yourself before the Lord when you heard what I have spoken against this place and its people, that they would become accursed and laid waste, and because you tore your robes and wept in my presence, I have heard you, declares the Lord." (2 Kings 22:19)

While antivirus software seeks and incinerates computer viruses, what is the analogue with regard to the human heart? Only the Holy Spirit can cleanse the inner being so that it is free from enslaving idols, and shielded against further infection. God himself must perform the diagnostic, restoring the heart to its original specifications, so that it is pure, peaceful, sagacious, and truly alive. In fact, with repentance the idolater soon finds that his heart possesses something far greater than its original design, the Holy Spirit actively working within it.

The sinner is not called to repent of actions, thoughts, appearances, emotions, or words. He is called to repent of the idolatrous heart that gave rise to them. This is why the wise counselor pays as much attention to motive as he does to action. The counselor recognizes that motive dictates the trajectory of future behavior. Thus, in pointing out motivation, the counselee's path is illuminated.

> In this work, *Tipping Point: How Little Things Can Make a Big Difference* (2000),[39] Malcolm Gladwell points out that anti-smoking campaigns have largely failed. Quite surprisingly, studies find that smokers are well aware of smoking's perils. In fact, smokers think that smoking is *more* dangerous than it actually is. Yet, they continue to smoke. The point is that smoking does not arise because of a lack of information. What Gladwell strikes up against (which only the Bible understands) is that smoking, like all displays of rebellion, arises from a worshipping heart harassing God's design work. This further buttresses the argument that rebellion never arises through a lack of information, but through a willful denial of, and attack upon, the person of God.

Exodus 6:9 is a difficult verse in light of this discussion of idolatry. "The Israelites did not listen to God's words through Moses because of their discouragement and cruel bondage." This verse seems to imply that it was the absence of encouragement, and the situation of bondage, which led the people to rebel against God, that the people's sin was in some way excusable as they were victims of circumstance.

If one misunderstands God's desire to radically change the heart, he will not understand what God is doing in his life. He will always be confused as to why the same problems keep arising, why the same trials and frustrations just will not go away. The breadth and depth of God's work is to change what one worships so that God never wastes his effort on merely altering circumstances, behaviors, thoughts, or words. If one does not recognize this he will wrongly focus attention on trying to overcome circumstances, gaining more knowledge, acquiring more resources, or forging more associations. These are not where God directs his attention. He directs himself at the epicenter of human existence, so as to reveal one's worship as either idolatrous or faithful. God does not rest until he has all of the Christian's worship for himself.

> "See to it, brothers, that none of you has a sinful, unbelieving heart that turns away from the living God." (Hebrews 3:12)

Repentance Implemented: The Quail and Serpent Approaches

In Numbers 11:4-34 the Israelites craved meat to such a degree that they were willing to return to the horrors of Egyptian slavery to get it. Later, Numbers 21:5 records the people's rebellion as they complained of their lack of bread and water. God rendered opposite judgments to both of these acts of rebellion.

In the first episode the Lord gave the people over to their sin, abundantly granting

---

[39] Malcolm Gladwell, *Tipping Point: How Little Things Can Make a Big Difference* (Little Brown, 2000)

them what they craved. In Numbers 11:20 the Lord promised that the people would eat quail for a whole month – until it came out of their nostrils and they loathed it. Making good on his promise, God sent quail three feet deep as far as a day's walk in every direction.[40]

Often the Lord gives his people over to their sinful passions, to let them drink deeply of their sin. This is similar to those who have everything the world can offer, fame, money, pleasure, and power. They have been given over to their passions to have their fill, so that the things of the world will become loathsome to them. Those who spurn the Lord will sometimes be given over to their sin, so that they might one day spurn the world they have embraced.

The Brazen Serpent
Benjamin West, d. 1820

Taking the opposite tact, in Numbers 21:2-13, God sent fiery serpents to harass the Israelites as they demanded bread and water, while deriding both God and Moses. After the outbreak of venomous serpents, the people admitted their sin. The source of the curse then became the source of the cure. God used opposite strategies to induce repentance, sometimes giving one the desire of his heart, with all its vapid and futile consequence, and at others bringing stinging pain as a bitter taste of a potentially more severe judgment to come.

Incentivized Repentance: Gratitude Reversal

On a grassy mountain plateau in eastern Pennsylvania there are several large boulders made of diabase, a volcanic rock. When struck with a hammer these stones emit a hollow metallic sound resembling tuned bells. Geologists are perplexed at how these boulders ended up on the mountain since there is no evidence of past volcanic activity

---

[40] Numbers 11:31

in the area. The deposits must be the work of an ice age glacier, but the rocks are so high that this seems improbable. This offers a picture of the way in which God induces a spirit of gratitude into the believer. The process often defies human logic or explanation. Yet, God routinely performs, not just the improbable, but the impossible, so that formerly self-consumed sinners are filled with reverence.

> "Sorrow looks back, worry looks down, pride looks around, but faith looks up."

The sinner's approach tends to be "grateful to" people (attributing to people something of the status of God himself), but not "grateful for" people (recognizing the person of God behind events and relationships). Through sanctification there is a gratitude pole reversal in which "grateful to" people becomes "grateful for" people, and "grateful for" God (having done what one desires) becomes "grateful to" God (to the person of God directly).

A Man-Centered Approach:

	Grateful to	Grateful for
People	Yes	No
Circumstances, objects	Yes	No
God himself	No	Not at all

> "Ingratitude is the daughter of pride and the mother of every vice." (French proverb)

A God-centered Approach:

	Grateful to	Grateful for
People	No	Yes
Circumstances, objects	No	Yes
God himself	Yes	Yes

The question of gratitude is really a question of what one installs as god and where one places his hope. One will be grateful to whatever, or whomever, he worships. The non-Christian is grateful to people, objects, or circumstances. The Christian is not just grateful *for* God, but grateful *to* God for salvation and sanctification. That is a big difference.

> The deeper and more sincere one's repentance, the greater one's self-denial. The greater one's self-denial the more intense and genuine one's love for God and others. This results in meaningful relationship (both vertical and horizontal), and the healing from what is termed "mental illness." Thus repentance, and the abrogated self, results in blossoming relationship.

Building Faith on a Solid Foundation of Repentance

Most towers are renowned for their height or beauty, but rarely is one celebrated for its flaws. The Leaning Tower of Pisa is a notable exception. Construction on the tower began in 1174 on marshy ground. The foundation only reached down fifty-eight feet, and tree trunks were used as footings. Soon after the fourth story was completed, the tower tilted slightly to the south. Builders compensated by raising subsequent floors on their southern side. This produced a northern curvature to the entire structure. Today, the 168 foot tower tilts by nearly fifteen feet, an eight-degree angle.[41]

The point is, just as a tower requires a solid foundation to stand, so too, the Christian needs a solid foundation in the task of removing idols and replacing them with faith. Without the proper foundation, all else is destined to remain destabilized, so as to finally crash in defeat.

A young Christian woman lashed out at me in unwarranted anger. Upon later confrontation, she said that she repented of her *anger*. However, there was no real change as she remained unabashedly given to outbursts. The reason hinges on the nature of her repentance. She exercised a clever slight of hand; she repented of the symptom (her anger), but not the cause (her demanding heart).

God seeks repentance at the source, that the font from which thought, action, and word arise would be renounced. What is the source? The worshipping heart. This woman setup a sanctimonious smokescreen behind which she offered the appearance of genuine repentance. However, she refused to repent of the faulty worship which gave rise to her anger. What she produced, in effect, was a means to exculpate herself. She reduced her problem to an incidence of misplaced anger, a moment of poor judgment. In this way, her worshipping heart remained untouched. On the exterior, her repentance looked genuinely contrite, but it actually concealed a devious heart whose desires remained untouched.

> "They dress the wound of my people as though it were not serious. 'Peace, peace,' they say, when there is no peace." (Jeremiah 8:11)

The more one suppresses the mere symptoms of idolatry (for example, squelching the anger), the more underlying idols can flourish undetected and unhindered. Put another way, the longer one deceives himself with specious repentance, the more heavily camouflaged and resilient idols become. In refusing to confront idols directly, the idolater institutionalizes those idols, setting them in worship concrete. In summary, the idolater, in merely repenting of cursory symptoms, crafts for himself a pale and

---

[41] Kevin McFarland, *Incredible! But True* (New York: Bell Publishing Company, 1976) 79.

weak faux-repentance, while failing to recognize his wicked God-deposing heart. Without this understanding, the counselor easily falls prey to the bait-and-switch.

Il Penseroso, Thomas Cole, 1845

> The antidote for the love of money is not the hatred of money. Rather, it is recognizing the warring desires which gave rise to the love of money. If, for example, one makes the praises of men into his god, he will easily love money. Thus, the antidote for the love of money is to go after the root cause and, in so doing, to liberate a heart that has surrendered itself to enslaving idols.

Worship Recidivism

The Song dynasty (960–1279) forensic science work, *Collected Cases of Injustice Rectified* (洗冤集录), published by Song Ci in 1247, contains the oldest known case of forensic entomology. In 1235, a Chinese villager was stabbed to death, his wounds inflicted with a sickle. This led authorities to suspect that a local farmer was the culprit. The magistrate had the farmers assemble in the town square where each placed his sickle on the ground in front of him. Within minutes a mass of blow flies gathered around one sickle (and none other), attracted to the blood residue invisible to the naked eye. It became apparent to all that the owner of that sickle was the perpetrator. He was promptly arrested as he pled for mercy.

This historical account offers a window into the nature of sin within the Christian's heart. Even after the Christian feels he has overcome indwelling sin, that sin leaves traces and unseen residue attracting ongoing temptation. Thus, the Christian, recognizing that sin often leaves scars on his spirit, rightly does battle with his sin in the strength of the Holy Spirit. Only the Holy Spirit can soften those scars in time, washing away their attractive residue.

> Consider recent news events in which, for example, it is often announced that the mastermind of a certain terror organization has been captured and killed. Then a few months later the mastermind of that exact same terror organization has again been captured and killed. The obvious implication is that, as the current mastermind is eliminated, the second-in-command steps up to fill the leadership void. No matter how many times the mastermind is captured and killed, there is always a new one. This is a picture of the worship recidivism associated with idols. As one idol is "captured and killed," another steps up to take its place, because the heart is a worship factory.[42]

Often a Christian has repented of his sin, renounced his idols, prayed for lasting change, and enlisted godly counselors. Yet, despite all this effort, and seeming victory, the same sin arises time and again. Regardless of the degree and sincerity of repentance, there is invariably a level of recidivism involved with sin. Why does this occur?

> The heart continually swaps failed idols for new ones that appear to be more functional.

The heart rarely turns from its sin completely and conclusively because it loves its sin, and resists change. For example, Jeremiah 18:12 states, "But they will reply, 'It's no use. We will continue with our own plans; we will all follow the stubbornness of our evil hearts.'" Yet, the regenerate heart, under the Holy Spirit's control, desperately desires freedom from sin and fights for this freedom. The war rages, and at moments it feels that victory is finally at hand, when suddenly there is another crushing defeat. Sin's recidivism is a mystery in the Christian life, why he continues to desire and act upon that which he knows to be wrong, even as he strives for deliverance.[43]

> "How do you get a grip when the barbarians are rioting in the streets of your mind?" (David Powlison)

Sometimes Christians speak of removing oneself from the throne of his heart and placing Jesus on that throne. Is this image adequate to capture the entirety of the Bible's teaching on heart worship? This kind of toggle-switch approach to worship is

---

[42] The concept "worship factory" borrowed from theologian John Calvin (1509-1564).
[43] Matthew 26:41; Romans 7:15

vastly too simplistic to capture the heart's depth and richness. This image of removing the self and replacing it with Jesus fails to recognize that there is a tangled web of idols resident within even the Christian's heart. This causes him to display faith in certain areas, but to defer to idols in others. So the heart is a rotating wheel of idolatry, warring idols each vying for supremacy. Put another way, each Christian's heart is an intricate mosaic of faith and idolatry, containing pockets of faith intermingled with pockets of atheism.[44] Wise counseling seeks to uncover this mosaic, so as to assist God's work in faith-expansion and sin-contraction.

The book of Joshua records two of Israel's battles in detail, Jericho and Ai.[45] The battle of Jericho stands as the exemplar of what happens when God's people are obedient. Jericho was difficult to defeat, but God handed Israel an easy victory. The battle of Ai, on the other hand, shows what happens when God's people are disobedient. Ai was easy to defeat, but God allowed Israel to falter.

The Jericho and Ai models could be applied to the Christian's sanctification. Sanctification is a battle in which God himself must conduct the fighting, and victory is his to determine. The battle with sin only succeeds as Christians live in the Spirit (a Jericho-inspired obedience). However, when confident in their own flesh (an Ai-inspired disobedience), Christians find crushing defeat.

> Jesus either removes the shackles of sin or they are daily forged in a heavier gauge.

A phenomenon that has perplexed me for years is that some genuine Christians seem to exhibit such minimal change for Christ. These Christians may read the Bible, pray, regularly attend a doctrinally-sound congregation, and do good works, but there is no real heart change. Such a heart seem recalcitrant and deadened to itself. It may put on the appearance of godliness but remains infested with idols, cankered with God-hatred, even in its seeming best intentions.

> The old adage goes that a politician yells the loudest just before he concedes defeat and abandons his argument.

The heart is such a dungeon of festering evil that it may display a simulacrum of repentance simply through stifling emotions. If emotions can be summoned, or suppressed, on demand to lend the appearance of sanctification, then no one will be the wiser. So instead of vanquishing one's idols, those idols are allowed to thrive under the cloak of feigned emotional responses. For example, Christians generally label anger as a clear indication of idolatrous avidity. So the Christian then stifles all anger so as to appear free from idols. Likewise, Christians are to display joy in all

---

[44] This concept from David Powlison, Westminster Theological Seminary, Philadelphia, Pennsylvania
[45] Joshua 6, 7

circumstances, so some erect a pleasant façade while simmering in defiance. Thus, emotions are routinely managed and manipulated as a cloaking device for resident idols.[46]

Henry IV Receiving the Portrait of Maria de Medici
Peter Paul Rubens, 1625

For example, recently, at a counseling seminar, a young man revealed that television watching had become an idol for him. One of the participants advised him to just put less attention on it, to simply like it less. While, in a certain regard, this advice contains some wisdom, there is something in it which misses the point. The issue of renouncing idols is not about merely "lowering the volume" on desire. The desire itself must be thoroughly dismantled and reconstructed.

> Geese fly in a V-formation because the air current created by the bird ahead forms a temporary vacuum which draws the next bird forward. Thus, each goose's effort is reduced by the one ahead. However, this benefit is only realized if the geese remain in close proximity. As distance between them increases, the effect dissipates. A similar analogy could be made for the Christian with regard to God. As the Christian draws close to God, he experiences a "vacuum effect" produced by the Holy Spirit, so that he no longer works in his own strength, but in God's. Thus, as the Christian desires fellowship with God, he receives the greatest blessing, and conversely, as he drifts far away, he increasingly labors in his own strength with fatiguing effect.

---

[46] For further discussion of this topic see "The *Coram Deo* Concept and the Issue of Emotions" in the first book in this series, *Ask for the Ancient Paths: From Art to Artifice to Arisen*, chapter 6: "Man Before the Face of God: The Imperium of the Psyche," and "The Hydraulic View of Emotions" in chapter 8: "What Has Jerusalem To Do With Vienna?: The Case Against Psychology"

The Counselor's Role in Exposing Idolatry

In 1875 the chief of the U.S. patent office considered permanently closing the office because he thought that every invention had already been created. While the reader may chuckle at such a gross miscalculation, an analogy could be drawn with the issue of repentance. While the Christian may think that his repentance is complete, it is an ongoing event. Repentance is far from a *fait accompli* as one understands the poverty of his own soul, the depth of his own depravity, his miserable state outside of Christ, and the continuous need to delve deeper into the recesses of the heart to expose its motives and machinations.

> "Philip said to Him, 'Lord, show us the Father, and it is enough for us.' Jesus said to him, 'Have I been so long with you, and yet you have not come to know me, Philip? He who has seen me has seen the Father; how can you say, "Show us the Father"?'" (John 14:8, 9)

The counselor does not ask a counselee what his idols are because the counselee reflexively eschews the topic.[47] The sinner subverts and twists questions of the heart into those which shift blame and shield him from guilt. Therefore, he recasts his idolatry so as to circumvent culpability before a holy God. It is up to the counselor to help those he counsels to identify and take responsibility for idols. The counselor must be clear about the evidence he observes, and point it out directly. He must also be vigilant not to permit the counselee to evade the topic, shift the terms of engagement, offer plausible excuses, or thrust red-herrings into the investigation.

> In exposing idols the counselor must remember that those very same idols are operative in his interaction with the counselee. This means that the counselee's idols function even in the course of the counseling process seeking to eradicate those idols.[48]

Listen carefully to people's stories, heroes, and descriptions because they reveal very clearly what their hearts worship. For example, the church elder who points out that his church was founded by an anesthesiologist reveals something about what he values (professional accomplishment, intelligence, prestige, one who overcomes adversity, a hero for his ethnic group, etc.).

A young Christian woman spoke about the allure of beauty. She praised shimmering young actresses, spoke of her fascination with makeup, and voiced her concern with regard to comparisons with other women. I pointed out that I feel she worships beauty,

---

[47] Paul Tripp, Westminster Theological Seminary, Philadelphia, Pennsylvania
[48] Paul Tripp, Westminster Theological Seminary, Philadelphia, Pennsylvania

that it is an idol controlling her heart. She immediately denied my claim, stating that she was merely interested in the topic and that she was well aware of the inherent dangers of focusing too much attention on it. I had to make a decision whether to press for further evidence or leave it alone. I told her I had strong justification to contradict her assertion, but that she would have to search the intentions of her own heart.

This may be a good juncture at which to mention that the counselor does not judge the heart but rather points out evidence of what lies in the heart.[49] Additionally, the counselor shows unflinching integrity so that the evidence he presents is eminently honest. Regardless of the cogency of his argument, he must, exercise wisdom to know how far to press his points. It is the work of the Holy Spirit, applied through Scripture, to affect the counselor's work within the counselee's heart. If the Spirit quickens the recipient's heart, the counseling may go forward with favorable results. If, however, the Spirit is not at work, the counselor's efforts are in vain.

The confrontation with sin and idolatry can easily become a chess match in which evidence is bandied back and forth, the counselor and counselee each lying in wait for the other to make a tactical error. Viewing one another as an opponent to be overcome is entirely the wrong approach. Thus, the counselor must be careful not to allow himself to become embroiled in a battle of competing evidence. The counseling session must always be an encounter with the living Christ, so that Jesus himself can administer the needed "checkmate."

The counselor must not win the battle only to lose the war. In focusing on the details, he never loses sight of his larger vision for Jesus. The goal in counseling is never to merely prove a particular point, but to win a heart to faith in Christ. Sometimes the greatest victories are realized, not in proving one's case, but in displaying humble submission to Christ. The counselor who respects personal choices and is willing, in appropriate ways, to listen patiently can often disarm an idolatrous heart so that it longs to surrender to Christ. (This is not to be confused with blind tolerance or permissiveness.) The wise counselor, always eyeing the prize,[50] rightly knows the tides and seasons, the ways and means for presenting a message that will prove winsome, attractive, and incarnational of Christ's own character.

> Since the unsanctified sinner functions in an idolatrous world, he assumes that others do as well. However, when the Christian does not exhibit an idolatrous focus, the world often does not know how to deal with this. For example, an employer often expects, and looks for, a man-pleasing spirit in employees. That employer wants an employee who seeks the company's interests at the expense of all else (while the

---

[49] For a comprehensive discussion of this topic see "The Question of Judgment" in the first book in this series, *Ask for the Ancient Paths: From Art to Artifice to Arisen*, chapter 2: "The Counseling Ambition"

[50] Philippians 3:14

> employer appears magnanimous in the face of his employee's personal needs). However, when one does not exhibit a man-pleasing spirit the assumption is that one either lacks motivation or harbors a perilous spirit of independence. This may not be the case, but the world cannot think in sanctified categories so it projects idolatrous ones. In other words, the world cannot countenance a third option, which is faith in Jesus Christ leading to eternally-directed motives.

The Trap of Fig Leaf Counseling

If one faced a pressing financial need and he could simply print currency, his need would be solved. This is the ultimate display of pragmatism. Sadly, in response to the heart's manifest idolatry the counselor often seeks to "print currency." This means he wrongly focuses the counselee on meeting perceived needs with little focus on uprooting idols. This might be termed "fig leaf counseling."[51] In other words, the counselor, often unwittingly complicit with idolatry, seeks pragmatic solutions which entrench and embolden that idolatry, so that it takes greater hold of the heart.

> "The heart has its reasons which reason does not know." (Blaise Pascal)

When someone says that he just wants to be happy, one's reflexive response is to look for some way to make him happy. Does he need a better job, a new living arrangement, a spouse, or more recreation? In reality, what one calls happiness is often a clever disguise for deceitful lusts of the heart. These lusts are dressed up and ennobled so that they look legitimate. However, the happiness sought is a deceitful end-run around God's "ecosystem." Now, of course, the counseling goal is not to actively make another unhappy. The goal is to change the terms of engagement, to radically alter the life metaphor, so that the counselee recognizes his quest for happiness as merely an escape from relationship with God, a way to make enslaving idols work. The counselor changes the questions and revises the acceptable answers.

Most theater fires start onstage, behind the proscenium arch. In other words, where the drama is most intense, the likelihood of a blaze is the greatest. Much of human drama is a cloaked form of pyromania, a desire to set and stoke existential fires. Let's be clear. People do not want their lives "fixed." No one wants his true problems solved, his dramas dampened, his distractions mitigated, his stories deciphered, and his turmoil and chaos organized. Because what would be have left except a vast, deep, unknown, and frightening world?[52] Most would rather remain a scion to the idol they know, than embrace a God they do not know. Therefore, the counselor will never break slavery to idols through a reasoned approach. He must go after the idol's wellspring, its stronghold on the heart. He must approach the idol as he would a

---

[51] This concept is based on Genesis 3:7
[52] Adapted from quote by Chuck Palahniuk

cornered predator fighting for its life.

> "Without the pain, what would we have to talk about?" (Robert De Niro)

Isabella and the Pot of Basil
William Holman Hunt, 1868

In John Milton's (1608–1674) *Paradise Lost* (1667) Satan said, "Better to reign in hell than serve in heaven." There is comfort and familiarity in one's idolatry. Even though it causes pain, distraction, turmoil, and chaos, it is one's own pain, distraction, turmoil, and chaos. The idol has become a home to one's soul, no matter how oppressive. Many would rather continue under the tyranny of their sin, than live in repentant submission to a God whom they view with suspicion.

However, God never allows idols rest. An automobile tire refuses to remain buried in the ground and will eventually resurface. When interred, a tire rises six inches per year because the rubber acts like a spring causing the surrounding soil to fall below it. A similar analogy could be drawn for idols. As the sinner seeks to bury his idolatry, in time it comes to light. No matter how deeply buried, idols eventually surface because of the built-in "spring action" of God's common (or special) grace which draws them to light.[53] God continually exposes idols revealing each person to himself, people inhabited by a blurred and spliced pastiche of whirling idols that pull the strings of one's seemingly most innocent acts.[54]

Idolatry and the Exemplar

After World War II the Soviet Union hosted screenings of the acclaimed movie "The Grapes of Wrath" (1940) to be viewed by its citizens. The hope was that the proletariat would recognize the inherent dangers in capitalism, thus making them acquiescent to communism. However, the plan backfired as Soviet viewers only

---
[53] Luke 12:3; 1 Corinthians 4:5
[54] This term "blurred and spliced pastiche" from Jacques Ellul (1912–1994)

noticed that even America's indigent owned cars, something which they did not have. The point is that sinners focus solely on the details that they desire, forsaking other details which do not fit their worship paradigm. This is a fitting introduction to the issue of exemplars.

Consider the following verses:

> 1. 'Now that I, your Lord and Teacher, have washed your feet, you also should wash one another's feet. I have set you an example that you should do as I have done for you. Very truly I tell you, no servant is greater than his master, nor is a messenger greater than the one who sent him. Now that you know these things, you will be blessed if you do them." (John 13:14-17)

> 2. "Follow my example, as I follow the example of Christ." (1 Corinthians 11:1)

> 3. "So from now on we regard no one from a worldly point of view. Though we once regarded Christ in this way, we do so no longer." (2 Corinthians 5:16)

> 4. "Follow God's example, therefore, as dearly loved children." (Ephesians 5:1)

> 5. "To this you were called, because Christ suffered for you, leaving you an example, that you should follow in his steps." (1 Peter 2:21)

While Scripture at times speaks about exemplars of faith (Jesus being the exemplar *par excellence*), this concept must be clearly defined. Certainly, Jesus is the Christian's exemplar for faith, but the Bible recognizes a glaring conundrum: the heart follows an exemplar only in the way that the heart itself desires. Thus, while "imitation is the sincerest form of flattery,"[55] that is often what imitation becomes, nothing more than a fleeting form of flattery. The reason being, that a perceived exemplar is viewed through a sinful set of lenses, so that that example is reshaped to cater to the heart's desires. In other words, the sinner interprets the exemplar so as to accommodate the dictates of his desire. Imitating an example in the lust of the flesh does not bring repentance, but rather a more ossified heart further emboldened in its rebellion.

If the Christian life were only about imitating the right actions, if it were only about proper performance, then the question, "What would Jesus do?" is entirely appropriate. However, the Christian life is about so much more than this. It is about being indwelled by the God of the universe so as to be transformed into his image. The counselor seeks that Jesus himself would indwell the believer.

---

[55] Charles Caleb Colton (1780-1832)

Thus, there are two aspects to consider:

1. When speaking about moralism (assuming the correct thoughts, words, and actions), the salient question becomes, "Which exemplar should one imitate?"

2. When speaking about being changed, the question is, "How does one more fully surrender to Christ?"

Mysteriously, the second question comprehensively answers the first, as surrender to Christ produces the needed exemplar, not through an external model, but by means of internal regeneration. Truly, Jesus was the sole example of perfected humanity, but that example comes within the context of a salvific message. The Christian is sanctified so that he has been given the power to faithfully follow an example. Without ongoing sanctification, the example ends up lying fallow. Thus, following Jesus as example assumes that one is being sanctified - confronted, and renewed by the Holy Spirit, so that the command to imitate God comes in the context of life-changing relationship.

As stated, when presented with an example to imitate the unsanctified heart only finds in that example that which suits its desire. In other words, one will not imitate that example's virtuous qualities unless the heart finds some self-serving benefit in that. Each seeks out examples to suit the idols resident within his heart. Thus, the heart's captivation to idols causes it to search for that which magnifies those idols, while discarding that which imperils them.

Consider, for example, that the heroes a society raises up reveal its deepest heart commitments, so that society retains those heroes (and their attributes) which manifest and magnify its collective *Zeitgeist*. Thus, heroes are not viewed as they really are, but as society wants to see them. The same could be said for Jesus, who is often viewed through an idolatrous lens so that those attributes which comply with idolatrous worship are retained, and those which do not are discarded.[56] So, for this reason, the counselor does not merely present Jesus as a model to follow, since the heart merely draws out what it wants in models.

Recasting the Worshipping Core

Ezekiel 11:17-20; and 36:26-28 offer a comprehensive picture of restoration and renewal, even a picture of sanctification in Christ. Ezekiel envisioned a day when, despite Israel's unfaithfulness, God would orchestrate a new Exodus with renewed covenant relationship. God himself would shepherd the exiles back to a reconstituted land whose boundaries were restored, and whose invading armies were vanquished.

---

[56] 2 Corinthians 5:16

The temple would be rebuilt upon Mount Zion, the holy dwelling place. At that time the people would be invested with a new heart and a new spirit. This is a foreshadowing of Jesus' work to sanctify his people. The promises proffered through Ezekiel find their fulfillment in Christ, who is Mount Zion and the reconstituted land.

Shipwreck, Claude Joseph Vernet, 1759

Sanctification is like a body of water; it can only be held back for so long. Eventually it cuts channels into any retaining structure, and those fissures widen until the water is a raging torrent which cannot be stilled. Just as one cannot ultimately keep water from finding its resting point, so too, one cannot staunch the Holy Spirit's work to sanctify believers. Faith in Jesus makes people easy to lead, but difficult to drive; easy to govern, but impossible to enslave.[57]

> The greatest freedom is a pure heart.

Christians often wrongly believe that Abraham, Joseph, Moses, David, and Solomon were far greater than believers today, towering figures of the faith that dwarf modern saints. Elevating the patriarchs to a position greater than that of the Christian unwittingly advances an existentialist view of humanity. Thus, those who focus attention on imitating the patriarchs tend to hold a functionally low view of Christ, little understanding of just what Christ accomplishes in believers. Most Christians, in lionizing the patriarchs, do not understand the power and potential that they have been given to be free from sin. The Christian possesses something far greater than the

---

[57] Adapted from Henry Peter Brougham (1778–1868)

patriarchs ever had, that for which the patriarchs longed, to witness the conclusive deliverance of their God, God himself living within believers.

> "For truly I tell you, many prophets and righteous people longed to see what you see but did not see it, and to hear what you hear but did not hear it." (Matthew 13:17)
>
> "We are not like Moses, who would put a veil over his face to prevent the Israelites from seeing the end of what was passing away. But their minds were made dull, for to this day the same veil remains when the old covenant is read. It has not been removed, because only in Christ is it taken away. Even to this day when Moses is read, a veil covers their hearts. But whenever anyone turns to the Lord, the veil is taken away." (2 Corinthians 3:13-16)

Consider Moses' radiant face, as spoken of in Exodus 34:29-35. While Moses was not aware that, after speaking with the Lord, his face was radiant, this radiance was so overwhelming that the people were frightened. So, when Moses spoke to the people he veiled his face, removing the veil when he entered the Lord's presence. While Moses' external radiance was an astounding display, it pails in comparison to the experience of those in Christ. While the Holy Spirit rested *upon* Moses,[58] the Spirit *indwells* the Christian.[59] Therefore, the Christian radiates the Holy Spirit from his inner being.

Excursus: The Day of Atonement

Leviticus 16:1-34	In Christ
1. A command to only approach God on a specified day each year. (16:2)	The Christian can approach Christ at any time with any request.[60]
2. A priest must bathe and wear sacred garments. (16:4)	The Christian is washed through Christ's blood and wears his robe of salvation.[61]
3. Aaron was to atone for his own sin before making intercession for the people's sin. (16:6, 11)	Christ is the perfect intercessor and is ready to make intercession on behalf of his people.[62]
4. Aaron presented two goats before the Lord. One goat was sacrificed, the other became the scapegoat. (16:9, 10)	The two goats in Leviticus 16 represent two aspects of Christ's atonement. He was sacrificed and he was led into the desert to die.[63]
5. Aaron was to conceal the atonement	Christ has removed the veil separating

---

[58] Numbers 11:17
[59] Ephesians 1:13, 14
[60] Hebrews 4:16
[61] Isaiah 61:10
[62] Isaiah 53:12
[63] Hebrews 9:11-14

cover with smoke from burning incense. God was to remain veiled in mystery. (16:13)	God and man, so that Christians may approach God with boldness.[64]
6. Aaron first made atonement for himself, then for his household, and lastly for the whole community. (16:17, 33)	Christ prayed for himself, his disciples, and then for all believers.[65]
7. Aaron pronounced the people's wickedness and rebellion on the head of the scapegoat, which was then led into the desert to a solitary place. (16:21, 22)	Christ began his public ministry by fasting and praying in the desert for forty days.[66] Christ was also "led into the desert" as he hung on the cross; he said that he was thirsty.[67]

8. The Day of Atonement – the tenth day of the seventh month set aside to cleanse the people (16:29)
    a. The people were to do no work.
    b. It was a Sabbath day of rest. (16:31)
    c. The people must deny themselves.
	Each day is a celebration of the atonement which Christ wrought. In the midst of this spirit of celebration, the Christian joyfully denies himself, daily taking up his cross to follow Jesus.[68]

The Jubilee Year was celebrated every fiftieth year,[69] inaugurated on the Day of Atonement with the sounding of the trumpets. It is a picture of the gospel: repentance, the joy of salvation, and the liberty which they bring.[70] There is indeed true and lasting joy in repentance, the greater one's repentance, the greater one's experience of joy.

> Turn your face to the sun (Son) and the shadows fall behind you. (adapted from Maori proverb)

Vanquishing the Ghost of Attila the Hun

A young Christian woman met me one afternoon and, upon hearing of my ministry, rattled off a litany of those who have achieved far more than I. She recounted, in detail, others' successes and triumphs in a way that seemed calculated to create a sense of superiority in the conversation. Even though unimposing and quiet, she might as well have been Attila the Hun (d. 453) returned from the dead. It was as if she

---

[64] 2 Corinthians 3:16; Ephesians 3:12; Hebrews 4:16
[65] John 17
[66] Matthew 4:2
[67] John 19:28
[68] Luke 9:23
[69] Leviticus 25:8-24
[70] The Matthew Henry Commentary, Bible Study Tools, 2012

sought to dominate me through associating herself with those whom she deemed had superseded me. This woman is a committed Christian recounting the work of other committed Christians, but her motive seemed entirely self-serving, a prideful attempt at gaining control.

It was fascinating to see the effect she had on me. As we spoke, I felt a battle waging within to retain a measure of self-respect. On the one hand, my mind crafted silent rebuttals, rehearsed the history of my successes, and rationalized away her evidence as propaganda. On the other hand, by God's

Attila fragment
Eugene Ferdinand Victor Delacroix, d. 1863

grace, Scripture came to mind calling me to peace with God, to rest in Jesus' accomplished work in my life, to recognize that no eye has seen and no ear has heard that which God has prepared for those who love him.[71] Thankfully, the battle ended in Jesus' victory as he caused me to listen and respectfully offer meaningful and loving commentary. He allowed me to consider her motives, so as to offer indirect counsel to repentance and growth in Christ, in short, to let Jesus take center-stage throughout the exchange.

> "Faith is taking the first step even when you don't see the whole staircase." (Martin Luther King, Jr.)

The Lord's command is to make obedience one's sole objective so that as one continues in godly behavior his heart is shaped. Thus, a feedback system operates within the psyche, behavior influences the heart and, in turn, the heart drives

---

[71] 1 Corinthians 2:9

behavior.[72] As one is free from idols he both experiences God's love and, in turn, is able to love God. To offer freedom from one's idols is God's great act of love to mankind. To know this freedom fills one with inexpressible love for a God who can redeem desperately depraved people. Additionally, casting off idols brings total change. The repentant soon sees what God sees, overlooks what God overlooks, hears as God hears, wants what God wants, rejects what God rejects, hates that which God hates, and loves as God loves.

> See, a king will reign in righteousness
> and rulers will rule with justice.
> Each man will be like a shelter from the wind
> and a refuge from the storm,
> like streams of water in the desert
> and the shadow of a great rock in a thirsty land.
>
> Then the eyes of those who see will no longer be closed,
> and the ears of those who hear will listen.
> The fearful heart will know and understand,
> and the stammering tongue will be fluent and clear.
> No longer will the fool be called noble
> nor the scoundrel be highly respected.
> For fools speak folly,
> their hearts are bent on evil:
> They practice ungodliness
> and spread error concerning the LORD;
> the hungry they leave empty
> and from the thirsty they withhold water.
> Scoundrels use wicked methods,
> they make up evil schemes
> to destroy the poor with lies,
> even when the plea of the needy is just.
> But the noble man makes noble plans,
> and by noble deeds they stand. (Isaiah 32:1-8)

---

[72] For further discussion of this topic see "The Heart-Eye Feedback System" in chapter 5: "Metaphors for Sin"

- 9 -

MARAUDING VISIGOTHS:
The Autocratic Self[1]

Jesus Exposes Each Person's True Identity[2]

Jesus' disciple Judas "betrayed innocent blood" in his disloyalty.[3] He was seized with remorse as he cast away his bribe,[4] and finally he hanged himself on a tree.[5] (According to Deuteronomy 21:23 anyone hanged on a tree was cursed.) Thus, Judas, in his interaction with Jesus, was thus shown to be the "anti-prophet."

According to Jewish law, it was forbidden for the high priest to hold a council at night, yet Caiaphas did just that. He

Kiss of Judas
Cornelis Engebrechtsz, c. 1500

sought false evidence against Jesus, an abuse of the high priest's power.[6] He tore his clothing after Jesus' response to the charges in defiance of Leviticus 21:10,[7] which stipulates that the high priest must wear a seamless garment. Thus, in his dealings with Jesus, Caiaphas was exposed as a fraudulent priest intent only on his own wicked

---
[1] This chapter might traditionally include a discussion of the theological topic of "calling."
[2] This general discussion of Judas, Caiaphas, and Pilate from Vern Poythress, Westminster Theological Seminary, Philadelphia, Pennsylvania
[3] Matthew 27:4
[4] Matthew 27:3
[5] Matthew 27:5
[6] Matthew 26:59
[7] Matthew 26:65

agenda. Thus, Caiaphas, in his interaction with Jesus, was shown to be the "anti-priest."

Three times the procurator Pilate was shown Jesus' innocence. First, Jesus made no reply to the charges brought against him.[8] Then, Pilate's wife warned Pilate of Jesus' innocence.[9] Finally, Pilate's own conscience was plagued ("Why? What crime has he committed?").[10] He knew Jesus was innocent, but was powerless to save him on account of his bondage to the people's will.[11] Pilate succumbed to the will of the people proving himself to have no authority in the situation.[12] He was himself on trial as he pleaded with Jesus uttering, "What is truth?"[13] Thus, Pilate, in his interaction with Jesus, was revealed as the "anti-king."

Luke 23:18-21 states,

> But they cried out all together, saying, 'Away with this man, and release for us Barabbas!'(He was one who had been thrown into prison for an insurrection made in the city, and for murder.) Pilate, wanting to release Jesus, addressed them again, but they kept on calling out, saying, 'Crucify, crucify Him!'

Barabbas is the Everyman, insurrectionist, murder, and ultimately one who seeks the murder of God himself. The crowd (representing the world) would rather see an evil man released than Jesus declared innocent. If Jesus is innocent then each is a confirmed sinner. Yet, each person desperately seeks exoneration from his sin, and the only way to do this is to condemn Jesus. The sinner must condemn Jesus to avoid being condemned himself. The crowds so vehemently sought Barabbas' release because they recognized that they were in effect coconspirators with Barabbas. Thus, in Barabbas' exoneration the crowds could likewise feel exonerated. But this is a fool's errand, the likes of which reside in every sinner's heart.

Many people love a Jesus of their own making, a Jesus after their own image. As long as the Jesus they worship does not make them change, they love him. While most seek to put Jesus into their "solar system" of truth, Jesus cannot be manipulated; he must pull each into his solar system. Just as with Judas, Caiaphas, and Pilate, Jesus exposes the root hypocrisy, duplicity, and idolatry in each person. Jesus exposes one to his true self; he reveals who each really is, and his besetting sin. One must either be conquered by Jesus or deny Jesus' true identity; there is no neutral ground.

---

[8] Matthew 27:14
[9] Matthew 27:19
[10] Matthew 27:23
[11] Matthew 27:18
[12] Matthew 27:24
[13] John 18:38

> "Anyone who falls on this stone will be broken to pieces; anyone on whom it falls will be crushed." (Matthew 21:44)
>
> "Then Simeon blessed them and said to Mary, his mother: 'This child is destined to cause the falling and rising of many in Israel, and to be a sign that will be spoken against,'" (Luke 2:34)

Consider that sinful man refuses to submit to Jesus Christ, a specific man, in a specific place, at a specific time in history. Jesus was not an abstraction but an actual person, God himself, who entered history. This is the locus of the offense, that Jesus was a historical person whom we are called to worship by name. Many would rather worship an abstract, faceless god whom they can shape into their own image and likeness. A faceless nameless god allows sinners to glorify their own name and identity. Yet, the sinner readily submits to himself, a specific person, in a specific place, at a specific time in history. Sinful man will not glorify Jesus' name, but instead glorifies of his own name.

Three Aspects of Self

There are essentially three dimensions to the self: creation, fall, and redemption. The first, creation, is that mankind is designed as an image-bearer of the infinite, eternal, all-powerful holy God. This means that the abilities and potential invested into mankind are, in some regard, unfathomable. The human intellect, creativity, potential for accomplishment, and ability to grow in wisdom, are truly awe-inspiring. The human design is magnificent, and that design is invested into every person regardless of raw ability, so that, as one encounters another person, he beholds a manifestation of the eternal God himself.

> Consider mankind's incalculable potential for achievement. Over the course of seventy years (1890s to 1960s) transportation evolved from horseback and railroads to sonic jets and space exploration. There has never been such rapid change in the speed of transportation in the history of the world. No period has even approached the three orders of magnitude increase which occurred during the first half of the 20th century. In just sixty-six years (1903 to 1969) mankind went from the discovery of flight to setting foot on the moon. That is an absolutely astounding accomplishment.

However, a sudden cataclysm, called "the fall," somewhat destroyed the manifestation of God in man. The fall was the loss of man's God-ward referent, so that mankind sought to be his own god, his own arbiter, committed to his own glory. This is the grievous tragedy which has partially decimated mankind's design. The fall did not utterly obliterate the image-bearing, but it did serious damage so that man uses his intellect, creativity, ambition, and self-delineated wisdom as a weapon against God, as a replacement for God, as a means for installing himself in God's place.

But God did not leave mankind to wallow in his tragic choice. Rather he sent his Son, Jesus Christ, to restore the image to its former glory, but even more so, to invest that image with greater soaring splendor than previously imagined. Thus, that which is gained in Christ is vastly superior to that which was lost in the fall. The Christian, living in God's Spirit, possesses something categorically more significant than Adam ever had in the garden. The Christian has seen the lengths that God would go through to save rebellious people, that God himself would suffer and die to reconstitute lost and shattered lives. The Christian has God himself living within him, and in that sense has something which even the angels long to experience.[14]

Rest on the Flight into Egypt, Michelangelo Caravaggio, c. 1597

Thus, in summary, mankind's design is unfathomable; the fall brought staggering loss; but Jesus now offers a restored and glorified re-creation of God's image in man.

> "People are always trying to 'find' themselves. The self is not something that one finds; it is something that one creates." (Thomas Szasz)

> The concept of diversity is greatly misunderstood in the modern world. The world generally views diversity along gender, ethnic, or socio-economic lines. However,

---
[14] 1 Peter 1:12

> true diversity is defined by the presence or absence of the Holy Spirit. Diversity is not firstly the product of man-defined categories (ethnicity) or human activities (economic development or educational background). True diversity is demarked with regard to those who know God and are wise, and those who reject God and are foolish.
>
> Thus, black or white, rich or poor, Western or Asian, are not the categories for what constitutes a diverse population. Diversity is determined by those who are in Christ and those who are not. This is the ultimate dividing line for demarking the self.

Modern Culture's *Lingua Franca*

Common Terms in Society	The Bible's Response: Corrective Worship
1. Self-concept	In Jesus there is corrective self-understanding which results in sober self-assessment. "I praise you because I am fearfully and wonderfully made; your works are wonderful, I know that full well." (Psalm 139:14) "As the heavens are higher than the earth, so are my ways higher than your ways and my thoughts than your thoughts." (Isaiah 55:9) "But Jesus would not entrust himself to them, for he knew all men." (John 2:24) "For by the grace given me I say to every one of you: Do not think of yourself more highly than you ought, but rather think of yourself with sober judgment, in accordance with the faith God has distributed to each of you." (Romans 12:3)
2. Self-confidence	In Jesus there is no confidence in oneself, but rather trusting in God's work through oneself. "Though an army besiege me, my heart will not fear; though war break out against me, even then I will be confident." (Psalm 27:3) "When all our enemies heard about this, all the surrounding nations were afraid and lost their self-confidence, because they realized that this work had been done with the help of our

	God." (Nehemiah 6:16) "And pray in the Spirit on all occasions with all kinds of prayers and requests. With this in mind, be alert and always keep on praying for all the Lord's people." (Ephesians 6:18) "For it is we who are the circumcision, we who serve God by his Spirit, who boast in Christ Jesus, and who put no confidence in the flesh--" (Philippians 3:3)
3. Self-determination	In Jesus there is the understanding that self-determination is a dangerous pursuit when not coupled with a regenerate heart. "They plot injustice and say, 'We have devised a perfect plan!' Surely the human mind and heart are cunning." (Psalm 64:6)
4. Self-empowerment	In Jesus, the Christian does seek self-empowerment (recognizing this as merely a euphemism for pride). The Christian, instead, seeks to be empowered by God's Spirit to experience lasting holiness. "Immediately what had been said about Nebuchadnezzar was fulfilled. He was driven away from people and ate grass like the ox. His body was drenched with the dew of heaven until his hair grew like the feathers of an eagle and his nails like the claws of a bird. At the end of that time, I, Nebuchadnezzar, raised my eyes toward heaven, and my sanity was restored. Then I praised the Most High; I honored and glorified him who lives forever." (Daniel 4:33, 34) "They are a feared and dreaded people; they are a law to themselves and promote their own honor." (Habakkuk 1:7)
5. Self-esteem	In Jesus, the Christian, refusing to honor himself, holds only esteem for Christ. "They came to him and said, 'Teacher, we know that you are a man of integrity. You aren't swayed by others, because you pay no attention to who they are; but you teach the way of God in accordance with the truth...'" (Mark 12:14) "It is written: 'As surely as I live,' says the Lord, 'every knee will bow before me; every tongue will acknowledge God.'" (Romans 14:11)

	 *The Libyan Sibyl*, Michelangelo Buonarroti, c. 1512 "I have been crucified with Christ and I no longer live, but Christ lives in me. The life I now live in the body, I live by faith in the Son of God, who loved me and gave himself for me." (Galatians 2:20) "…that at the name of Jesus every knee should bow, in heaven and on earth and under the earth," (Philippians 2:10)
6. Self-help	In Jesus, the Christian recognizes that he is unable to help himself without the indwelling work of the Holy Spirit. "Who can discern his errors? Forgive my hidden faults." (Psalm 19:12) "When you were dead in your sins and in the uncircumcision of your flesh, God made you alive with Christ. He forgave us all our sins, having canceled the charge of our legal indebtedness, which stood against us and condemned us; he has taken it away, nailing it to the cross. And having disarmed the powers and authorities, he made a public spectacle of them, triumphing over them by the cross." (Colossians 2:13)
7. Self-image	In Jesus, one is given the correct self-image, the understanding

	that he is constructed in the image of God so as to glorify him. "…for he knows how we are formed, he remembers that we are dust." (Psalm 103:14) "I praise you because I am fearfully and wonderfully made; your works are wonderful, I know that full well." (Psalm 139:14) "I am a man of unclean lips, among a people of unclean lips." (Isaiah 6:5) "For from him and through him and for him are all things. To him be the glory forever! Amen." (Romans 11:36)
8. Self-improvement	In Jesus, the heart is progressively sanctified to become more like Christ; this is the only improvement that matters. "They who heard it said, 'Then who can be saved?' But He said, 'The things that are impossible with people are possible with God.'" (Luke 18:26, 27) "But even if I am being poured out like a drink offering on the sacrifice and service coming from your faith, I am glad and rejoice with all of you." (Philippians 2:17) "But there is a place where someone has testified: 'What is mankind that you are mindful of them, a son of man that you care for him?'" (Hebrews 2:6)
9. Self-love	In Jesus, the Christian recognizes that he instinctually loves himself to his own peril. Loathing the sin within himself, the Christian only truly loves Jesus. "If your hand or your foot causes you to stumble, cut it off and throw it from you; it is better for you to enter life crippled or lame, than to have two hands or two feet and be cast into the eternal fire. If your eye causes you to stumble, pluck it out and throw it from you. It is better for you to enter life with one eye, than to have two eyes and be cast into the fiery hell." (Matthew 18:8, 9) "He answered, 'Love the Lord your God with all your heart and with all your soul and with all your strength and with all your

	mind'; and, 'Love your neighbor as yourself.'" (Luke 10:27) "No, I strike a blow to my body and make it my slave so that after I have preached to others, I myself will not be disqualified for the prize." (1 Corinthians 9:27)
10. Self-pity	In Jesus, the Christian does not pity himself but rests in the provision of a good God who cares for his every need (the chief of which is the need to be free from sin). "'All these I have kept,' the young man said. 'What do I still lack?' Jesus answered, 'If you want to be perfect, go, sell your possessions and give to the poor, and you will have treasure in heaven. Then come, follow me.' When the young man heard this, he went away sad, because he had great wealth." (Matthew 19:20-22)
11. Self-pride	In Jesus, the Christian embraces humility, that despite his incomparable gifts, he ultimately occupies a lowly position with regard to his Creator. "'Woe to me!' I cried. 'I am ruined! For I am a man of unclean lips, and I live among a people of unclean lips, and my eyes have seen the King, the Lord Almighty.'" (Isaiah 6:5) "We know that the law is spiritual; but I am unspiritual, sold as a slave to sin. For I know that good itself does not dwell in me, that is, in my sinful nature. For I have the desire to do what is good, but I cannot carry it out." (Romans 7:14, 18) "But whatever were gains to me I now consider loss for the sake of Christ. What is more, I consider everything a loss because of the surpassing worth of knowing Christ Jesus my Lord, for whose sake I have lost all things. I consider them garbage, that I may gain Christ" (Philippians 3:7, 8)
12. Self-promotion	In Jesus, the Christian seeks self-sacrifice. "He must become greater; I must become less." (John 3:30) "For he chose us in him before the creation of the world to be holy and blameless in his sight." (Ephesians 1:4) "Since you died with Christ to the elemental spiritual forces of this world, why, as though you still belonged to the world, do

	you submit to its rules…" (Colossians 2:20) *The Boyhood of Alfred the Great (A Little Prince Likely in Time to Bless a Royal Throne)*, Edmund Blair Leighton, 1913
13. Self-regard	In Jesus, the Christian does not countenance his own concerns but rather exercises a proper self-abasement. "Therefore I despise myself and repent in dust and ashes." (Job 42:6) "…wretched man that I am. Who will deliver me from this body of death?" (Romans 7:24) "So from now on we regard no one from a worldly point of view. Though we once regarded Christ in this way, we do so no longer." (2 Corinthians 5:16) "All of us also lived among them at one time, gratifying the

	cravings of our flesh and following its desires and thoughts. Like the rest, we were by nature deserving of wrath." (Ephesians 2:3)
14. Self-worth	In Jesus, one recognizes that he has no intrinsic value, except that which God invests. "But the LORD said to Samuel, 'Do not consider his appearance or his height, for I have rejected him. The LORD does not look at the things people look at. People look at the outward appearance, but the LORD looks at the heart.'" (1 Samuel 16:7) "What is man that you are mindful of him, human beings that you care for them?" (Psalm 8:4) "This is what the LORD says: 'What fault did your ancestors find in me, that they strayed so far from me? They followed worthless idols and became worthless themselves.'" (Jeremiah 2:5) "All the peoples of the earth are regarded as nothing. He does as he pleases with the powers of heaven and the peoples of the earth. No one can hold back his hand or say to him: 'What have you done?'" (Daniel 4:35) "The Spirit gives life; the flesh counts for nothing. The words I have spoken to you—they are full of the Spirit and life." (John 6:63)

"Self" words are inextricably God-directed, so that self-worth, self-love, and self-confidence are worship nomenclature. They are the pride of man and the fear of man artfully packaged to appear noble. Self-confidence easily grows into belief in oneself. Belief in oneself quickly slips into the delusion that one is, and ought to be, his own god. The idol underlying self-confidence is the same as the belief that one is God himself.

> There is a pantheon of false functional gods residing in the heart, each marshaled to serve the self and each serving as a prism through which the self, with its attendant desires, is viewed.

Thus, modern concepts of self run counter to the entire teaching of the Bible. The Bible speaks about self-control, self-denial, self-discipline, and self-sacrifice, each built upon a resting in the Holy Spirit to do this work. For example, Matthew 6:10

reads, "…your kingdom come, your will be done, on earth as it is in heaven." The model prayer reminds one to petition that *God's* will would be done, not that of the one praying. The Bible never prizes man's will, but sees that will as a liability to be quenched and cast off. Man's prime objective should be to submit to, and enter into, God's declarative will (the Bible).

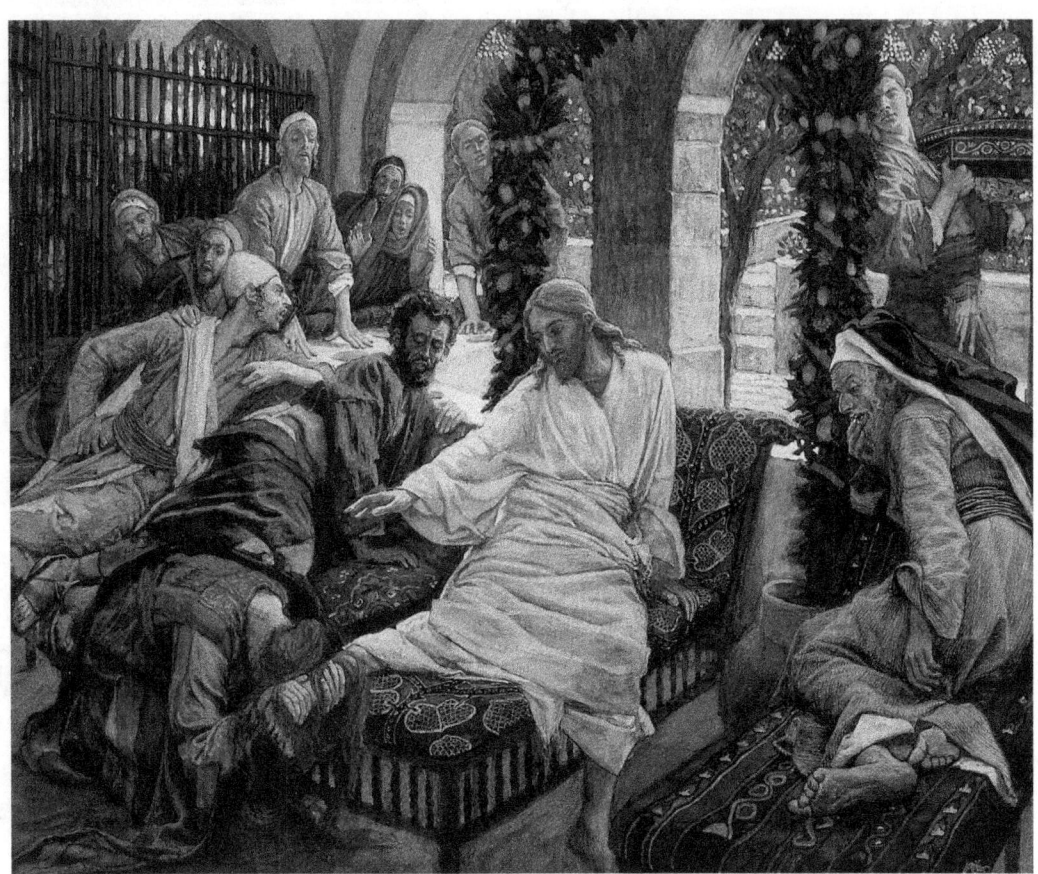

Mary Magdalene's Box of Very Precious Ointment
James Jacques Joseph Tissot, d. 1894

The Bible's "self" words are neither self-navigated nor self-implemented. Rather, they are a drawing close to God, a resting in him, a decision to seek him in recognition of his exclusive proprietary claim to the heart's change process. James 4:8 states, "Draw near to God, and he will draw near to you. Cleanse your hands, you sinners; and purify your hearts, you double minded." James' admonition to purify one's own heart is the direct result of drawing near to God. The process of drawing near results in an indwelled, impacted, chastened, and purified heart.

> "This is the final test of a gentleman: his respect for those who can be of no possible value to him." (William Lyon Phelps)

In whatever way one's self-image is flawed, this invariably leads to pain and loss. At one extreme, the one who worships himself as god espouses a delusional and enslaving self-love. He is unable to love others and unable to find satisfying purpose in life. At the other extreme, the one who sees himself and others as no more than random accidents of nature will engage in self-destructive thoughts and behaviors. He will eventually seek to expunge the image of God within himself and others.[15] (I find it fascinating that these two extremes routinely live within the same person, a wild veering back and forth between apotheosis and cosmic accident. In fact, the ancient Romans described this phenomenon as *"aut Caesar, aut nihil,"* ("either a Caesar or nothing"). Without solid grounding in God's Word, mankind's self-understanding swings perilously, like an existential metronome that has lost its pivot point.)

The Rise of Self-Celebration

King Herod was installed as king of the Jews in 40 B.C. at age twenty-five. From the start of his reign, Herod was a brutal tyrant exhibiting an unquenchable lust for power. He was shrewd and adept at forging political alliances to his own advantage. Herod, during his reign, built seven palaces and a grand temple. He married ten wives, each for political expedience. Yet, Herod was highly-paranoid, so that as his power grew so did his fear of insurrection. So great was his fear, that Herod had one of his wives and two of sons executed on suspicion of treason. Incidentally, at the time of Jesus' birth Herod had finally defeated his political enemies and was ready to luxuriate in his triumph. Thus, upon hearing the news of Jesus' birth Herod literally "shook uncontrollably."[16]

Herod could construct, marry, or murder at will, with impunity. He did as he liked in his pursuit of mastery of his world. However, commoners were forced to endure the powers above them, subject to the whim and will of tyrants. It would appear that in modern times the commoner has become the Herod. The average citizen is now able to go where he wants, do what he wants when he wants, without hindrance. As with kings of the past, the common man today can impose something of his will on his world. This "democratization of imposed wills" is having dire effect as modern people are each becoming a "miniature Herod."

> "A man's worst difficulties begin when he is able to do as he likes." (Thomas Henry Huxley)

I recently attended a dinner party at which I chatted with a young man and woman. In the middle of the conversation the woman raised her cell phone, holding it away from her face as if to take a picture. Assuming the woman was snapping our picture,

---

[15] For further discussion of this topic see, "The Center Point Theory of Design" in the first book in this series, *Ask for the Ancient Paths: From Art to Artifice to Arisen,* chapter 5: "Redefining the Pygmalion Effect: Exploring the Image of God in Man"

[16] Matthew 2:3; see "The Herod Effect" in chapter 8: "The Search for Eldorado Ends: Repenting of Idols of the Heart"

the young man and I shifted closer and smiled. Yet, she giggled impishly as she disclosed that she had just taken a picture of herself. This anecdote succinctly captures the modern ethos. It was not long ago that one might raise his cell phone to snap a picture of a friend. Today, one raises his cell phone, more often than not, to snap a picture of himself, and that unceremoniously in the middle of conversation. When the urge to celebrate herself arose, this woman could not resist. There was no sense of discipline or other-centeredness. The impetus to memorialize herself at that moment took precedence over all else, even if it meant alienating her company. The spirit of Herod has been resurrected.

> As people increasingly love themselves and do as they please, civilization hurdles toward its doom.

The modern world is afflicted by angst over not being adequately celebrated. With growing alarm, people long to be noticed, praised and prided for their achievements, and appreciated for their inherent worth. Those who do not receive adequate adulation often feel anxious that a moment has passed in which no one has honored them, no one has duly recorded their existence. In this regard, Jeremiah 2:17 states, "Have you not brought this on yourselves by forsaking the LORD your God when he led you in the way?"

> "Everyone runs his own theater. In it he is playwright, director, actor, stagehand, box office, usher, and audience." (Julius Hare)

Cursed by the tyrannical self, the heart is flooded with ever-greater demands which either confuse and paralyze it, or else propel it with intoxicating impulsivity. The ever-growing social anxiety associated with longing for praise and approbation often leads to impulse buying, fits of rage, prevarication, sexual desire and, when roiled with a demanding spirit, suicidal ideations. The celebrated self falls into many temptations set by the world. It is easily distracted, deluded, and seduced into a lifestyle of ever-deepening hatred of God.

> "Sin" and "pride" both have "I" in the middle;[17] idol begins with "I" and rightly could be thought of as an "I-doll."[18]

A recent study found that the explosion of promiscuity and adultery is, to some extent, driven by the quest for a partner who simply notices, emotionally engages, who conveys the message that one is remembered and worthy of attention. In a world swirling with chronic distraction and wistful indulgence, people today are desperate to simply be noticed, to matter to someone, to leave some personal impression on the

---

[17] Rick Warren, Fox News, Sean Hannity interview
[18] Michael Bobick, *From Slavery to Sonship: A Biblical Psychology for Pastoral Counseling* (1995) (class notes)

world. In this one glimpses the curse of self-worship, chronic self-focus, and the tireless quest for some feeling of recognition. Negotiating the labyrinth of perceived needs leads to debilitating self-imprisonment.

> "You turn things upside down, as if the potter were thought to be like the clay! Shall what is formed say to the one who formed it, 'You did not make me'? Can the pot say to the potter, 'You know nothing'?" (Isaiah 29:16)

A self-obsessed heart easily develops:

1. Brooding
2. Competitiveness and comparisons
3. Despair
4. Eating disorders
5. A fantasy world
6. Hatred for one's own body image
7. Out of control consumer spending
8. A preoccupation with physical appearance
9. Self-consciousness

The Return of the Prodigal Son
Pompeo Batoni, 1773

The Toxic Delusion of Believing in Oneself

One often hears the phrases "believe in yourself," "discover yourself," "find yourself," "be true to yourself," "love yourself," and "follow your dreams" (phrases which filled the prodigal son's heart as he demanded his share of the estate and set out for a distant land[19]). Though seemingly guileless, these phrases are the treachery of a humanistic worldview which fails to recognize the desperate depravity and the often unmitigated self-aggrandizement of the human heart. Self-focus often leads to piercing loss, desperate loneliness, and inner vacuity. One's dreams, when not under God's auspices, only vivify a relentless pursuit of self-destruction.

> "Almost every man wastes part of his life attempting to display talents he does not possess, trying to gain applause which he cannot keep." (Samuel Johnson)

---

[19] Luke 15:11-31

Genesis 3:6 reads, "When the woman saw that the fruit of the tree was good for food and pleasing to the eye and also desirable for gaining wisdom, she took some and ate it." Eve put confidence in herself. She trusted her interpretation of the fruit, that it would give her the wisdom that she sought. Her self-confidence was belief in her own ability to rightly assess and define the created order without God. Her belief in herself caused here to elevate herself to the status of God. She felt that she could, in grabbing for the fruit, become a god herself. Following Eve's lead, self-confidence is the way of the world and functions in defiance of God.

Inline with Eve's misguided faith, the "believe in yourself" mantra has become the creedal statement of the modern world, a kind of evangelistic message derived directly from *The Satanic Bible*. This creed shows itself in often brazen acts intended to aggrandize the self. For example, recently, a teenage tourist carved his name onto an ancient Egyptian bas-relief, defacing art that dates back 4,500 years. This is the fruit of the "believe in yourself" culture, a culture that sees little harm in self-assertion, self-aggrandizement, and self-adulation. This believe-in-oneself mentality causes one to never question himself. The assumption is that if a thought derives from oneself, and promotes oneself, then it must be right. However, Proverbs 14:12 warns, "There is a way that appears to be right to a man, but in the end it leads to death."

> "Heaven-sent calamities you may stand up against, but you cannot survive those brought on by yourself." (Shu Qing)

In a culture in which people increasingly believe in themselves (trust their own judgment, pursue a vacuous self-confidence, and seek ways to further love-themselves) there is a blindness to the dangers of visual media such as television. Since people believe themselves to be inherently good and wise,[20] they judge goodness or evil based upon what they see (and in the process only misjudge). Thus, as with Eve, each person is easily mesmerized, hypnotized, by what his eyes have seen. The greater one's self-confidence the greater one's self-deception, as he fails to see the dangers lurking in adjudging with unregenerate eyes.

> "Woe to those who call evil good and good evil, who put darkness for light and light for darkness, who put bitter for sweet and sweet for bitter." (Isaiah 5:20)

Mankind's knowledge of himself should lead to two outcomes. The first is to recognize the inherent "very goodness" of his original design, prompting a spirit of thankful worship of God. The second is to recognize one's depravity, resulting in profound inability to arrive at truth, or to act wisely, without intimate relationship with God. The knowledge of self should not result in self-worship; it should result in

---

[20] Romans 1:22

humility and praise of a God who saves in spite of oneself.

> Plyometrics refers to using the body's own weight as the means for working the body (such as pushups, pull-ups, and squats). The greater the body's mass, the greater the means by which that mass is transformed (to shed adipose tissue, for example). The human psyche may also experience a kind of plyometrics as the crushing weight of sin should drive the sinner to repentance before a holy God. The greater one's sense of his sin (awareness of its "mass"), the more vigorously he should run to Christ for salvation (the greater the "workout"). Thus, that which is to one's detriment (the soul's "adipose") should drive one to the foot of the cross desperate for mercy (the "exercise" of one's soul). The greater the detriment, the greater the cry for mercy.[21]

While some point out that the believe-in-oneself appeal only applies to recognizing one's God-given talents or abilities, the truth is that the sinful heart never stops there. It takes such a premise further, easily sliding into self-worship. So the heart knows no boundary in its self-focus. Without the mitigating presence of a holy God one is easily seduced with the allure of self-worship.

Some also point out that unless one believes in himself he is likely not to take responsibility for himself. The concepts of believing in oneself and taking responsibility for oneself are diametrically opposed, opposite ends of the spectrum in terms of how the psyche functions. Those who believe in themselves invariably renege on taking responsibility for themselves, since taking true responsibility arises from humility and self-denial.

> "Look for yourself, and you will find in the long run only hatred, loneliness, despair, rage and decay. But look for Christ and you will find Him, and with Him everything else thrown in." (C.S. Lewis)

Although the obsession with self is thought to be a modern scourge, throughout history people have displayed the same tendency. Matthew 20:20-28 recounts the mother of Zebedee's sons request that her two boys sit at Jesus' right and left in heaven. This mother knelt before Jesus lending the appearance of self-effacing reverence. Yet, her request was entirely self-promoting and built upon sinful comparison, an attempt to gain the upper-hand over her peers. Jesus refused to take the bait; he saw through her request. Matthew 20:22 reads, "'You don't know what you are asking,' Jesus said to them. 'Can you drink the cup I am going to drink?'" Jesus' reply was that eternal accolades are at his Father's discretion; but clearly those who want to reign with Jesus must also suffer with him. Those who, like this mother,

---

[21] See Luke 7:47; In Romans 6:1, 2, Paul is clear that there is never any net benefit from sin. Therefore, it is vital to point out that the Bible never presents sin as holding any disguised blessing. Sin is unmitigated loss. However, God leverages sin's effect on the psyche to drive the sinner to Christ. Thus, God often brings good out of a seemingly irredeemable evil.

believe in themselves invariably miss God's calling to forsake themselves, repent, and receive Jesus as savior. God calls sinful self-centered people to deny their own priorities in order to adopt his.

> "If I cannot do great things, I can do small things in a great way." (James Clark)

Sculptors in Ancient Rome
Lawrence Alma Tadema, d. 1912

Is the greater evil extrinsic to, or intrinsic to, mankind? If the greater evil surrounds man, then his problem is his finiteness; he has a circumstance problem. (This was Adam's error; he thought he needed to be more like God.) If, however, the greater evil is within, then mankind has a worship problem, a need for repentance. Because the Bible places the force majeure upon internal evil, Matthew 15:11 states, "What goes into a man's mouth does not defile him, but what comes out of his mouth, that is what defiles him." Picking up this theme, Hebrews 12:11 states, "No discipline seems pleasant at the time, but painful. Later on, however, it produces a harvest of righteousness and peace for those who have been trained by it." God knows that the believer's greatest need is for internal discipline, that which reduces the evil within, in order to outwardly produce good fruit.

When the intrinsic evil (the flesh) is eliminated, the extrinsic evil (Satan and the world) loses its persuasion and power. Thus, for mankind the problem of evil is not firstly an outward-to-inward problem, but an inward-to-outward problem.[22] Therefore, God knows that the Christian's greatest need is to be freed from himself through lifelong rehabilitation.

> Society uses the term "at risk" to describe those who come from disadvantaged

---

[22] Luke 11:39

> backgrounds or dissolute communities. This term arises out of a liberal secular progressive ideology, purveyor of the "tyranny of low expectations."[23] The term "at risk" is frequently nothing more than a convenient excuse for obvious immoral behavior.

In the face of insult or attack the world says one should retaliate, one should show pride, assert himself, earn respect, and seek revenge. This is the curse of following one's own desires. In contrast, a holy God calls those who are persecuted to humbly endure, to leave room for the Lord's wrath, to pray for those who injure him, to love his enemies.[24] In this way, the Christian is vividly revealed as one who places his life firmly in the hands of a good God, one who, when his pride, social standing, and even his very life, are threatened, places uncompromised trust in the deliverance of a God who is unseen yet present.

> "But man, despite his riches, does not endure; he is like the beasts that perish. This is the fate of those who trust in themselves, and of their followers, who approve their sayings." (Psalm 49:12, 13)

Excursus: Automobile Ownership and Self-Obsession

Automobile ownership is on the rise throughout the world. This phenomenon seems to be attended by the precipitous rise in individualism (individualism might be a euphemism for self-obsession). Besides automobile ownership, the rise of individualism brings with it a host of correlated societal maladies, such as promiscuity, the love of money, and divorce. Automobile ownership tends to feed into a lie already resident within the heart, that since one is able to travel at will, and therefore in control of his destiny, he is functionally his own master.[25]

> "Each generation wastes a little more of the future with greed and lust for riches." (Don Marquis)

At the same time that automobile ownership sparks individualism, the spirit of individualism (self-obsession, pride, control) promotes automobile ownership. The desire for autonomous control spurs the love of the automobile, and the love of the automobile justifies and intensifies autonomous control. This is the heart's worship "double helix,"[26] a vicious cycle of intensified worship encouraged by thoughts, words, and actions.

---

[23] This term from Daniel Patrick Moynihan (1927-2003), former New York State senator
[24] Romans 12:19
[25] It is fascinating to note that the Amish have rejected automobiles because they would disrupt the pace of Amish life, spawning inequality and competition. The Amish believe that with an automobile one easily becomes prideful and desires control over others.
[26] This term borrowed from David Covington, Biblical Counselor

However, the Bible does not consign this vicious cycle to an infinite loop but places great confidence in the sanctified heart's invested ability to separate from the allures of the world (namely the temptations associated with the automobile), so that in Christ the believer can participate in the world, while not succumbing to its attendant worship traps.

The Proliferation of Self-Love

> To love myself with abandon, that would prove a joy unbridled "with the cross my only rival."[27]

A Christian friend stated, "Do you love what Jesus loves?" My answer, "Yes." Her next question, "Does Jesus love you?" My answer, "Yes." Her conclusion, "Then you should love yourself." This logic sounds reasonable until one looks into Scripture to discover that the imperative to love oneself is wholly absent. While it is certainly true that Jesus loves each person, and each is called to love what Jesus loves, that is hardly a call to self-love. From beginning to end, the Bible paints self-love as mankind's most glaring problem, the driver of his defiance toward the good news of salvation. In fact, self-love always causes one to turn away from God.[28]

Today, people frequently speak of having a healthy self-image, believing in oneself, having confidence in oneself, accepting oneself, and loving oneself. People place a high priority on personal fulfillment and making oneself happy first. Three themes surface time and again in conversation:

1. The desire to be wealthier
2. The longing to be more attractive
3. The plan to gain more friends

The desire for wealth is a desire for power over people and over God himself. The longing for a pleasing appearance is the quest to be respected, celebrated, and desired. The plan for more friends is to be assured an antidote to loneliness, the looming scepter of the modern world.

> My objective as sinner is to make a name for myself rather than to submit to the "one name under heaven by which men are saved."[29]

People increasingly crave technology that promises the ability to love one's body, one's life, and one's friends. Technology allows one to fashion himself in any way he wishes. It offers the opportunity to create a second identity (avatar), to permit one to

---

[27] The phrase "with the cross my only rival" borrowed from Leonard Bernstein, *Candide* (1956)
[28] Tedd Tripp, *Shepherding a Child's Heart* (Wapwallopen, Pennsylvania: Shepherd Press, 1995) 52.
[29] Genesis 11:4; Acts 4:12

be the person he always longed to be. People easily hide behind this virtual veil as a convenient avoidance for face-to-face communication. This veil lets them finally love themselves as they have always wanted.[30]

The Guitarist
Jean-Baptiste Greuze, 1757

For example, the explosion of personalized entertainment has become an enabler in the growth of self-love. In past generations families sat around a single radio or television, or listened to a local band. This fostered a sense of community, other-centeredness, and subjugating one's personal tastes to the good of others. Today, however, each enjoys his own entertainment, abiding by his own tastes, with little regard for others; there is rarely a need to regard others, to ever have a thought outside of oneself. Thus, the personal entertainment movement (like the automobile) drives increased self-obsession with little to counter it.

With alarming intensity, the love of self is gaining strength as it is now embraced and praised throughout the world. It would appear that 2 Timothy 3:2-5 becomes more prescient with each passing generation.

> People will be lovers of themselves, lovers of money, boastful, proud, abusive, disobedient to their parents, ungrateful, unholy, without love, unforgiving, slanderous, without self-control, brutal, not lovers of the good, treacherous, rash, conceited, lovers of pleasure rather than lovers of God — having a form of godliness but denying its power. Have nothing to do with such people.

Each year one looks forward to a birthday celebration, a socially sanitized form of

---

[30] Sherry Turkle, *Alone Together: Why We Expect More from Technology and Less from Each Other* (Basic Books, 2012)

> self-admiration with little or no recognition of a holy God who brought one into existence. One may view his birthday as a celebration of life itself (a vague abstraction), a glimpse into heaven (a sense of the eternal), or as a way to thank one's parents (a form of scientific materialism). However, one's birthday should distinguish itself with thankfulness to a God who has graciously extended the gift of life for one more year.[31]

Narcissism: Self-Love in the Extreme

In Greek mythology, the hunter Narcissus fell so in love with his image in a still pond that he remained transfixed for eternity. Thus, self-love in the extreme is called "narcissism." The modern descendant of Greek philosophy, psychology, has co-opted this label so that it is an official mental disorder in which one exhibits an inflated sense of his own importance, and a presiding need for admiration. "A mercurial mix of charm and devastating ego,"[32] narcissists believe themselves to be superior to others and therefore, to their thinking, rightly show little regard for other's feelings.[33] Narcissism involves the following personality traits:

1. Narcissists love the center of attention and seek ways to maintain that attention through such means as humor, passion, and theatrics.

2. Narcissists are motivated to maintain respect from others since they crave a steady diet of affirmation and encouragement. They are desperate to maintain the lie that they are rightly the center of attention.

3. Narcissists tend to be charming and engaging because this maintains other's attention and approbation.

> "...Behind [the] mask of ultra-confidence lies a fragile self-esteem, vulnerable to the slightest criticism." (from a Mayo Clinic study)

4. Narcissists enjoy speaking about themselves with vivid stories.

5. Those who feed the narcissist's self-aggrandizing storyline are rewarded with his presence. However, the narcissist's elevated sense of self tends to treat others poorly, looking down upon, and maligning others on account of a sense of entitlement.

---

[31] Instead of a birthday celebration, why not initiate the tradition of volunteering and serving those in need on one's birthday? Would this not be a more fitting response to the gift one has received?
[32] This quote from *The Hollywood Reporter*, March 15, 2015
[33] David Kupelian, *How Evil Works: Understanding and Overcoming the Destructive Forces That Are Transforming America* (Threshold Edition, 2010) 79.

6. Just as Narcissus hated those who adored him, those who both do, and do not, offer the narcissist affirmation and encouragement are at risk of attack.

> "The one who has no shame before men, has no fear of God." (Jewish proverb)

The narcissist's offer of friendship, while often highly-attractive, is ultimately a vacuous experience, as the entire purpose of the friendship is self-serving drama. The narcissists can be highly-entertaining, but he makes no lasting investment in others. His sole objective is to, at all costs, maintain his self-image, which invariably casts him into a burning hell of unmet need.

I find a good rule of thumb for uncovering narcissism is this: the narcissist speaks about other's need for change, but never his own. In any conflict, or in any situation of loss, the narcissist immediately points to the outside world as the culprit. Every problem is what another has done, how others have failed, and what others ought to do differently. The narcissist could be thought of as rampaging through life sustaining collisions for which he feels others are at fault.

> Richard Dawkin's *The Selfish Gene* (1976),[34] an affirmation of evolution, in some sense reads like a narcissist's manifesto. Narcissism follows the natural trajectory of the theory of evolution since in evolutionary thinking one should prize and promote himself so as to affect the upward surge of the race. In a subtle twist, however, modern narcissism can cast itself as merely the product of genetic drivers. In this way, it is exonerated from all culpability for its exploits. If humanity is genetically chained to narcissism then there is no guilt in it. One simply plays out a predetermined self-love script to which he is bound.

A veritable laboratory for studying narcissism is the world of media (namely the products of Hollywood). Media stars are, with rare exception, narcissists in the extreme, having perfected the art of self-promotion to a thoroughly air-brushed image. Anyone in the media, from a local meteorologist to a blockbuster movie star, rises or descends on his ability to remain in the public spotlight. Thus, stars have an insatiable lust for attention and approval because they see their livelihood as inextricably linked to maintaining the world's attention.[35] Thus, creatures of Hollywood, while wholly obsessed with self-promotion, often cleverly camouflage themselves with a media-crafted display of altruistic concern. (In fairness, there have been a few shining exceptions to this generality, a few in the Hollywood machine who have shown genuine humility. However, such a posture tends to undermine the entire enterprise.)

---

[34] Richard Dawkins, *The Selfish Gene* (Oxford University Press, 1976)
[35] David Kupelian, *How Evil Works: Understanding and Overcoming the Destructive Forces That Are Transforming America* (Threshold Editions, 2010) 78.

382 What Agreement Is There Between the Temple of God and Idols?

Portrait of the Sculptor Viktor Malmberg, Hugo Simberg, d. 1917

> "We often grieve the death of our enemies because we wish they could be around to witness our future successes." (Arthur Schopenhauer)

Psychology offers no explanations for narcissism's rise and, more importantly, no cure. In fact, psychology is the chief culprit for narcissism because psychology removes guilt before a holy God, advancing the lie that one's fault merely grows from a lack of adequate self-love and self-esteem. Thus, psychology cultivates an environment in which narcissism can blossom and flower. The reason is simple; without the proper fear of God narcissism flourishes unchecked. (In fact, all false religions and worldviews foster narcissism.) Since there is no true fear of God, the narcissist is uninhibited, regularly engaging in self-aggrandizing flights of fantasy (which often result in grave harm).[36]

Consider Romans 12:19, "Do not take revenge, my dear friends, but leave room for God's wrath, for it is written: 'It is mine to avenge; I will repay,' says the Lord." Would a narcissist ever forgo revenge? The narcissist specializes in exacting revenge since he sees himself as a commanding deity perched on Mount Olympus. Having installed himself as god, revenge is often his principle means for maintaining his supposed hegemony.

---

[36] For further discussion of psychology's effect on the self see "Psychology as Competing Religion" and "Psychology's Chief Purpose" in the first book in this series, *Ask for the Ancient Paths: From Art to Artifice to Arisen,* chapter 8: "What Has Jerusalem To Do With Vienna? The Case Against Psychology"

> Self-love is functionally the same as God-hatred. However, the question could be raised, "Which is first - the love of self or the hatred of God?" The two would seem to be coterminus, opposite sides of the same coin.

The greater one's focus on himself the greater one's emptiness, the more intense the haunting scepter of perdition and pain. The more one tries to achieve an eternal détente through temporal means the greater one's sense of impending doom. The more one feels that rebellion offers an attainable solution, the more one is consumed with dread that the farce and chicanery will all be exposed as a worthless lie. Those who lavish attention on themselves increase their slavery to their sin. While those who focus their attention on Jesus Christ find true and lasting freedom.[37]

Excursus: The Veblen Effect and Vanity

Consumer demand for most goods and commodities follows a microeconomic principle called simply "the law of demand." This means that price and demand are negatively correlated. As price decreases demand increases, and vice versa.

However, there is an intriguing economic concept called "The Veblen effect," described in *The Theory of the Leisure Class* (1899) by American economist Thorstein Veblen (1857–1929). Veblen postulated that certain luxury goods exhibit an inverse law of demand. As price increases, demand also increases, and vice versa. Goods which follow this trend are called "Veblen goods."

The Veblen effect is based on the concepts of conspicuous consumption and status-seeking. This means that certain items sell *because* of their price, so that if price falls, interest in those goods falls, as well. Examples of Veblen goods are certain luxury cars, exclusive jewelry, and designer clothing. As the price of such goods increases, so does demand because of the perception of exclusivity and status.

> "There is something about your successes which disquiets even your closest friends." (Oscar Wilde)

In other words, Veblen-seekers only desire a good or service if it is so prohibitively expensive that few others can afford it. As that good or service becomes affordable, demand drops. Companies which manufacture Veblen goods profit handsomely by stoking and legitimizing vanity.[38] The Veblen effect offers yet another portal into the heart's depravity, a depravity which clothes itself in often innocent raiment. The heart,

---

[37] Galatians 5:1
[38] Incidentally, Veblen felt that a capitalist system is weakened and made inefficient by consumption for status. (Veblen partially based his economic theories on Darwinian evolution, which historically stokes class envy and struggle.)

regardless of its *Sitz im Leben*, is cankered with festering desire to distinguish itself, to cast itself in patrician superiority.

The Curse of Self-Love: Burning Insecurity

On May 23, 1883, the Brooklyn Bridge opened with a grand ceremony attended by President Chester Arthur (1829-1886). As one of the tallest structures in the city, imagine the excitement as the bridge's travelers viewed ships and birds below them. Originally designed for pedestrians, the Brooklyn Bridge saw 150,000 people cross the span on its opening day. But one week later tragedy struck as some, fearing the bridge was falling, sparked a stampede that crushed twelve people. (One year later, to allay fears, circus showman P.T. Barnum (1810–1891) marched twenty-one elephants across the bridge.)

This anecdote serves as a fitting introduction to the curse of self-love. While on the surface self-love appears to be a soaring tour of boundless splendor, it is always attended by panic culminating in crushing loss. Consider 1 Samuel 18:7-11,

> As they danced, they sang: 'Saul has slain his thousands, and David his tens of thousands.' Saul was very angry; this refrain displeased him greatly. 'They have credited David with tens of thousands,' he thought, 'but me with only thousands. What more can he get but the kingdom?' And from that time on Saul kept a close eye on David.
>
> The next day an evil spirit from God came forcefully on Saul. He was prophesying in his house, while David was playing the lyre, as he usually did. Saul had a spear in his hand and he hurled it, saying to himself, 'I'll pin David to the wall.' But David eluded him twice.

It is ironic that Saul, handsome and a "head taller" than his rivals, was consumed with burning anger and envy for David. Those who invest their worth and meaning in an idol (such as their own beauty, ability, intelligence, or power) are deeply insecure, never at peace with that idol. Saul was consumed with envy because he worshipped his own appearance, and lusted after the praises of men. The outcome of Saul's idolatry was insanity. The evil spirit upon Saul alighted at his own invitation, a manifestation and curse of his angry demands.

> "We are so vain that we are bothered by the opinions of those we don't even like." (Maria Ebner-Eschenbach)

In keeping with this analysis of Saul, a study of professional athletes finds that the greatest stars are the most insecure, the most anxious and fearful. Defining themselves based on their physical performance, they render themselves empty, lost, longing, weak, purposeless, besieged by self-treachery, and searching for answers outside of themselves. Thus, the paradox is that the premiere athletes are the most insecure in their ability. From a Biblical perspective this makes perfect sense, as those who most worship themselves are the most cursed with themselves. Those who are the most deeply self-invested, and most unabashedly self-reliant, are the most self-deluded. It is possibly the ones who are less self-confident who may at times feel the need to reach out for the provision and guidance of a holy God.

George as Prince Regent in the Robes of the Order of the Garter
Thomas Lawrence, 1816

"One may understand the cosmos, but never the ego. The self is more distant than any star." (G.K. Chesterton)

Those who wear a mask of self-confidence are actually the most fearful and the most uncertain in themselves. That is why they must maintain the front, to cover the truth. The more focused one is on himself, the more invested in his own glory, the greater his fear, insecurity, emptiness, darkness, deception, and depression. The one who is most enamored with himself is a prisoner to the slightest criticism or offense which casts him into an oblivion of depression. That is the curse of self-love, the greater its intensity, the greater the ruin. It should be noted that self-confidence-driven depression is not a function of *actual* standards of pulchritude, ability, or wealth, but rather grows from one's *perception* of his relative level of pulchritude, ability, or wealth. Self-obsession drives this perception, skewing one's ability to rightly assess reality as God alone sees it.[39]

"Young people try on one face after another, until they find their own." (Logan Pearsall Smith)

---

[39] Romans 12:3

Excursus: The Dunning-Kruger Effect

In *As You Like It* (c. 1600) William Shakespeare (1564-1616) wrote, "The fool doth think he is wise, but the wise man knows himself to be a fool." Later Charles Darwin (1809-1882) stated, "Ignorance more frequently begets confidence than does knowledge." Even 1 Corinthians 8:2 offers a similar comment, "Those who think they know something do not yet know as they ought to know." Shakespeare, Darwin, and Paul observed a phenomenon now known as the Dunning-Kruger effect which states that incompetent people overestimate their own skill, fail to recognize others' ability, and are blind to their own inadequacies.[40] Thus, the incompetent tend to rate their skill as far higher than it actually is. However, as skill improves, a previously incompetent person tends to become more aware of his own *inability*. Paradoxically, competent people tend to dwell on their incompetencies, rating themselves far below their actual ability level.

> "A timid question will always receive a confident answer." (Justice Darling)

Jonah 4:11 recounts, "And should I not have concern for the great city of Nineveh, in which there are more than a hundred and twenty thousand people who cannot tell their right hand from their left—and also many animals?" Nineveh, although a proud city, was functionally deceived concerning even the most rudimentary truths. This hints of the way in which the Bible presents a concept more rudimentary than the Dunning-Kruger effect - spiritual blindness. There is something in the delusion of sin which amplifies and elevates the self, so that the self is no longer evaluated using a God-centered set of lenses. For this reason, those whom the world labels as having the "most," in actuality have the least. Luke 1:53 states, "He has filled the hungry with good things but has sent the rich away empty." Those who think that successful rebellion is within reach, that beauty will make one the object of desire, that intelligence will tighten one's command over others, that wealth will lend unassailable security, these are the ones who are the most forlorn and destitute.

> A perennial threat to the church's vitality is that most Christians feel they are experts in sound Bible interpretation when they are not. Additionally, they often wrongly assume that intelligence and career competence necessarily predispose one to sagacious biblical insight. For example, a local church often recounts that it was founded by an anesthesiologist, implying that this somehow renders the congregation more solidly grounded, more nobly hewn. In reality, Christians with a faulty understanding of the gospel, of sin and sanctification, propagate their errors causing gangrenous lesions on the body of Christ.[41]

---

[40] David Dunning and Justin Kruger, "Unskilled and Unaware of It: How Difficulties in Recognizing One's Own Incompetence Lead to Inflated Self-Assessments," *Journal of Personality and Social Psychology* 77 (1999): 1121-1134.
[41] 2 Timothy 2:17

Romans 12:3 reads, "For by the grace given me I say to every one of you: Do not think of yourself more highly than you ought, but rather think of yourself with sober judgment, in accordance with the faith God has distributed to each of you." Thus, the Christian neither depreciates nor denigrates his ability, but glorifies God with it in a spirit of thankfulness. Second Timothy 2:20, 21 reads,

> In a large house there are articles not only of gold and silver, but also of wood and clay; some are for special purposes and some for common use. Those who cleanse themselves from the latter will be instruments for special purposes, made holy, useful to the Master and prepared to do any good work.

> As one studies people, one discovers that their degree of self-focus is the degree to which they maintain the mentality of a child. Most adults are functionally like either a three year-old, or a three year-old with a soiled diaper. While some may be offended by the analogy, there really is no psychic difference between adults and children. Even 1 Corinthians 13:11 states, "When I was a child, I talked like a child, I thought like a child, I reasoned like a child. When I became a man, I put the ways of childhood behind me." Paul implies that some are still in a childlike state, not yet grown-up in their faith in Christ.
>
> Without Jesus' heart overhaul, the way that one was as a child is the same way that he will be as an adult. There is no unaided growth out of selfishness. The only way to break this pattern is to be regenerated in Christ so that one grows into "adulthood" with regard to his dealings with God and others.

The Curse of Self-Love: Crippling Comparison with Others

> "When a proud man hears another praised, he feels that he has been injured." (English proverb)

Until the late 18th century women often suffered from severely pocked skin caused by various childhood ailments. As a young woman approached marriageable age cratered skin was smoothed with wax. (For this reason, women did not sit close to an open fire without a hand fan to shield the face.) Today, however, women do not generally suffer from pocked skin, and on the whole, due to dermatological advances, display more unblemished beauty than in the past. This results in, not diminished, but intensified infatuation with beauty. And while the love of beauty has always existed, it has become a more ubiquitous conveyance of self-love.

> Barbie®, the demure slender doll, was first marketed in 1959. Before this girls played with baby dolls. But, as an idealized representation of a woman, in

proportions and with features that real women could never match, Barbie® would forever change girls' self-image. While Barbie® has proved immensely popular, with over one billion sold in 150 countries, it is both fascinating and chilling that the vast number are mutilated and beheaded by young girls out of hatred for the dolls' unattainable beauty. That which they idolize and seek to emulate, they also despise and seek to destroy.

A Woman of Ambition
James Jacques Joseph Tissot, 1885

Among the millennial generation (those born after 1980) there is an epidemic of self-objectification, especially in young girls. Girls, in particular, now exhibit a far higher sense of competition than ever before. This drives them to obsess about body image, continually monitoring their body for imperfections, and other real or perceived vulnerabilities to social scorn. This body monitoring now starts in early childhood as girls are bombarded by a paralyzing assault of media-generated images. The tragic result has been ever-increasing dissatisfaction with body image which casts girls into a downward spiral of depression, often attended by eating disorders. The quest for an alluring body image seems to be driven by an intermingling of vaunting ambition for superiority subfused with a deep aversion to rejection (for not measuring up to a media-generated image).

Beauty, intelligence, talent, and wealth when coupled with an idolatrous heart offer the delusional thrill of being god. They advance the lie that rebellion against God can succeed, that one can attain for himself all that was lost in the fall, all that one desires as a result of pursuing the fall's trajectory of self-consumption.

In reality, the concept of competition holds no meaningful place in the Christian worldview. Since one was not created by mankind nor for mankind, one is under no obligation to placate mankind nor meet his standards. On Judgment Day one will not stand before a human judge, but before the Creator of the universe. So, why would one compete in worldly affairs for meaningless gains? Why would one wrap his life around futile pursuits, and not around God himself?

Consider Isaiah 3:16-26:

> The Lord says,
>   'The women of Zion are haughty,
> walking along with outstretched necks,
>   flirting with their eyes,
> strutting along with swaying hips,
>   with ornaments jingling on their ankles.
> Therefore the Lord will bring sores on the heads of the women of Zion;
>   the Lord will make their scalps bald.'
>
> In that day the Lord will snatch away their finery: the bangles and headbands and crescent necklaces, the earrings and bracelets and veils, the headdresses and anklets and sashes, the perfume bottles and charms, the signet rings and nose rings, the fine robes and the capes and cloaks, the purses and mirrors, and the linen garments and tiaras and shawls.
>
> Instead of fragrance there will be a stench;
>   instead of a sash, a rope;
> instead of well-dressed hair, baldness;
>   instead of fine clothing, sackcloth;
>   instead of beauty, branding.
> Your men will fall by the sword,
>   your warriors in battle.
> The gates of Zion will lament and mourn;
>   destitute, she will sit on the ground.

Self-love's menacing consequence is isolation from God and others. Thus, the extent of one's self-love is the extent to which one will functionally be alone. The more self-obsessed the more one is a prisoner, trapped in an existential terrarium of his own design with no God to offer any assurance. Self-love, thus, breeds unsettling fear of rejection.

> The Hebrew patriarch Jacob adorned his son Joseph in a richly ornamented robe because he loved him.[42] Today we adorn ourselves in richly ornamented robes because we love ourselves. How much better to be clothed in serendipitous exaltation than to exalt oneself and find in it nothing more than tattered rags.

---

[42] Genesis 37:3

Case Study: The Explosion of Love Addiction[43]

A college student wore a shirt that read, "No love, no life." This encapsulates a curious and disconcerting social phenomenon steadily taking greater hold: love addition. This is the desire to be in love, to experience the rush and thrill of emotion. Love addiction seems to be closely linked with two growing social trends. The first is the rise in loneliness, the second, the proliferation of social media. The growth of loneliness as a social epidemic drives yearning for an emotional stimulant, a feeling of connectedness, of being desired, and of desiring. In this way, love becomes little more than an emotional narcotic for a quick high.

> "I don't love you for who you are but for what I am when I am with you."

Many people merely seek an instantaneous romantic "fix," to be the center of attention, the object of desire, with no sense of serving, or sacrificing for, another. The very concepts of serving and sacrificing are entirely foreign to love addicts, since potential partners are merely objects to be manipulated. Thus, love addiction causes one to have little ability to enter into a meaningful marriage relationship. As quickly as the thrill of marriage wears off the addict plunges into an emotional abyss of searing pain. Relationships are both entered into, and broken, as frequently as the emotional intoxication ebbs and flows.

> Some people want to fall in love, if only for a minute.

Social networking is about intense bursts of interaction given and received instantly. This fosters a relational style which places little or no value on long-term commitment. Today, social networking, which does not prize permanence but intensity and immediacy (a rush of contact, like a hit of cocaine), profoundly shapes romance.

The prevalence of love addiction, or romance "intoxication," could explain the tendency for modern romantic relationships to last on average about six months. Romance today is marked by soaring emotional elation followed by plunging depression when that romance ends. The transitory nature of love addiction drives the proliferation of sexualized clothing among women who seek to be the object of a moment's desire, not a participant in, or the beneficiary of, a lifetime of sacrifice. Love addiction also drives flirtatious behavior, the quest to conquer another's emotions for a momentary thrill. Love addicts often use the rush of romance as an anesthetic to numb chronic loneliness. Desperate for attention, they seek any sign of hope that their loneliness will soon subside.

> "I am using an example from everyday life because of your human limitations. Just

---

[43] Some of the following inspired by Judy Dutton, "Addicted to Love," match.com (October 15, 2012)

> as you used to offer yourselves as slaves to impurity and to ever-increasing wickedness, so now offer yourselves as slaves to righteousness leading to holiness." (Romans 6:19)

Scintillating Self-Denial

The world's motives almost always concern putting on a display and receiving recognition. The world cannot countenance an act which does not overtly promote the self, does not gain the praise of men, or demonstrably advance one's future prospects. However, Philippians 2:2-4 states,

> ...then make my joy complete by being like-minded, having the same love, being one in spirit and purpose. Do nothing out of selfish ambition or vain conceit, but in humility consider others better than yourselves. Each of you should look not only to your own interests, but also to the interests of others.

The Infanta Isabel Clara Eugenia with Magdalena Ruiz
Follower of Alonso Coello, 16th C.

In stunning defiance of the world and its ways, one finds an anecdotal gem in Exodus 38. The Tent of Meeting was to be attended by young Israelite women charged with guarding its entrance and ensuring that all supplies were in order. Exodus 38:8 reads, "They made the bronze basin and its bronze stand from the mirrors of the women who served at the entrance to the Tent of Meeting." This is a fascinating verse. These women relinquished their personal mirrors to fashion the bronze basin used to wash the high priest's hands and feet, that he might be purified. Thus, these servant girls committed their own mirrors to construct this ceremonial cleansing basin.

> "My sacrifice, O God, is a broken spirit; a broken and contrite heart you, God, will not despise." (Psalm 51:7)

The mirror is the quintessential accessory of human vanity. Israelite women, like their

Egyptian contemporaries, carried highly-polished bronze mirrors in order to frequently check their appearance. The mirror was then, as today, an implement and symbol of self-absorption. These women were willing to give up their mirrors in order to form the basin which would be used to hold the water for ceremonial purification. In effect, they did more than simply donate a personal accessory. They symbolically relinquished their self-focus, cast away an accoutrement of self-love, in order to affect the purity of God's people. This was a noble act.

> Conventional wisdom says, "youth: immature, yet accustomed to making choices while blithely unaware of the consequences." From the Bible's perspective choices, whether right or wrong, are not a function of age, but a function of wisdom. The young may make sound choices, if wise, and the old, poor ones, if foolish.

This casting away mirrors to form a purification basin is, in some sense, a metaphor for the Christian life. The Christian is asked to crucify his self-obsession, sacrifice his self-love, in order that Jesus might purify him. Jesus longs to clean those who are willing to die to themselves, and forsake their own lives, in order to follow him.

> "And if anyone wants to sue you and take your shirt, hand over your coat as well." (Matthew 5:40)

An outgrowth of relationship with Jesus is that the time and effort once exhausted in maintaining mere appearances is now to be focused on inward transformation. The time previously spent in front of a mirror entranced by one's image should rightly be used to assess and confront one's heart. Self-absorption should turn into self-inspection, self-assessment, self-discipline, and self-control, as one sits at Jesus' feet and listens to him, learns from him, and dwells in him.

> Galatians 6:4 reads, "Each one should test his own actions. Then he can take pride in himself alone, without comparing himself to someone else." This is not a call to self-pride, but pride in the work that God does in, and through, the believer.

Paul echoed this in 1 Corinthians 9:27, "No, I beat my body and make it my slave so that after I have preached to others, I myself will not be disqualified for the prize." The implication is that one can become enslaved to his own body. Yet, Paul entreats his readers to reverse the equation. The body should serve man, not man serve the body. The body should be used in the purpose for which it was created, not to imprison mankind to lustful desire. That being said, there is nothing in the body which is inherently enslaving. Since the body is created "very good" (in contradistinction to the Platonic view), there is no defect in man's physical constitution which would predispose him to evil.

Christ Washing the Feet of His Disciples, Paolo Veronese, 1580

Platonism saw the body as a distraction to the mind, since the body tempts with base and depraved needs such as food, sleep, and carnal desire. The Greeks saw the mind as inherently noble, and the internal as vastly more important than the external. Thus, to the Platonists, Jesus' *bodily* resurrection was confusing and counterproductive since they saw the entire purpose of death as freeing the mind and soul from the body. According to Platonism, to most separate oneself from the material world (including the body) was to most closely approach God. Why then would God want to reunite the soul and body after death?[44] Philippians 3:20, 21 offers a direct elenchus to Platonism. "But our citizenship is in heaven. And we eagerly await a Savior from there, the Lord Jesus Christ, who, by the power that enables him to bring everything under his control, will transform our lowly *bodies* so that they will be like his glorious body."

> "But we have this treasure in jars of clay to show that this all-surpassing power is from God and not from us." (2 Corinthians 4:7)

The Bible never encourages loving oneself or accepting fallen aspects of oneself. It builds upon the assumption that all people instinctively love themselves, to their own detriment. This is the background for the second Great Commandment in which Jesus stated to love others as oneself.[45] Jesus' words have built within them a condemnation. He admonished his listeners to love others in the way that they already wrongly love themselves.[46] Jesus' words presuppose that no one ever hated himself. No one ever sought to knowingly undermine his own position or sabotage himself (even suicide

---

[44] Incidentally, Aristotle reversed the Platonic thesis. Aristotle saw human potential, and man's innate competence, even within the confines of the body. (As a side note, the ancient Egyptians feared altering the body in anyway, since they believed this bore eternal repercussions. In fact, the Egyptians were the only ancient civilization which did not perform brain surgery.)

[45] Luke 10:27

[46] Jay Adams, *The Biblical View of Self-esteem, Self-love, Self-image* (Harvest House Publishers, 1986)

being a supposed victory). Consider Ephesians 5:29, "After all, no one ever hated their own body, but they feed and care for their body, just as Christ does the church..."

Psalm 26:2 states, "Test me, LORD, and try me, examine my heart and my mind;" That which is by God's design one ought to accept as God's eternal plan, but that which accrues as a result of sin ought to be gouged out, cut off, and thrown into the fire.[47] In mankind's sinfulness he seeks to change that which he should accept, and to accept that which he should desire to change. If one's outward appearance does not match one's self-concept, then in humility he should accept God's design. If one's position in life does not accord with one's dreams, he can take comfort that there are higher and grander pursuits than upward mobility.[48]

> Numbers 12:3 states, "Now Moses was a very humble man, more humble than anyone else on the face of the earth." It could be that this statement describes the end of Moses' life, but it does not seem to reflect the entirety of Moses' dealings with God. In Exodus 4:10, "Moses said to the LORD, 'Pardon your servant, Lord. I have never been eloquent, neither in the past nor since you have spoken to your servant. I am slow of speech and tongue.'" Moses may have appeared humble and self-effacing as he spoke about his limitations (the way in which he could not accomplish the Lord's bidding), and how ineffectual he would be in petitioning Pharaoh. However, he was not. Moses harbored a well-camouflaged worship of power and influence.[49]

Ironically, the more the sinner seeks to distinguish himself, the more he ends up the same as others. Truly standing out is not a matter of more effectively asserting oneself, but of systematically and consistently denying oneself. When that happens one is truly unique among peers.

The Self-Esteem Reign of Terror

Until the mid-1950s America celebrated heroes with integrity, strong moral fiber, and unflinching courage in the face of evil. But in the mid-1950s a perplexing shift occurred, the rise of the anti-hero, one who defies authority, rejects traditional morality, and exhibits brooding self-absorption. (The first cinematographic anti-hero was legend James Dean (1931–1955).)

Since the 1950s the media has featured an escalating trend of existential heroes, those who are self-promoting, sexually immoral, anti-authoritarian, anti-American, and

---

[47] Matthew 5:29, 30
[48] For further discussion of this topic see "Fixed Design Elements: Submission to God's Plan" in the first book in this series, *Ask for the Ancient Paths: From Art to Artifice to Arisen*, chapter 5: "Redefining the Pygmalion Effect: Exploring the Image of God in Man"
[49] Numbers 20:10 offers evidence of Moses' lust for power.

committed to personal desires, all while appearing other-centered. This stands in sharp contradistinction to the heroes of prior generations who were patriotic, concerned for the commonweal, and self-sacrificial.

> With rising fervor mankind wants each episode of his life to be a *cause celebre*.

Recently the news reported that a prominent middle-aged Hollywood star has trouble recognizing faces. He cannot remember faces outside of a small circle of friends and associates. This actor does not have a visual acuity problem and is not senile. It would appear that his notoriously self-centered life causes him to focus little attention outside of his immediate desires. He cannot remember faces for a simple reason: he cares little for remembering people. His consuming self-focus makes him "face-presbyopic," as anyone outside of his solar system of self-promotion is simply not worth remembering.

> Hollywood's stories infiltrate our culture and are absorbed into individual lives. The one who fashions his life after movie heroes often forges for himself a delusive and fading glory.

Possibly the greatest tragedy of self-esteem thinking is the fact that people today no longer see others for who they are. Most today do not want to understand others; they want others to become what they desire for them to become. They only see what others can do for them, viewing life through a self-directed prism. Most cannot understand others, cannot appreciate God's gift in and through others, or the need to listen carefully in order to properly understand others. The self-esteem delusion creates a restlessness within the soul which causes one to overlook interpersonal details, so as to only see that which one deems salient to his solipsistic existence.

> "To his dog, every man is Napoleon; hence the constant popularity of dogs." (Aldous Huxley)

The self-esteem delusion drives a stake into the human heart, deadening it to God's work in the world. Consider Matthew 5:44-48,

> 'But I tell you, love your enemies and pray for those who persecute you, that you may be children of your Father in heaven. He causes his sun to rise on the evil and the good, and sends rain on the righteous and the unrighteous. If you love those who love you, what reward will you get? Are not even the tax collectors doing that? And if you greet only your own people, what are you doing more than others? Do not even pagans do that? Be perfect, therefore, as your heavenly Father is perfect.'

How can self-esteem thinking ever arrive at such a perspective on life? Self-esteem runs in the exact opposite direction as God's wisdom, as it leads to self-worship which impels self-serving behavior. Higher than man's ways,[50] God's perspective rises above self-esteem's petty quest so as to offer a towering vision of how life was meant to be.

From a related angle consider Hebrews 12:6, 7, which states, "…the Lord disciplines those he loves and punishes everyone he accepts as a son. Endure hardship as discipline; God is treating you as sons. For what son is not disciplined by his father?" God has a greater goal in mind for those who belong to him than self-love and self-esteem. God's goal is the knowledge of himself within his people. It is to this end that hardship and suffering are often necessary, not to be reflexively eschewed, but to be recognized as a hidden treasure. Any degree of self-focus will invariably miss this, because to the unregenerate heart pain is always seen as an evil intruder.

Descent from the Cross
Peter Paul Rubens, 1618

Case Study: King Nebuchadnezzar: One Afflicted with Himself[51]

> Twelve months later, as the king was walking on the roof of the royal palace of Babylon, he said, 'Is not this the great Babylon I have built as the royal residence, by my mighty power and for the glory of my majesty?' Even as the words were on his lips, a voice came from heaven, 'This is what is decreed for you, King Nebuchadnezzar: Your royal authority has been taken from you.

---

[50] Isaiah 55:9
[51] For further discussion of King Nebuchadnezzar see, "Insanity's Inception" in the first book in this series, *Ask for the Ancient Paths: From Art to Artifice to Arisen,* chapter 8: "What Has Jerusalem To Do With Vienna? The Case Against Psychology"

You will be driven away from people and will live with the wild animals; you will eat grass like the ox. Seven times will pass by for you until you acknowledge that the Most High is sovereign over all kingdoms on earth and gives them to anyone he wishes.' Immediately what had been said about Nebuchadnezzar was fulfilled. He was driven away from people and ate grass like the ox. His body was drenched with the dew of heaven until his hair grew like the feathers of an eagle and his nails like the claws of a bird.

At the end of that time, I, Nebuchadnezzar, raised my eyes toward heaven, and my sanity was restored. Then I praised the Most High; I honored and glorified him who lives forever.

His dominion is an eternal dominion;
his kingdom endures from generation to generation.
All the peoples of the earth
   are regarded as nothing.
He does as he pleases
   with the powers of heaven
   and the peoples of the earth.
No one can hold back his hand
   or say to him: 'What have you done?'

At the same time that my sanity was restored, my honor and splendor were returned to me for the glory of my kingdom. My advisers and nobles sought me out, and I was restored to my throne and became even greater than before. Now I, Nebuchadnezzar, praise and exalt and glorify the King of heaven, because everything he does is right and all his ways are just. And those who walk in pride he is able to humble.' (Daniel 4:29-37)

> "As long as a word remains unspoken you are its master; once you utter it, you are its slave." (Solomon Ibn Gabirol)

King Nebuchadnezzar brought destruction on himself through unbridled hubris, subjecting him to four crucial consequences of his rebellion:

1. He became isolated.[52]

2. He functioned as an animal.[53]

3. He took on the appearance of an animal.[54]

---

[52] Daniel 4:33
[53] Daniel 4:33
[54] Daniel 4:33

398 WHAT AGREEMENT IS THERE BETWEEN THE TEMPLE OF GOD AND IDOLS?

4. He became insane.[55]

Nebuchadnezzar's brazen pride drove him to isolation; he became like an animal, bore the appearance of an animal, and lost his sanity until he acknowledged "that the Most High is sovereign over all kingdoms on earth."[56] In many ways, this reflects something of man's modern plight. Mankind, like Nebuchadnezzar, is also deluded by his own self-glorification, and increasingly isolated through his self-focus.

Macbeth Consulting the Vision of the Armed Head
Johann Heinrich Fussli, d. 1825

> "Better a patient man than a warrior, one with self-control than one who takes a city." (Proverbs 16:32)

Reflecting the curse upon Nebuchadnezzar, mankind today views himself as merely a highly-evolved animal. (Man has also become insane through his sin.) When Nebuchadnezzar repented, raised his eyes toward heaven and acknowledged God's sovereignty, his sanity as well as his "honor and splendor," were restored for the glory of his kingdom.[57] What's more Nebuchadnezzar, when he repented "became even greater than before."[58]

> Jesus' disciple Peter retraced Nebuchadnezzar's act of repentance. "When Simon Peter saw this, he fell at Jesus' knees and said, 'Go away from me, Lord; I am a sinful man!'"[59] In that moment Peter transitioned from prideful self-assurance to humble self-assessment.

---

[55] Daniel 4:34
[56] Daniel 4:32
[57] Daniel 4:34, 36
[58] Daniel 4:36
[59] Luke 5:8

Through the lens of Nebuchadnezzar's life one sees the curse of the "believe in yourself" mantra. This was Nebuchadnezzar's crushing mistake, and it cast him into a hell-like condition. Likewise, those who subscribe to the "believe in yourself" lie find themselves in the same condition, isolated, animal-like, and insane.

> "The smallest package I ever saw was a man completely wrapped in himself." (Billy Graham)

Self-Esteem's Deception

> There is a mine for silver
>   and a place where gold is refined.
> Iron is taken from the earth,
>   and copper is smelted from ore.
> Mortals put an end to the darkness;
>   they search out the farthest recesses
>   for ore in the blackest darkness.
> Far from human dwellings they cut a shaft,
>   in places untouched by human feet;
>   far from other people they dangle and sway.
> The earth, from which food comes,
>   is transformed below as by fire;
> lapis lazuli comes from its rocks,
>   and its dust contains nuggets of gold.
> No bird of prey knows that hidden path,
>   no falcon's eye has seen it.
> Proud beasts do not set foot on it,
>   and no lion prowls there.
> People assault the flinty rock with their hands
>   and lay bare the roots of the mountains.
> They tunnel through the rock;
>   their eyes see all its treasures.
> They search the sources of the rivers
>   and bring hidden things to light.
> But where can wisdom be found?
>   Where does understanding dwell?
> No mortal comprehends its worth;
>   it cannot be found in the land of the living. (Job 28:1-13)

When Harvard University was founded in 1636, its shield of three books included one facing away from the observer. The idea was that there are some things hidden to mankind that only God can know. In 1911 Harvard reversed the direction of that book to face the viewer in order to show that through human reason all things could be known, that truth could no longer be hidden from autonomous humanity.

The following year the *Titanic* was heralded as unsinkable. This exuberance emerged as part of a modernist era in which technology was thought to conquer any opponent to progress. Just prior to its maiden voyage, the *Titanic*'s captain pretentiously declared, "God himself cannot sink this ship."

> "Then they sweep past like the wind and go on— guilty people, whose own strength is their god." (Habakkuk 1:11)

There is a link between the impudent reversal of Harvard's crest and the sinking of the *Titanic*. The link is the celebration of human reason as savior, arbiter of truth, and means of purification of the race. Untempered human reason leads to the inevitable outbreak of destructive hubris. Humanity operates to its own detriment with each passing generation as it further plumbs its flawed existence without God, against God, and in defiance of God.

> "In their case the god of this world has blinded the minds of the unbelievers, to keep them from seeing the light of the gospel of the glory of Christ, who is the image of God." (2 Corinthians 4:4)

Listen carefully to psychology's analysis of nearly any psychic problem, the automatic answer almost always offered is the need for higher self-esteem. In other words, nearly every problem is made into a low self-esteem problem (even when the psychologist correctly identifies rampant selfishness and pride). How can society's manifest self-centeredness be remedied in greater focus on self? Psychology's conclusions simply defy logic, and its fallacious labels only fortify the refuge of a desperate and dark heart seeking to more effectively defy God's self-revelation.

The modern focus on self-confidence and self-esteem is part of the general package of suppressing the knowledge of God expressed in Romans 1. Mankind persistently seeks to snuff out the light illuminating his sin. In this regard, the modern focus on self-confidence is merely another means of truth-suppression permitting mankind to feel more comfortable in his sin. As an implicit denial of man's inherent sinfulness, self-esteem is Satan's cunning deception channeling attention away from mankind's daily need for repentance.

The Christian refutation of self-confidence and self-esteem never implies nor advocates blind self-attack. Instead, the Christian seeks a proper self-understanding. There are certain aspects of one's being which one cannot change, and should joyfully accept, as part of an eternal plan. For example, one's height, intelligence, general appearance, and time in history are God's work, and therefore God's responsibility. God calls each to rest in his provenance, trusting that he will faithfully meet his responsibility to all that he created. Thus, one should be at peace with his life to the extent that he cannot change it.[60]

> "Woe to those who quarrel with their Maker, those who are nothing but potsherds among the potsherds on the ground. Does the clay say to the potter, 'What are you making?' Does your work say, 'The potter has no hands'?" (Isaiah 45:9)

However, one should not be at peace with those aspects of his life that he is called to change such as false worship commitments, misplaced loves, and destructive desires. These are areas where God deliberately brings discomfort and pangs of existential angst in order to effect change.

> People everywhere are climbing ladders to nowhere. If God is gracious the ladders' rungs will break. (David Powlison)

The problem with the self-esteem movement is that it blindly confuses those aspects which one should and should not accept. Thus, while one should rest in his level of intelligence or appearance, one should not rest in his desire to make himself his own god. There are certain design qualities in which one should take comfort; there are certain worship commitments in which one should find himself troubled and longing for deliverance.

It is worth noting that never have I seen self-esteem as the end-product, in and of itself. Self-esteem is a front to some larger objective such as the love of money, sexual lust, control, or ethnic pride. Thus, self-esteem is summoned to serve a far more poignant and pressing god. For example, a teenage boy might be counseled to show higher self-esteem so that he can finally attract the girl he desires. The struggling salesman is given a pep-talk on self-esteem so that he can land more client accounts. In other words, few are concerned with self-esteem as such; they are concerned with what it offers.

> Mankind's supreme foolishness and deepest ignorance is his self-confidence, his sense of innate nobility and perfection outside of God.[61]

When properly understood, evolution states that mankind, individually and corporately, is worthless, temporal, and expendable. However, because each is made

---

[60] For further discussion of this topic see "Fixed Design Elements: Submission to God's Plan," in the first book in this series, *Ask for the Ancient Paths: From Art to Artifice to Arisen,* chapter 5: "Redefining the Pygmalion Effect: Exploring the Image of God in Man"

[61] John Calvin, *The Institutes of the Christian Religion* (William B. Eerdman's Publishing Company, 1995)

in the image of an eternal God, each knows that he is an eternal being, designed to live forever. Thus, self-esteem thinking may be marshaled as an avenger to the degrading implications of evolution, a means of hoisting the torch of self-honor, nobility, and inherent value. Evolution delivers an indignity; self-esteem thinking seems to correct that indignity. Since each instinctively senses the dehumanizing error in evolution, he grabs for a worldview counterbalance, a soothing succor.[62] However, the self-esteem counterbalance is equally in error. The truth is found in a third option, one's identity as God's own image-bearer.[63]

Massacre of the Innocents, Peter Paul Rubens, 1612

> "What is man in nature? A nothing compared to the infinite, an everything compared to nothing, a midpoint between nothing and everything." (Blaise Pascal)

Evolutionary thinking is thus an unwitting contributor to the explosion of the self-esteem movement. People who, because of evolution, hear that they are worthless mistakes of nature instinctively know that this is not true and thus seek out an equalizer. Self-esteem thinking serves as just such a makeshift equalizer. However, the truth is found in neither existentialism (evolution) nor humanism (self-esteem). Rather

---

[62] For a further discussion of this topic see "The Center Point Theory of Design" in the first book in this series, *Ask for the Ancient Paths: From Art to Artifice to Arisen*, chapter 5: "Redefining the Pygmalion Effect: Exploring the Image of God in Man"
[63] Genesis 1:27

it is found in the biblical option, that people are carefully designed by a holy God for a purpose, not to honor themselves, but to honor their Creator.

> In business "workers soar to heights through frenzied programs of ego building, then as suddenly dive, becoming expendable serfs of workplace Darwinism."[64]

The Low Self-Esteem Label: "I Have So Many Talents but I Just Can't Remember Where I Hid Them"[65]

In a certain neighborhood a newly constructed Cape Cod-style house might be an object of desire among one's neighbors. One who owns such a house feels a sense of accomplishment because no one else in the neighborhood lives in a new Cape Cod. (In the land of dated homes, the new house is king.) The new homeowner glows with high self-esteem since he set a standard for himself which he has attained. His idolatrous desire for a sense of accomplishment and respect appears to function well, an angry fist raised against God which appears to work for the moment.

However, consider another neighborhood across town in which one living in that same Cape Cod-style home feels embarrassed among his neighbors who live in stately Victorians. So the Cape Cod homeowner now feels low self-esteem because he does not measure up to his neighbors. That is a standard that he sets for himself; he must be viewed as a success (in terms of his home) in the eyes of his neighbors, and he has failed. This homeowner's low self-esteem is nothing more than failed self-pride, a dysfunctional idol, again, an angry fist raised against God, either searching for self-dignifying excuses or a strategy to gain the upper-hand.

> "Poverty is a state of mind caused by a neighbor's new car."

One's choice of house or neighborhood is not the issue. The issue is how one views himself in relation to others based upon a standard set purely by human pride. The sinful heart longs to achieve that which is valued in the eyes of others. Thus, comparisons are based on an idolatrous desire to gain life, meaning, power, and blessing outside of God himself through the attainment of one's own egoistic standards. The fact that each desires and pursues a worldly standard is the source of his stress, anxiety, pain, frustration, loss, and futility.

> Incidentally, one could approach this homeowner example from a different angle. Consider the fact that some desire a neighborhood in which their home will be

---

[64] Mark Caldwell, *A Short History of Rudeness: Manners, Morals, and Misbehavior in Modern America* (New York: Picador USA, 2000) 83.
[65] For additional discussion of low self-esteem see the section "The Dynamics of Fear: Manifestations of the Fear of Failure" in the first book in this series, *Ask for the Ancient Paths: From Art to Artifice to Arisen,* chapter 6: "Man Before the Face of God: The Imperium of the Psyche"

> surrounded by more expensive homes (since one's own home assumes greater market valuable). Thus, for some the love of money trumps the fear of being seen as inferior.

The following tend to lead to low self-esteem:

1. Failed perfectionism
2. Flailing self-righteousness
3. Struggling selfish ambition
4. The absence of praise for one who craves the praise of men
5. Defeat for the war-maker

> With the overly compliant person, other people are gods, so there is a tendency toward "flight." With the war-maker, he himself is god, so there is a tendency toward "fight."[66] Flight or fight, cowering or combat, fear of man or envy, mankind seeks to deal with his separation from God through means of a false narrative that he rehearses within himself.

Low self-esteem is, from the Bible's perspective, either failed self-pride or failed fear of man. Low self-esteem is looking at oneself through the eyes of other people and determining that one has failed to meet a standard that one has set for himself.[67] The quest for high self-esteem is simply clever packaging for making self-worship appear justified.

The objective behind gaining self-esteem is at its root setting a standard in defiance of God. Therefore, low self-esteem results from failing at a standard which denies and defies Jesus' death on the cross. In denying Christ, low self-esteem is just a euphemism for the curse of living under a human-imposed standard, and judging oneself according to that standard. From God's perspective the standard has already been met in Jesus' death on the cross. The cross is not just a means by which to attain eternal life, but the standard set for life on earth as well. Thus, on account of Jesus' death, there is no human standard to meet because Jesus satisfied all possible standards that could be imposed upon the believer. The entire question of measuring up to standards has become a non-category, a non-concern, for the Christian.

> In Numbers 12:1, 2, Moses was undermined by his siblings, Miriam and Aaron, who impugned him on account of his Moabite wife. In this episode Moses did not defend his wife, his status as a prophet, or his personal history. God himself defended Moses.[68] Similarly, defending one's reputation is not the Christian's responsibility.

---

[66] David Powlison, Westminster Theological Seminary, Philadelphia, Pennsylvania
[67] David Powlison, Westminster Theological Seminary, Philadelphia, Pennsylvania
[68] Numbers 12:7-9

> The Christian rests in the defense he has already received in Christ. This is the Christian's *mirabile dictu*, the brilliant antidote to the whims and wiles of a world held captive to self-esteem thinking.

In summary, what stands behind the low self-esteem label is man's arrogant ascendance to a standard outside of the gospel, seeking to be judged by his own works and worth. Man wants to be his own savior, and when he fails, to serve as his own acquitting judge.

Reply of the Zaporozhian Cossacks to Sultan Mehmed IV of the Ottoman Empire
Ilya Repin, 1891

It is vital to understand that the low self-esteem label diagnoses and cures nothing. While it merely describes a set of symptoms, it offers no analysis concerning what gave rise to those symptoms. This points, once again, to psychology's grand guile. Psychology presents a label that masquerades as diagnosis and solution, when in reality it has done nothing but describe symptoms. Wrongly directed description then leads to the wrong analysis - the presumed answer to low self-esteem being high self-esteem. However, psychology has led its adherents down a false path eventually stranding them in the desert of humanism.

The Counselor's Charge

People who search out and promote higher self-esteem in one life arena usually feel some glaring deficiency in other arenas, for which they compensate. For example, one who feels he is of diminutive stature may become overly focused on wealth or intellect. He sets his standard as a way to uphold personal pride in light of his perceived deficiency. His compensating narrative to the supposed deficiency is really a story of hatred of God's design and will. The self-esteem panacea is, for the sinner, a weapon raised in defiance of God, the manifestation of burning disdain for a God whom he believes is set against him.

> Some wrongly assume that because the Bible refutes the concept of self-esteem, that it says that one should feel bad about himself. The Bible is not that roughly hewn. Still others think that if they just feel bad about themselves then they have, in some way, justified themselves. The Bible does not let the sinner off that easily. The issue is never about one's feelings; it is about one's objectives and desires. The Bible seeks to change worship commitments; that is the level on which it operates.

The wise counselor is aware that the one who labels himself as suffering from low self-esteem is really a failed idolater desperate to make his idolatry work. The counseling trap is to merely help the *failed* idolater become a *successful* idolater (in the eyes of the world), so that he can harmoniously join the ranks of other successful idolaters. The counselor must be vigilant not to help fledgling and struggling idolaters successfully compete with other apparently established and accomplished idolaters. That is the devil's errand.

> "Man's toil and skill in work comes from envy of his neighbor." (Ecclesiastes 4:4)

My students sometimes complain that the wealthy among them have abundant employment opportunities, can afford to study abroad, and even have their pick of desirable spouses, while those from humbler backgrounds tend to be denied these opportunities. Some students, therefore, gravitate to me in the hope that through our interaction they can gain some supposed advantage in their battle for upward mobility.

My objective is never to help aspiring egoists better compete with fully-operational egoists. My goal is not to arm one set of emerging idolaters for battle with entrenched idolaters so that the former can ascend. My aim is not to make the unsuccessful successful at a losing game. My goal is to expose root idolatry, to confront what my students long for, so as to affect repentance and submission to Christ. I seek to change the narrative so that the idolater abandons a futile pursuit and longs to win at a new game. I want to make Christ far more attractive than the things of the world, so that his towering victory overshadows its empty promises. Colossians 2:15 states, "And having disarmed the powers and authorities, he made a public spectacle of them, triumphing over them by the cross."

> "No one can make you feel inferior without your consent." (Eleanor Roosevelt)

Excursus: Counterculture as a Manifestation of Self-Pride

Most young people seek to fit in, and often blindly follow the behaviors and thought patterns of their peers. However, in nearly every community there is a counterculture made up of what one might term "misfits," those who deliberately defy all sense of conformity and seek to stand out as strange.

For those who deliberately embrace being labeled "strange" or "deviant," there is a certain self-righteousness in being hated, rejected, insulted, and ostracized. In rejection they feel superior, noble, or martyred for being an outcast to a society for which they hold contempt.

Often the counterculture of Goths or Punks reject conformity to social norms, but they themselves extend no tolerance to those among them who do not conform to the Goth or Punk subculture. This reveals the curse of idolatry; that which the idolater most despises also holds him captive; that which he most eschews he also succumbs to.

> Consider 1 Kings 18:28, 29, in which the priests of Baal cut themselves with swords when their god did not respond to their requests. What drove this practice of self-mutilation? Verse twenty-eight informs that it was "their custom" to cut themselves until blood flowed. This act, driven by pride and angry demand, sheds light on the alarming practice of self-mutilation common among modern young people. The same dynamic at work in the priests of Baal, is at work today. The cutting arises out of pride and seething anger. It is an attempt to pay for one's sin through the shedding of one's own blood, to somehow cast off the scepter of guilt before God with one's own torture and pain. While the one who cuts himself may often appear to be a victim, in reality he is the perpetrator of assault upon God's intended temple. The cutting is a "terror attack" upon God's planned earthly dwelling. There is never any reason to shed one's own blood, as it is meaningless in the expiation from one's own guilt. The gospel alone is freedom. Jesus shed his blood so that sinner would find rest in an efficacious provision of forgiveness.

Counseling Those with Perceived Low Self-Esteem

The danger in counseling a depressed person is to run after, and seek to alleviate, symptoms. Often the counselor simply wants to make the counselee feel better, so that if he feels better, the counseling is deemed a success. However, from God's perspective counseling which does not lead to fundamental heart change is always a failure. The counselor is not trying to make another feel better, but to either initiate or reestablish relationship with the living God. The counselor is a conduit and catalyst for God's own presence, power, and work in the counselee's life. The counselor, therefore, introduces people to an actual person. Anything short of this merely rehabilitates failed idols, reanimating that which God longs to destroy. The counselor, therefore, goes after root worship, consuming desires, and formative allegiances so as to expose idolatry and replace it with faith.

A Merry Christmas (*Pears Annual*), Frank Dadd, 1907

Low self-esteem (a modern nomenclature for depression) is the result of not measuring up to standards set in defiance of Christ's sacrifice on the cross. When counseling one with low self-esteem symptoms (as opposed to depression brought on by physiological ailments) an early question would be, "Whose standard is one trying to live up to?" The answer will often reveal that the low self-esteem person has set goals that are culturally-defined, or defined by those he longs to please, dominate, or control.

> "Why aren't you happy? It's because ninety-nine percent of everything you do, think, and say, is for yourself." (We Wei Wu)

An ancillary issue involves those who routinely disparage themselves. For example, I sometimes ask members of our congregation to take on certain responsibilities for the good of the church. Some may be asked to lead worship, organize a holiday dinner, or offer some teaching. A common response is that one does not feel capable enough to perform the task at hand. This is usually accompanied by a mock-humility which appears self-effacing. I find myself unsettled by such responses because they seem couched in pride, and therefore defiant of Christ's sanctifying work.

Christian humility is not self-deprecation, or stating what one cannot do. Such responses grow out of the assumption that one's gifts are his own, and that it is one's place to depreciate those gifts for the sake of receiving affirmation. In actuality, one's gifts are given by God and for God, to glorify himself. Thus, when called upon to use those gifts, one does so with a spirit of joyful confidence that the God who bestows gifts will accomplish all that he desires. Christian humility is trusting God to do something through oneself, in spite of oneself. The Christian does not show humility when falsely assessing his gifts, or through shying away from using them. This is actually cleverly disguised self-pride raised in defiance of a God who promises to prosper all that one does in his name.[69]

> "I can do all this through him who gives me strength." (Philippians 4:13)

It is fascinating that the very same Christians who take offense at being counseled to abandon their quest for high self-esteem, have no problem depreciating the gifts God has invested within them. They would rather exalt themselves in their own way for their own purposes, than be exalted in God's way for his purposes (that they would serve and glorify Christ).

> "For we are God's handiwork, created in Christ Jesus to do good works, which God prepared in advance for us to do." (Ephesians 2:10)

How Does the Christian Rightly Tell Others of God's Love?[70]

First John 4:8 is clear, "Whoever does not love does not know God, because God is love." While the Christian rightly tells others of God's loves for them, if not carefully explained, this statement can have a detrimental effect on account of the proliferation of self-love. Today, the statement "God loves you" might be met with the unspoken response, "Of course God loves me; I deserve to be loved. He should love me." The Christian, in presenting God's love in abstraction, may unwittingly feed man-centered self-love. The recognition of God's love, while intended to soften the heart for repentance, could have the opposite effect, emboldening an already bloated self-concept, so that it remains unassailed. God's love must be explained so that it stands in sharp contradistinction to secular misconceptions of love (namely that of unconditional love).

The narcissist, when told that God loves him, will likely feel enthralled, excited that his plan to gain another's acceptance and admiration is working, even with God

---

[69] Proverbs 16:3; Philippians 4:13
[70] For a comprehensive discussion of God's love see the case study "God's *Sui Generis* Love" in the third book in this series, *The Days of Reckoning Are at Hand: From Fig Leaf to Olive Branch to Laurel Wreath*, chapter 2: "Suffering: The Kintsugi Objective"

himself. Thus, the narcissist interprets God's love as justification for his already thriving self-love. In his mind it is natural and appropriate for God to love him.

The wise counselor, recognizing the hidden dangers, parses the Bible's development of God's love, drawing out its vital components and contours. God's love longs to free one from himself, searches the heart to reveal sin and induce repentance, wrestles with the sinner to subdue his spirit, and does not rest until God's work is completed. God's love fights for the sinner and fights with the sinner. It has vision and passion to make the sinner holy, not that the real "you" would emerge, but that Jesus might emerge in you. In this way, the planned outcome of God's love is repentance, growth in holiness and, quite surprisingly, the joy of abandoning self-love.

The Christian Possesses That Which Is Far Greater Than Self-Esteem

Plowing the Field, Frederick Arthur Bridgman, d. 1928

The horse has been used to plough fields for millennia. However, its strength was harnessed inefficiently during most of that time. The Romans, for example, fitted the horse's neck with a leather strap, enabling it to pull only about 500 pounds. However, in the Middle Ages European monks devised the horse collar which squares the load on the horse's shoulders. Suddenly a horse could pull an astounding 1,500 pounds, revolutionizing farm productivity. In some ways, this serves as a fitting analogy for human existence, one in which God was meant to exhibit his power. Humanity was meant to serve God's purposes on earth, an awe-inspiring task. However, hobbled by burdensome self-love (a figurative strap around the neck), mankind never achieves his intended purpose. For God's glory to be showcased in the human existence requires God himself "refitting" man (the load properly positioned in accordance with design) so that man is able to use that which he possesses for vastly greater eternal purpose.

A grave danger in this discussion is that one receives the wrong message, a message that one is incapable and incompetent, and therefore turns to the state for his sustenance. Renouncing self-confidence should not spawn passive people who have abandoned all sense of initiative. This discussion of self is not the enemy of initiative. Rather, it is a macadamized road ushering in a sober understanding of the desperate need for a holy God to indwell and direct the self for fruitful purpose.

The threat of statism is ever on the march as once productive citizens become increasingly dependent on a bloated bureaucracy to provide for their needs, rather than taking responsibility for themselves and loved ones.[71] Thus, this discussion of self runs the risk of foundering on the rocks of dependency unless firmly grounded in Christ, who empowers people of faith, driving them forward with great effect.

The Bible, from the creation in Genesis to the final wedding supper of the lamb in Revelation, describes mankind in terms of three fundamental functions, prophet, priest, and king. While the functions of prophet and priest may be clear enough, the station of king is often the most vulnerable to misunderstanding.[72]

> The Bible advances the idea that each person is made in the image and likeness of a holy eternal God. This belief led to the development of the novel in the West. The idea that an entire book could be written around one central character developed from the belief that each person's life has significance and eternal purpose.

Adam was commissioned by God as a vice-generant, one placed in authority over God's creation with the charge to benevolently govern for God's glory. The first command given to Adam, to name the animals,[73] was a commission to excise authority (as naming throughout the Bible is an authoritative act). In naming, Adam asserted his position as vice-generant, one superior to the animals and regaled with jurisdiction over the creation in God's place. Sadly, at the fall mankind sought to claim authority for himself, to exercise his own decretive will.

In the fall man retained God's image, but lost God's likeness. Mankind's position as derivative king, and the exercise of authority inherent in his position, was stripped from him. Adam and his progeny would labor in a position of weakness, subject to a cursed creation.

---

[71] For further discussion of this topic see "The World System: Intrusive Government" in chapter 2: "The World, the Flesh, and the Devil: Assessing the Threat Matrix"
[72] For further discussion of this topic see "The Image of God: Prophet, Priest, and King" in the first book in this series, *Ask for the Ancient Paths*: *From Art to Artifice to Arisen,* chapter 5: "Redefining the Pygmalion Effect: Exploring the Image of God in Man"
[73] Genesis 2:19, 20

Those in Christ, however, are restored kings under God's authority; they are august sons. Thus, the Christian recognizes that his life and abilities do not exist for himself, but to manifest God to the world. That is why each Christian was created as a prophet, priest, and king, to highlight the personhood of God. Consider, for example, Luke 15:22, which alludes to the stations of priest, king, and prophet in symbolic form. "But the father said to his servants, 'Quick! Bring the best robe and put it on him. Put a ring on his finger and sandals on his feet.'" A ring is a symbol of authority, the provenance of a king. (The robe symbolizes the priest, and the sandals, a prophet.) The prodigal son, in his repentance, was given a ring by his father to manifest the son's newfound authority in his father's house.

Christ in the Storm of the Sea of Galilee
Rembrandt van Rijin, 1632

Matthew 8:23-27 states,

Then he got into the boat and his disciples followed him. Suddenly a furious storm came up on the lake, so that the waves swept over the boat. But Jesus was sleeping. The disciples went and woke him, saying, 'Lord, save us! We're going to drown!' He replied, 'You of little faith, why are you so afraid?' Then he got up and rebuked the winds and the waves, and it was completely calm. The men were amazed and asked, 'What kind of man is this? Even the winds and the waves obey him!'

In stilling the storm, Jesus demonstrated his authority over the created world. This is the exercise of an exalted king. Jesus, both God and man, displayed the full extent of humanity, the greatness which humans were designed to execute had they not rebelled against God. Had Adam not fallen he would have exercised the same authority displayed in Jesus. In John 14:12 Jesus said, "Very truly I tell you, whoever believes in me will do the works I have been doing, and they will do *even greater things* than these, because I am going to the Father."

Unsanctified culture perverts each aspect of what mankind was meant to be in Christ. Every facet of godless culture is, in some sense, a distortion of God-ordained qualities within man. For example, throughout history kings and emperors sired royal families and dynasties. This is the world's faux royalty. Thus, humanly-defined royalty foists a pale, even grotesque, counterfeit royalty upon humanity. The Christian is, in fact, born into a royal bloodline, that of Jesus himself. First Peter 2:9 states, "But you are a chosen people, a royal priesthood, a holy nation, God's special possession, that you may declare the praises of him who called you out of darkness into his wonderful light." Romans 8:30 states, "And those he predestined, he also called; those he called, he also justified; those he justified, he also *glorified*." The Christian is already gloried, already wearing the crown of eternal righteousness. Therefore, Christians are members of God's own royal family, a royalty based solely upon Christ's majesty and splendor, not upon human aspiration or ambition.

> "Everyone who competes in the games goes into strict training. They do it to get a crown that will not last, but we do it to get a crown that will last forever." (1 Corinthians 9:25)

The fact that the Christian is given the position of a restored king in no way implies taking on the authority of God himself, nor does it imply the status of one who acts out of his own will, without regard for God. Christians do not seek to establish an earthly caliphate propped up for worldly gain. The Christian's kingly function is exercised under God himself, as one who enjoys the status of a privileged son with derivative authority. In this regard, 2 Timothy 1:7 states, "For the Spirit God gave us does not make us timid, but gives us power, love and self-discipline." This power, love, and self-discipline obtain directly from the Holy Spirit.

The fact that the Christian already occupies the position of a king in Christ should never make him arrogant or demanding (as kings are want to be). Rather, the Christian is, with regard to his earthly function, a servant. He considers others greater than himself,[74] exercising daily repentance in the humble recognition that everything he has is a gift from Christ who wore a crown of thorns to bestow upon the Christian an imperishable crown of glory. The patriarch Joseph offered the correct posture with regard to God when he said, "I cannot do it, but God will give Pharaoh the answer he desires."[75] This was a tacit recognition of one's rightful reliance upon God for all things. Even Jesus himself submits to his Father's supremacy, when in John 12:49 he said, "For I did not speak on my own, but the Father who sent me commanded me to say all that I have spoken."

Nations go to war to gain territory, garner wealth, or in retribution for various

---

[74] Philippians 2:3
[75] Genesis 41:16

grievances. Christians do battle each day with the forces of evil in the heavenly realms.[76] Each Christian is actively engaged in a war far more fierce and consequential than any earthly war. Human war is a mere shadow of the war that God waged upon the cross, and continues to wage against Satan. For this reason, the Christian is labeled "more than a conqueror,"[77] one who does battle but already basks in the victory Jesus accomplished.

> "Fixing our eyes on Jesus, the pioneer and perfecter of faith. For the joy set before him he endured the cross, scorning its shame, and sat down at the right hand of the throne of God." (Hebrews 12:2)

---

[76] 2 Corinthians 10:3, 4; Ephesians 6:12
[77] Romans 8:37

- 10 -

A NOUTHETIC ANALYSIS OF MOSES

Liberation from Egypt: The Call of Moses

Moses encountered God as a burning bush on the mountain of Horeb where God identified himself as the God of his fathers Abraham, Isaac, and Jacob.[1] God longed to rescue his people from misery, suffering, and oppression.[2] Here is the key verse: God said, "I am sending you [Moses] to Pharaoh to bring my people the Israelites out of Egypt."[3]

Moses on Mount Sinai, Jean-Léon Gérôme, c. 1900

In response, Moses sounded humble. "Who am I, that I should go to Pharaoh?"[4] In reality Moses displayed the fear of man, questioning God's ability to protect him. At that moment, Moses lived a man-centered story in which people wield ultimate power and God is small and weak. God, however, assured Moses; "I will be with you."[5]

A second time Moses questioned, "'Suppose I go to the Israelites and say to them, 'The God of your fathers has sent me to you,' and they ask me, 'What is his name?'

---

[1] Exodus 3:2, 6
[2] Exodus 3:8, 9
[3] Exodus 3:10
[4] Exodus 3:11
[5] Exodus 3:12

Then what shall I tell them?'"[6] A third time Moses questioned, "What if they do not believe me or listen to me and say, 'The LORD did not appear to you'?"[7] God then promised three miraculous signs to substantiate Moses' claims.[8]

A fourth time Moses pled, "'Pardon your servant, Lord. I have never been eloquent, neither in the past nor since you have spoken to your servant. I am slow of speech and tongue.'"[9] The Lord reminded Moses of his power, that he himself could cause Moses to speak.[10] A fifth time Moses spoke, saying, "'Pardon your servant, Lord. Please send someone else.'"[11] Pay careful attention to what came next: the Lord's anger burned against Moses.[12]

Through this exchange it is clear that Moses was living a man-centered story, one in which he, himself, was the main character, the flawed hero. His words revealed certain cravings of the heart, namely for the respect and acceptance of men, that his own safety and social standing be prioritized. In Moses' story God is functionally distant, weak, and untrustworthy, and people - Pharaoh, the Israelites, and the elders - are his de facto gods. In Moses' appraisal, they had ultimate power over him.

Interpreting Moses' First Four Statements

In Exodus 3:7 to 4:14, each of Moses' first four statements implicitly began with the phrase, "I cannot obey you because…"

1. I cannot obey you because…"Who am I?"[13] This is really a statement of "Who are you, that Pharaoh should obey your command? I don't think I can trust you with my life." Moses argued that his was a power problem. The demand of Moses' heart: "God, give me assurance that you can protect me against those who might kill me."

> Throughout the book of Exodus Pharaoh is the anti-creation anti-redemption character. Pharaoh is a leitmotif of Satan himself, and as such, was the quintessential earthly enemy of God. This explains why Moses' reluctance to oppose Pharaoh was so impassioned.

2. I cannot obey you because…"What if the Israelites ask who sent me?"[14] Moses showed fear of man. He lusted after respect and acceptance, a position of relational safety. Moses argued that his was an information problem. The demand of Moses'

---

[6] Exodus 3:13
[7] Exodus 4:1
[8] Exodus 4:2-9
[9] Exodus 4:10
[10] Exodus 4:11
[11] Exodus 4:13
[12] Exodus 4:14
[13] Exodus 3:11
[14] Exodus 3:13

heart: "God, give me more information."

> "Nothing hurts more than to be laughed at." (Latin proverb)

When planning an event with a friend, I was about to say, "Make sure you get me all the information." Then I stopped myself, as it occurred to me that I do not need all the information. I only need the information that God desires for me to have so as to walk in obedience. In fact, all the information might make me a fool; all the information would imperil the right decision. The point is that Moses' deepest problem was not a dearth of knowledge. He had already received undeniable revelation at the burning bush on Mount Horeb.[15] Moses' deepest problem was flawed relationship with God on account of unbelief. In proper relationship, one only needs that which God seeks to reveal to him in order to live by faith.

> One would not instruct a blind person in optics in order to heal his blindness. A paraplegic is not handed a book on anatomy in the hope that through study he can be cured.[16] A falling person is not given a lecture on gravity in an attempt to break his fall. The human plight, in all its flaunt and fury, does not fundamentally arise from a lack of information (for which he is presumed innocent). Mankind is in desperate need of salvation through God's own personal intervention.

3. I cannot obey you because... "What if they do not believe me?"[17] In this query Moses revealed a longing for evidence, proof, the demonstrable, the concrete. Moses did not trust that God could be taken at his word, or that God's word was sufficient. The demand of Moses' heart was for a miraculous sign, a display of power. In this Moses sought covering from the people's possible rejection. Moses thought his problem was a need for respect from people. The demand of Moses heart: "God, give me a way to gain respect."

God accommodated Moses on this point. In response to Moses' faithless words, God nevertheless furnished Moses with three miraculous signs: the staff and snake, the hand and cloak, and the water and blood, each an image of Jesus, his identity, his work, and the salvation he wrought.

> a. **Jesus' identity.** The staff and snake are images of Jesus as king. The staff is a symbol of power, the snake a symbol of Satan. While Moses could only pick up the snake by the tail, Jesus crushed the serpent's head.[18]

> b. **Jesus' work.** The hand and cloak are images of Jesus as priest. The cloak covers

---

[15] Exodus 3:1-10
[16] Paul Tripp, Westminster Theological Seminary, Philadelphia, Pennsylvania
[17] Exodus 4:1
[18] Genesis 3:15

the sickness of Moses' hand. Sickness is a symbol of sin's disease. With his white robe (a symbol of forgiveness),[19] Jesus covers the sin of those who put their faith in him. (Incidentally, the hand is an appendage used for work. Moses' hand was diseased representing the inability of one's work to save him from his sin.[20] Conversely, the healed hand represents Jesus' work of salvation through his death and resurrection.)

> Exodus 6:1 reads, "Then the LORD said to Moses, 'Now you will see what I will do to Pharaoh: Because of my mighty hand he will let them go; because of my mighty hand he will drive them out of his country.'" Here one sees the contrast between Moses' sickly hand, which was unable to heal itself, and God's mighty hand, efficacious for salvation.

    c. **Salvation through Jesus**. The water and blood are symbols of Jesus as prophet. At the crucifixion water and blood flowed from Jesus' side, *proof* that he had died.[21] (Note that the prophet speaks the truth; even in his death, Jesus' body produced truth.) Jesus' blood covers the believer's sin effecting salvation.[22]

4. I cannot obey you because… "I have never been eloquent."[23] Exodus 4:10 reads, "I have never by been eloquent (*debarim aish la*, דברים איש לא), neither in the past nor since you have spoken to your servant. I am slow of speech (*aral*, ערל) and tongue." The word "eloquent" in the Hebrew is literally "not a man of words" (*debarim aish la*, דברים איש לא). Later, Exodus 6:12 also records that Moses was slow of speech (*aral*, ערל), literally "one with uncircumcised lips." The phrases "not a man of words" and "uncircumcised lips" likely refer to either a defect in the speech organs, or inadequate knowledge of the Egyptian language after a hiatus of forty years in the desert.[24]

If Moses' slowness of speech and tongue was in fact a speech impediment, there are two possible causes. The impediment may either arise from a physical defect, or from some "nouthetic" or "worship" disorder. While Moses was traditionally thought to have a stammer or stutter, this is not clear from the Hebrew text. The Hebrew word *aral* (ערל) could indicate either an actual stammer or merely slowness in articulation. Regardless of the exact nature of the impediment, Moses implicitly blamed God. Moses either attributed to God a design flaw or the arrangement of circumstance in which Moses found himself inarticulate in the Egyptian language. Exodus 4:11, 12, states, "The Lord said to him, 'Who gave man his mouth? Who makes him deaf or mute? Who gives him sight or makes him blind? Is it not I, the Lord? Now go; I will help you speak and will teach you what to say.'" This may indicate that the problem

---

[19] Revelation 6:11
[20] Ephesians 2:8, 9
[21] John 19:34
[22] 1 John 1:7
[23] Exodus 4:10
[24] Adam Clark Commentary on Exodus, Bible Study Tools, 2012

was both, since God offered his help to overcome the stammer, and his teaching to articulate the Egyptian language.

Moses Breaking the Tablets of the Law
Gustave Dore, c. 1866

It is crucial to point out that stammering, when not attributable to a physical defect, arises from harbored anger which seeks, but cannot find, expression. Such anger disrupts the lingual mechanics resulting in a stammer. Thus, the answer for this type of stammer is repentance, the renunciation of one's idols, the surrendering of one's heart to the holy God, the laying down of weapons raised against God. Exodus records that Moses was, in fact, prone to explosive anger. He impulsively killed an Egyptian slave master,[25] and struck a desert rock in a fit of rage.[26] Moses, condemned for his anger, was forbidden from entering the Promised Land.[27] Moses' anger made his "ineloquence" all the more disconcerting because, in this case, it would have been his own heart which was the source of his speech impediment.

> The Academy Award® winning movie, "The King's Speech" (2010), highlights the challenges of stammering. In the movie, Prince Albert (1895-1952), Duke of York (soon-to-be King George VI) suffered from an unrelenting stammer which he managed with the help of a gifted speech therapist. As with Moses, the prince harbored smoldering rage as he was prone to explosive outbursts which revealed a heart enslaved to self-serving anger. While the movie portrays the king as having overcome the impediment, it was merely managed through various breathing exercises and cognitive techniques. The truth is that a stammer, like all symptoms of sin-based anger, is only finally conquered at its root through repentance and faith in Jesus Christ.

---

[25] Exodus 2:12
[26] Numbers 20:11
[27] Numbers 20:12

If, in fact, Moses' own heart was to blame for his speech impediment, his conversation with God showed him to be a dissembler and blame-shifter. Acts 7:22 states, "Moses was educated in all the wisdom of the Egyptians and was powerful in speech and action." This verse, spoken by the martyr Stephen at the time of his death, may indicate that Moses spoke with eloquence when under the Holy Spirit's direct intervention. It is also possible that Moses, later in life, repented and his speech impediment faded. Regardless, Moses implicitly attributed his inability to God himself. The demand of Moses heart: "God, free me from my finite ability. Give me the gift you are withholding from me."

> Jeremiah 1 echoes Exodus 3 and 4. God called Jeremiah to bring his word to Jerusalem as Israel faced exile. In Jeremiah 1:6, the prophet stated, "'Alas, Sovereign LORD,' I said, 'I do not know how to speak; I am too young.'" Jeremiah 1:8 records God's response, "'Do not be afraid of them, for I am with you and will rescue you,' declares the LORD." Additionally, in Jeremiah 1:17 God states, "'Get yourself ready! Stand up and say to them whatever I command you. Do not be terrified by them, or I will terrify you before them.'" Like Moses, Jeremiah sounded self-effacing while surreptitiously blaming God for the circumstances (or design) by which he was incapable of effecting God's will.

In contradistinction to Moses, Jesus Christ spoke with perfect eloquence and absolute authority. While Moses failed to repent of his anger until it was too late (and it finally cost him entrance into the Promised Land), Jesus perfectly expressed anger with calculated purpose.[28]

Moses' Conclusion: Defiant Distrust

To ancient Israel, Egypt was a place of plagues, death, darkness, desolation, graves, the underworld, and oppression. Thus, one can understand God's driving intent to free the Israelites from their slavery in Egypt. To this end, God sought to use Moses. God, in fact, did free his people from their tyrannical overlord in a life-and-death struggle which proved to be a defining moment in Israel's history. God delivered his people from a state of death to a state of life and, in this way, Exodus is a resurrection narrative.

However, at the time God summoned Moses, the outcome of events was uncertain to human eyes. Could God possibly prevail over the god-like Pharaoh, one clothed in untold majesty and wealth, commander of the greatest fighting force on earth? Pharaoh was a kind of ancient Near Eastern demiurge, the most powerful among all earthly powers. For Yahweh to prevail over Pharaoh was incontrovertible proof that

---

[28] John 2:17

Yahweh alone was supreme over all gods of the ancient Near East.

Moses, in facing Pharaoh, must confront a "bully," one vastly more powerful than himself. Yet, despite God's many assurances, Moses refused to confront his own fearful and conflicted heart. Four times God identified himself as the God of Abraham, Isaac, and Jacob, and five times Moses intrinsically denied God's identity. Instead of repenting of his unbelief, Moses sought a "doable" law in seeking to remove, or at least neutralize, the threat. God desired nothing less than the overhaul of Moses' heart, a heart which when yielded to God, could be used for epic purpose. Yet, Moses remained unyielding and impassive, shielding his heart with his seemingly innocuous questioning.

> "Half of our difficulties are imaginary, and if we keep quiet about them they will disappear." (Robert Lynd)

Moses concluded that God should send someone else.[29] Moses' message to God was, "Your plan does not fit with my understanding of the situation. I need more power, more information, more respect, and more ability. I need a different plan that allows me to be my own hero, in my own way, for my own purpose, in my own ability, with assurance of respect from others, and in accordance with my own sense of safety and efficaciousness. I want to be hero of this story and not God. If I cannot emerge as my own hero, this is all a grand boondoggle."

> Heroes in God's sight arise both through what they do and what they refuse to do. Sometimes the greatest heroes are seldom seen – purveyors of stalwart plodding quiet courage in the face of temptation or threat.

What was God's response to Moses' queries, maneuvering, and cajoling? The Lord's anger burned.[30] (Later, in Exodus 32:10, concerning the worship of the golden calf, God asked Moses to leave him alone so that his "anger may burn against" the Israelites.) God's anger burns whenever he encounters torpor and defiance with regard to his stated will. The same God, whose anger burned with regard to the golden calf, burned in response to Moses. In effect, Moses had raised golden calves in his heart, each as reprehensible and abhorrent as Aaron's statuary.

Despite his seemingly self-effacing statements, Moses did not suffer from low self-esteem. He was not in need of more encouragement. He did not require more ability, or more information. He needed new questions, a new interpretation of life. He needed a revamped internal narrative in which he would be willing to lay down his life in obedience to God, to cede his will, and relinquish his fears so as to serve the

---

[29] Exodus 4:13
[30] Exodus 4:14

purpose of the God of his fathers. Regardless of what Moses thought he saw, or thought he understood, in spite of the fact that everything around him told him that God's plan would fail, would he nevertheless comply with God's will? Would Moses theocentrically reinterpret his world?

Pharaoh and His Host Lost in the Red Sea
Benjamin West, 1792

"Now faith is confidence in what we hope for and assurance about what we do not see." (Hebrews 11:1)

Moses, as he lived in the realm of probabilities, inhabited a world subject to his own interpretation viewed through the lens of his own sin. But as Moses later discovered, God reinterpreted the terms of engagement, rewrote the story, and stood in command of history, so that success was not a possibility but a certainty.

The tragic reality is that for much of his life, and through the course of many events, Moses refused to reinterpret his world. Immediately subsequent to his opening dialogue with God, Moses defied God with regard to his family. Moses knew the Lord's commands concerning circumcision, yet he did not circumcise at least one of his sons (possibly the first born).[31] It could be that Moses neglected this responsibility on account of opposition from his wife, Zipporah, a Midianite. From Exodus 4:25 one might deduce that Zipporah found circumcision reprehensible as she called Moses a "bridegroom of blood." It may be that Moses, fearing his wife's scorn, disobeyed the Lord's command and in so doing failed to uphold the covenant. Thus, one again sees Moses' fear of man (namely, the fear of his foreign-born wife)

---

[31] Exodus 4:24

> dictating his decisions.

Moses' Misplaced Priorities and Squandered Opportunities

In Numbers 11:11-15, Moses complained to God concerning the people. Here, again, Moses pointed to his situation as the source of his trouble,[32] and brazenly blamed God for the people's treason. Moses asked God why he brought this trouble upon him and, in so doing, questioned God's intentions.[33] Moses claimed the people to be his burden,[34] and thus arrogated to himself the functional status of God. The people were never Moses' burden, yet Moses voiced a patrician self-righteousness in stating that their rebellion was not his fault since he had not fathered them.[35]

Moses questioned where he could find meat for the people,[36] and in so doing, again fell into the prior trap of asking for a pragmatic solution, rather than a nouthetic one.[37] He should not have sought to assuage the people's complaints, but rather to confront the rulers of their hearts.

Moses complained that the burden of leading the people was too heavy for him.[38] This again points to Moses' lust for power since he felt ill-equipped to deal with the people's demands, and sought to wield power more decisively. Moses' subsequent pleas for death were a supreme act of pride.[39] Like one who impudently demands his way, Moses adopted a suicidal posture in his refusal to submit to God.[40]

Moses' final statement in this episode, "Do not let me face my own ruin,"[41] would appear to be a humble and innocent cry. However, it could just as easily be a strong-armed, tight-fisted demand of God. There seems to be something of simmering defiance nestled in Moses' words. As long as he harbored a desirous heart that feared people, Moses could not submit to God's will. Additionally, Moses trenchantly failed to understand that the fault was not with God and his provision, but with sinners eager to find fault with God and his provision. Moses still seemed largely oblivious to the fundamental human condition, a condition resident in himself, as much as within the

---

[32] Numbers 11:10
[33] Numbers 11:11
[34] Numbers 11:11
[35] Numbers 11:12
[36] Numbers 11:13
[37] Exodus 18:17
[38] Numbers 11:14
[39] Numbers 11:15
[40] As one sees with Moses, the suicidal heart does not suffer from low self-esteem; it is consumed with God-hatred, overrun with demands, and engaged in a skirmish of cravings for an alternate situation. When those demands and cravings go unmet, suicidal talk becomes a coercive means for garnering attention and manipulating God. Not unlike a spoiled child throwing a tantrum, suicidal ideations are generally the demand of the self-entitled. The problem is not God's character, provision, or creative acts; the problem is the demanding heart's desperate flailing by means of sprawled and sprattled theatrics. For further discussion of this issue see the case study "Suicide: Idols in Death Throws," in the third book in this series, *The Days of Reckoning Are at Hand: From Fig Leaf to Olive Branch to Laurel Wreath*, chapter 2: "Suffering: The Kintsugi Objective"
[41] Numbers 11:15

people. Moses, time and again, fundamentally misunderstood sin in believing that the people would be mollified with a change of situation. I contend that Moses was blind to the truth about sin because he harbored a measure of smoldering contempt for God.

Moses' Blindness to Foreign Gods Among the People[42]

In Genesis 35:2 Jacob admonished his household to rid themselves of their enslaving gods, to purify themselves, and to change their clothes. Then, in Genesis 35:4, Jacob's household surrendered their idolatrous statues and earrings, so that Jacob might bury them under the oak at Shechem. In burying their statues and earrings, Jacob supposed that he interred his household gods. After this, presumably the practice of false worship ceased among the Israelites, but only for a time. Later, possibly influenced by the animistic practices in surrounding Chaldea and Babylon, the Israelite's once again wore gold earrings associated with the worship of foreign gods.

> Exodus 21:6 refers to a freed slave who, because of his love for his bonded wife and children, refused to relinquish his slavery. The verse reads, "Then his master must take him before the judges. He shall take him to the door or the doorpost and pierce his ear with an awl. Then he will be his servant for life." If the slave's ear was pierced, he became his master's slave for life. This may hearken back to the Egyptian practice of wearing earrings to represent devotion to false gods. Could this ear piercing, representing lifelong bondage to one's master, be a veiled reference to the idolatry associated with earrings in which one renders himself a slave to a false god?

However, Jacob's victory over false worship eventually faded as more than 430 years later Aaron commanded the Israelites, "Take off the gold earrings that your wives, your sons and your daughters are wearing, and bring them to me."[43] Aaron fashioned these earrings into a gold idol in the shape of a calf, declaring that this calf was Israel's gods (plural).[44] It seems that Aaron, in referring to the golden calf as "gods," drew attention to the individual gods inhabiting the assortment of collected earrings.

> **Shedding a New Light on the Exodus**
>
> It would appear that centuries after Jacob's time, while slaves in Egypt, the Israelites once again reverted to the practice of wearing earrings, and thus succumb to worshipping foreign gods.[45] This has seismic implications for the correct interpretation of Israel's deliverance in Exodus. It is generally assumed that the

---

[42] For further discussion of this topic see the case study "The Golden Calf: Idolatry in All its Malevolent Glory," in chapter 6: "Uncovering Idols of the Heart: Make Us Gods to Go Before Us"
[43] Exodus 32:2
[44] Exodus 32:34
[45] Exodus 32:2

> Exodus was driven by God's desire to liberate his people from *physical* slavery to an earthly tyrannical king. God's intentions were vastly deeper, and of a far more significant nature.
>
> Although certainly God longed to deliver his people from physical bondage, the Exodus was less about a physical deliverance and more about a deliverance of worship. God's deliverance from Egypt was on account of Israel's worship of Egyptian gods (as evidenced by their earrings and ornaments). Thus, God primarily sought to deliver his people from their idol worship, and only secondarily sought to free them from their circumstance. (Although physical deliverance would have induced worship deliverance as the people experienced God's love.) Thus, the focal point of the Exodus was not about changing circumstance (physical freedom); it was about freeing the heart from false gods.
>
> This interpretation would accord with many statements throughout Scripture (see Ephesians 6:5; 1 Timothy 6:1, 2; Titus 2:9, for example) in which physical slavery is regarded as a recognized reality in a sinful and fallen world. Thus, as evidenced throughout Scripture, God focuses less attention on freeing slaves from physical bondage, and far more on freeing mankind from his slavery to sin (which, in time, will invariably result in liberation from physical bondage). So God sought to deliver Israel not so much from Pharaoh's tyranny, but from their spiritual slavery to Egyptian gods. That is why they were led into the desert, so that in the midst of a barren hinterland, utterly cutoff from all civilization, their hearts could be exposed, confronted, and brought into submission to their God.[46]

Upon descending from Mount Sinai, Moses incinerated and pulverized the golden calf, scattering its gold in the people's drinking water.[47] He subsequently collected the remaining gold jewelry (itself dedicated to Egyptian gods) to be melted down for the completion of the tabernacle.[48]

> Moses' collection of Israel's remaining gold jewelry could be analogous to the idea that God "melts down" the idols of sinful hearts, razes strongholds erected against him, and with those same ravished materials raises temples dedicated to himself. This is the story of the Christian life, depraved, dark, devious, and dead people who through God's mercy are torn down and disassembled so as to be raised and rebuilt as living temples.[49]

As one of the cognoscenti, Moses should have known that the people had reverted to

---

[46] As Numbers 32:13 states, Israel's forty-year nomadic existence was a process of purification, so that once the rebellious generation had passed away the next generation would be permitted to settle in Canaan.
[47] Exodus 32:20
[48] Exodus 33 :5, 6, 22
[49] 1 Corinthians 3:16

pagan worship, that their earrings served as an outward sign of an inward reality. However, Moses did not read the signs as he was distracted by self-serving motives. He, therefore, missed the opportunity to preempt, in his absence, the golden calf atrocity, the Bible's pinnacle example of idolatry. (Thus, the thesis of this chapter is, had Moses seen the people with the right eyes, and had he taken the right steps to confront their hearts, the golden calf debacle could have been avoided entirely.)

The Worship of the Golden Calf, Jan Steen, c. 1677

An ancillary blindness, Moses failed to see that foreigners ("rabble") had infiltrated the Israelites.[50] The term *hasaphsuph* (הָאסַפְסֻף), in Exodus 12:38, means the "collected or gathered people" who fled Egypt with the Israelites.[51] Thus, this rabble was foreign people, interspersed among the Israelites, undermining the nation's vitality. It could be that these foreigners lived on the fringes of the camp, since, as Numbers 11:1 mentions, the fire of the Lord burned among the people, consuming some on the outskirts of the camp. It might be that this consuming fire was a later warning to the remaining foreigners to abandon their false gods (gods which

---

[50] Numbers 11:4
[51] Adam Clarke Commentary, Bible Study Tools, 2012

presumably the Israelites had also worshipped).

> The infiltrating rabble among the Israelites foreshadows the church, in which will always be found outsiders who wangle their way into its ministry and community. These outsiders undermine and threaten the church's vitality with ungodly teaching and living, just as they undermined Israel's worship.

Moses' Strategic Error: Serving as Civil Judge

Obvious signs of rebellion among the people existed from the beginning, rebellion which threatened to capsize the entire operation unless it was addressed. Yet, somewhat inexplicably, Moses installed himself as civil judge for those who gathered around him from morning till evening.[52] Moses stated, "…the people come to me to seek God's will. Whenever they have a dispute, it is brought to me, and I decide between the parties and inform them of God's decrees and laws."[53] From the beginning, Moses focused on legal matters, property rights, and civil justice at the expense of issues of the heart. Instead of confronting wayward worship, Moses focused on temporal matters which only ossified already refractory hearts. He should have forsaken civil concerns in order to address worship commitments. While Moses was merely meting out legal justice, he should have been exhorting, teaching, rebuking, counseling, and shepherding hearts.

Exodus 18:17 reveals that Moses worked in his own strength from morning till evening, wearing himself out (as his father-in-law Jethro observed). Seeking to alleviate Moses' burden, Jethro advised Moses, "Teach them the decrees and laws, and show them the way to live and the duties they are to perform."[54] (It should be noted that acting for God's purposes, in God's way, empowered by his Spirit, one cannot be worn out.[55] People become worn out when then they act in their own strength, for their own purposes.) Yet, Moses found himself bedraggled in acting as magistrate in civil disputes.[56] Moses functioned in his own strength, for his own purpose, possibly to assuage public criticism, to maintain undisputed control, to justify selfish motive, or to exonerate his searing guilt.

It would also seem that Moses assumed his role as judge out of some degree of pride. He wanted to exercise a measure of control over the people, to be needed, or to wield decision-making power. In functioning as the people's judge, Moses sought to maintain his position, authority, and command. Had Moses been acting in accord with God's will, he would have forsaken legal matters, opting instead to shepherd derelict

---

[52] Exodus 18:13
[53] Exodus 18:15
[54] Exodus 18:20
[55] Isaiah 40:31; Matthew 11:28-30
[56] Exodus 18:17

hearts. Here, as before, he assumed a role which only served as a distraction, deflected attention away from the true issues, and did not rightly diagnose or counsel the people's nouthetic condition. Moses' "house was burning" around him (the people's worship of foreign gods, and the neglect of wayward hearts), but he could not see it because he had taken up mere utilitarian pursuits which, while they appeared to diffuse daily conflict, proved to be superfluous and ruinous dissipation.

> In Moses' defense, at the time that he served as civil magistrate (in Exodus 18), Moses had not yet received the Decalogue or plans for the Ark of the Covenant. Later, God would personally descend upon the Ark's cover to meet with Moses, and issue commands for proper governance.[57]

Moses' Squandered Opportunity to Shepherd Hearts

Moses, if a pastoral presence, a shepherding figure, would have seen the obvious signs in the people's earring and ornaments so that, with preemptive action, he could have out-maneuvered the golden calf fiasco. Exodus 32:2 and 33:4-6 reveal that, even after the golden calf atrocity, the people continued to wear ornaments, which like their earrings, connoted Egyptian, Chaldean, and Babylonian deity worship. Displaying their heart allegiances on their bodies, the people desperately needed a visionary shepherd.

Why did Moses so consistently miss the idols of the heart and the opportunity to provide shepherding counsel?

1. Remember that years earlier Moses murdered an Egyptian slave master.[58] The next day Moses rebuked a Hebrew for beating his fellow man.[59] The perpetrator contemptuously queried, "Who made you ruler and judge over us?"[60] Could it be that on account of committing murder, Moses lost his will to make judgments concerning the people's worshipping intentions? Maybe the guilt of Moses' own sin caused him to retreat into a self-exonerating blindness, a flailing effort to blunt his haunted conscience. Later, Moses may have focused on civil justice as a protective covering for his own heart, a way to externalize transgression and, in so doing, reduce sin to the behavioral (to the neglect of its worship driver).

> King David refused to discipline his sons Amnon and Absalom, to their ultimate demise. Is it possible that David's guilt over his dual sins of adultery and murder squelched his resolve to confront sin in others?[61] There was possibly a subtle,

---

[57] Exodus 25:22
[58] Exodus 2:12
[59] Exodus 2:13
[60] Exodus 2:14
[61] 2 Samuel 11:4, 15

> but entrenched, self-protective quality in Moses' and David's refusal to confront and shepherd hearts, as confrontation of others' hearts would necessitate confrontation of their own.

2. Is it possible that Moses, as civil judge, sought a position of demonstrable authority out of strong-willed ambition, refusing to countenance the more unassuming and servant-like role of pastor and shepherd?

3. Moses focused on a particular redemptive-historical plan – possessing Canaan. In this obsessive focus he had not equipped himself, nor concerned himself, in dealing with the somewhat mysterious and murky waters of heart worship. As God commissioned Moses to lay physical claim to the Promised Land, Moses may have abandoned a regard for that which seemed secondary to taking the land.

Victory, Oh, Lord! (Moses, Aaron, and Hur)
John Everett Millais, d. 1896

4. Moses may have held a somewhat crude and boorish understanding of motives. Possibly on account of simmering anger, Moses was simply hebetated and desensitized to heart issues.

5. Moses may have been somewhat deceived and distracted by his Midianite (foreign) wife.[62] There is evidence that on account of pleasing his wife, Moses, at critical junctures, lost focus on God and exhibited lapses in judgment.

---
[62] Exodus 4:25

It was not until the eve of his death that Moses finally recognized the people's need for a shepherd, a shaper of hearts, a confronter and director of their worship. In Numbers 27:17, as the end approached, Moses asked that the Lord appoint a man over the Israelites, one who will go out and come in before them, one who will lead them out and bring them in, so that the Lord's people would not be like sheep without a shepherd. (Of course, unbeknownst to him at the time, Moses petitioned for the savior, Jesus Christ, one who would not just shepherd his people but invest in them new hearts of obedience to their God.)

Moses' Recumbent Fear of God, Recalcitrant Fear of Man[63]

It would seem that Moses' actions reveal a heart consumed with the fear of man. Exodus 8:26 contains hints of Moses' nascent modus operandi as he said, "'…The sacrifices we offer the LORD our God would be detestable to the Egyptians. And if we offer sacrifices that are detestable in their eyes, will they not stone us?'" Moses betrayed that he was fearful of Egyptian retribution. In fact, his fear of man was greater than his fear of disobeying God. Later, this fear of man cloaked itself in a seemingly noble pursuit as Moses assumed the role of civil judge. As previously stated, in overlooking the people's earrings and ornaments, Moses neglected the issue of heart worship. This allowed the people to dictate the terms and purpose of Moses' interaction with them. Moses succumbed to their whim and will, seeking to appease their lust for money, earthly justice, and temporal equity.

This theme of fearing men more than God recurs time and again with Moses. In Numbers 10:29-32, Moses pled with his father in law, Hobab, to travel with Israel in order to show them where to camp in the desert and so, to be their "eyes." It seemed that Moses had forsaken the Lord's direct leading through the cloud over the tabernacle.[64] Also, it would appear that Moses was willing to give away some of Israel's inheritance to his father-in-law, who was likely not a God-fearer.[65]

Later, in Numbers 11:10-15, Moses lamented his position as the Israelites wailed for meat. In Numbers 11:11, Moses stated that the people were a burden to him, and again in Numbers 11:13, Moses questioned where he could procure meat for the people. Moses once again failed to counsel the people. He should have addressed heart issues in the "rabble."[66] As the people engaged in revisionist history ("We remember the fish we ate in Egypt at no cost."[67]), Moses should have daily confronted their sinful craving.

---

[63] For further development of this topic see "Pockets of Atheism Within the Heart" in chapter 6, "Uncovering Idols of the Heart: Make Us Gods To Go Before Us"
[64] Numbers 9:15-23
[65] Numbers 10:30
[66] Numbers 11:4
[67] Numbers 11:5

> In Numbers 16 Korah enlisted 250 Israelite elders to rebel against Moses. In Numbers 16:22, Moses and Aaron fell facedown and beseeched God not to be angry with the entire assembly, when only *one man* had sinned. However, Moses and Aaron failed to see that, not just Korah had sinned, but those following him as well. The 250 elders were far from innocent. For this reason, the Lord, recognizing their culpability, consumed the elders with fire.[68]

Thankfully, Moses glimpsed something of his error and heeded his father-in-law's advice. Moses delegated authority so as to manage the workload. But tragically, he did not adopt the pastoral role that he should have. He did not have the vision to shepherd the people, nor did he disabuse them of their treachery. In blindly pursuing situations and circumstance, he refused to confront hearts, and therefore was somewhat culpable for the people's latent idolatry (which later reared its head at the foot of Mount Sinai).

Rather than adjudicating legal matters, Moses should have seen God's law for what it is – the revealer of hearts. Moses should have leveraged the law to expose to the people their desperate need for repentance and holiness.[69] Moses should have recognized, and grieved over, the smoldering rebellion around, and in, him. He should have been deeply troubled by the people's earrings and ornaments, known that these were portals for the worship of demiurges, and recognized them as an outward sign of a deeper, more insidious, depravity.

> Moses' blindness with regard to nouthetic issues may be similar to David's misuse of music to soothe Saul's guilty conscience.[70] David looked for a way to assuage the sinner's guilt, rather than confronting sin directly, so as to bringing lasting healing through repentance. In this sense, David's actions seem similar to the way of the world, which likewise soothes the sinner with song.

Moses seemed to finally grasp the gravity of sin when in Exodus 32:31, 32 he said, "Oh what a great sin these people have committed! They have made themselves gods of gold. But now, please forgive their sin – but if not, then blot me out of the book you have written." Moses was then willing to forsake himself in order to intercede on behalf of the people, to be anathematized rather than that the people perish. In that moment of bolide clarity Moses seemed to carry the mantle of intercessor with self-effacing dignity (and in this sense, sheds a flash of light on Jesus' future sacrifice).

---

[68] Numbers 16:35
[69] Galatians 3:24
[70] 1 Samuel 16:14-23

In Exodus 33:13 Moses spoke to God as one friend to another,[71] saying "'If you are pleased with me, teach me your ways so I may know you and continue to find favor with you. Remember that this nation is your people.'" At key junctures, Moses seemed to grow steadily in his passion for God, in his desire to know and be known by God. He humbled himself before God in stating, "Teach me your ways." Moses was also "faithful in all [the Lord's] house."[72] Additionally, while the Lord generally communicated with prophets in visions and dreams, with Moses the Lord spoke face-to-face, clearly, and not in riddles.[73] Moses also received the unique gift of witnessing the form of the Lord.[74] At moments, Moses sparkled with hope and beamed cavorting wisdom in the midst of an otherwise often hobbled and injudicious intercessory role.

Moses Shown the Promised Land, Benjamin West, 1801

In Living by Sight, Moses Remained Blind To People

Despite Moses' privileged witness and moments of towering faith, in Numbers 13:17-32 Moses once again apparently failed to recognize the nouthetic barrenness of the people's hearts. Moses treacherously sent twelve spies to explore Canaan with the directive to determine:

1. The nature of the land[75] (a man-centered means of assessment)

---

[71] Exodus 33:11
[72] Numbers 12:7
[73] Numbers 12:6
[74] Numbers 12:8
[75] Numbers 13:18

2. What kind of land it was – good or bad[76] (an accommodation to the lust of the eye)

3. Whether the people were strong or weak, few or many[77] (an expression of the fear of man)

4. The kind of towns – unwalled or fortified[78] (the trust in human means)

5. The soil quality – fertile or poor, and whether there were trees[79] (a veiled love of money)

6. The quality of the land's fruit[80] (the lust of the flesh) (Pointing out that it was the season for the first ripe grapes, Moses asked the spies to return with some fruit.)

In spying out the land, Moses merely focused on circumstances and visible evidence over God's stated Word. God had already told Moses all he needed to know about the land. In Exodus 3:8, when summoned at the burning bush, God told Moses that Canaan was a good and large land, a land flowing with milk and honey. Subsequently, in Exodus 13:5, Moses had already informed the people of the land's goodness.

However, upon approaching the land, it would appear that Moses lost sight of God's promise and greater mission. For example, Moses' request that the spies ascertain knowledge of the people living in the land, whether strong or weak, was clearly a faithless request, one based in the fear of man. Likewise, Moses' request for surveillance on the nature of the towns, whether unwalled or fortified, revealed a fear of worldly strength and earthly opposition, a trust in human means to vanquish the enemy. Did Moses compartmentalize his faith, judging God to be faithful in certain situations, powerful only under certain conditions? It appears that here, as before, Moses resorted to a faulty means of evaluation, one which assuaged the fears of men, and appealed to the feckless and faithless.

The spies' report was attended by a subsequent insurrection among the people,[81] an insurrection for which Moses had set the stage. Had Moses not asked situational questions of the land and its inhabitants, had he not sent spies at all, Moses would have been more likely to lead the people by faith rather than by sight. Moses could

---
[76] Numbers 13:19
[77] Numbers 13:18
[78] Numbers 13:19
[79] Numbers 13:20
[80] Numbers 13:20
[81] Numbers 14

have leveraged the imminent entrance into the land as a life-altering opportunity to confront hearts, marshal faith, and redirect worship. Instead, Moses squandered the opportunity, failing to recognize that it was not the details of the land and its inhabitants which were at issue, but the Lord's work in the people's hearts. Once again, in his misplaced allegiances, Moses failed to confront hearts, so that, in the process of seditious inquiry he sparked a firestorm.

I Wouldn't Have Seen It If I Hadn't Believed It

Allegory of the Five Senses, Gerard de Lairesse, 1668

To say that reality is only that which can be known through the five senses (empiricism evaluates solely by means of sense-discerned evidence) assumes perfect and complete knowledge of the universe. To live by empirical evidence alone assumes man's senses to be the ultimate arbiter of truth and, thus, the limit of what can and cannot be known (called epistemology). This, in effect, makes man and his senses divine.

While Christians would rightly denounce empiricism, they often function by means of it. Although they may profess faith, Christians often live as though they trust only what can be known by means of the five senses. This often occurs when Christians turn to psychology to define their lives, effect their sanctification, and calibrate their worldview. (Psychology is an implicit paean to empiricism.)

Rightly understood, the Christian message is "contra-sensory." Faith vitiates against everything the senses reveal about the nature of reality. Under the aegis of sin, appearances are deceptive, the senses falsely perceptive, and one's worldview myopic. Those who would know reality are called to be a people of the "ear," to listen to God and seek Him. Through seeking and knowing God, there is a slow but deliberate realignment, recalibration, and reorientation of one's perception of reality so that it properly aligns with God's. That is why faith seeks understanding, not the other way around. Only the Christian, re-created by means of faith, rightly appraises the world and lives accordingly. "Learning the gaze of God we come to weigh life aright."[82] God's gaze reveals that there is, in all things, a holy God leading the lost (and the saved) to himself.

> Social scientist Marshall McLuhan (1911–1980) ingeniously reversed the well-known expression "Seeing is believing," to read, "I wouldn't have seen it, if I hadn't believed it."

This leads to Numbers 20:2-13, the *coup de grace* in Moses' intercessory role. In this episode the people lacked water and gathered to oppose Moses and Aaron.[83] The people stated that they would have preferred to perish with the previous rebellious generation.[84] They asked why Moses brought them out of Egypt to this terrifying place with no grain, figs, grapevines, pomegranates, or water.[85] Moses and Aaron interceded before the Lord,[86] who commanded Moses to take his staff and gather the assembly.[87]

The Lord commanded Moses to speak to the rock "before their eyes," and it would pour out its water. Moses gathered the assembly and lashed out with, "'Listen, you rebels, must we bring you water out of this rock?'"[88] Moses raised his arm and, with his staff, struck the rock twice; water gushed out. Instead of speaking to the rock, as God commanded, Moses struck the rock in anger for his own aggrandizement in the people's eyes.[89] The Lord rebuked Moses and Aaron stating that, because they did not trust him enough to honor him as holy in the sight of the Israelites, they would not accompany the community into the Promised Land.[90]

In this episode, there was either an element of false piety in Moses and Aaron, or else shallow faith. Notice that in Numbers 20:6 Moses and Aaron fell face down before the Lord (in what might be mock-repentance), yet moments later, Moses proceeded to

---

[82] David Powlison, Westminster Theological Seminary, Philadelphia, Pennsylvania
[83] Numbers 20:2
[84] Numbers 20:3
[85] Numbers 20:5
[86] Numbers 20:6
[87] Numbers 20:8
[88] Numbers 20:10
[89] Numbers 20:11
[90] Numbers 20:12

strike the rock in anger.[91] Moses frequently perpetrated displays of godliness, only to grant full flourish to his self-serving heart. It would appear that when Moses' personal renown was threatened he lashed out, the curse of a vigilant and vibrant fear of man.

Moses Striking the Rock for Water, Nicolas Poussin, 1649

Case Study: Numbers 32: The Transjordan Tribes

The Reubenites and Gadites:

1. Possessed large herds and flocks, so that they enjoyed a measure of prosperity and wealth[92]

2. Viewed the lands of Jazer and Gilead as suitable for their livestock,[93] showing themselves to be ruled by the lust of the eye and selfish ambition, rather than by God's promise of taking the land

3. Told Moses that the Transjordan land (which the Lord had subdued before Israel) was suitable for livestock, and in this way co-opted the Lord's work for their own personal gain[94] (They were not focused on why the Lord subdued the land, nor what it meant to repent and live by faith as a result.)

---

[91] Numbers 20:11
[92] Numbers 32:1
[93] Numbers 32:1
[94] Numbers 32:4

4. Did not plan to cross the Jordan to enter Canaan, but hoped instead to possess the land on the opposite side of the Jordan. In so doing, the Reubenites and Gadites forfeited their promised Canaan inheritance for a plot of land that they judged suitable through their own reason.[95]

5. Planned to build fortified cities for the protection of their women and children[96]

6. Were accused by Moses of discouraging Israel, as their fathers had done[97]

7. Were called a brood of sinners by Moses; the Reubenites and Gadites were standing in the place of their fathers, making the Lord even angrier with Israel[98]

At Moses' behest, the Reubenites and Gadites pledged an oath of alliance to Israel in taking Canaan.[99] Moses stated that if they reneged they had sinned.[100] However, Moses missed the point. The sin had already occurred in seeking that which was in defiance of the Lord's command, in desiring that which undermined the Lord's redemptive-historical plan.

Overlooking the tribes' underlying sin issue, Moses unwittingly catalyzed the Reubenites' and Gadites' defection by encouraging them to build cities and pens for their flocks.[101] Moses gave them a means for finding comfort in their sin, merely placated sin, so that it anchored itself within the heart, ensconced itself within a plausible storyline. In this, as before, Moses showed a blindness to the heart's wicked machinations. Moses' plans finally divided Israel, so that the nation was now severed by the Jordan. Moses unwittingly became a co-conspirator in subverting God's intention for his people.

> John Calvin (1509–1564) believed that the Reubenites and Gadites vouchsafed their own personal convenience at the expense of the public good, discarding the honor and interest of Israel, as well as the Lord's promise to Abraham.[102] In like manner,

---

[95] Numbers 32:5, 19
[96] Numbers 32:17
[97] Numbers 32:7
[98] Numbers 32:14
[99] From Joshua 4:13 one learns that from the tribes of Reuben and Gad, and the half of the tribe of Manasseh, only 40,000 armed men passed over the Jordan to assist their brethren in the submission of the land. However, the tribe of Reuben consisted of 43,730 men; the tribe of Gad, 40,500; and the tribe of Manasseh, 52,700 (half of which is 26,350). Add these amounts (43,730 + 40,500 + 26,350) and the total is 110,580. This leaves 70,580 men (110,580 − 40,000) left behind for the defense of the women, children, and the flocks, more than sufficient to defend them.[99] It would seem that the tribes partially reneged on their promise to Moses. (They did not send the full number of men that they agreed to.) This should not come as a surprise since the tribes had already rebelled against God in setting aside his promises.
[100] Numbers 32:22-24
[101] Numbers 32:24
[102] Genesis 22:17

> many Christians plan and seek their own convenience and ambition, rather than that of Jesus Christ.[103] Christians, influenced by worldly concern and advantage, forfeit their promised Canaan (Jesus himself) when their spirit too easily agrees with the world, with that which is seen and temporal.
>
> Like the Reubenites and Gadites, Abraham's nephew, Lot, chose "by the sight of the eye,"[104] and suffered grave loss. So too, Christians are quick to say, "It is good to be here,"[105] and so surrender the greater blessing. If the Christian is to receive his inheritance, and rightly choose his portion, he must wholeheartedly listen to, and obey, God's Word.[106] The Reubenites and Gadites abandoned God's Word for the lust of the eye, and so subverted the entire redemptive-historical blueprint.

There is much similarity between Numbers 32 and Luke 14:15-24:

> When one of those at the table with him heard this, he said to Jesus, 'Blessed is the one who will eat at the feast in the kingdom of God.'
>
> Jesus replied: 'A certain man was preparing a great banquet and invited many guests. At the time of the banquet he sent his servant to tell those who had been invited, 'Come, for everything is now ready.'
>
> 'But they all alike began to make excuses. The first said, 'I have just bought a field, and I must go and see it. Please excuse me.'
>
> 'Another said, 'I have just bought five yoke of oxen, and I'm on my way to try them out. Please excuse me.'
>
> 'Still another said, 'I just got married, so I can't come.'
>
> 'The servant came back and reported this to his master. Then the owner of the house became angry and ordered his servant, 'Go out quickly into the streets and alleys of the town and bring in the poor, the crippled, the blind and the lame.'
>
> 'Sir,' the servant said, 'what you ordered has been done, but there is still room.'
>
> Then the master told his servant, 'Go out to the roads and country lanes and compel them to come in, so that my house will be full. I tell you, not one of

---

[103] Phillipians 2:21
[104] Matthew Henry Commentary, Bible Study Tools, 2012
[105] Matthew 17:4
[106] Numbers 32 is similar to Luke 14:15-24: The Parable of the Great Banquet

those who were invited will get a taste of my banquet.'

Often God's people willingly settle for that which appears pleasing to the eye, a place of safety and seeming prosperity, rather than faithfully pursuing all that God has planned for them. The unwillingness to wait for the fruition of God's full desires is pride which prioritizes personal desire. The Lord wants to redirect his people's attention from a low-ceilinged world to an eternal plane.[107] (For example, in Acts 7:55, Stephen, full of the Holy Spirit, removed his focus from the people in front of him to gaze on Jesus standing at the right hand of God.)

Just as the Reubenites and Gadites refused to enter the Promised Land, instead choosing another location that appeared commodious, so too, many Christians refuse to enter the Promised Land of Jesus. They rather seek to live outside the land in the mere appearance of submission to God's will, living out their own self-serving purpose.

With regard to the Reubenites and Gadites, Moses offered a textbook example of defective counsel. Moses missed the glaring sin issue in deferring to a pragmatic solution. While his approach seemed wise, it led to a split in God's people, which would have devastating effect for generations to come. Moses' false counsel indirectly led to a later civil war.

Concluding Remarks

As a child, I was shocked to learn that the American Colonists burned the British king, George III (1738–1820), in effigy. In fact, in the lead up to the Revolution, several prominent figures were burned in effigy. I wondered, "Where is 'Effigy,' and why do important people keep getting burned there?" I eventually discovered that effigy was not a place but a thing (an often crude representation of someone). It is not my intention to burn Moses "in effigy" (and I hope my analysis does not render only a crude representation). In humility, I recognize that the exact same failings exhibited by Moses live within me in spades.

While some may find the foregoing analysis of Moses hypercritical and highly-subjective, the purpose of this analysis is to specifically understand why the golden calf episode occurred, and how it could have been avoided. The evidence, heretofore presented, makes the case that Moses failed to shepherd the people's hearts, that he overlooked the confrontation of their false idols, and neglected to draw them from recognized ancient Near Eastern gods. Time and again, Moses showed himself a complicit accomplice in the people's idolatry, and therefore was, to a degree, culpable

---

[107] The concept "low-ceilinged world" from David Powlison, Westminster Theological Seminary, Philadelphia, Pennsylvania

for it. As he attended to judicial matters, he inadvertently institutionalized and ossified heart idols. Those idols, given sturdy sanctuary, remained poised and potent. As Moses excused guilty parties (i.e. the 250 elders who conspired with Korah), he unwittingly allowed insurrection to flourish. As he focused attention on that which was demonstrable, visible, and tangible (i.e. sending spies into the land), he drew attention away from the Lord's promises, the imperative of faith, and the discipline to trust the unseen. Thus, Moses, while he displayed discrete moments of towering faith, largely failed to engage the enemy on the battlefield of the heart.

Christ Falls on the Way to Calvary
Raphael, 1516

Most ancient literatures (such as Greek or Egyptian mythologies) present heroes in god-like grandeur who accomplished superhuman feats. The Bible, however, presents its heroes in sober earthy candid terms. Biblical heroes were sinful flawed men and women who chose faith in God at a pivotal moment of indecision. When these people faced a life-or-death situation, they made a historic and heroic decision to trust and obey an unseen God, patiently waiting for his promises to be fulfilled.

Yet, the Bible is careful to point out that each of its characters, save one, crucially failed to be the kind of hero that God desires. However, despite having mishandled God's mission at numerous junctures, each failed hero was finally counted righteous merely by faith, a defining and unwavering worship decision. Hebrews 11 recalls victorious Old Testament saints who walked in genuine faith and were commended by

God, not for flawless obedience, but for crucial submission at an eternal crossroad.

> "By faith Moses, when he had grown up, refused to be known as the son of Pharaoh's daughter. He chose to be mistreated along with the people of God rather than to enjoy the fleeting pleasures of sin. He regarded disgrace for the sake of Christ as of greater value than the treasures of Egypt, because he was looking ahead to his reward. By faith he left Egypt, not fearing the king's anger; he persevered because he saw him who is invisible. By faith he kept the Passover and the application of blood, so that the destroyer of the firstborn would not touch the firstborn of Israel." (Hebrews 11:24-28)

Finally, while the progeny of those Moses led for forty years entered the Promised Land, they did so without him. Moses died disappointed. Yet, in a final act of humility, Moses petitioned for a shepherd for the people,[108] a role he had inadequately and reluctantly assumed. This parting call was nothing less than the cry for a savior. Thus, it would appear that on his deathbed, Moses finally spied something of the heart's true condition, and its desperate need for change. My intention has never been to wantonly cast aspersions upon Moses, but to present a convincing case for Jesus, the minister of a covenant inordinately greater than that administered by Moses.[109]

> "Jesus has been found worthy of greater honor than Moses, just as the builder of a house has greater honor than the house itself." (Hebrews 3:3)

The Old Testament closed with a 400 year-long silence marked by dark disappointment and longing. The savior promised at the fall had not come. But hope was not lost. The Bible's millennia-long quest for a savior *par excellence* was fulfilled with Jesus' birth. Here was finally the one worthy of praise, able to deliver the people from their sin, and destined to restore the glory of Israel in the hearts of its people. The one Bible hero who succeeded perfectly in the mission placed before him was God's own son, Jesus Christ.

---

[108] Numbers 27:17
[109] 2 Corinthians 3:7-18

EPILOGUE

The Clockmaker, Jules Zermati, 1900

Revelations Are Nothing Without Revolutions[1]

> "…we declare God's secret wisdom, a wisdom that has been hidden and that God destined for our glory before time began." (1 Corinthians 2:7)

Consider a fine Swiss timepiece. Each lever and gear is crafted to exacting specification. In orchestrated precision, parts swivel and rotate on gemstone pivots, each perfectly coordinated like intricate celestial movements. The meticulous detail that goes into just one such chronometer is truly astounding. Yet, each component exists for a singular pedestrian objective – to produce the correct time. As each constituent serves a function, to remove even one of the least significant gears would render the entire timepiece inoperable. Thus, concerning the watch's function, each internal component is vital; concerning the watch's appearance (such as the color of the face, the style of the hands, or the appearance of the dial), all is, however, merely a matter of taste.

If you have completed the first two books in *The Christian Exceptionalism in Counseling Series™*, you have covered the crucial tenets of biblical counseling. In

---

[1] The phrase, "Revelations are nothing without revolutions" from Greg Gutfeld's commentary "Small Government is Back" on Fox News, June 6, 2013.

writing this material, there has been a deliberate attempt to mimic the workings of a fine timepiece (in both function and appearance). This model's various functional components are each carefully developed so as to induce sanctification in the believer (at the Holy Spirit's behest). If, however, any of these cogs is removed the entire endeavor is imperiled, the guiding creation-fall-redemption model quickly crumbles. (In terms of "appearance," I have offered some diversion along the way, occasional stylistic delights for the imagination.)

Thus, the foundational elements of these first two books are absolutely vital for grasping this paradigm - what it means to be indwelled by, and personally changed by, Christ himself. For example, one must apprehend the heinousness and pervasiveness of sin in order to appreciate the gospel; a weak view of sin results in a weak view of Christ.[2] Thus, each biblical pillar intertwines to form a latticework maintaining the integrity of the Bible's entire paradigm.

Some foundational elements of the biblical counseling paradigm:[3]

1. The heart is designed to worship and, in fact, is consigned to worship.

2. Mankind, as image-bearer, forms a covenant either with the true God or with idols.

3. Each person lives before the face of the holy God to whom he responds moment-by-moment.

4. One's greatest need is for relationship with God through Jesus Christ.

5. Man is totally depraved, so that even his reasoning ability is damaged.

6. The sinner turns to idols in a desperate gamble that they will bestow the power, meaning, and blessing he seeks.

7. The sinner is consumed with meeting perceived needs.

8. The Bible speaks to every concern of the psyche, and is necessary and sufficient to handle every matter pertaining to right living.

9. God's love is not blindly unconditional, but operates with regard to a sanctification agenda.

---

[2] For further discussion of this point see "Understanding the Nature of Depravity" in chapter 3: "Total Depravity: This Imperiled Arcadia"

[3] For a more comprehensive list see the first book in this series, *Ask for the Ancient Paths: From Art to Artifice to Arisen,* chapter 1: "The Exordium to Biblical Counseling"

10. The summation of all of God's work is the transformation of every redeemed sinner into the image of Christ.

One must grasp the rudiments of creation, fall, and redemption, in order to apprehend the psyche's constitution, the human dilemma, and that which Jesus accomplished on the cross. One must understand the Bible's teaching on sanctification, so as to comprehend the nature of God's love. One must appreciate man's continual confrontation with the living God, in order to appraise man's fears. One must fathom the infused longing for holiness, in order to plumb mankind's most pressing psychic need. Every element is intricately interlaced so as to function as a seamless tapestry.

You may ask, "Does one need Swiss precision to merely tell the time of day? Couldn't one function reasonably well with a dime-store electric watch strapped to his wrist?" This is where such an analogy breaks down; the Bible offers an all-or-nothing proposition, a kind of holy Hobson's choice, with regard to the psyche. One either wholly accepts the Bible's paradigm, or one is rendered utterly lost. Thus, the dime-store electric watch (which might be likened to a syncretistic view of the Bible and psychology) always gives the wrong time, and not even an ordered error (such as, always five minutes slow), but a wholly chaotic readout. Thus, while a fine timepiece produces a singular result - precision timekeeping, the Bible's plenary teaching also produces a singular result – relationship with Jesus Christ. That is why the Bible exists. Each gear and lever, the synchronized movements, and the pivoting pinions, all serve one objective, that the observer would find, and be conformed to, Jesus, resulting in abundant fruit. To remove even one constituent imperils the entire enterprise.

Lest you despair, I have some good news. As you faithfully study the Bible, Jesus inserts within you all of the needed gears and levers, all of the crucial gemstones and pinions. He longs and labors to install within you each component, so as to produce the fruit for which you were born. Thus, it is not up to you to position all of the needed elements; the Holy Spirit effects this work, so that one is finally perfected in the faith. As you learn more about your design, your sin, and your salvation, each part is being appropriated and calibrated under the aegis and precision of the Holy Spirit, that you, the faithful Christian, would be a spectacle to the universe,[4] a glorious temple in which Jesus reigns.[5]

I encourage you to continue on to the third, and final, book in this series, *The Days of Reckoning Are at Hand: From Fig Leaf to Olive Branch to Laurel Wreath*, which more directly applies this latticework of truths. It is by means of the third book that

---

[4] 1 Corinthians 4:9
[5] 1 Corinthians 3:16; 6:19

possibly the sweetest fruit will be harvested for Christ, as this paradigm more vividly distinguishes itself from secular models. As the mystery unfolds, the Bible's counseling paradigm will be more perspicuously revealed as a peerless *tour de force* of human freedom, freedom through relationship with Jesus Christ.

- APPENDIX -

A DEMON POSSESSION CASE STUDY[1]

Saint Michael, Agnolo Bronzino, 1546

The Setting

On November 18, 2011, and again on December 22, 2011, I observed incidences of demon possession in a church setting.

The Possessed

The possessed woman, "Fiona," is about twenty-eight years old, living at home with her mother. Fiona is currently unemployed because of frequent demon possession attacks which leave her vulnerable to social ostracism. Fiona wears glasses, and dresses neatly and respectfully. She appears to be of above average intelligence and generally polite and responsible. She is quiet and reserved, but well-spoken and responsive in conversation.

Information Gathered from Fiona's Pastor

1. Fiona had shown signs of possession for three years.

---

[1] Consider 1 Samuel 16:14; Luke 9:49; 11:19; Acts 19

2. On several occasions the demon has spoken:
   a) Its voice is audibly different from that of Fiona – a deeply angry and frightening voice.
   b) The demon said that it has inhabited Fiona for thirteen years.
   c) It refuses to leave and claims that no one can cast it out.

3. On occasion, during possession episodes Fiona has become violent, even striking those who are praying for her.

4. Fiona was sent to a Pentecostal church two years prior where members prayed over her. They claim to have cast out several demons but that one demon could not be exorcised. (They do not know why the last demon remains obdurate.)

5. Fiona consistently attends Sunday worship and evening prayer meetings. Several times she has vomited during the Scripture reading or during the preaching.

6. According to the pastors, Fiona had shown some improvement over the past three years. The episodes are now not as frequent, nor as violent in nature. In fact, the pastors claim that during the first possession episode that I observed they sensed progress in weakening the demon.

7. When asked why the demon persists, despite years of prayer to cast it out, the pastors responded that this demon is particularly strong, requiring extraordinary faith on the part of those praying.

> "Jesus rebuked the demon, and it came out of the boy, and he was healed from that moment. Then the disciples came to Jesus in private and asked, 'Why couldn't we drive it out?' He replied, 'Because you have so little faith. I tell you the truth, if you have faith as small as a mustard seed, you can say to this mountain, 'Move from here to there' and it will move. Nothing will be impossible for you.'" (Matthew 17:18-22)

Preliminary Fact-Finding

1. On November 18, 2011, Fiona approached student "Elle" (a young Christian woman) and I with a request for help. She said that the church claims she is demon possessed, but she does not believe this is true.

2. I asked Fiona when she became a Christian. She did not offer a clear answer. I asked her how she knows she is a Christian. Again, her answer was vague. At one point she made the comments, "I am not good enough to be a Christian," and "I do not meet God's standard."

> Satan daily accuses the saints, pointing out their sin to God, so as to induce God's wrath upon them.[2]

3. I asked her to state the gospel. She stated it correctly. However, I suspected she only provided an intellectual response. She appeared to be rehearsing a doctrine that she had previously heard.

4. I asked Fiona some questions about her past. When Fiona was eight years old her parents divorced. Her father left and she saw him infrequently, if at all. She often interjects this into conversation. It seems to define her.

5. Fiona's mother remarried soon after the divorce. As a young girl, Fiona's step-father subjected her to sexual harassment, often forcing her to watch pornography. As an adolescent (the age is unknown, but I would guess about fifteen years old), Fiona's step-father either sexually assaulted her or severely abused her.

6. Fiona subsequently attacked her step-father with a knife. What happened at that point is unclear, but the outcome was that he never again came near her. (The step-father has since left the family.)

Possession Episode #1 (November 18, 2011)

1. Suspecting that Fiona was not a Christian, I shared Ephesians 2:8, 9 and Acts 4:12. As I read, Fiona began to convulse. The convulsions were at first slow and then grew more violent, having a kind of spasmodic quality. It seemed that her head and body movements were intended to instill fear in onlookers as she often jerked or slightly lunged toward onlookers.

2. Fiona's head rapidly twisted from side to side in a violent motion. Her neck painfully craned. Her mouth opened as if she were trying to vomit. Her eyes became red and her entire face took on a ghoulish appearance as it convulsed and contorted. She emitted frequent loud shrieks and yells. Her hands writhed and twisted, as if she were caught in an epileptic seizure. Her hands remained deformed during the episode.

3. During this time, I sat directly next to Fiona, but was careful not to touch her (especially given her history of sexual abuse). Student Elle sat on her left reading Scripture during the entire episode. Several church members surrounded us praying in an almost frenzied rhythm. Additional church members seemed to appear like angels descending from the sky. At first I saw six members, then

---
[2] Revelation 12:10

twelve, twenty, and later possibly thirty, each praying loudly.

4. I continued praying, my hands raised in caution. I was at times fearful Fiona would attack one of us, maybe student Elle, who was very frightened. I was careful not to back away as I suspected that any obvious display of fear might embolden the demon to attack.

5. At one point Fiona's contorted hand slowly moved in my direction. I could not tell if it sought to stop my prayer, or if it reached out for help, if it was under the will of the demon or Fiona. I grabbed the cuff of her coat sleeve and held it tightly in the event she became violent.

6. At one point the pastor put her hands on Fiona. This seemed to make her particularly agitated as the shrieks grew louder and the convulsions more violent. The pastor approached Fiona from behind, placed her hands around Fiona's neck, and held firmly as she prayed loudly. Another held Fiona's hands, while a third woman shouted, "in the name of Jesus," into Fiona's mouth.

7. During the possession episode, Fiona was either fully or partially conscious. She seemed to know and understand what was happening. At one point, while her head shook, her glasses nearly fell off her nose. She lifted her hand to replace them. This told me that she was aware of what was happening. Additionally, Fiona later stated that the pastor had held her neck so tightly that she had trouble breathing.

8. It was unclear to what extent Fiona was fighting the possession, or at least seeking help to fight it. To what extent was she in opposition to, cooperating with, or in submission to the possession?

9. After about forty minutes the situation calmed down. Fiona returned to her senses and appeared relieved. She looked exhausted, her eyes filled with tears, and her face red. She sat quietly for a time and said nothing, as onlookers dispersed.

10. I was saddened in observing this episode. I pity Fiona and desire to free her from this torture chamber. I felt as though I were witnessing hell itself, the Bible's description of weeping, anguish, gnashing of teeth, unquenchable fire,[3] extreme physical and emotional pain, and suffering under the tyranny of Satan himself.

> "But the subjects of the kingdom will be thrown outside, into the darkness, where

---

[3] Matthew 13:42

there will be weeping and gnashing of teeth." (Matthew 8:12)

Dante and Vergil in Hell, Eugène Ferdinand Victor Delacroix, 1822

11. The following day, November 19th, I asked Fiona about her prior statements: "I am not good enough to be a Christian" and "I do not meet God's standard." She denied making such statements. I wondered how much of her denial might be confusion caused by the demon. Was she in fact speaking, or was the demon trying to deceive those around her into assuming that she was speaking?

12. Two days after the possession episode, on November 20th, at an open witnessing meeting, Fiona shared her faith with those gathered, stating that real and permanent change had in fact occurred though the counseling training she attended that week.

"Whatever is true, whatever is noble, whatever is right, whatever is pure, whatever is lovely, whatever is admirable—if anything is excellent or praiseworthy—think about such things." (Philippians 4:8)

Possession Episode #2 (December 22, 2011)

1. On December 19, 2011, I saw Fiona at our training class. A few of us noted that she looked better than one month prior. She appeared brighter, more at peace, and more optimistic. We asked her about the change. She said that she had been daily

praying in tongues, and that consequently she had seen a reduction in the possession episodes. She claims that when she speaks in tongues her heart is at peace, and that she becomes angry less often. I was suspicious about this.

2. I had hoped to counsel Fiona further. However, there was no opportunity to speak at the meeting on December 19th. The next morning I saw her waiting for a bus outside the church. I asked if she had time to meet one evening during the week. She seemed distant and aloof. She said that she was busy but, if time allowed, she would come to the church one night. Her response seemed odd, almost as if she did not care about the counseling session. I wondered if her aloofness indicated that she had been dissatisfied with our previous discussion. I also wondered if Fiona's mother had discouraged her from speaking with me.

3. I saw Fiona at our training session on December 22, 2011. She listened quietly to my lesson on the parable of the prodigal son, but appeared emotionally distant, almost catatonic.

4. After the students dispersed. I asked Fiona if we could discuss her problem in more detail. She agreed. Together with student Elle and "Barney" (a young Christian man), we sat in the front of the classroom.

5. I first asked Fiona to tell me when she became a Christian. She responded that she had become a Christian in March, 2010. I noted that this was fairly recent, and asked her to provide some brief background concerning the circumstances around which she received Christ.

6. Her story started with her father leaving when she was eight years old. (She again placed great emphasis on this.) This is the seminal event for nearly every conversation about her life and, in fact, seems to define her.

7. She quickly transitioned to her college years and recounted a series of dating relationships. She spoke in detail about three boyfriends. I sensed that she moved from relationship to relationship as a way to fill some emotional longing. I suspected that she kept putting herself into abusive relationships with men. She mentioned that one of her boyfriends was a member of a gang, a drug addict, and had been convicted of murder. I found this almost unimaginable as such a boyfriend seemed grossly out of character with Fiona's image and personality.

I wondered if she was exaggerating for sympathy, or if she had embellished this boyfriend's persona as part of a fantasy world to cover her own sin. Without further evidence, I had to take her comments on face-value. My greatest fear was that she had been sexually-involved with these boyfriends, which only served to further her emotional anguish, self-absorption, and hatred of God.

8. As Fiona spoke about relationships (father, step-father, boyfriends, friends, pastors) there was one common theme: each person had in some way failed her, disappointed her, or hurt her. (Oddly, Fiona did not mention her mother at all in any conversation.)

9. I asked Fiona to clearly state which events led her to Christ. She offered a vague answer. This confirmed for me that something was very wrong. I sensed that the Holy Spirit did not live in her, that she was either deeply confused, or deliberately obfuscating the gospel.

10. If there were to be any progress, I knew the counseling would need to move in the direction of a confrontation with sin and rebellion, and a call to repentance. I would need to be clear on the distinction between being a victim, and responding to victimization with a strong-armed hatred of God. I emphasized the comprehensive state of the heart with regard to sin, a worship orientation built around rebellion toward a holy God. We would start at the beginning – a careful walk through the gospel culminating in a call to conclusively abandon a life of self-righteousness, and a plea to finally surrender to Jesus in faith.

11. I asked Fiona to allow me to explain the gospel. She seemed annoyed, as if I was wasting her time. I read Romans 1:16-19. We walked through each aspect of her need for repentance, receiving Jesus' sacrifice by faith, salvation as God's gift through his grace, and the impossibility of earning God's favor. She paid attention, and was generally at peace with our discussion. However, as I delved deeper into the issue of sin and idolatry, I sensed her anger growing and she was agitated.

12. Fiona's mother entered the room late and sat about three rows behind Fiona, so that Fiona was not immediately aware that her mother was present. Her mother listened to our conversation with a rapped intensity. She seemed angry or condescending concerning our conversation, oddly distant and aloof during the explanation of the gospel (even though the mother claims to be a Christian).

13. I tried to keep Fiona calm, sensing that she may lapse into a demon attack. On three occasions, sensing her anger rising, I gently stopped her and asked her to relax, remain calm, and simply rest. This seemed to work for a time. She told me she could feel the demon entering her brain. I asked her why the demon was entering. She did not offer a clear answer.

14. Within a few moments the convulsions and shrieks began. This time the possession seemed more violent than the previous episode. Fiona's mother ran

forward to hold her daughter.

15. The young man, Barney, loudly commanded the demon to leave in Jesus' name. The demon, through Fiona, asked Barney, "Who are you?" Barney responded, "a son of God." Barney began to chant "In the name of Jesus, depart!" Fiona grew more agitated. At one point her eyes rolled back in her head.

16. After about twenty minutes Fiona calmed down. I prayed out loud that she would be given God's grace to repent of the sin within her heart, that she would receive Jesus by faith and be free from her rebellion. As I prayed, Fiona grew violent. She struck her mother uncontrollably, and four of us moved forward to restrain her.

17. As Fiona repeatedly struck her mother, she yelled to her, "Leave me alone!" and "No, get away." I found this strange. There were four people restraining her (her mother, an older woman, Barney, and myself), yet Fiona only struck and verbally attacked her mother, not the other three. I do not know if she could not strike the other three because of the Holy Spirit's restraint. Is the mother not truly a Christian, and therefore not protected by the Spirit?

> "We know that anyone born of God does not continue to sin; the one who was born of God keeps him safe, and the evil one cannot harm him. We know that we are children of God, and that the whole world is under the control of the evil one." (1 John 5:18, 19)

18. Elle stepped backward and prayed the following: "Fiona knows that Jesus died for her," "Fiona knows that Jesus' blood can save her from her sin," and "Fiona knows that in Jesus she has eternal life." Fiona raised her head and glared at Elle with an intense hatred. Fiona's eyes were not her own. The demon, through Fiona, said, "Are you talking to me?"

19. During our session the demon spoke twice. Each time it displayed brazen arrogance, a raging defiance, and contempt for those listening. At times the demon, through Fiona, uttered vile profanity. At one point her tongue twitched like that of a snake (quickly moving in and out of her mouth) and her eyes glowed intensely.

> "…yet even angels, although they are stronger and more powerful, do not bring slanderous accusations against such beings in the presence of the Lord" (2 Peter 2:11)

20. Soon Fiona spoke in an unintelligible voice, a kind of glossolalia which sounded

like the demon's voice. As Fiona spoke in tongues, her mother joined in and also spoke in tongues. Did the mother speak in tongues from the Holy Spirit, or did she speak in a demonic tongue intended to mimic the Holy Spirit and deceive those present? Was the mother communicating with the demon? I sensed that the mother was in some way participating in the demon possession, placating the agitated demon, maybe offering praise and comfort.

The Nightmare, John Henry Fuseli, 1781

> "Dear friends, do not believe every spirit, but test the spirits to see whether they are from God, because many false prophets have gone out into the world. This is how you can recognize the Spirit of God: Every spirit that acknowledges that Jesus Christ has come in the flesh is from God, but every spirit that does not acknowledge Jesus is not from God. This is the spirit of the antichrist, which you have heard is coming and even now is already in the world." (1 John 4:1-3)

21. Soon Fiona calmed down. Her body was lifeless and she appeared almost paralyzed, as she fell to the floor and wept. She whispered, "Thank you, Jesus." "Praise God," "Thank the Lord for his grace and help." I wondered if this was a deception perpetrated by the demon to make the listeners believe that Fiona is a true Christian. Was this a way to gain covering so that others could not glimpse the sinful condition of her heart?

22. When Fiona came to her senses I asked her what she was thinking during the possession episode. She said that she wanted to attack student Elle and myself. I

asked if *she* wanted to attack us or if the *demon* wanted to attack us. She did not offer a clear answer. She said that when she submitted herself to the demon, the possession grew more violent. When she resisted the demon, the possession seemed to subside.

> "Submit yourselves, then, to God. Resist the devil, and he will flee from you." (James 4:7)

23. At this point everyone was exhausted and it was late. The bystanders soon dispersed. As we were leaving, the mother sat with Fiona and spoke to her. Fiona was beginning another possession episode. We did not stay to witness it.

> In each of the possession episodes there were, to my knowledge, only Christians present (maybe with the exception of the mother). This was strange because several non-Christians had attended the training sessions immediately prior to the possession episodes. After each session, the non-Christians mysteriously left before the episode began. I believe that this was God's mercy and protection to the non-Christians, keeping them from becoming another vector for Fiona's demon. I sensed that anyone present who was not protected by Jesus' blood might be subject to the demon's influence. This may account for the fact that Fiona only attacked her mother, as I suspect that the mother is influenced by a demon (maybe the same one that possesses her daughter). If the mother is not protected by Jesus' blood, then she would be susceptible to demonic attack.

Fiona's Mother

1. Two days after the first possession episode, on November 20, 2011, student Elle and I spoke with Fiona's mother. The mother's appearance is emotionally cold. She seems stern, distant, and maybe even supercilious. My first thought was that she is not a Christian, and I suspected she might be surreptitiously opposing Christ's work in her daughter's life.

2. I shared with the mother my thought that the demon possession is linked to sin and rebellion in her daughter's heart. I asked some counseling questions to ascertain the nature of Fiona's rebellion. For example, I asked the mother what Fiona usually discusses, or thinks about, in the moments immediately preceding an attack. (I was looking for the trigger, or precipitating event, which seems to invite evil in.) The mother stated that she did not know, and implied that any inquiry into the heart was trivial or incidental to the problem.

3. Fiona's mother referred to her daughter as a victim who only has Jesus in her life. The mother seemed indignant at the mere suggestion that her daughter's problem

is sin related. She appeared to be further angered when questioned about whether her daughter is in fact a Christian.

4. The mother claimed that her daughter shared the gospel with her, and that she received Christ about one year prior through her daughter's witness.

5. The mother stated that she (the mother) was given the gift of tongues to help heal her daughter, and that she had taught her daughter to pray in tongues. On December 19th Fiona stated that she now daily prays in tongues and that that has helped her gain more control over the possession episodes.

6. The mother seems convinced that direct spiritual warfare is the key to solving her daughter's problem. She rejects the idea that this problem will be solved through repentance, growth in faith, resisting Satan's advances, or walking in obedience to the Word. The mother feels that her daughter needs a "deliverance."

> "But even the archangel Michael, when he was disputing with the devil about the body of Moses, did not dare to bring a slanderous accusation against him, but said, 'The Lord rebuke you!'" (Jude 9)

7. I pointed out to the mother that her daughter harbors idols within her heart which contribute to the possession. This internal evil is of greater importance as it provides a lush environment in which the demon continues to live and thrive. The mother did not want to discuss this topic.

8. I strongly suspect that the mother enables the possession through allowing her daughter to feed an angry and rebellious heart. The mother also perpetuates a victim identity in her daughter. I believe that the mother blocks her daughter from repentance, and from receiving Christ. Even more sinister, I suspect that the mother has some connection with the demon, and may even aid and abet it (as horrible as that sounds).

Questions Raised

1. Is the human will inviolable? Can a demon take control of, or possess, another's will, or does that demon just influence, coax, or persuade the will?

> Jesus' death on the cross, the final and complete victory over Satan and evil, serves as a cosmic exorcism conclusively destroying Satan's ultimate power (while Satan yet remains present).[4]

---

[4] David Powlison, *Power Encounters: Reclaiming Spiritual Warfare* (Baker Books, 1994)

> "And having disarmed the powers and authorities, he made a public spectacle of them, triumphing over them by the cross." (Colossians 2:15)

2. Can a demon physically inhabit a vector's body, showing itself at particular times, or does the demon live outside of the body, revisiting that body when afforded a window of opportunity?

Healing of a Demoniac in the Synagogue, James Jacques Joseph Tissot, d. 1902

3. Can a Christian be possessed by a demon, even momentarily, or can a Christian merely be influenced by demons?

> David was led by Satan to take a census of Israel which brought God's judgment on the nation.[5]
>
> Peter was Satan's mouthpiece to persuade Christ to walk away from his impending death on the cross.[6]
>
> Satan persuaded Christians Ananias and Sapphira to lie to the Holy Spirit.[7]

---

[5] 1 Chronicles 21:7
[6] Matthew 16:21-23
[7] Acts 5:1-11

4. To what extent is Fiona fighting the demon's influence? To what extent is she cooperating with the demon, and submitting to its will?

> "...so let us put aside the deeds of darkness and put on the armor of light." (Romans 13:12)
>
> "Submit yourselves, then, to God. Resist the devil, and he will flee from you." (James 4:7)

5. To what extent does Fiona tacitly invite the demon into her life through ongoing idolatry? Will repentance weaken the demon's hold? Does she even desire repentance?

> "Endure hardship with us like a good soldier of Jesus Christ. No one serving as a soldier gets involved in civilian affairs—he wants to please his commanding officer. Similarly, if anyone competes as an athlete, he does not receive the victor's crown unless he competes according to the rules." (2 Timothy 2:3-5)

It would appear that Fiona gets everything that she wants from the demon, an excuse for her sin, a sense of power, a welcomed distraction from an otherwise uneventful life, attention from others, a persuasive manipulator and scapegoat. It would appear that her ultimate objective is to deflect attention away from her own sinful heart, to make herself appear as nothing more than a helpless victim. It is possible that she deliberately invites the demon for self-serving purpose.

> First Timothy 6:12 states, "Fight the good fight of the faith. Take hold of the eternal life to which you were called when you made your good confession in the presence of many witnesses." Christianity is a fight waged by means of faith because the Christian rests in the victory that has already been won on the cross.

6. Is the glossolalia exhibited by Fiona, and her mother, from the Holy Spirit or merely a clever demonic imitation to deceive those present? Are the mother and daughter both praying in demonic tongues and communicating with one another? Is the mother actually encouraging the demon possession to persist? (The mother may be shielding her daughter from her need for repentance, and possibly placating, even emboldening, the demon.)

7. It is sin for Fiona to strike her mother. Is the demon causing Fiona to sin? Why did Fiona only strike her mother and not others? Does this indicate that the mother is not protected by Jesus' blood?

> "Be self-controlled and alert. Your enemy the devil prowls around like a roaring lion looking for someone to devour. Resist him, standing firm in the faith…" (1 Peter 5:8, 9)

8. Persistent prayer seems to weaken the demon's hold but does not seem to cast it out. Why? What exactly weakens the demon? Is the demon only pretending to be weakened through perpetrating a mock sanctification within Fiona, or through causing her to exhibit a counterfeit speaking in tongues? (It would appear that true sanctification is not occurring.)

9. How should Christians handle a demon? For example, should a Christian, in Jesus' name, ask a demon to reveal its name, or the reason it inhabits a person? If the Christian asks questions in Jesus' name, is the demon compelled to reveal the truth? What should a Christian then do with this information? Should a Christian ever speak to a demon, or only directly speak to God in prayer?

> "She kept this up for many days. Finally Paul became so annoyed that he turned around and said to the spirit, 'In the name of Jesus Christ I command you to come out of her!' At that moment the spirit left her." (Acts 16:18)
>
> "For though we live in the world, we do not wage war as the world does. The weapons we fight with are not the weapons of the world. On the contrary, they have divine power to demolish strongholds." (2 Corinthians 10:3-5)
>
> "Jesus said, 'My kingdom is not of this world; if my kingship were of this world, my servants would fight.'" (John 18:36)
>
> "Do not conform any longer to the pattern of this world, but be transformed by the renewing of your mind. Then you will be able to test and approve what God's will is – his good pleasing and perfect will." (Romans 12:2)

10. At the end of the second possession episode Fiona praised Jesus for her deliverance from the demon (albeit temporarily). Is it possible for one to praise Jesus and not be indwelled by the Holy Spirit?

> "Many will say to me on that day, 'Lord, Lord, did we not prophesy in your name, and in your name drive out demons and perform many miracles?' Then I will tell them plainly, 'I never knew you. Away from me, you evildoers!'" (Matthew 7:22, 23)

11. In what way are those around Fiona helping her to be free from the demon? In what way are those around her causing her to take a passive, even resigned,

stance toward the demon possession? In what way do others perpetuate the possession by making excuses for Fiona, externalizing the evil, and blinding themselves to her indwelling sin? In what way do those around Fiona see her only as a victim, but not as a sinner responding to her situation in defiance of God?

> "For our battle is not against flesh and blood, but against the rulers, against the authorities, against the powers of this dark world and against the spiritual forces of evil in the heavenly realms." (Ephesians 6:12)
>
> "But our citizenship is in heaven. And we eagerly await a Savior from there, the Lord Jesus Christ, who, by the power that enables him to bring everything under his control, will transform our lowly bodies so that they will be like his glorious body." (Philippians 3:20, 21)

An Assessment of Fiona

1. I suspect that soon after Fiona was sexual assaulted or abused as an adolescent she invited demons into her life in a kind of pact of protection and revenge. She sought Satan as an avenger and weapon against her attacker, and against God himself. She developed a deep hatred of God that he was not able to, or unwilling to, protect her. Fiona still feeds this trenchant distrust of God, despite possibly having some intellectual understanding of the gospel.

> "Rather clothe yourselves with the Lord Jesus Christ, and do not think about how to gratify the desires of the sinful nature." (Romans 13:14)

2. Fiona seems highly self-absorbed, harboring an intense focus on her feelings and desires. I observe that she often sits alone, does not speak with others, and is largely unconcerned with, or aware of, others. It seems that she broods in her self-misery and feeds her hatred. This builds an ever-thicker social cocoon around her. Additionally, not being able to work is a debilitating trial, robbing her of social dignity.

3. Fiona stated that at age eight she started to see herself as god, and stated that she "believes in herself." (On one occasion, she even used the term "god" to describe herself.) This seems to be the wormhole through which the demon gains entrance into her will (or on whatever level its influence exists). Fiona's feeling of being god reveals consuming idols of the heart, which must be confronted and brought to repentance.

> "Don't you know that when you offer yourselves to someone to obey him as slaves, you are slaves to the one whom you obey – whether you are slaves to sin, which

> leads to death, or to obedience, which leads to righteousness?" (Romans 6:16)

4. As Fiona is consumed by anger (based in vengeance against those who abused her), this becomes fertile ground for ongoing demon possession. It appears that she may dredge up memories of childhood abuse, sparking the possession episodes. She may be replaying the abuse in her mind like a film reel. This is closely related to her statements that she is god (as one consumed with anger, in fact, assumes the position of God himself).

> "Do not let the sun go down while you are still angry, and do not give the devil a foothold." (Ephesians 4:26, 27)

I suspect that seething anger over prior sexual abuse, coupled with her own guilt over subsequent sexual sin, serves as the trigger or catalyst for her demon possession episodes. It is this tandem rage and guilt which raises an obstacle to receiving the gospel. I believe that she actively fights against receiving Jesus and will not submit to him. The demon possession episodes are used to keep any presentation of the gospel at a distance, to confuse, distract, and subsume the truth.

> "Saul was very angry; this refrain displeased him greatly. 'They have credited David with tens of thousands,' he thought, 'but me with only thousands. What more can he get but the kingdom?' And from that time on Saul kept a close eye on David."
>
> "The next day an evil spirit from God came forcefully on Saul. He was prophesying in his house, while David was playing the lyre, as he usually did. Saul had a spear in his hand and he hurled it, saying to himself, 'I'll pin David to the wall.' But David eluded him twice." (1 Samuel 18:8-11)

5. Fiona frequently speaks about what others have done to her, or how they have failed her. There appears to be a pattern of blame-shifting for every problem in her life as there is rarely, if ever, any statement of her own responsibility, failing, seeking forgiveness, or growth in wisdom. She seems obsessed with exonerating herself, shifting blame to others, or even seeking retribution.

> In Matthew 18:21-35 the servant's large debt is forgiven; yet, he condemns one who owes him a small debt. This shows the nature of playing God. Each sinner owes the Father a massive debt (that debt being his sin). How then can that sinner condemn another who, by comparison, owes him a small debt?

I sense that Fiona approached the counseling session as a means of gaining an ally, an attempt to placate guilt, or as a way to vindicate herself. I did not sense that she honestly wants to change, sees a need for change, or seeks to glorify Jesus in her life and relationships.

Alte Pinakothek, Munich (church altar piece), c. 1475

6. It appears that Fiona continues to invite the demon (it is not clear to what extent this is deliberate) into her life through her rage, fear, desire for revenge, or desire to be god herself. It seems that when there is a call to repentance, or when she is aware of her guilt before God, the demon attacks to maintain its stronghold in her heart. Likewise, the demon fights to keep the gospel away from Fiona. Is this at Fiona's invitation or outside of her will?

> "Then I heard a loud voice in heaven say: 'Now have come the salvation and the power and the kingdom of our God, and the authority of his Christ. For the accuser of our brothers, who accuses them before our God day and night, has been hurled down.'" (Revelation 12:10)

7. Speaking in tongues is likely a scheme Fiona uses (either masterminded by her mother or by the demon) to conceal idols, so as to afford them an opportunity to work unassailed. This is a way to avoid heart issues in favor of external display

for a supposed deliverance. Speaking in tongues affords Fiona a "church-approved" covering for her idols. Consequently, unsuspecting Christians no longer see sin as the root cause and, thus, silence their call for repentance. Speaking in tongues is merely a smokescreen behind which the demon now hides, so that others will not bring the gospel to bear upon Fiona's heart.

Glossolalia also serves to garner attention from others as this appears to distinguish Fiona as a "spiritual" person, making her appear to be a genuine (and gifted) Christian. I sense that speaking in tongues also serves a more foundational craving for attention from others.

> "Be self-controlled and alert. Your enemy the devil prowls around like a roaring lion looking for someone to devour. Resist him, standing firm in the faith, because you know that your brothers throughout the world are undergoing the same kind of sufferings." (1 Peter 5:8)

It is clear that Fiona is not growing in Christ, nor is she seeking to be sanctified. She has little or no understanding of the idols within her heart or what, if any, repentance should occur. It also seems that those around her are not aware of sin patterns within her. Daily speaking in tongues siphons off attention from Fiona's pressing need for repentance.

8. What is odd is that at the end of our counseling training class, during an open sharing session on November 20th, Fiona expressed a heart of humility, showing evidence of repentance and sanctification. This may have been a false witness intended to deceive those listening.

9. It seems increasingly apparent that Fiona is not a Christian. How can a Christian be demon possessed? Is it possible for a demon to inhabit one who already possesses the indwelling Holy Spirit? (Scripture clearly indicates that once God claims a person, and his Spirit inhabits her, there is no chance that an evil spirit can also inhabit that space.[8])

> "And no wonder for Satan himself masquerades as an angel of light. It is not surprising, then, if his servants masquerade as servants of righteousness. Their end will be what their actions deserve." (2 Corinthians 11:14, 15)

Excursus: The Armor of God

Each Christian is a participant in spiritual warfare by nature of his citizenship. Ephesians 6:11 states, "Put on the full armor of God so that you can take your stand

---

[8] Mark 3:25

against the devil's schemes." Full armor refers to both defensive instruments and weapons of attack against evil. This includes:

Jason and the Dragon
Salvator Rosa, 1664

1. The belt of truth which holds the sheath of the sword[9]

2. The breastplate of righteousness which covers the heart[10]

> "But since we belong to the day, let us be self-controlled, putting on faith and love as a breastplate…" (1 Thessalonians 5:8)

3. Feet fitted with the readiness which comes from the gospel of peace, a readiness to run into battle[11]

> Isaiah 59:7, 8 speaks about those who do not know God. "Their feet rush into sin; they are swift to shed innocent blood…The way of peace they do not know; there is no justice in their paths…no one who walks in them will know peace."

4. The shield of faith to "extinguish all the flaming arrows of the evil one," a defensive weapon[12]

> "Blessed are you, O Israel! Who is like you, a people saved by the Lord? He is your shield and helper and your glorious sword. Your enemies will cower before you, and you will trample down their high places." (Deuteronomy 33:29)
>
> "O house of Israel, trust in the Lord, he is their help and shield. O house of Aaron, trust in the Lord – he is their help and shield. You who fear him, trust in the Lord – he is their help and shield." (Psalms 115:9-11)

---

[9] Ephesians 6:14
[10] Ephesians 6:14
[11] Ephesians 6:15
[12] Ephesians 6:16

5. The helmet of salvation which might guard the five senses as well as one's mind[13]

> "But since we belong to the day, let us be self-controlled, putting on faith and love as a breastplate, and the hope of salvation as a helmet." (1 Thessalonians 5:8)
>
> "We demolish arguments and every pretension that sets itself up against the knowledge of God, and we take captive every thought to make it obedient to Christ." (2 Corinthians 10:5)
>
> "…the Lord looked and was displeased that there was no justice. He saw that there was no one, he was appalled that there was no one to intervene; so his own arm worked salvation for him, and his own righteousness sustained him. He put on righteousness as his breastplate, and the helmet of salvation on his head; he put on the garments of vengeance and wrapped himself in zeal as in a cloak." (Isaiah 59:15-17)

6. The sword of the Spirit, which is the Word of God, is the only part of the armor used for attack.[14] (When Satan tempted Jesus in the desert, Jesus rebuked Satan with Scripture.[15])

> "I have hidden your word in my heart that I might not sin against you." (Psalm 119:11)

> Medieval armor that was well-designed and built was nearly impenetrable. It cost the equivalent of a farm and was guarded as a man's greatest possession. A returning victorious knight would often first report how many suits of armor he took from the enemy.

Each piece of armor must be in place. Over this armor there is to be the mantle of humility, as pride in battle ensures loss.

> "Be careful when you stand lest you fall." (1 Corinthians 10:12)

Toward a Biblical View of Demon Possession

In the following analysis, I will first present David Powlison's views on demon possession, as found in his work, *Power Encounters: Reclaiming Spiritual Warfare* (!994).[16] Afterward, I will present a somewhat modified view (which I term a "hybrid view").

---

[13] Ephesians 6:17
[14] Ephesians 6:17
[15] Matthew 4:4
[16] David Powlison, *Power Encounters: Reclaiming Spiritual Warfare* (Baker Books, 1994)

As David Powlison presents, the Bible speaks about two different kinds of evil: situational and moral. Situational evil is the presence of destructive and painful events in the world, such as disease, deformity, or natural disasters. Moral evil is the sin which men perpetrate, like lying, greed, or murder. Reversing situational evils does not culminate in the absence of moral evil. (Likewise, moral evils can lead to situational evils.) In the Bible, demon possession is always spoken about as a situational evil, and is never linked to moral evil. Incidentally, the fact that animals can be possessed (such as the legion demons who inhabited a herd of swine), would tend to support the situational theorem.[17]

> "When they came to Jesus, they saw the man [the Gerasene demoniac] who had been possessed by the legion of demons, sitting there, dressed and in his right mind; and they were afraid." (Mark 5:15)

Demon possession is primarily found in the books of Matthew, Mark, Luke and Acts, where such accounts speak about people as victims of demon possession. The demon possessed are put in the same category as the lame, blind, hungry, and sick. For example, Luke 13:10-17 speaks about demon possession in the same way that it would discuss a donkey or ox in need of water.

Casting out demons does not lead to moral improvement (except as the person is led to faith through the miracle). Likewise, demons are never presented as holding people in bondage to sin. Whenever people were morally challenged, Jesus used the classical model of spiritual warfare: repentance, faith, obedience, and adherence to the Word of God. Thus, there is no command in Scripture, nor implication, for believers to cast out demons. In fact, Scripture warns Christians against speaking with demons. Instead, Jesus calls Christians to live by faith alone, and to leave the command of demons to God alone.

> "...so that by following them [Paul's instructions] you may fight the good fight, holding on to faith and a good conscience. Some have rejected these and so have shipwrecked their faith." (1 Timothy 1:18, 19)

A Refutation of Deliverance Ministry

Deliverance ministry is essentially "Christianized goetry," the practice of summoning and commanding demons. Deliverance ministries tend toward a syncretism between pagan magic rites and the Christian worldview.

Deliverance ministry's fundamental errors:

---
[17] Mark 5:12

1. Demons can indwell a person and take over the functions of the human heart.

The Gadarene Swine, Julius Schnorr von Carolsfeld, d. 1872

2. Demons are like a pocket of alien inhabitation within the human personality – an area beyond one's control and will.

3. Habitual sinful practices can give demons a foothold which, over time, can strengthen into a stronghold. At that point, sin is the work of the demon, and no longer the sinner's sole responsibility.[18]

4. The belief that demons can be inherited from past generations (generally through occult practices).

> "…in order that Satan may not outwit us. For we are not unaware of his schemes." (2 Corinthians 2:11)

Those who believe in demon possession tend to ascribe autonomy to demons, that they have power to indwell human beings beyond God's control. In this way, demon possession has the look and feel of superstition. In the end, most deliverance ministry has more affinity with an occult worldview than with the Bible's.

---

[18] Ephesians 4:27

> What has light to do with darkness?[19]

The Bible never speaks of indwelling "demons of sin." It speaks about demon possession with little or no statement about how the possession came about. The Bible emphasizes personal responsibility for sin. Since man's will is inviolable, each has the power to choose his own actions. The Bible's focus is always upon repentance, renunciation, faith, prayer, and embracing the truth – in short, putting on a new way of life.[20] This is always deemed sufficient to clean out the inner man.[21]

The Bible teaches that the core issue in the human drama is a personal moral issue. Whose voice will one listen to?[22] Whom will one believe and obey? In this way, the thrust of the Bible's work is to emphasize human depravity, which can never be mitigated by anything except faith in Jesus Christ. (Of course, the human love for sin is recalcitrant, so that sin does not fully recede, even for the justified believer.)

> "...in truthful speech and in the power of God; with weapons of righteousness in the right hand and in the left;" (2 Corinthians 6:7)

A Hybrid View

While I hold David Powlison's analysis in the highest regard, I would like to offer a slight variation upon it (what I term a "hybrid" approach). The difference in my analysis is based on the issue of how demon possession arises. While David Powlison points out that the Bible's record of demon possession always presents possession as situation, and the possessed as purely a victim (as a lame or blind person would be), I would submit that the Bible's handling allows for another possibility, that the possession could arise from a willful pact with Satan or demons. Such a pact might be for protection from a real or perceived threat, or it might be a prideful desire for dominance over others. Regardless of the reason, I would theorize that Fiona made a deliberate decision to cast her lot with Satan in an alliance of protection from her step-father's assaults.

Since the Bible does not elucidate the manner in which possession arises, I would, postulate that it allows for willful possession. In other words, Fiona made a moral decision (for which she is fully responsible), but which resulted in repercussions for which she was wholly unprepared. I do not want to, in any way, depreciate Fiona's own moral culpability in the matter, while recognizing that she has actually delivered her will to a demon, from which she seeks some benefit. Seething anger and desire for revenge became the portal through which the demon entered the theater of her heart, a

---

[19] 2 Corinthians 6:14-16
[20] Ephesians 4:24
[21] Matthew 23:26
[22] Genesis 3:1

possession of her will which she invites and condones, but from which she cannot find an escape (in the same way that an addict feels powerless, while fully culpable).

> Possibly the most important issue to remember in demon possession is that no focus should be placed upon the demon. Rather, the entire focus should be upon counseling the sinner with the gospel. The gospel carries with it such unmitigable force that no evil can stand in its presence. My confidence in the gospel is so great that I believe one brought under its salvific power will become a hostile and uninhabitable environment for any evil (whether of Satan, the world, or the flesh).

My goal is to guard the desperate need for the gospel in Fiona's life, and that requires maintaining her guilt in the possession. Without qualification, Fiona needs a savior from her sin. When she has received a new heart and mind in Christ, she will also find deliverance from an alliance which currently renders her a prisoner. Like an addict who is fully responsible for his addiction but simultaneously trapped by it, Fiona also is responsible for an addiction to a demonic alliance which she feels powerless to break. Deliverance from her sin will finally break her addiction to the possession, will decisively remove the gateway. Thus, as Jesus enters Fiona's life, renews her heart, and removes her desire for revenge, the demon will no longer find an open portal, will no longer find a welcoming heart. In this way, the demon will be both propositionally and functionally excluded from Fiona's life as she is finds deliverance in Jesus.

The Author

James Venezia studied physics at Haverford College and later divinity and apologetics at Westminster Theological Seminary. He currently serves as a college instructor and pastor.

Please direct comments or questions concerning this series to jamesvenezia@yahoo.com.

The Christian Exceptionalism in Counseling Series™

The first book in the series, *Ask for the Ancient Paths,* is an introduction to biblical counseling.

Chapter four (here shown in booklet form) offers a comprehensive exposition of the gospel.

Chapter eight presents a biblical response to psychology.

Chapter ten examines the concept of sanctification.

The second book, *What Agreement Is There Between the Temple of God and Idols?*, is an in-depth study of sin and idolatry.

Chapter two introduces the triple concept - the world, the flesh, and the devil.

Chapter six introduces the issue of idolatry.

Chapter nine investigates the modern construal of the self.

The third book, *The Days of Reckoning Are at Hand,* focuses on application of the biblical counseling paradigm.

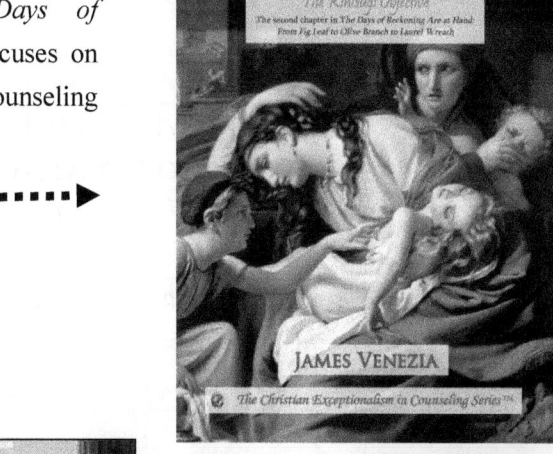

Chapter two analyzes suffering from a biblical perspective.

Chapter three considers the issue of loneliness.

Chapter four argues for living relationship with Jesus himself, the life-blood of the Christian faith.

A Summary of *The Christian Exceptionalism in Counseling Series*™

Textbook	Textbook Chapter in Booklet Form[1]
ASK FOR THE ANCIENT PATHS *From Art to Artifice to Arisen*	**THE GOSPEL AS INCEPTION POINT** *From Immorality to Immortality* (chapter 4)
	WHAT HAS JERUSALEM TO DO WITH VIENNA? *The Case Against Psychology* (chapter 8)
	THE THIRD-WAY OF SANCTIFICATION *From Abominable to Indomitable* (chapter 10)
WHAT AGREEMENT IS THERE BETWEEN THE TEMPLE OF GOD AND IDOLS? *The Accidence of Sin and Idolatry*	**UNCOVERING IDOLS OF THE HEART** *Make Us Gods to Go Before Us* (chapter 6)
	MARAUDING VISIGOTHS *The Autocratic Self* (chapter 9)
THE DAYS OF RECKONING ARE AT HAND *From Fig Leaf to Olive Branch to Laurel Wreath*	**SUFFERING** *The Kintsugi Objective* (chapter 2)
	THE HOBGOBLIN IN THE INGLENOOK *Assessing Loneliness* (chapter 3)
	THE UMBILICUS OF PERSONAL RELATIONSHIP WITH CHRIST (chapter 4)

All materials in *The Christian Exceptionalism in Counseling Series*™ available for sale at Amazon bookseller

---

[1] Please note that each booklet is an exact reprinting of its respective chapter in the textbook.

Also by the Author

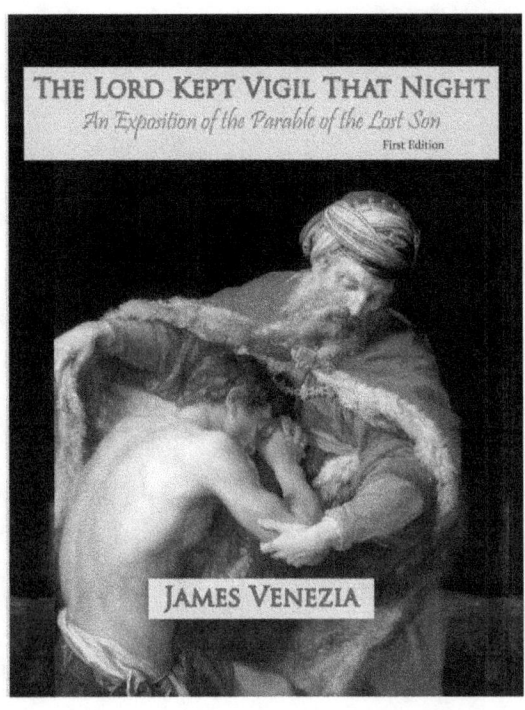

*The Lord Kept Vigil That Night:
An Exposition of the Parable of the Lost
Son*

*Rescue Us from the Present Evil Age:
Array of Hope*

*Hurl All Our Iniquities
into the Depths of the Sea*

www.ingramcontent.com/pod-product-compliance
Lightning Source LLC
Chambersburg PA
CBHW081123170426
43197CB00017B/2732